NINJA SLAYER KILLS!

ニンジャスレイヤー

ORI
BRADL

MANGA ADAPTATION SUPERVISION:
YU HONDA / LEIKA SUGI

MANGA:
KOUTAROU SEKINE

CHARACTER DESIGN:
WARAINAKU / KOUTAROU SEKINE

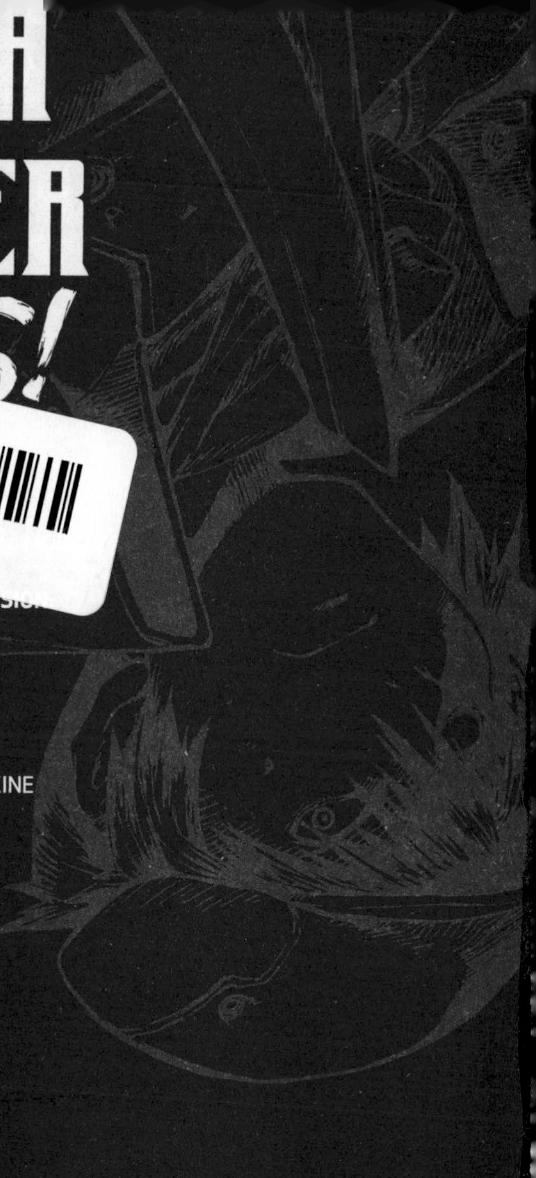

VOLUME
2

Ninja Slayer Kills was created based on contents from the original Ninja Slayer novels and some details, including time periods,

FOREWORD

Domo.

I am Truncator.

So you've survived the first volume, have you?

Well, you may have made it this far, but don't think you can relax just yet.

As the great Miyamoto Masashi once said, "Check your *mempo* after winning." In other words, one victory doesn't mean that the war is over.

The paltry amount of terms you learned in the last volume were just enough to let you survive with only a few cuts and scratches, but things will only get tougher from here on out.

It is essential that you sharpen your *wazamae* and increase your ninja vocabulary to ensure that you reach the end of this perilous journey with your entrails still intact.

To survive the blood-soaked path that lies ahead, it is imperative that you feast your eyes on the *kotodama* on the pages that follow these words.

If you fail to follow my instructions, then I offer you this suggestion: start practicing your *haiku* skills...

KOTODAMA

What is written upon these pages are more than mere words, they have been brought to life on the breath of those who inhabit the world of Ninja Slayer, and as such, hold power that bring them close to the heart and soul of ninja life. Learn these words as if your life depended on it, for they might be your best weapons in this age of wanton violence and depravity.

KORAH

An ending often heard when in the presence of an angered *Yank* (young delinquent) or Yakuza (Japanese mafia) member. Under normal circumstances, it is used to call one's attention in the same way as "hey" but for Yakuza and *Yanks*, its overuse has turned it into a modifier to express the user's outrage.

KACHIGUMI/MAKEGUMI

In Neo-Saitama, social class can largely be divided between the haves and have-nots, i.e. the *Kachigumi* (winning team) and *Makegumi* (losing team). The *Makegumi* are the majority, people who live and die in squalor. The *Kachigumi*, on the other hand, are the social elite who have passed difficult exams, allowing them to land jobs as salarymen (stereotypical businessmen) and women at top companies. These lucky few make up only 5% of the population. Even those who make it into the *Kachigumi* are not guaranteed an easy living, as members of this elite cadre are obligated to follow strict social etiquette and rules at the threat of ostracization.

SUMOTORI

A sumo wrestler. A competitive fighter who hides massive strength behind his corpulent appearance. Those who fail to win tournaments often end up as bodyguards and bouncers for the Yakuza.

ZBR (ZUBARI)

Officially called "*zubari* adrenaline," *zubari* or *ZBR* is a tranquilizing drug that is normally taken intravenously, but can also be consumed as a powder or in pills. It is often abused in Neo-Saitama and addicts can be identified by the color of their hair, which has been turned white due to a side effect of the drug.

OHAGI

Typically, *ohagi* is a Japanese confection consisting of sweet rice with azuki bean paste in its center. However, in the world of Ninja Slayer, the word "*ohagi*" is put to more sinister use as the name of an addictive drug. *Ohagi* is known to send its users into an ecstatic stupor that allows them to forget the sorrows of their pain-filled existence.

MAPPOU

In Buddhism, *mappou* is an age of decadence and degeneracy—an age in which the teachings of the Buddha are absent. This also happens to be the age in which Ninja Slayer takes place.

ZAKENNAH, SUZZO

Forms of Yakuza slang that are usually followed by the aforementioned *korah*. *Zakennah* is a shortened version of *fuzakeruna*, which translates to "don't fuck around" and *suzzo* is a shortened version of *korosuzo*, which means "I'll kill you."

YEEH MOTOH

A shout known and used by practitioners of the ancient art of *chado*. Its exact meaning is shrouded in mystery.

MEMPO

A face mask or covering used by ninja.

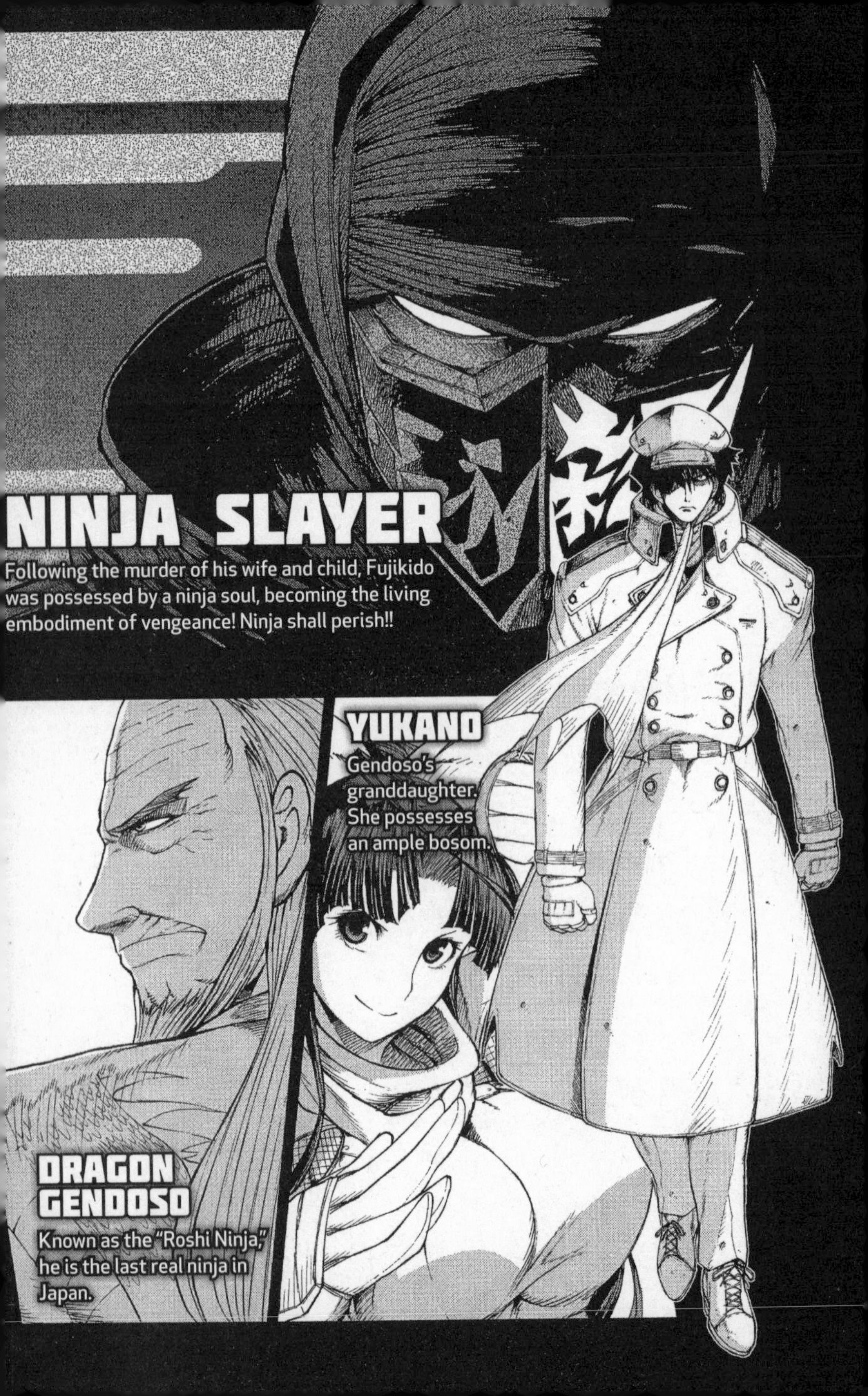
NINJA SLAYER
Following the murder of his wife and child, Fujikido was possessed by a ninja soul, becoming the living embodiment of vengeance! Ninja shall perish!!
YUKANO
Gendoso's granddaughter. She possesses an ample bosom.
DRAGON GENDOSO
Known as the "Roshi Ninja," he is the last real ninja in Japan.

THE STORY THUS FAR

While pursuing vengeance for the murder of his wife and child, Fujikido Kenji, also known as Ninja Slayer, acquired the vaccine for the anti-ninja virus that had been eating away at his master, Dragon Gendoso. However, moments after Fujikido delivered the medicine to his master's secret hideout, he found himself under attack by Darkninja of the Soukai Syndicate, who lashed out with his fierce *karate*. Only when Gendoso gave his life on a desperate counterattack was Darkninja just barely driven off. This small victory came at a terrible price, as Fujikido suffered a dire loss, the likes of which was second only to the loss of his wife and child. In his suffering, he thought back to the memories of the past year—the time since his possession by the ninja soul.

LAOMOTO KHAN

The mastermind behind the Soukai Syndicate who uses his control over the dark megacorps and the power of his ninja to rule Neo-Saitama in both the light of

DARKNINJA

Ninja Slayer's archenemy who wields the Demon Sword Beppin. A mysterious ninja who swears allegiance to Laomoto Khan.

NINJA SLAYER *KILLS!*
CONTENTS

BONUS EXTRAS 特 別 収 録

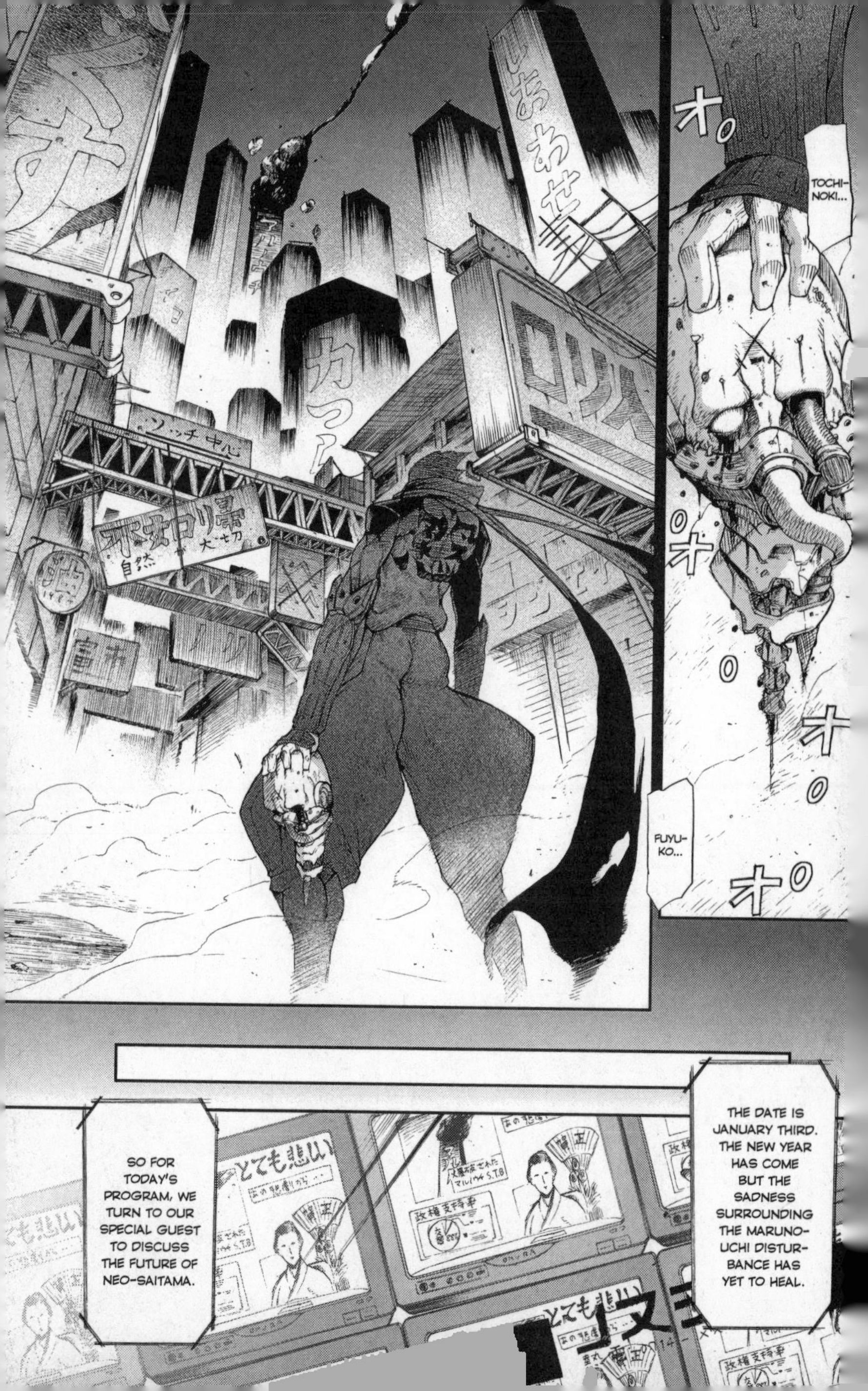
TOCHI-NOKI...
FUYU-KO...
THE DATE IS JANUARY THIRD. THE NEW YEAR HAS COME BUT THE SADNESS SURROUNDING THE MARUNO-UCHI DISTUR-BANCE HAS YET TO HEAL.
SO FOR TODAY'S PROGRAM, WE TURN TO OUR SPECIAL GUEST TO DISCUSS THE FUTURE OF NEO-SAITAMA.

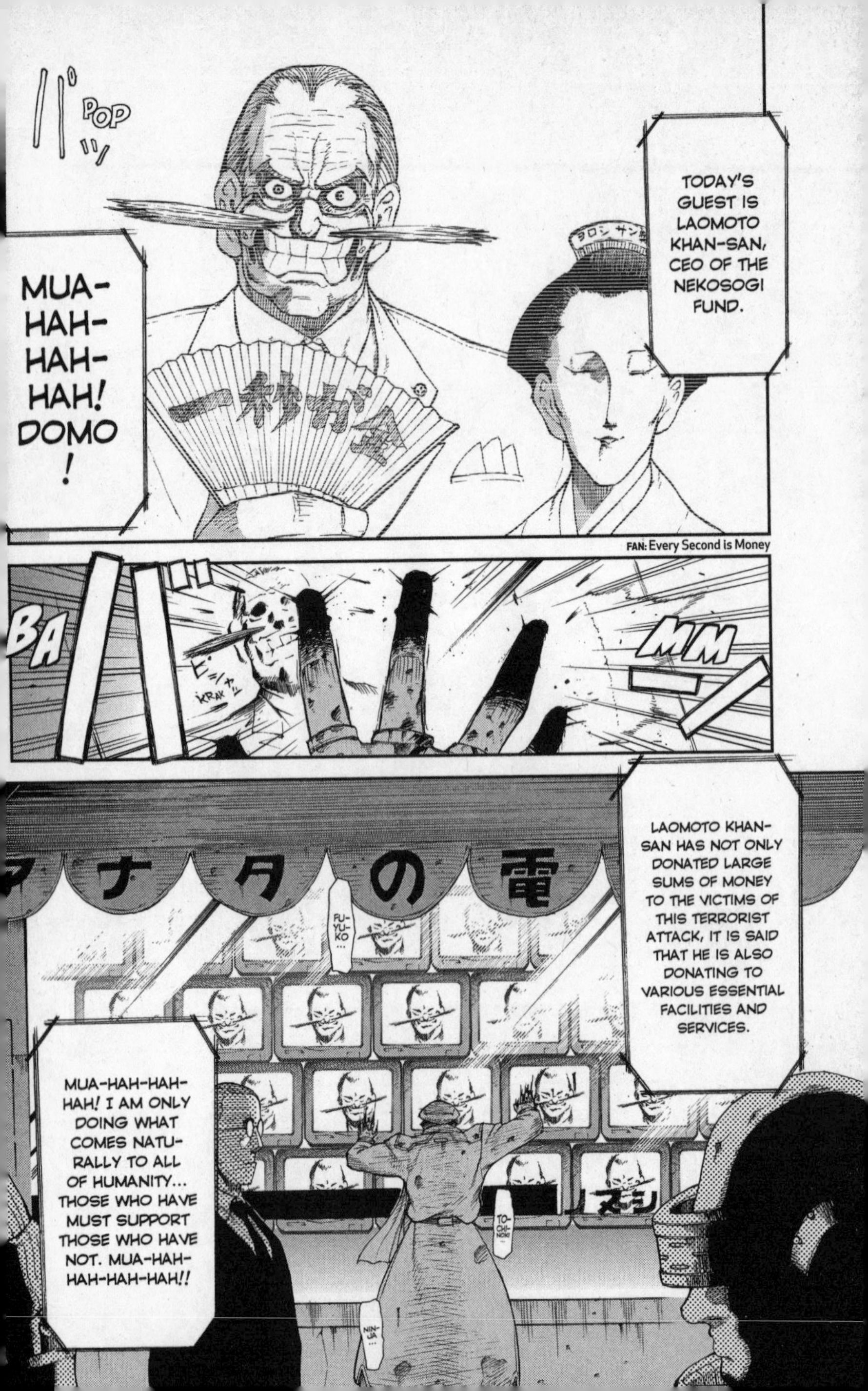
TODAY'S GUEST IS LAOMOTO KHAN-SAN, CEO OF THE NEKOSOGI FUND.
POP
MUA-HAH-HAH-HAH! DOMO!
FAN: Every Second is Money
MM
KRAK
BA
LAOMOTO KHAN-SAN HAS NOT ONLY DONATED LARGE SUMS OF MONEY TO THE VICTIMS OF THIS TERRORIST ATTACK, IT IS SAID THAT HE IS ALSO DONATING TO VARIOUS ESSENTIAL FACILITIES AND SERVICES.
FU-YUKO...
MUA-HAH-HAH-HAH! I AM ONLY DOING WHAT COMES NATU-RALLY TO ALL OF HUMANITY... THOSE WHO HAVE MUST SUPPORT THOSE WHO HAVE NOT. MUA-HAH-HAH-HAH-HAH!!
TO-CHI-NO!...
NIN-JA...

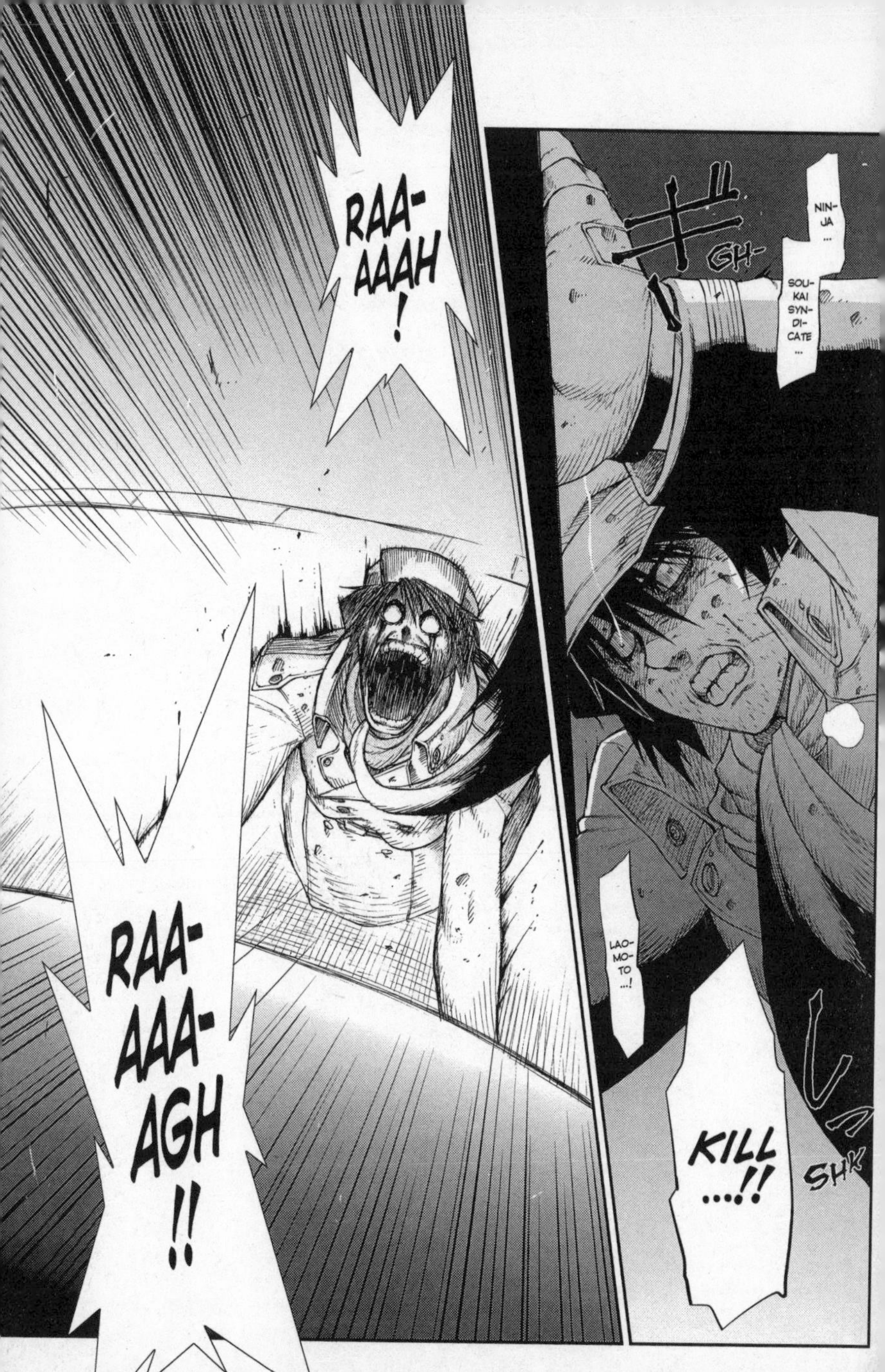
NIN-JA ...
GH-
SOU-KAI SYN-DI-CATE ...
LAO-MO-TO ...!
KILL ...!!
SHK
RAA-AAAH!
RAA-AAA-AGH!!

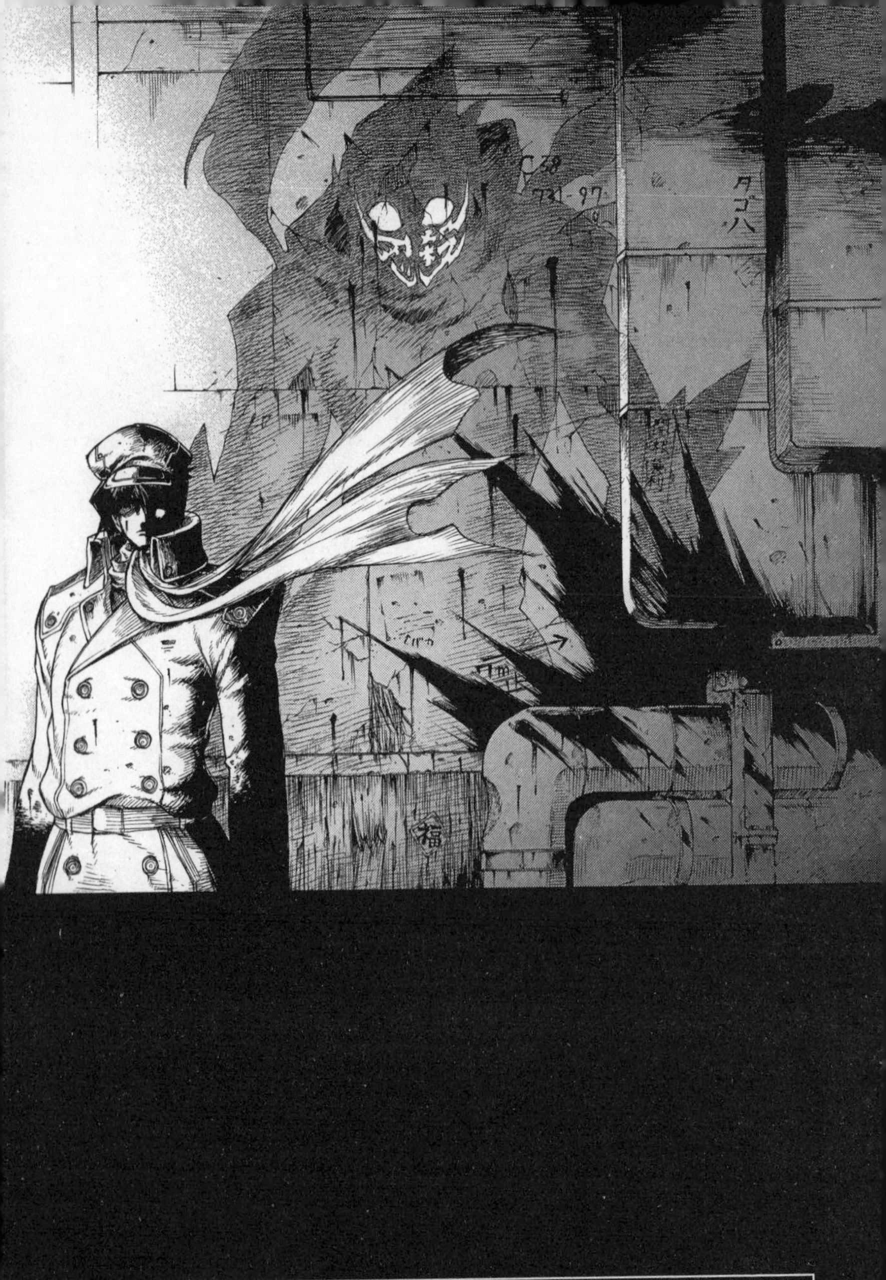
タコ八
福

KILLs 007 ✦ KICKOUT THE NINJA MOTHERFUCKER PART 1

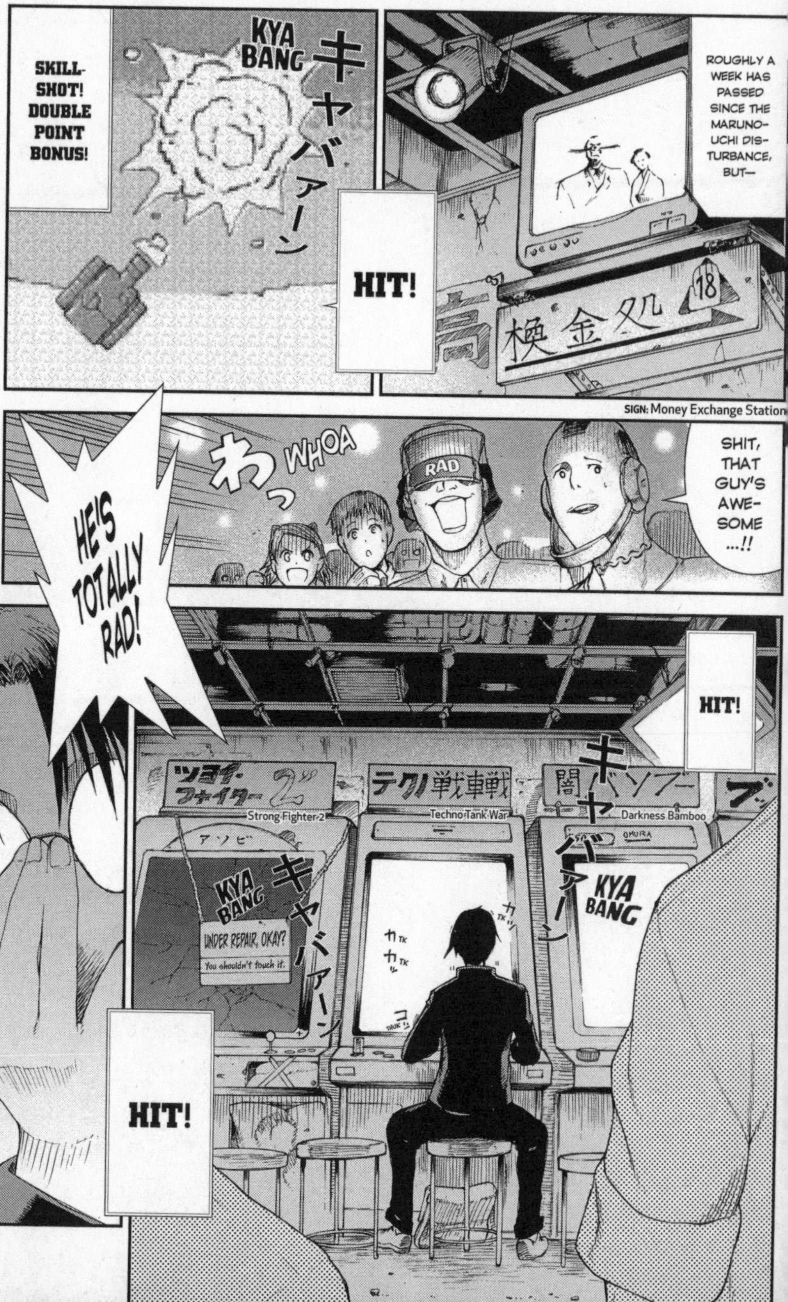

ROUGHLY A WEEK HAS PASSED SINCE THE MARUNOUCHI DISTURBANCE, BUT—
18
SIGN: Money Exchange Station
HIT!
KYA BANG
SKILL-SHOT! DOUBLE POINT BONUS!
SHIT, THAT GUY'S AWESOME ...!!
わっ WHOA
RAD
HE'S TOTALLY RAD!
HIT!
KYA BANG
Darkness Bamboo
Techno Tank War
Strong Fighter 2
KYA BANG
UNDER REPAIR, OKAY?
You shouldn't touch it.
HIT!

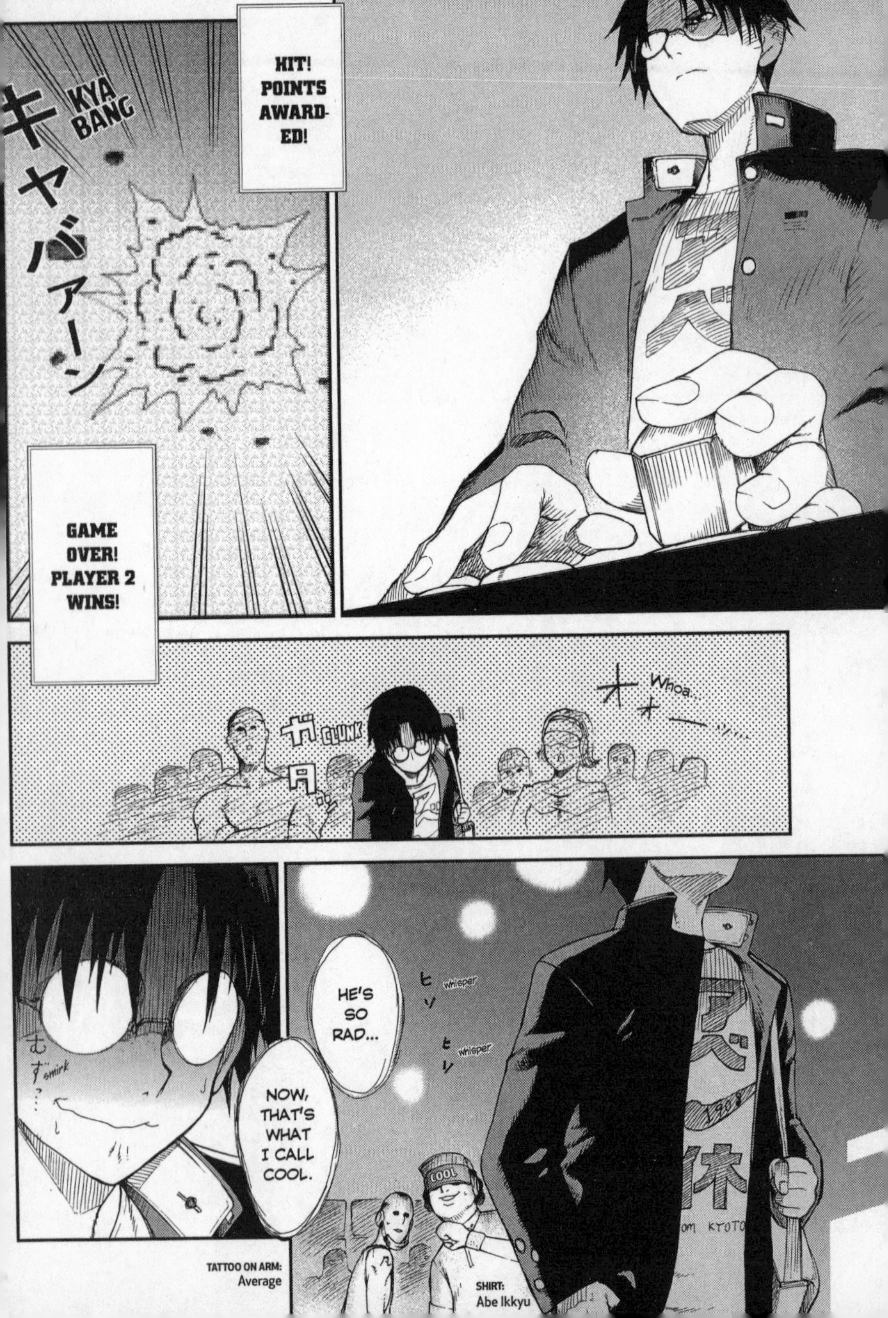
HIT! POINTS AWARDED!
キャバァーン
KYA BANG
GAME OVER! PLAYER 2 WINS!
オォー
Whoa..
ガタ
CLUNK
ヒソ
whisper
ヒソ
whisper
HE'S SO RAD...
NOW, THAT'S WHAT I CALL COOL.
COOL
SHIRT:
Abe Ikkyu
むすっ
smirk
TATTOO ON ARM:
Average

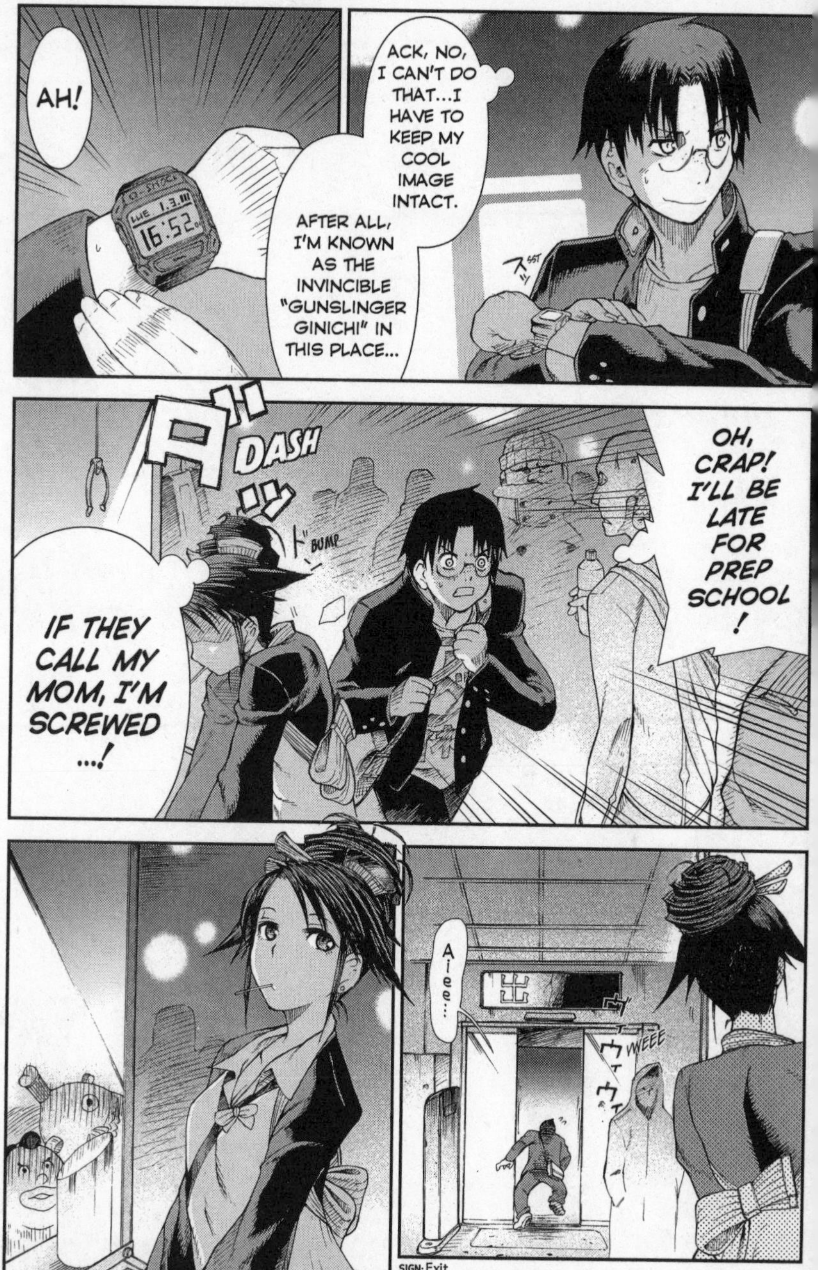

ACK, NO, I CAN'T DO THAT...I HAVE TO KEEP MY COOL IMAGE INTACT.
AFTER ALL, I'M KNOWN AS THE INVINCIBLE "GUNSLINGER GINICHI" IN THIS PLACE...
SSST
AH!
OH, CRAP! I'LL BE LATE FOR PREP SCHOOL!
DASH
BUMP
IF THEY CALL MY MOM, I'M SCREWED...!
Aiee...
WEEE
SIGN: Exit

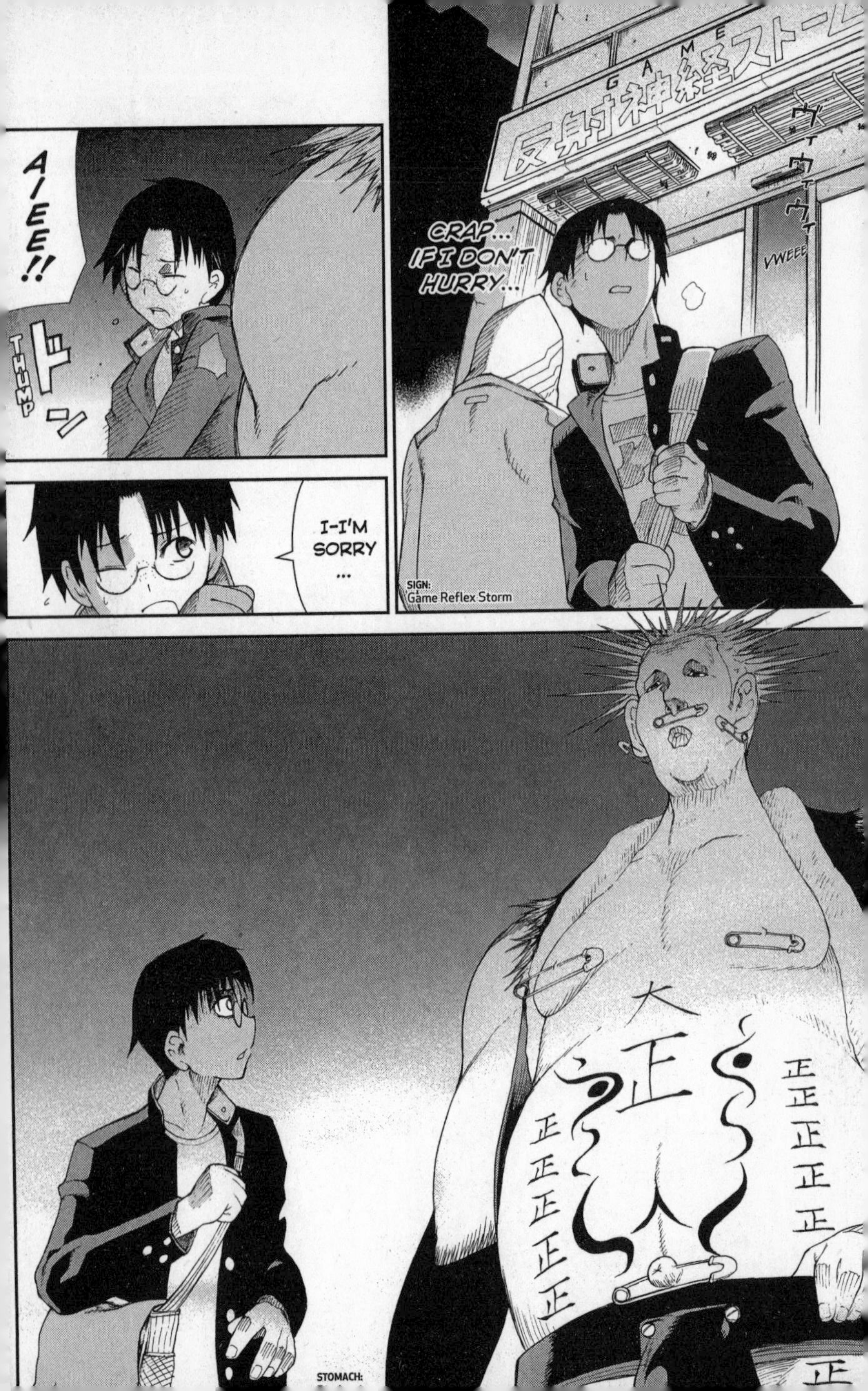
GAME
反射神経ストーム
VWEEE
CRAP... IF I DON'T HURRY...
SIGN: Game Reflex Storm
AIEEE!!
ドン
THUMP
I-I'M SORRY ...
STOMACH:

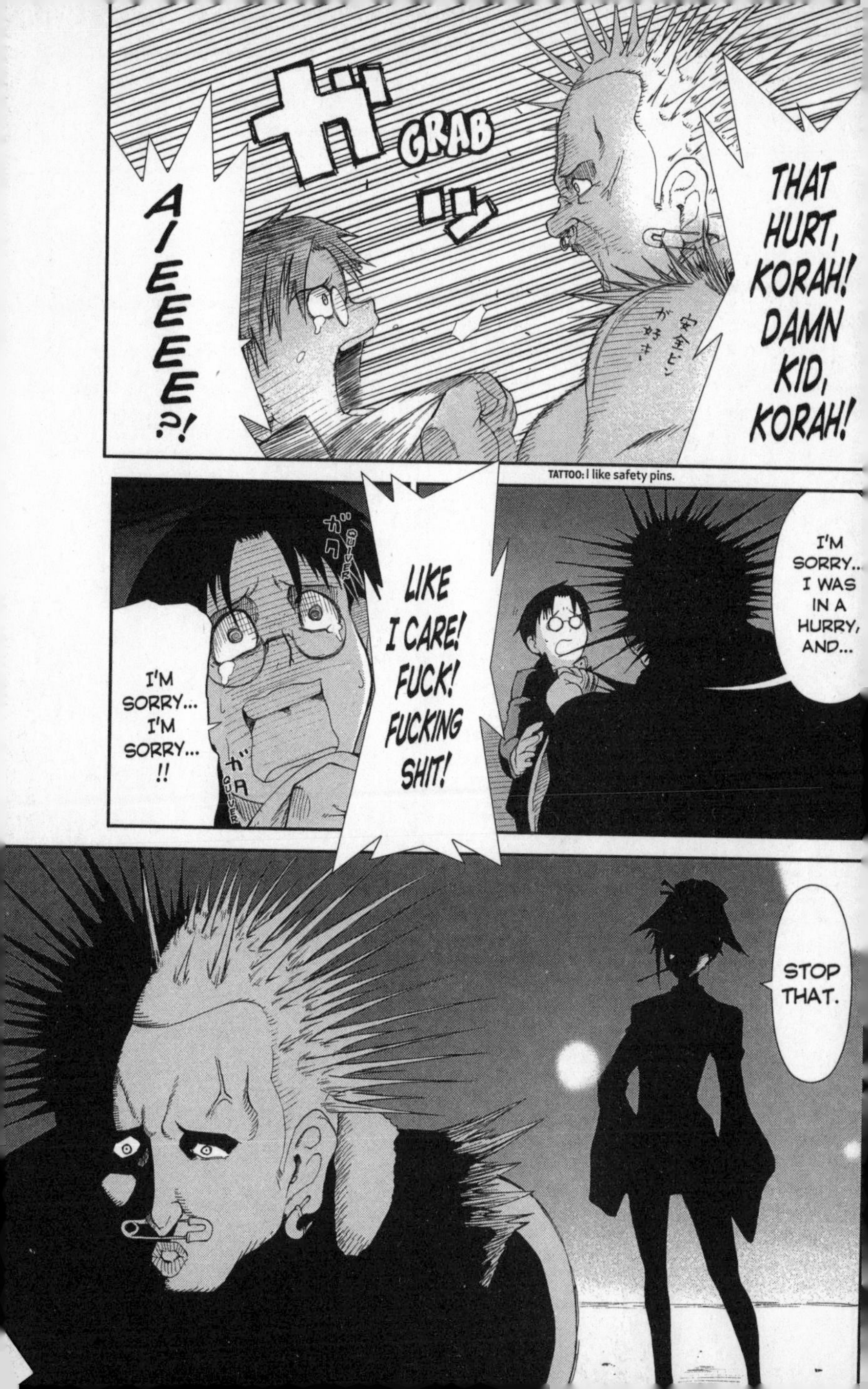
THAT HURT, KORAH! DAMN KID, KORAH!
安全ピンが好き
ガッ
GRAB
AIEEEEE?!
TATTOO: I like safety pins.
I'M SORRY... I WAS IN A HURRY, AND...
LIKE I CARE! FUCK! FUCKING SHIT!
ガク
QUIVER
I'M SORRY... I'M SORRY... !!
ガク
QUIVER
STOP THAT.

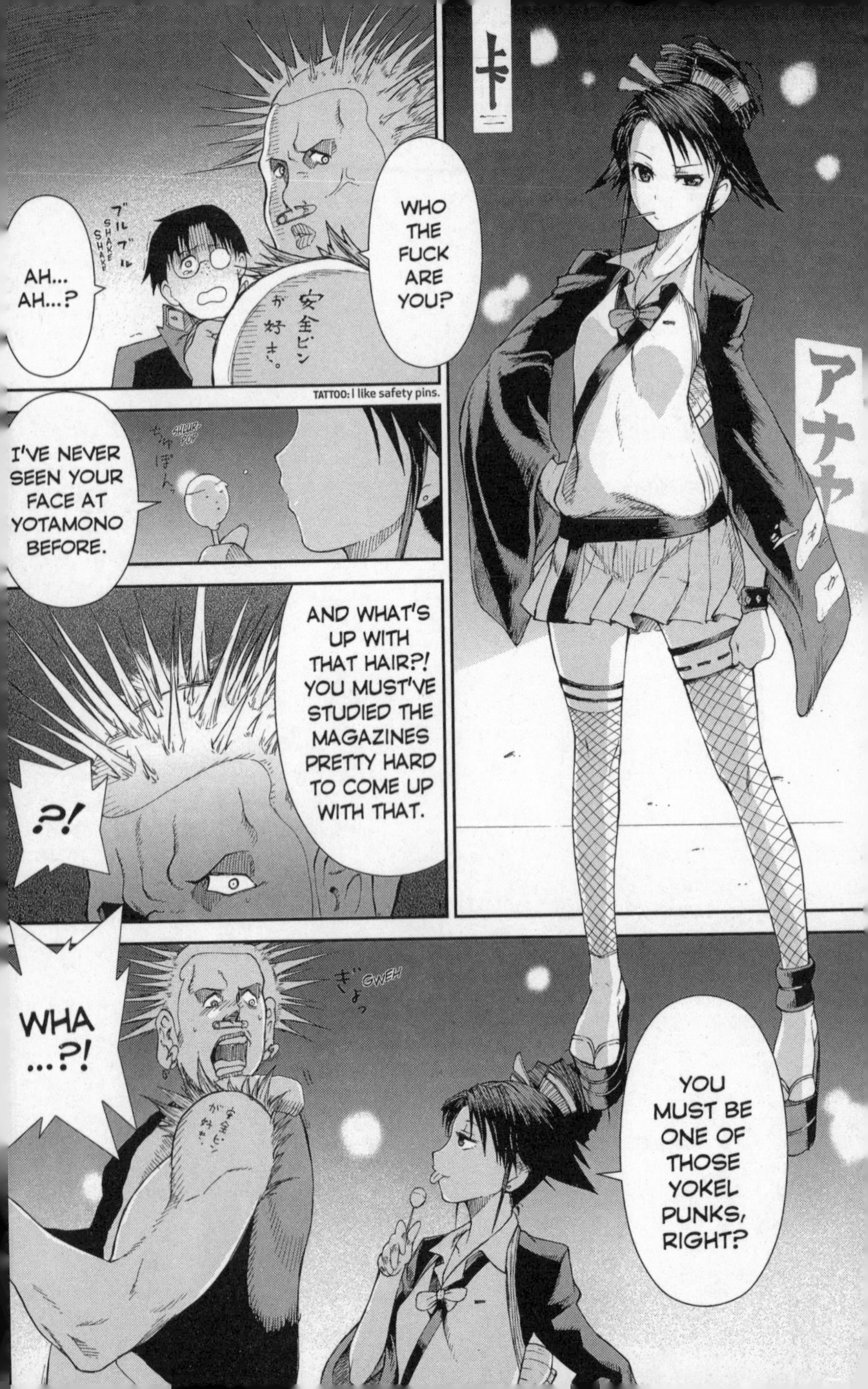
キ
アナヤ
WHO THE FUCK ARE YOU?
ブルブル
SHAKE SHAKE
AH... AH...?
安全ピンが好き。
TATTOO: I like safety pins.
ちゅぽん
SHLURP POP
I'VE NEVER SEEN YOUR FACE AT YOTAMONO BEFORE.
AND WHAT'S UP WITH THAT HAIR?! YOU MUST'VE STUDIED THE MAGAZINES PRETTY HARD TO COME UP WITH THAT.
?!
ぎょっ
GWEH
YOU MUST BE ONE OF THOSE YOKEL PUNKS, RIGHT?
WHA ...?!

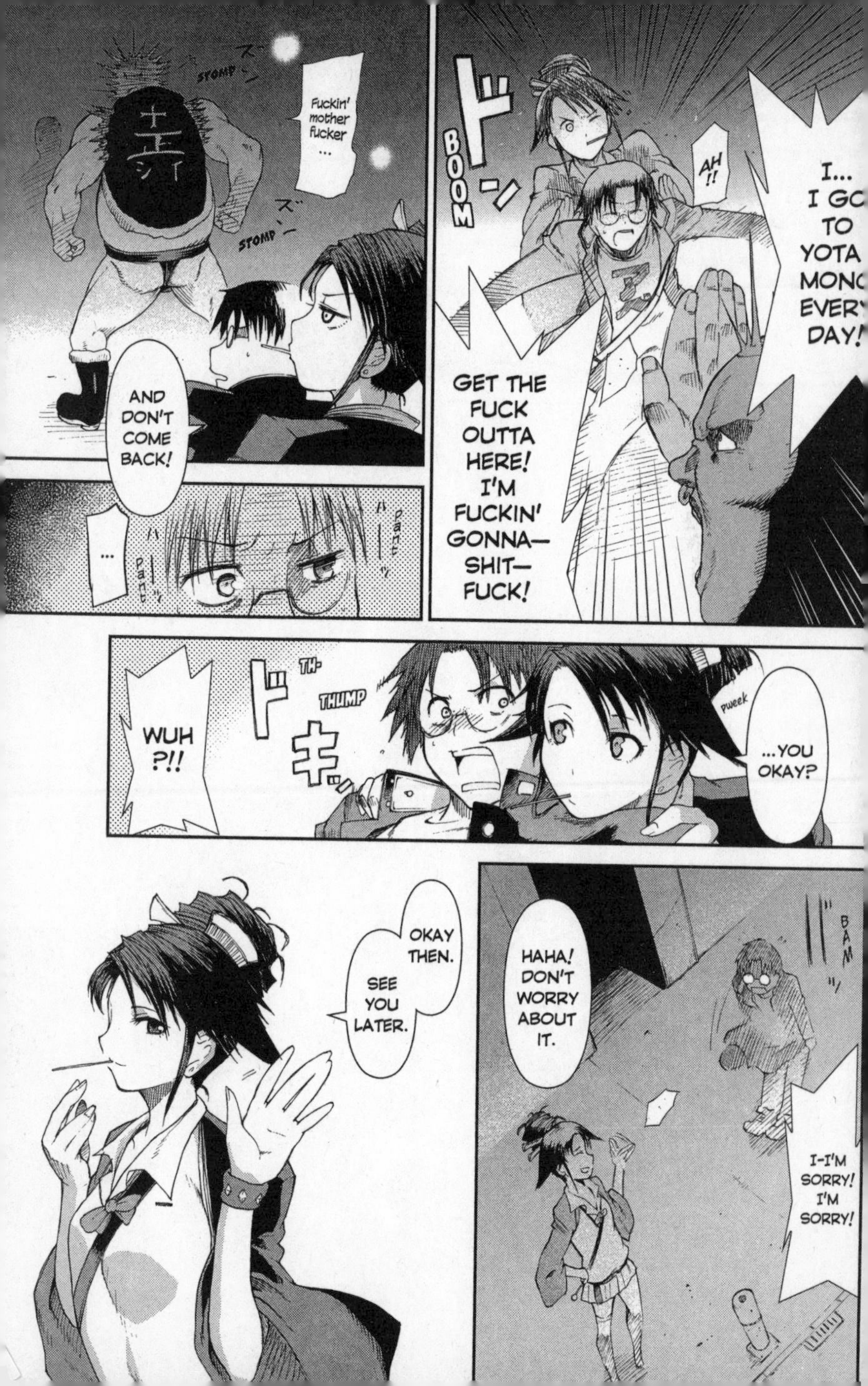
BOOM
AH!!
I... I GO TO YOTA MONO EVERY DAY!
GET THE FUCK OUTTA HERE! I'M FUCKIN' GONNA— SHIT— FUCK!
STOMP
Fuckin' mother fucker ...
STOMP
AND DON'T COME BACK!
pant pant
...
pweek
...YOU OKAY?
TH-THUMP
WUH?!!
BAM
I-I'M SORRY! I'M SORRY!
HAHA! DON'T WORRY ABOUT IT.
OKAY THEN.
SEE YOU LATER.

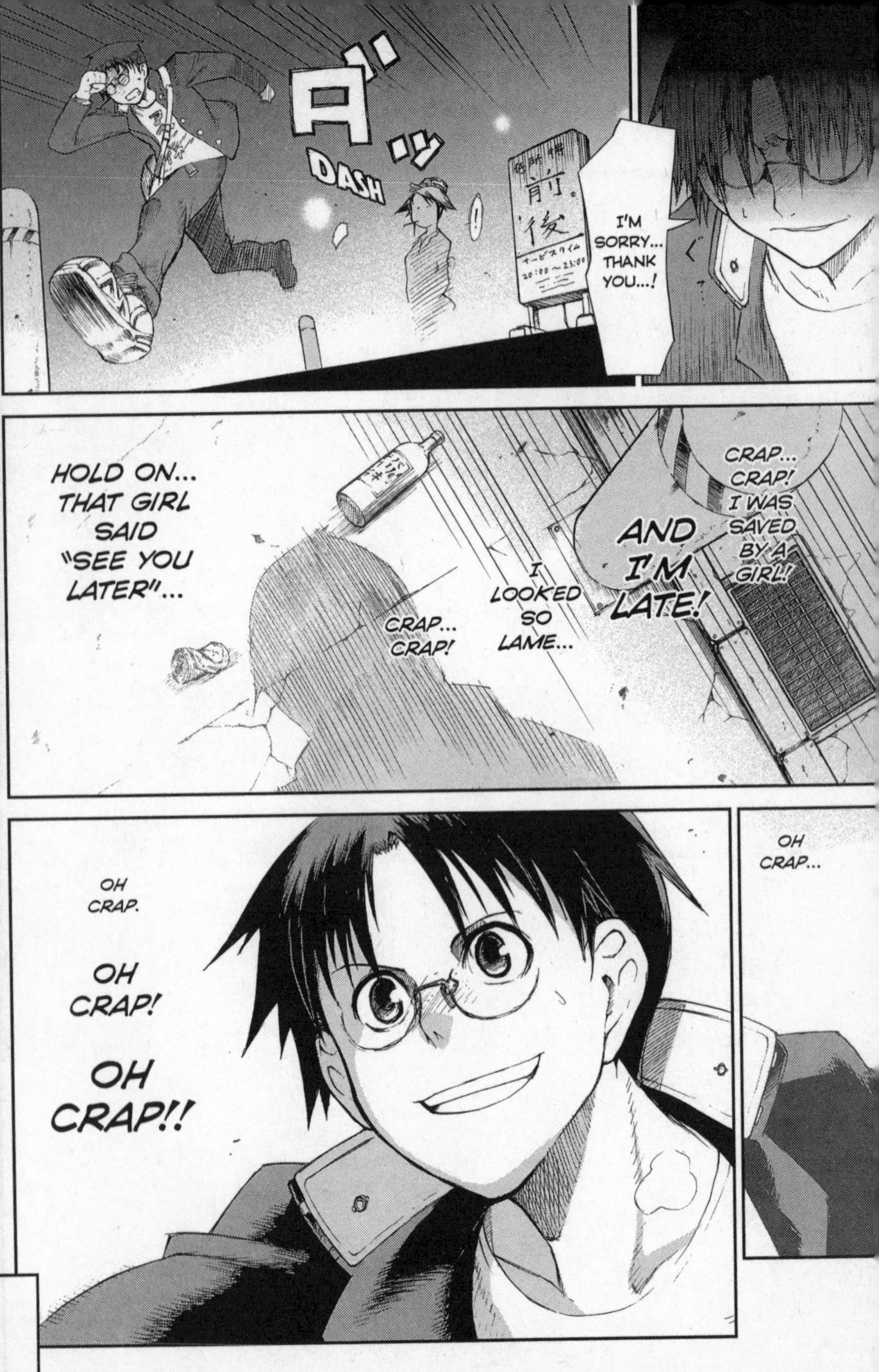
I'M SORRY... THANK YOU...!
ダッ
DASH
!
CRAP... CRAP! I WAS SAVED BY A GIRL!
AND I'M LATE!
I LOOKED SO LAME...
CRAP... CRAP!
HOLD ON... THAT GIRL SAID "SEE YOU LATER"...
OH CRAP...
OH CRAP.
OH CRAP!
OH CRAP!!

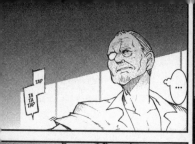

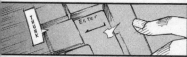

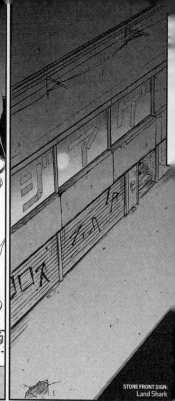

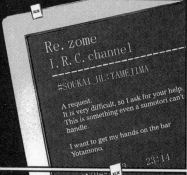

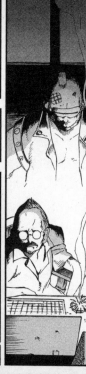

STORE FRONT SIGN: Land Shark
...
TAP
TA TA TAP
THUNK
Enter
KLIK
Re. zome
I. R. C. channel
#SOUKAI_HL:TAMEJIMA
A request.
It is very difficult, so I ask for your help.
This is something even a sumotori can't handle.
I want to get my hands on the bar Yotamono.
23:14
KLIK
Yotamono.
BOOP
#SOUKAI_HL:SOUDAN
I will dispatch a ninja, then.
You will be billed at a later time.
23:15
AIEE?! NINJA ?!
B-BOSS ...?!
KLUNK

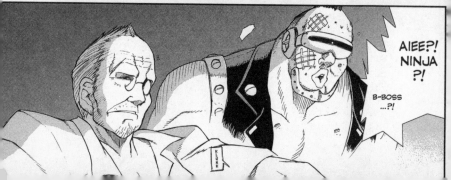

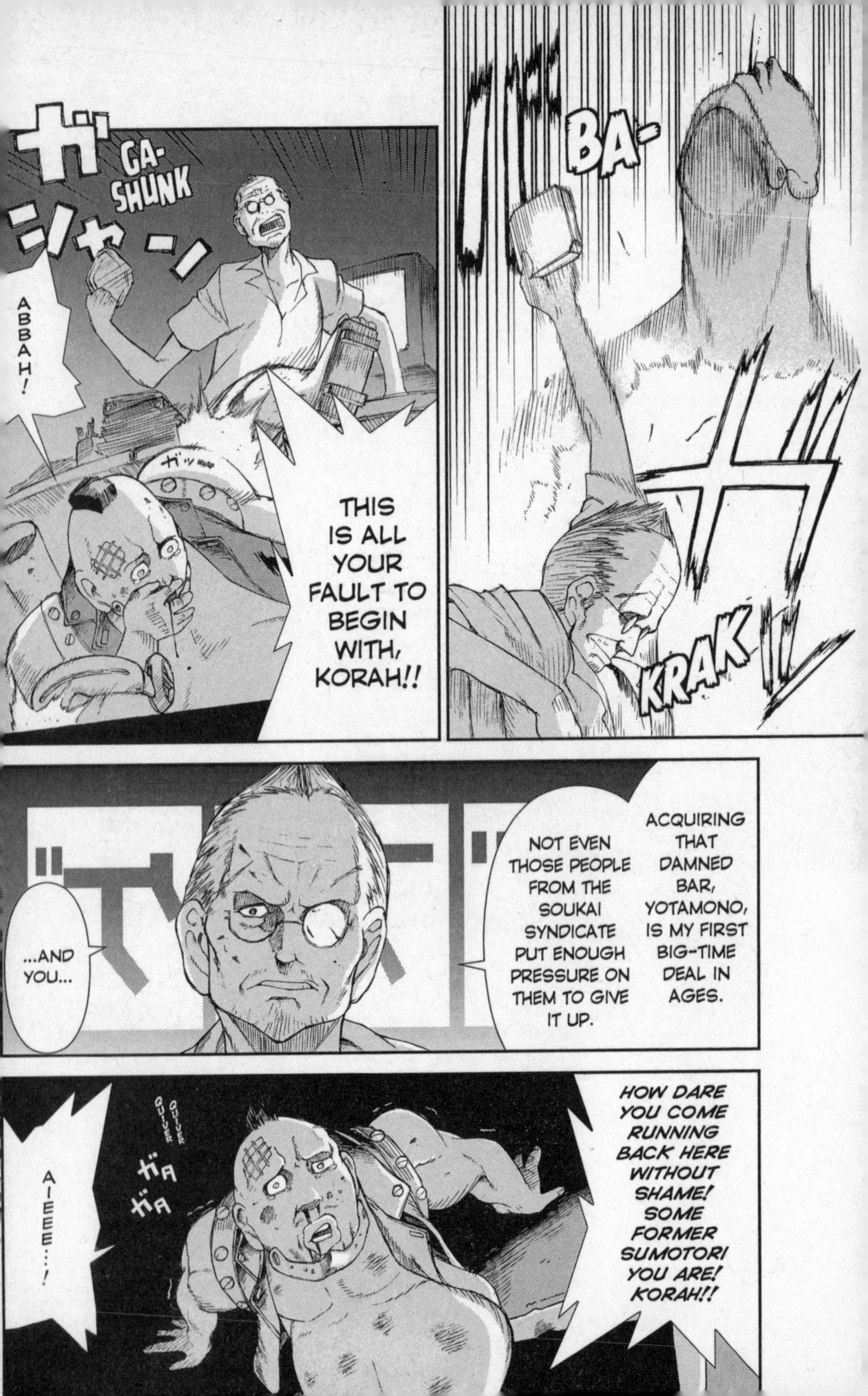
BA-
KRAK!!
GA-SHUNK
ABBAH!
WHAP
THIS IS ALL YOUR FAULT TO BEGIN WITH, KORAH!!
ACQUIRING THAT DAMNED BAR, YOTAMONO, IS MY FIRST BIG-TIME DEAL IN AGES.
NOT EVEN THOSE PEOPLE FROM THE SOUKAI SYNDICATE PUT ENOUGH PRESSURE ON THEM TO GIVE IT UP.
...AND YOU...
HOW DARE YOU COME RUNNING BACK HERE WITHOUT SHAME! SOME FORMER SUMOTORI YOU ARE! KORAH!!
QUIVER QUIVER
AIEEE...!

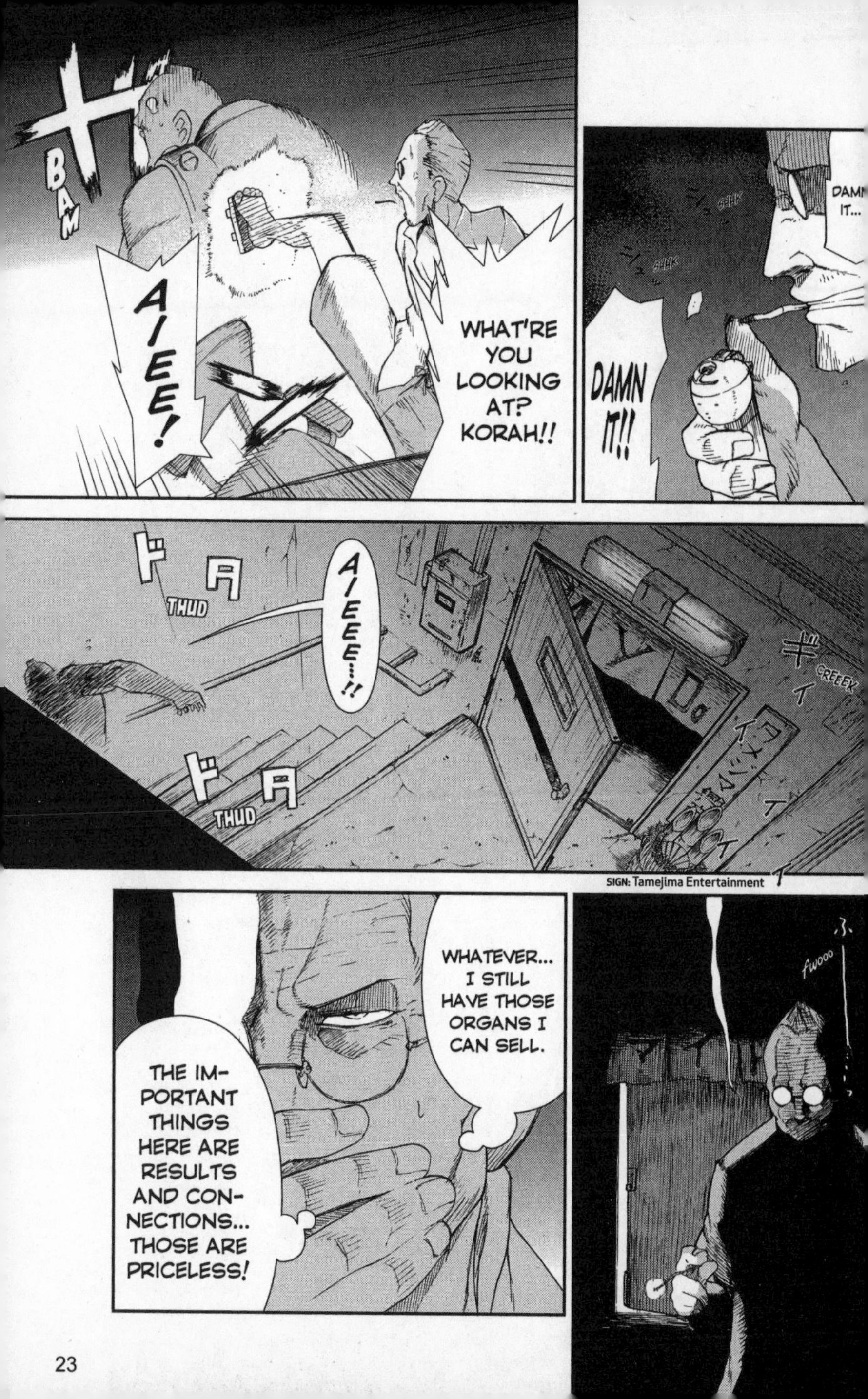
DAMN IT...
SHAK
SHAK
DAMN IT!!
BAM
AIEE!
WHAT'RE YOU LOOKING AT? KORAH!!
CREEEK
AIEEE...!!
THUD
THUD
SIGN: Tamejima Entertainment
fwooo
WHATEVER... I STILL HAVE THOSE ORGANS I CAN SELL.
THE IMPORTANT THINGS HERE ARE RESULTS AND CONNECTIONS... THOSE ARE PRICELESS!

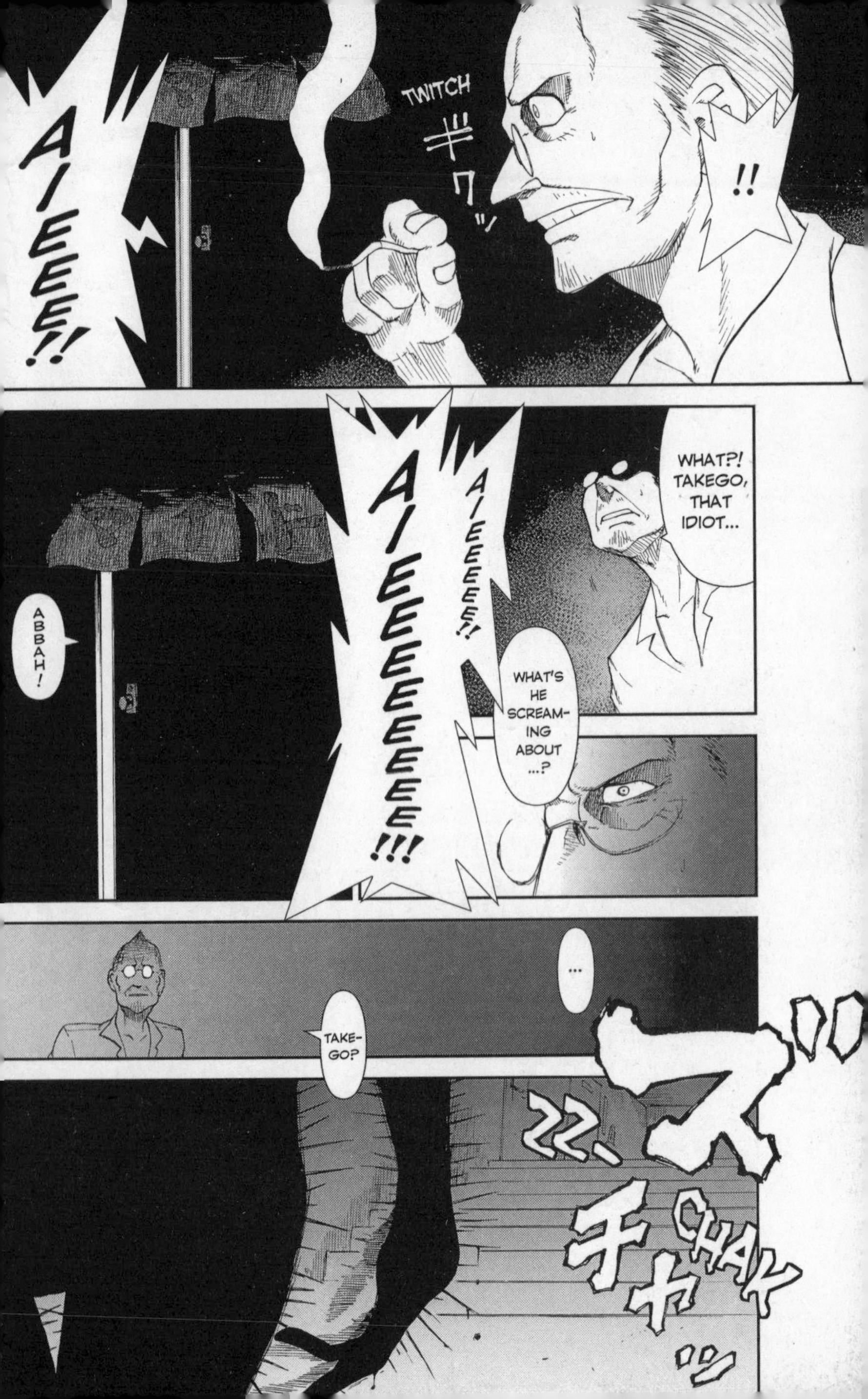
!!
TWITCH
ギクッ
AIEEEE!!
WHAT?! TAKEGO, THAT IDIOT...
AIEEEEE!!
AIEEEEEEEEEE!!!
WHAT'S HE SCREAM-ING ABOUT ...?
ABBAH!
...
TAKE-GO?
ズ
ZZZ
チャッ
CHAK

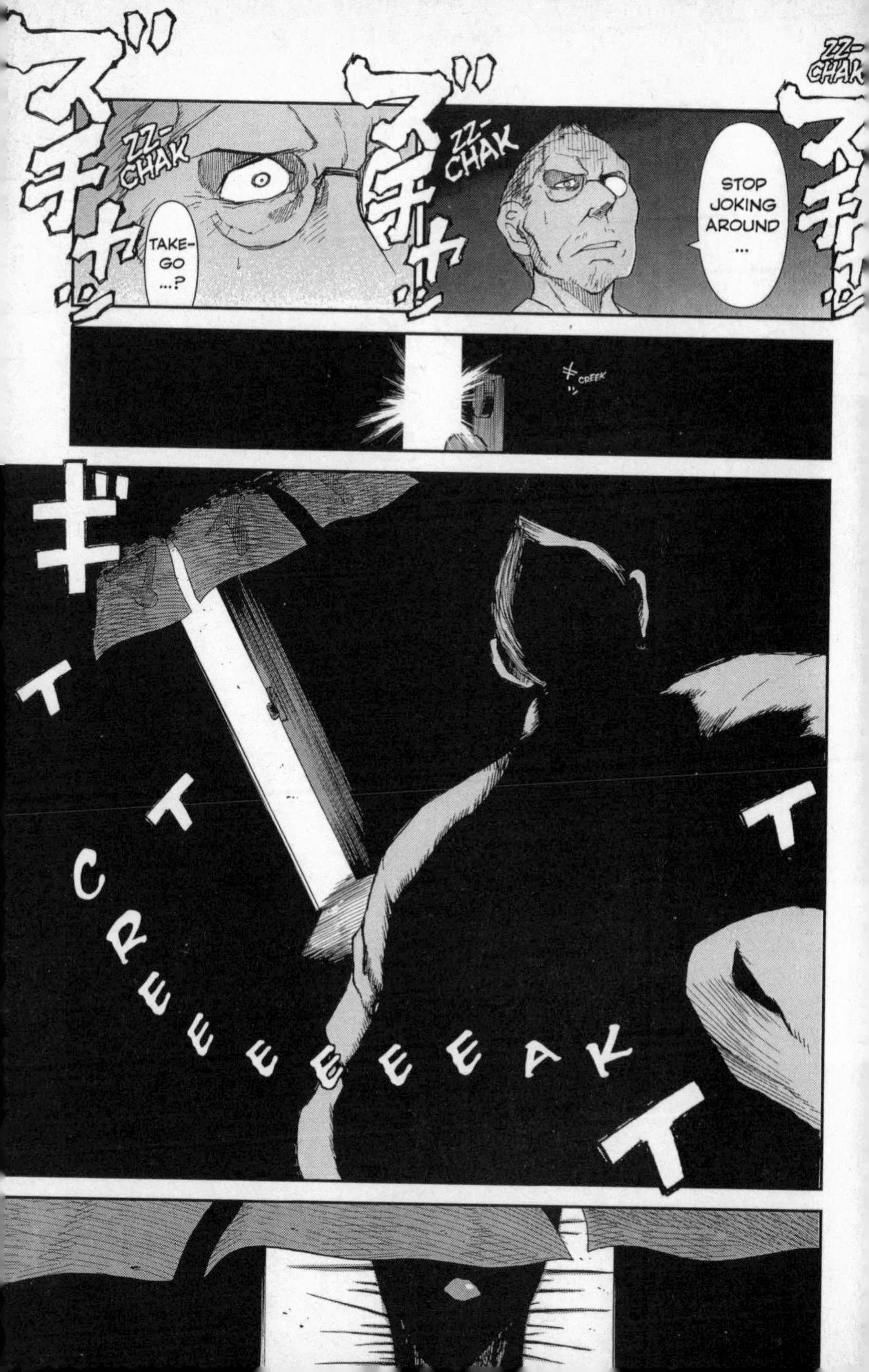
ZZ-CHAK
STOP JOKING AROUND ...
ZZ-CHAK
ZZ-CHAK
TAKE-GO ...?
CREEK
CREEEEEAK

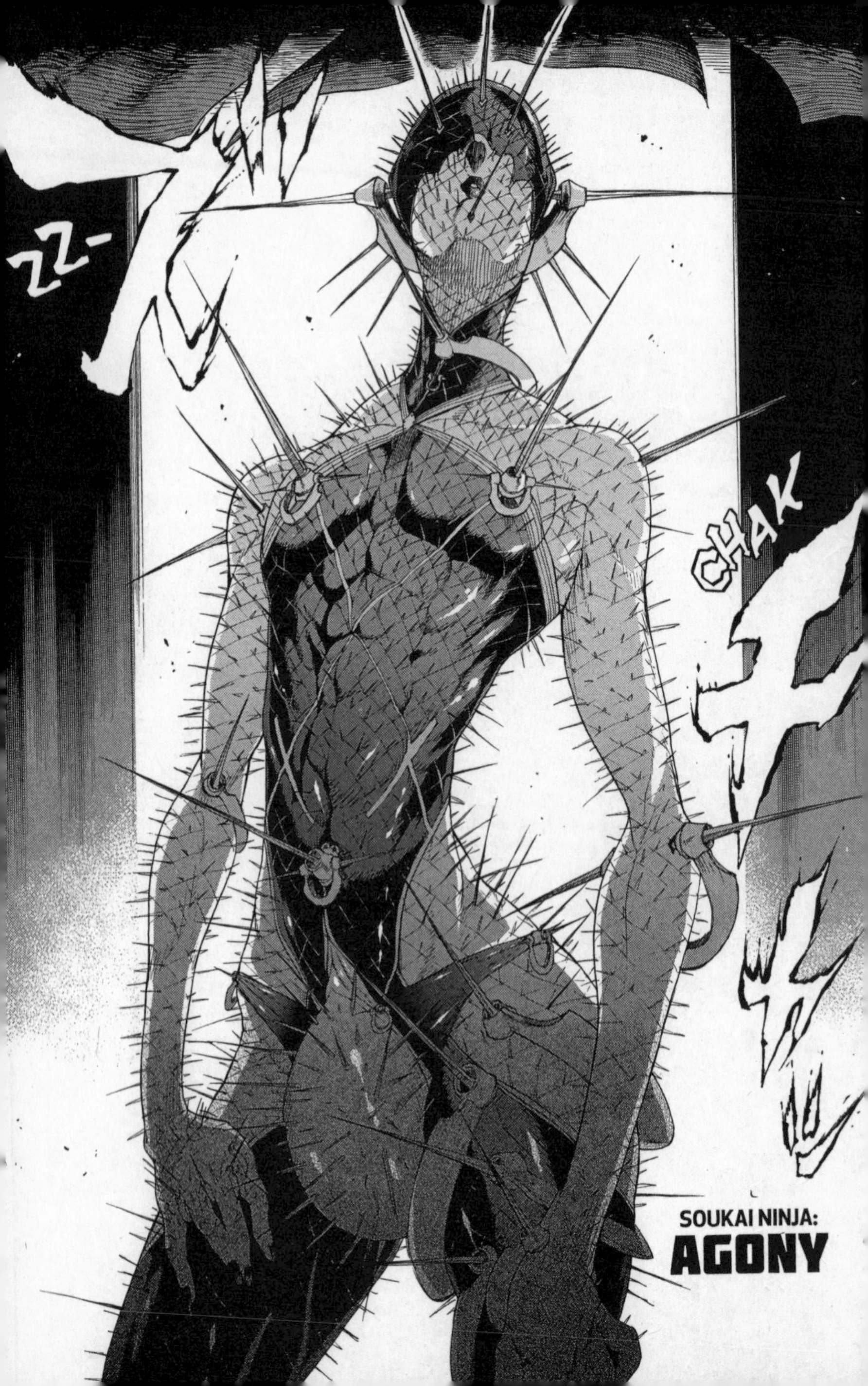
ZZ-
CHAK
SOUKAI NINJA:
AGONY

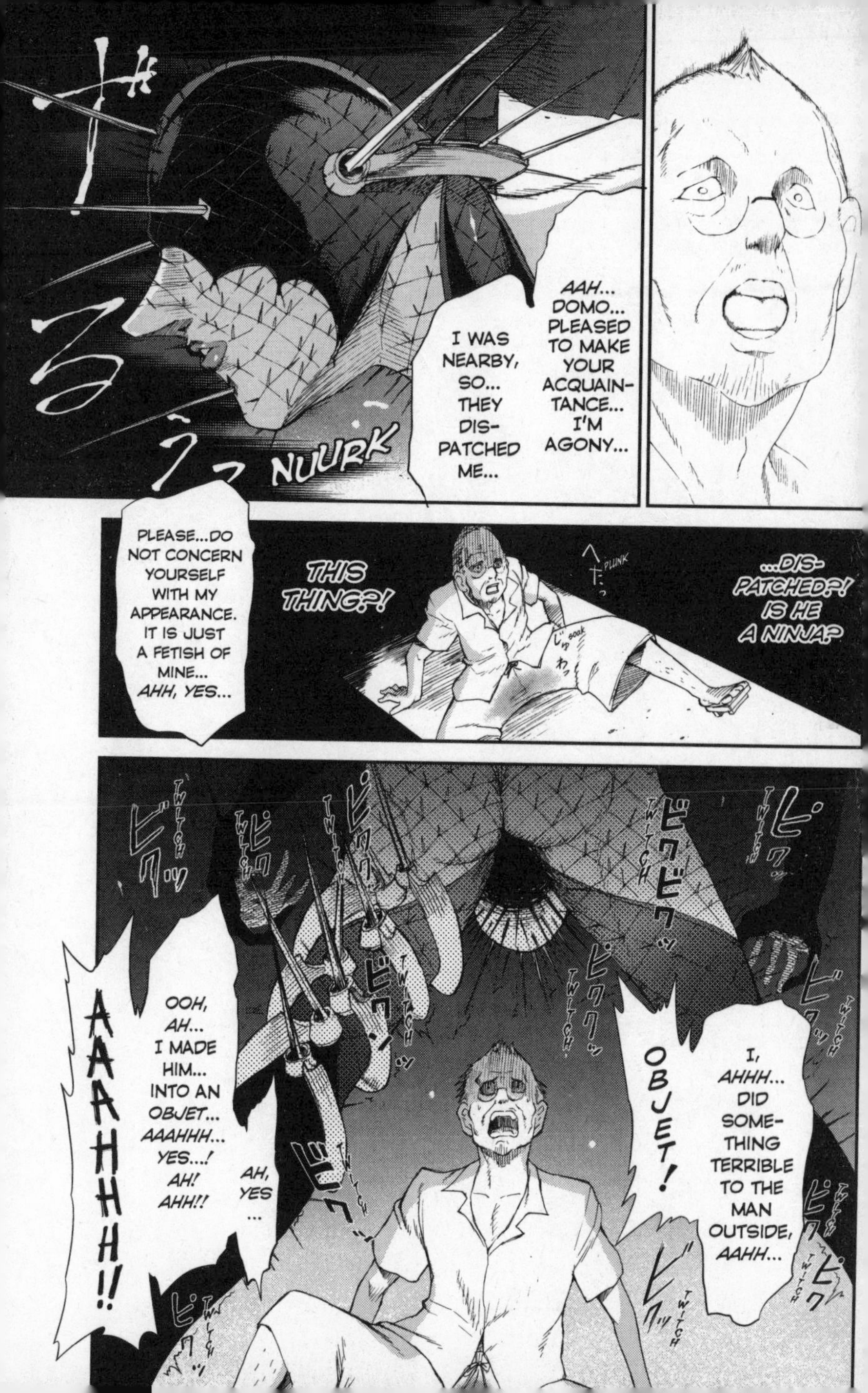
AAH... DOMO... PLEASED TO MAKE YOUR ACQUAINTANCE... I'M AGONY...
I WAS NEARBY, SO... THEY DISPATCHED ME...
NUURK
...DISPATCHED?! IS HE A NINJA?
PLUNK
SOAK
THIS THING?!
PLEASE...DO NOT CONCERN YOURSELF WITH MY APPEARANCE. IT IS JUST A FETISH OF MINE... AHH, YES...
TWITCH
TWITCH
TWITCH
I, AHHH... DID SOMETHING TERRIBLE TO THE MAN OUTSIDE, AAHH...
OBJET!
TWITCH
TWITCH
TWITCH
TWITCH
TWITCH
TWITCH
OOH, AH... I MADE HIM... INTO AN OBJET... AAAHHH... YES...! AH! AHH!!
AH, YES ...
AAAHHHH!!
TWITCH

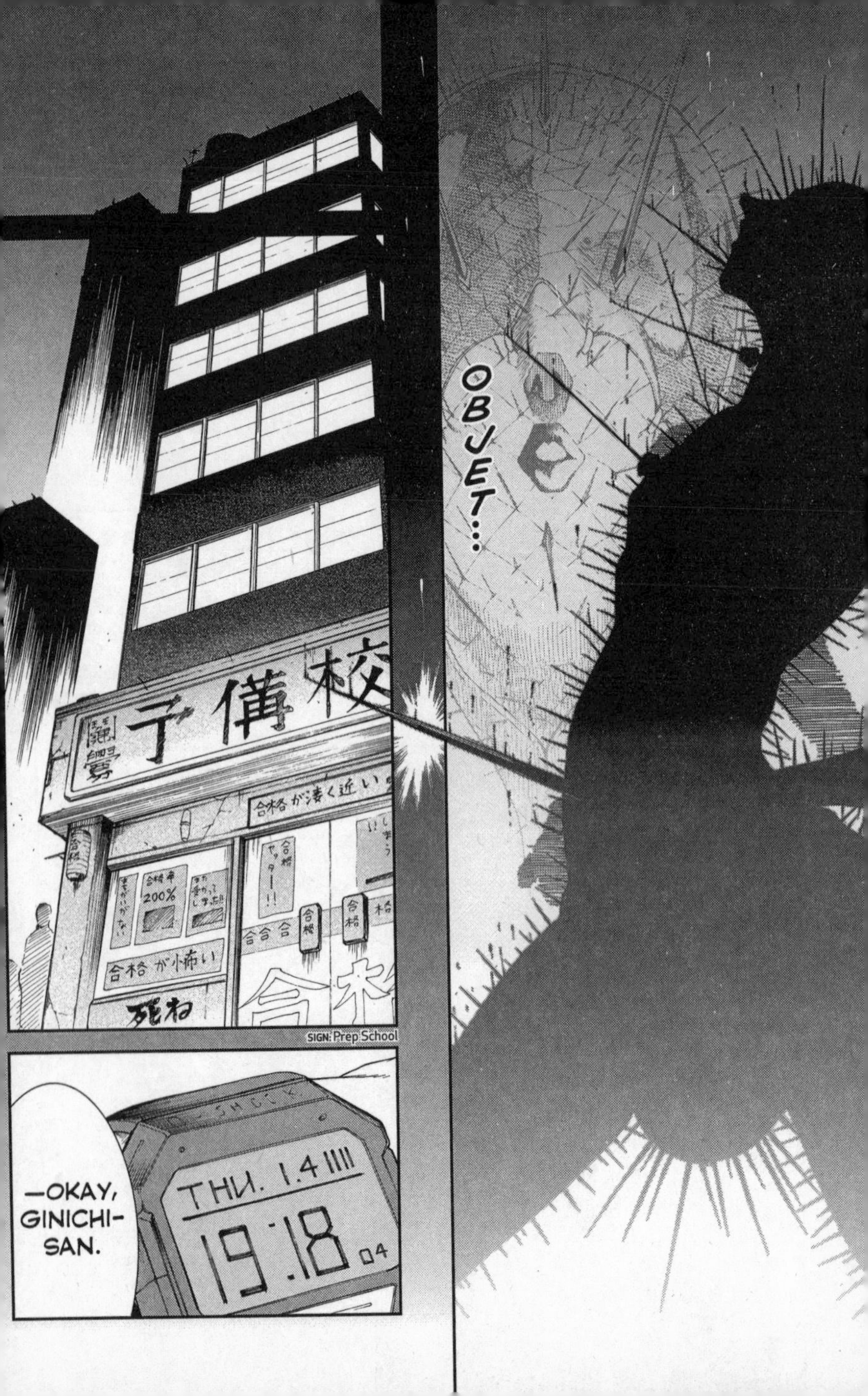
OBJET...
予備校
合格が凄く近い
合格率200%
合格が怖い
SIGN: Prep School
THU. 1.4
19 18 04
—OKAY, GINICHI-SAN.

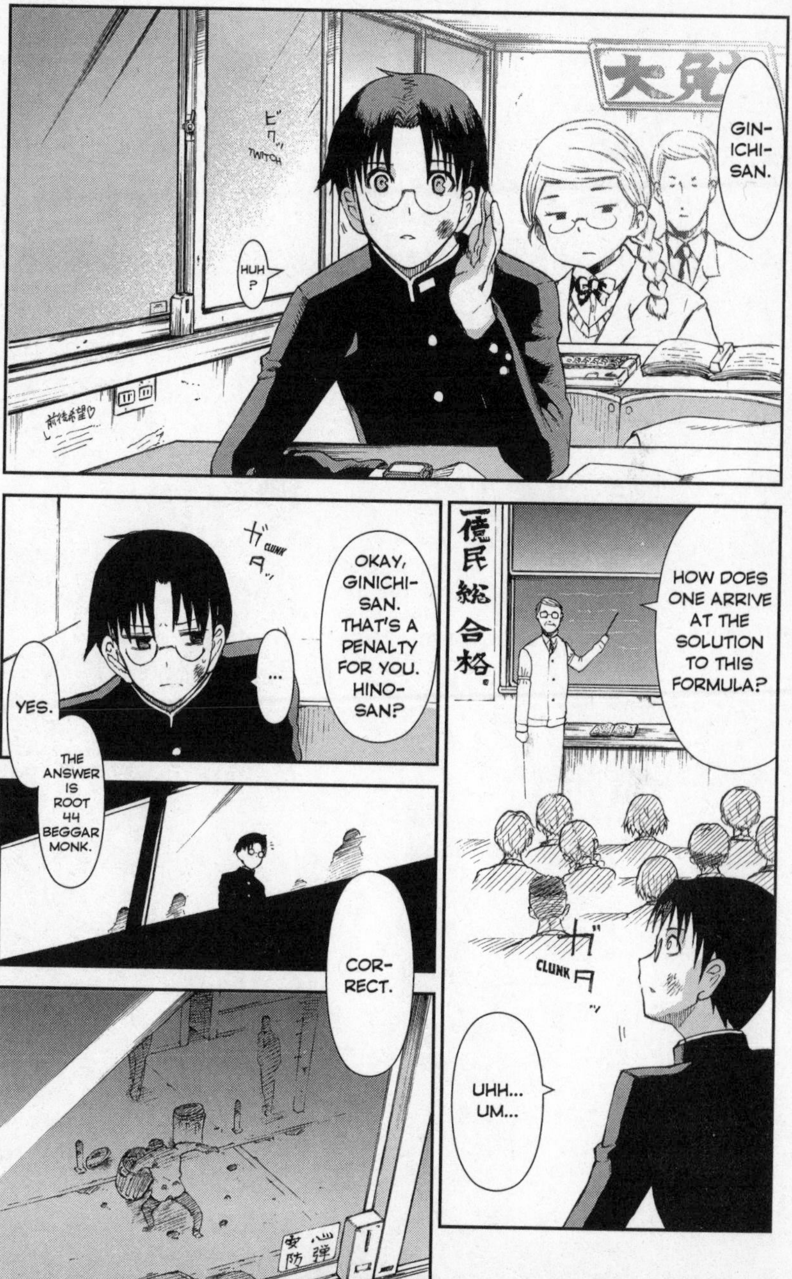
GIN-ICHI-SAN.
ビクッ
TWITCH
HUH?
HOW DOES ONE ARRIVE AT THE SOLUTION TO THIS FORMULA?
一億民総合格
ガタッ
CLUNK
UHH... UM...
OKAY, GINICHI-SAN. THAT'S A PENALTY FOR YOU. HINO-SAN?
ガタッ
CLUNK
...
YES.
THE ANSWER IS ROOT 44 BEGGAR MONK.
COR-RECT.

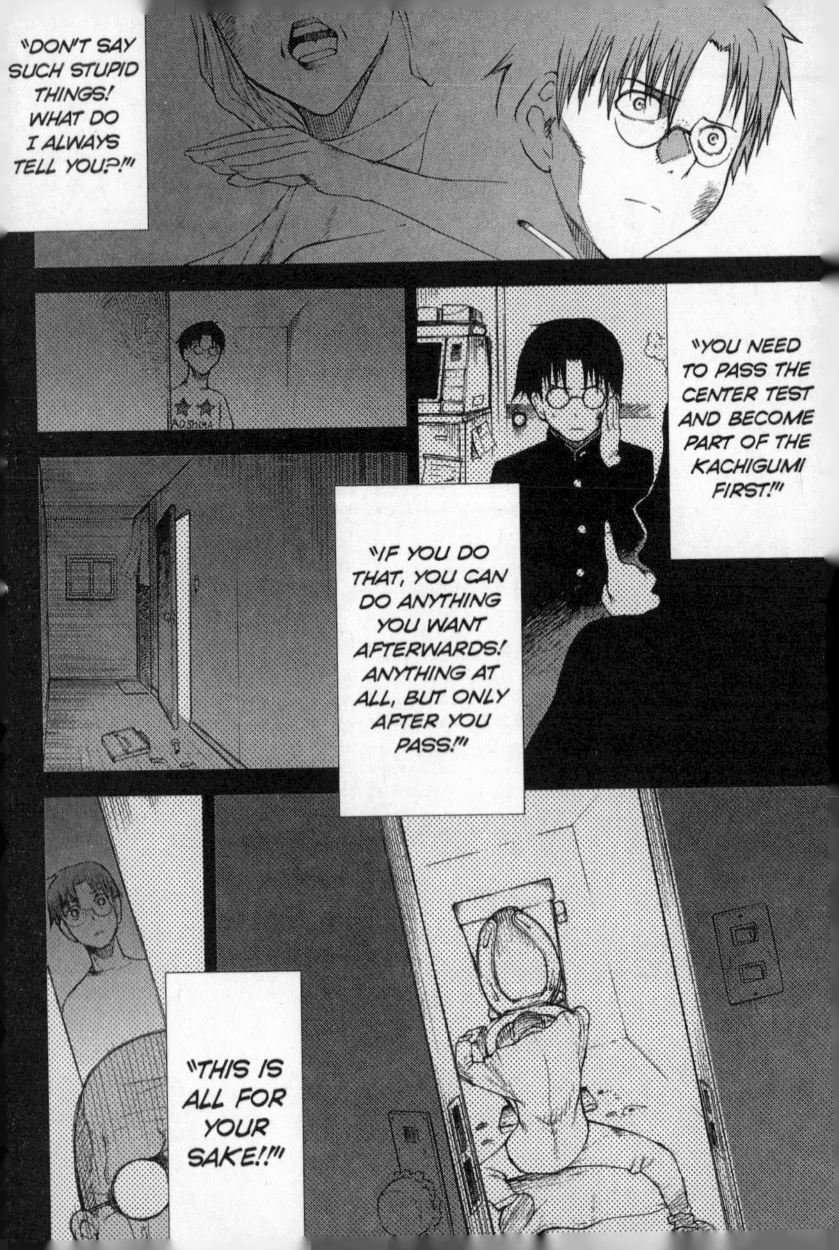
"DON'T SAY SUCH STUPID THINGS! WHAT DO I ALWAYS TELL YOU?!"
"YOU NEED TO PASS THE CENTER TEST AND BECOME PART OF THE KACHIGUMI FIRST!"
"IF YOU DO THAT, YOU CAN DO ANYTHING YOU WANT AFTERWARDS! ANYTHING AT ALL, BUT ONLY AFTER YOU PASS!"
"THIS IS ALL FOR YOUR SAKE!!"

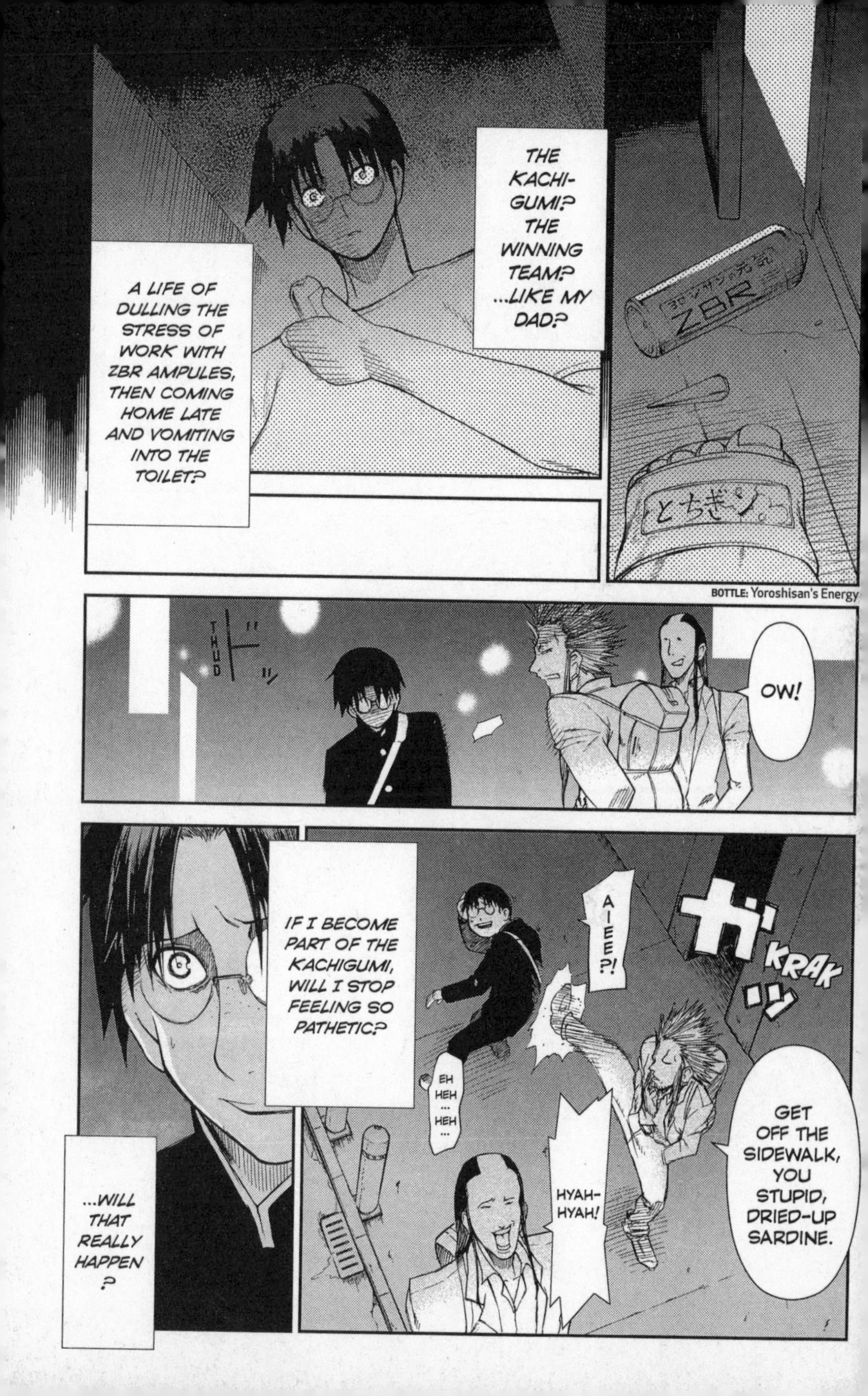
ZBR
BOTTLE: Yoroshisan's Energy
THE KACHI-GUMI? THE WINNING TEAM? ...LIKE MY DAD?
A LIFE OF DULLING THE STRESS OF WORK WITH ZBR AMPULES, THEN COMING HOME LATE AND VOMITING INTO THE TOILET?
OW!
THUD
KRAK
AIEE?!
IF I BECOME PART OF THE KACHIGUMI, WILL I STOP FEELING SO PATHETIC?
GET OFF THE SIDEWALK, YOU STUPID, DRIED-UP SARDINE.
EH HEH ... HEH ...
HYAH-HYAH!
...WILL THAT REALLY HAPPEN ?

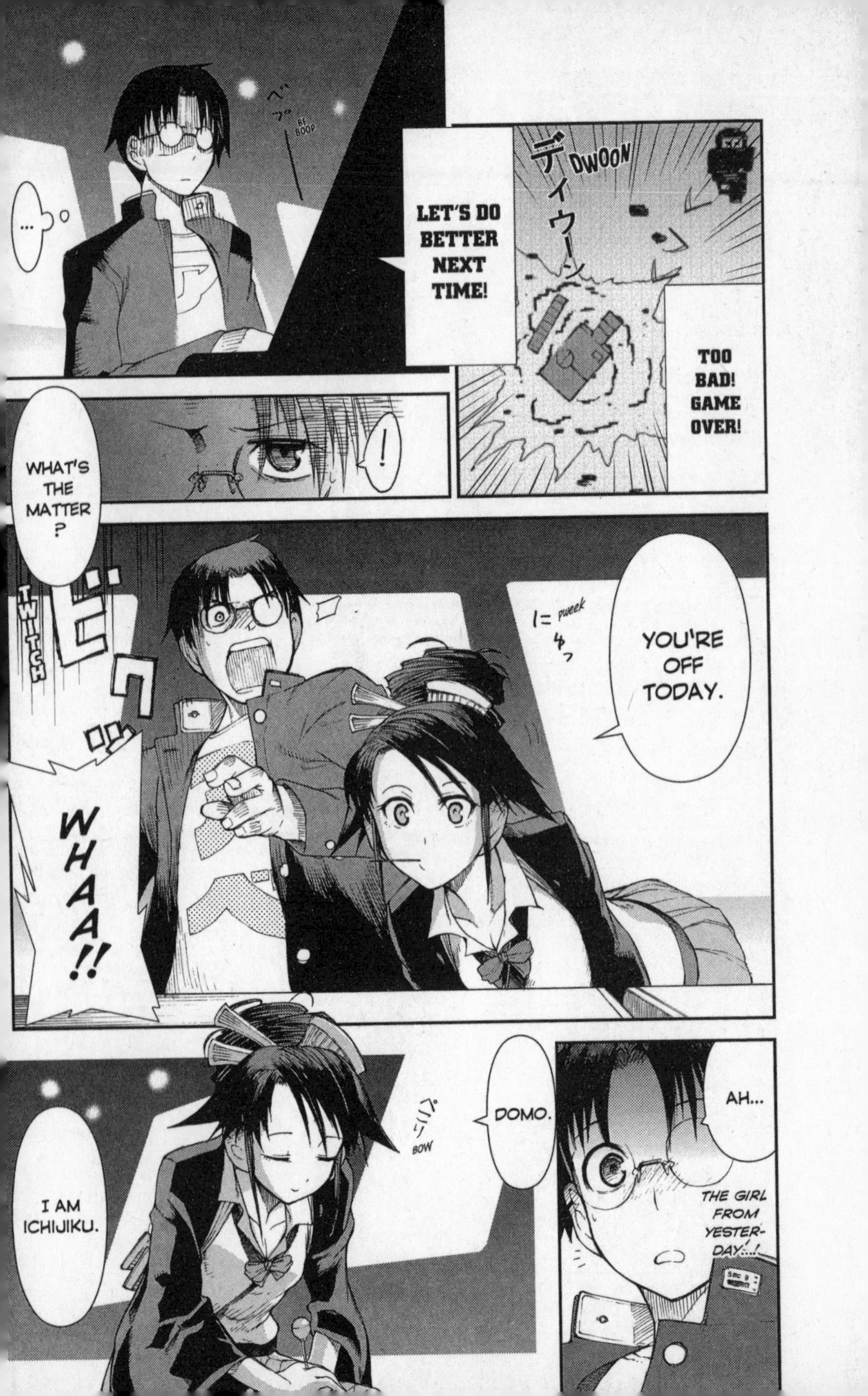
デイウーン
DWOON
TOO BAD! GAME OVER!
LET'S DO BETTER NEXT TIME!
BE BOOP
...
!
WHAT'S THE MATTER?
YOU'RE OFF TODAY.
pweek
TWITCH
WHAAA!!
AH...
THE GIRL FROM YESTER-DAY...!
DOMO.
BOW
I AM ICHIJIKU.

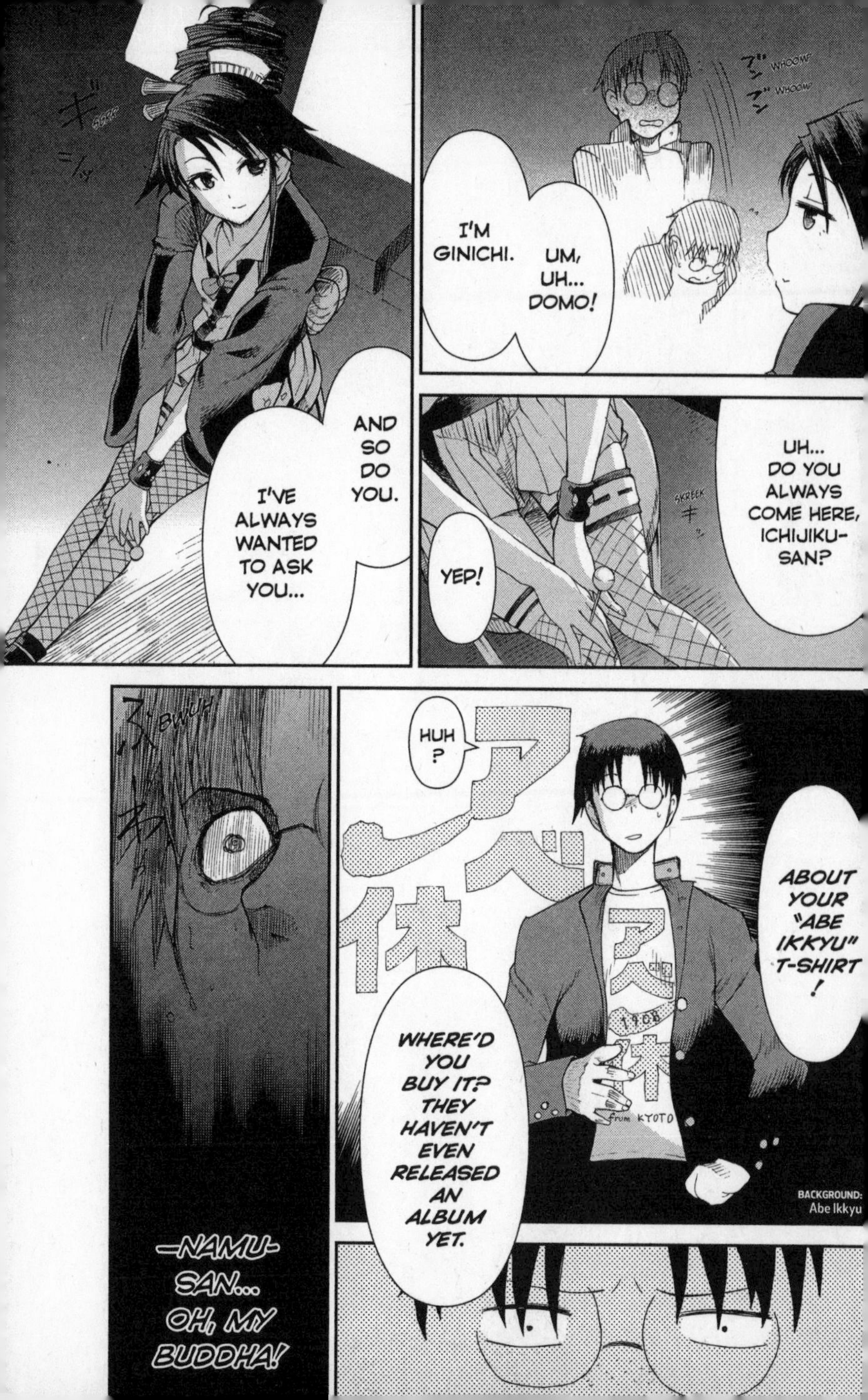
WHOOMF
WHOOMF
UM, UH... DOMO!
I'M GINICHI.
UH... DO YOU ALWAYS COME HERE, ICHIJIKU-SAN?
SKREEK
YEP!
AND SO DO YOU.
I'VE ALWAYS WANTED TO ASK YOU...
ABOUT YOUR "ABE IKKYU" T-SHIRT!
HUH?
WHERE'D YOU BUY IT? THEY HAVEN'T EVEN RELEASED AN ALBUM YET.
BACKGROUND: Abe Ikkyu
BWUH
—NAMU-SAN... OH, MY BUDDHA!

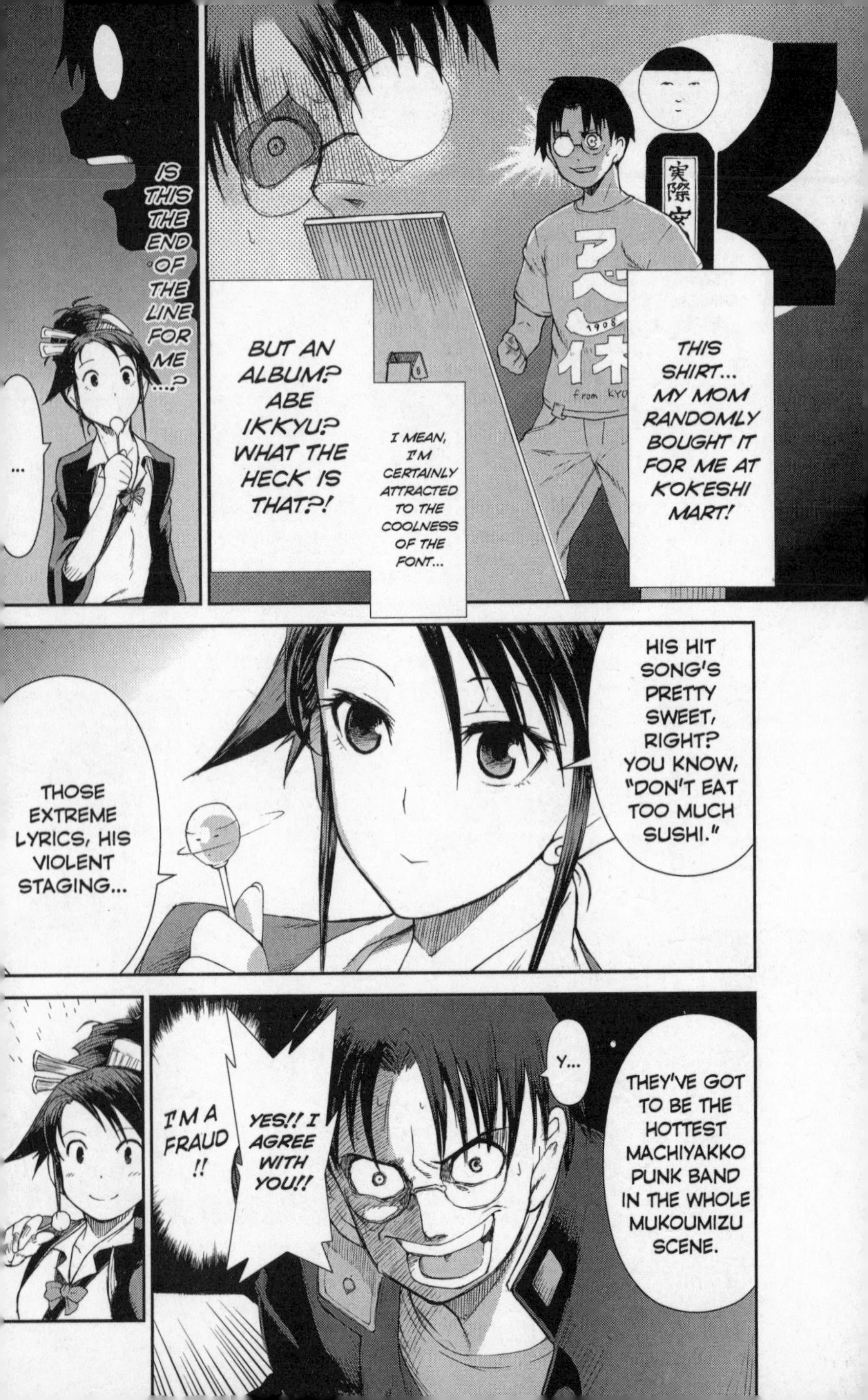
THIS SHIRT... MY MOM RANDOMLY BOUGHT IT FOR ME AT KOKESHI MART!
I MEAN, I'M CERTAINLY ATTRACTED TO THE COOLNESS OF THE FONT...
BUT AN ALBUM? ABE IKKYU? WHAT THE HECK IS THAT?!
IS THIS THE END OF THE LINE FOR ME...?
...
HIS HIT SONG'S PRETTY SWEET, RIGHT? YOU KNOW, "DON'T EAT TOO MUCH SUSHI."
THOSE EXTREME LYRICS, HIS VIOLENT STAGING...
THEY'VE GOT TO BE THE HOTTEST MACHIYAKKO PUNK BAND IN THE WHOLE MUKOUMIZU SCENE.
Y...
YES!! I AGREE WITH YOU!!
I'M A FRAUD!!

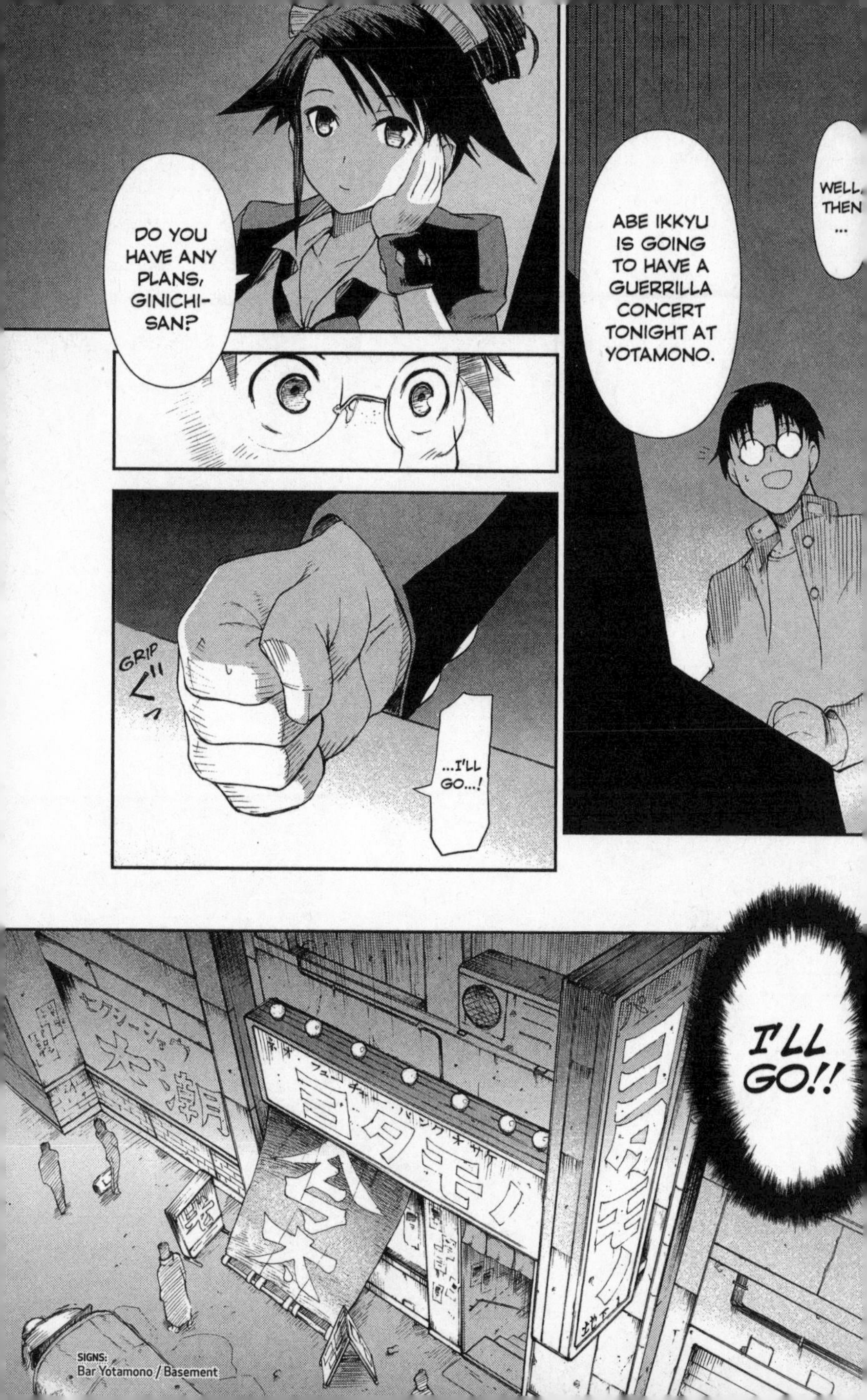
WELL, THEN ...
ABE IKKYU IS GOING TO HAVE A GUERRILLA CONCERT TONIGHT AT YOTAMONO.
DO YOU HAVE ANY PLANS, GINICHI-SAN?
GRIP
...I'LL GO...!
I'LL GO!!
SIGNS:
Bar Yotamono / Basement

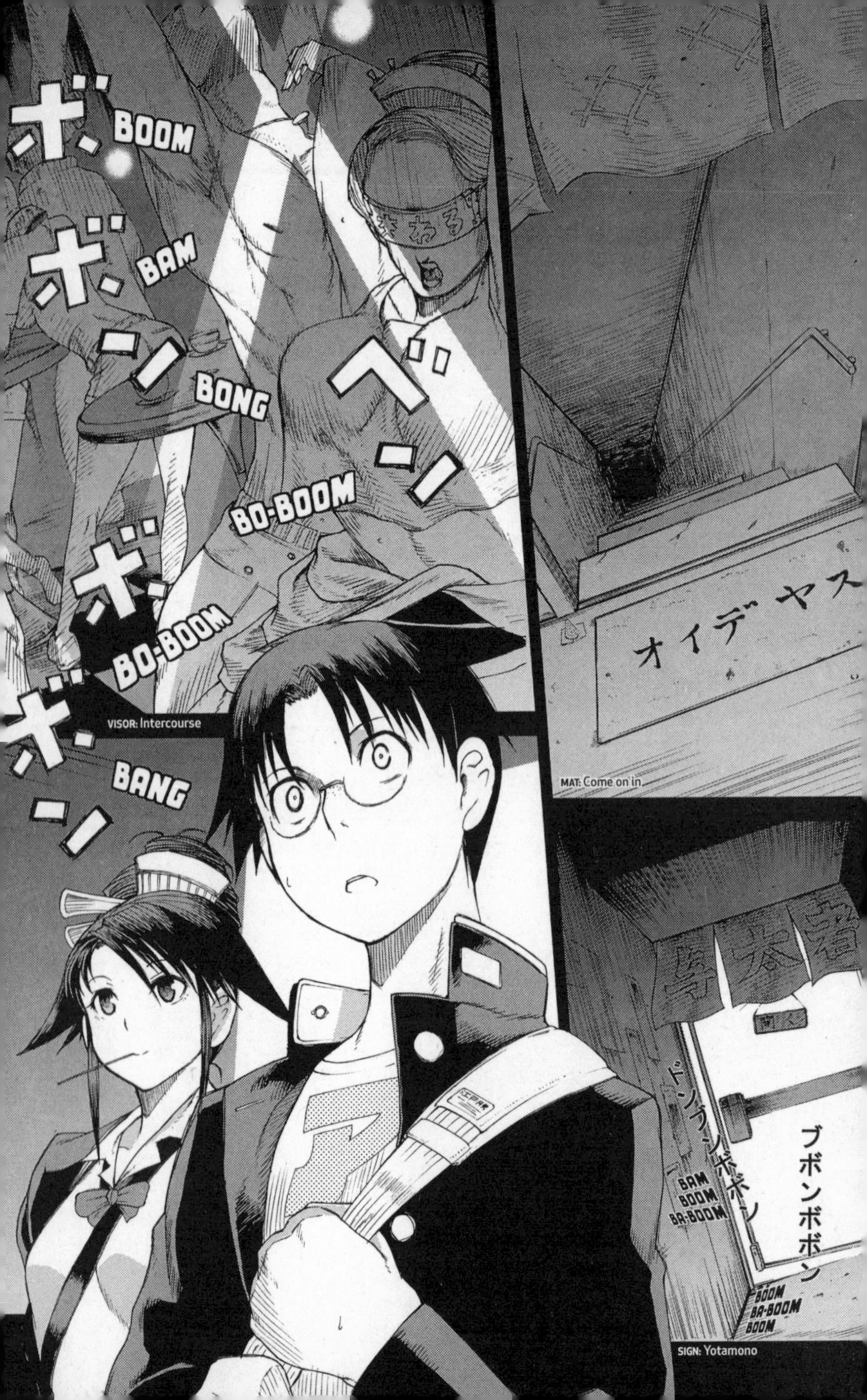
オイデヤス
MAT: Come on in
ボン BOOM
ボン BAM
ン BONG
ベン
BO-BOOM
ボン BO-BOOM
ボン BANG
VISOR: Intercourse
ブボンボボン
BOOM
BA-BOOM
BOOM
ドンブンボボン
BAM
BOOM
BA-BOOM
SIGN: Yotamono

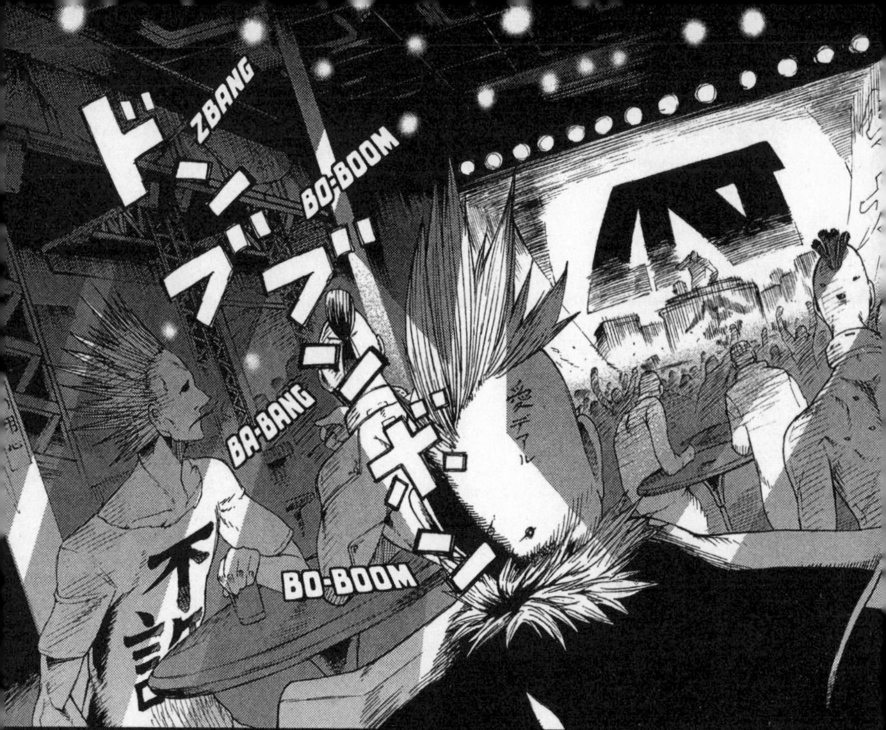

ZBANG
BO-BOOM
BA-BANG
BO-BOOM

T-SHIRT: Rights Reserved

TATTOO: It's Love

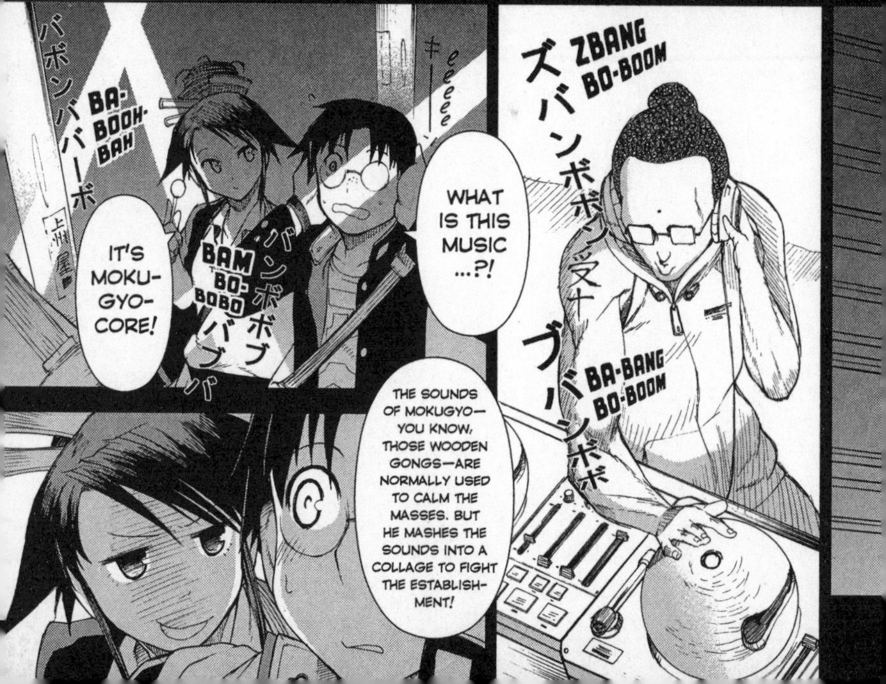

ZBANG
BO-BOOM
BA-BANG
BO-BOOM
eeeee
WHAT IS THIS MUSIC ...?!
BA-BOOH-BAH
BAM BO-BOBO
IT'S MOKU-GYO-CORE!
THE SOUNDS OF MOKUGYO— YOU KNOW, THOSE WOODEN GONGS—ARE NORMALLY USED TO CALM THE MASSES. BUT HE MASHES THE SOUNDS INTO A COLLAGE TO FIGHT THE ESTABLISH-MENT!

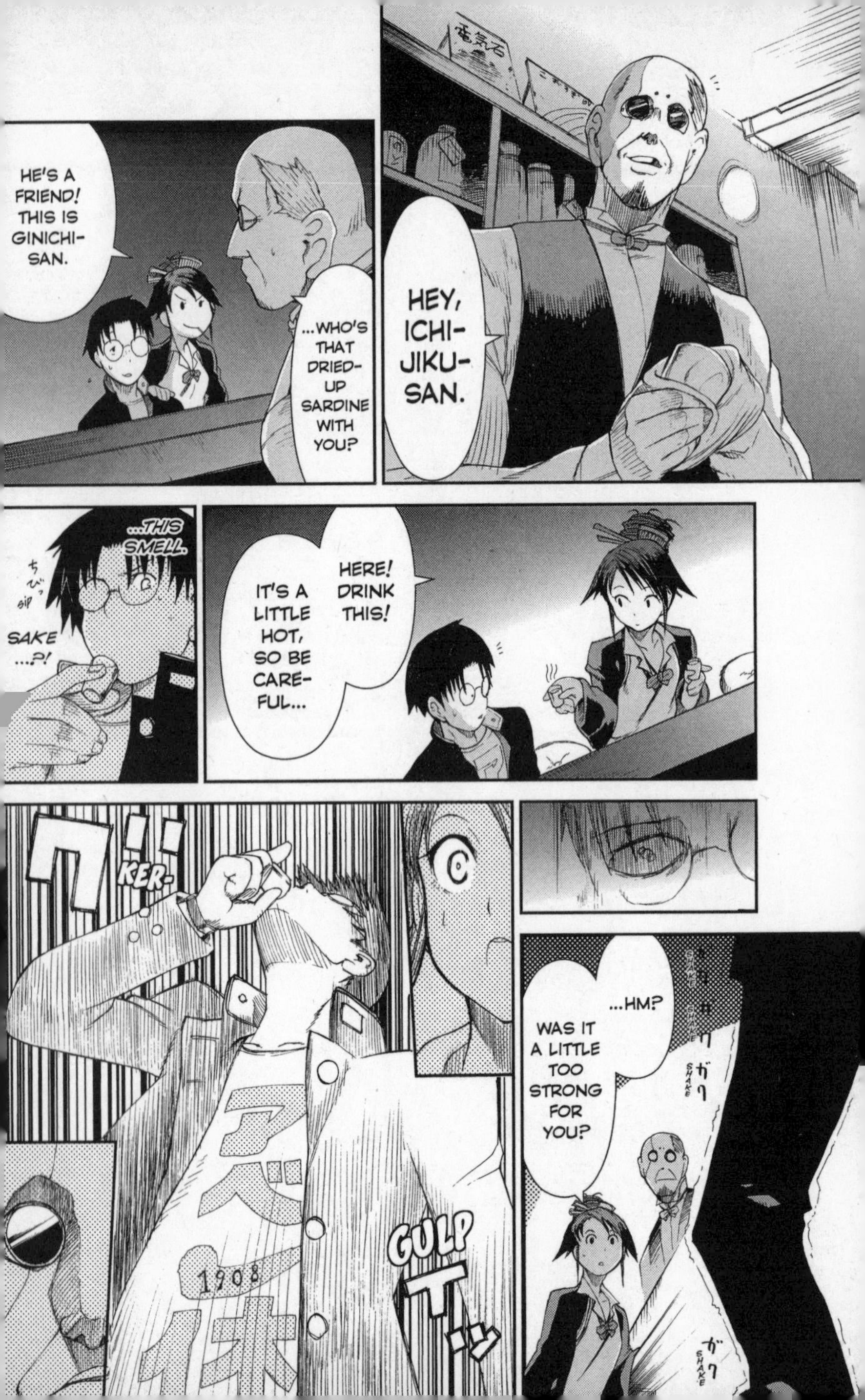
HEY, ICHI-JIKU-SAN.
...WHO'S THAT DRIED-UP SARDINE WITH YOU?
HE'S A FRIEND! THIS IS GINICHI-SAN.
HERE! DRINK THIS!
IT'S A LITTLE HOT, SO BE CARE-FUL...
...THIS SMELL.
ちびっ
SIP
SAKE ...?!
SHAKE SHAKE
...HM?
WAS IT A LITTLE TOO STRONG FOR YOU?
ガク
SHAKE
KER-
GULP
1908

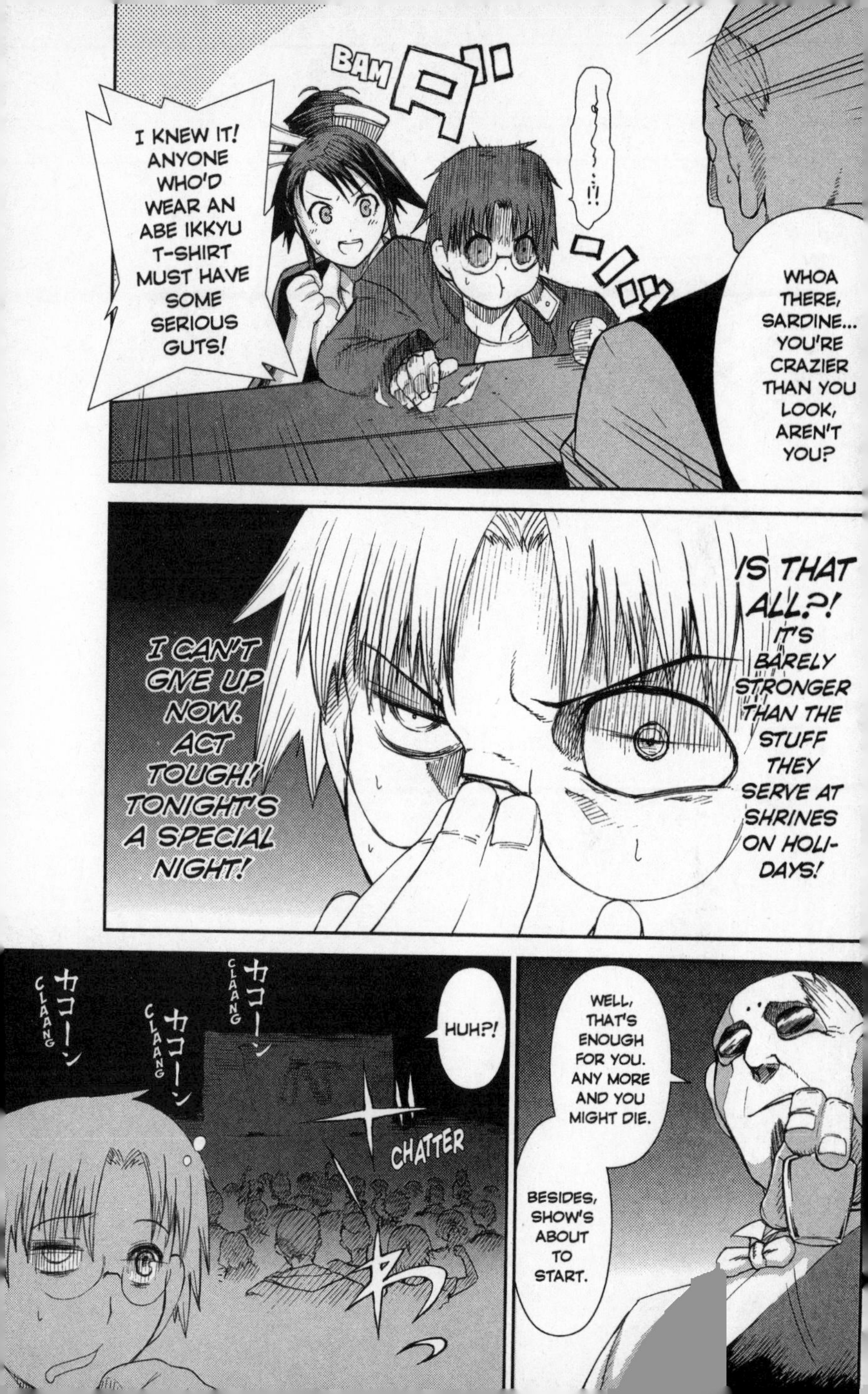
WHOA THERE, SARDINE... YOU'RE CRAZIER THAN YOU LOOK, AREN'T YOU?
BAM
I KNEW IT! ANYONE WHO'D WEAR AN ABE IKKYU T-SHIRT MUST HAVE SOME SERIOUS GUTS!
IS THAT ALL?! IT'S BARELY STRONGER THAN THE STUFF THEY SERVE AT SHRINES ON HOLI-DAYS!
I CAN'T GIVE UP NOW. ACT TOUGH! TONIGHT'S A SPECIAL NIGHT!
WELL, THAT'S ENOUGH FOR YOU. ANY MORE AND YOU MIGHT DIE.
BESIDES, SHOW'S ABOUT TO START.
カコーン CLAANG
カコーン CLAANG
カコーン CLAANG
HUH?!
CHATTER

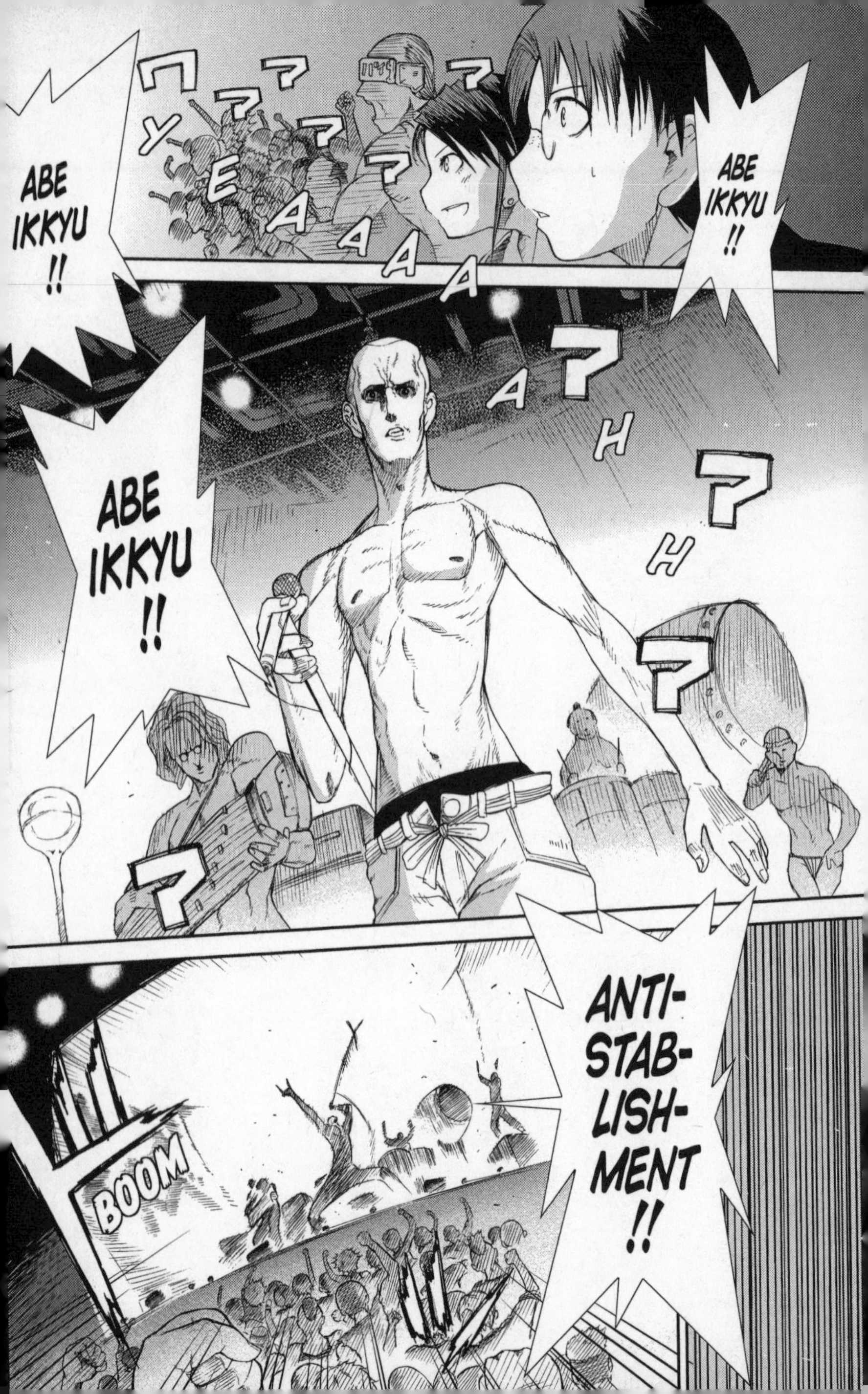
ABE IKKYU !!
ABE IKKYU !!
YEAAAAAHH
ABE IKKYU !!
ANTI-STAB-LISH-MENT !!
BOOM

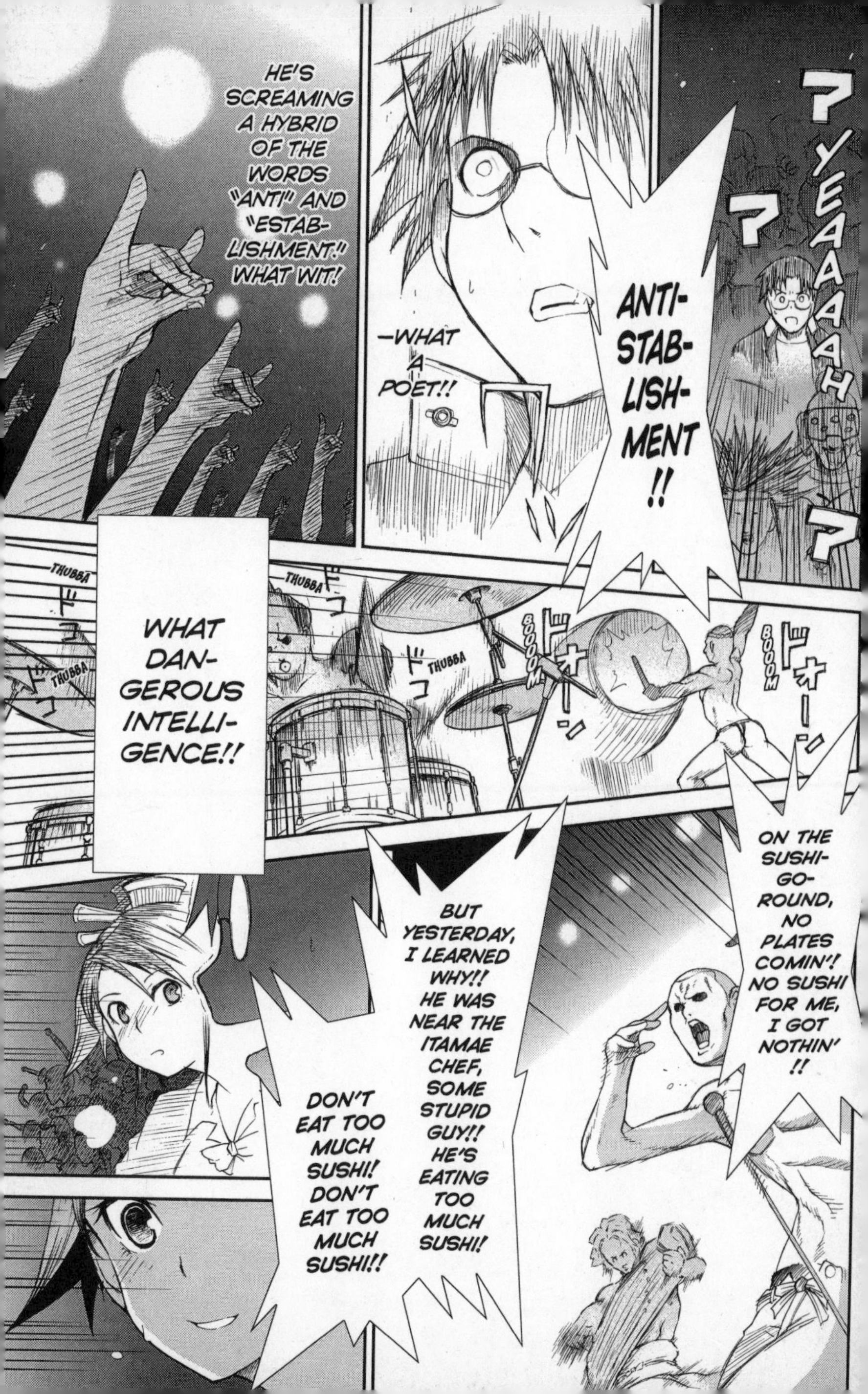
YEAAAAAH
ANTI-STAB-LISHMENT!!
—WHAT A POET!!
HE'S SCREAMING A HYBRID OF THE WORDS "ANTI" AND "ESTAB-LISHMENT!" WHAT WIT!
BOOOM
BOOOM
THUBBA
THUBBA
THUBBA
THUBBA
WHAT DAN-GEROUS INTELLI-GENCE!!
ON THE SUSHI-GO-ROUND, NO PLATES COMIN'! NO SUSHI FOR ME, I GOT NOTHIN'!!
BUT YESTERDAY, I LEARNED WHY!! HE WAS NEAR THE ITAMAE CHEF, SOME STUPID GUY!! HE'S EATING TOO MUCH SUSHI!
DON'T EAT TOO MUCH SUSHI! DON'T EAT TOO MUCH SUSHI!!

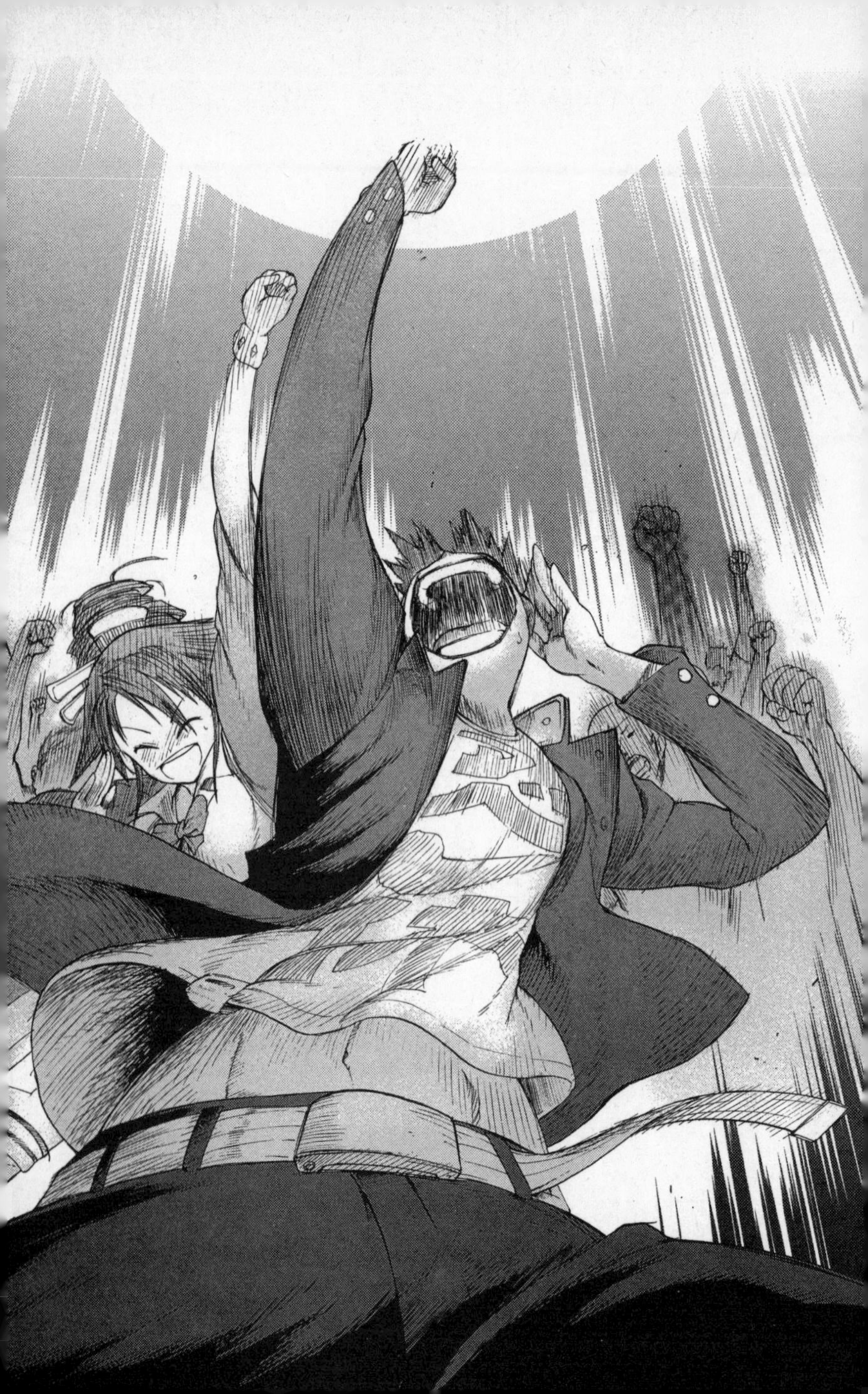

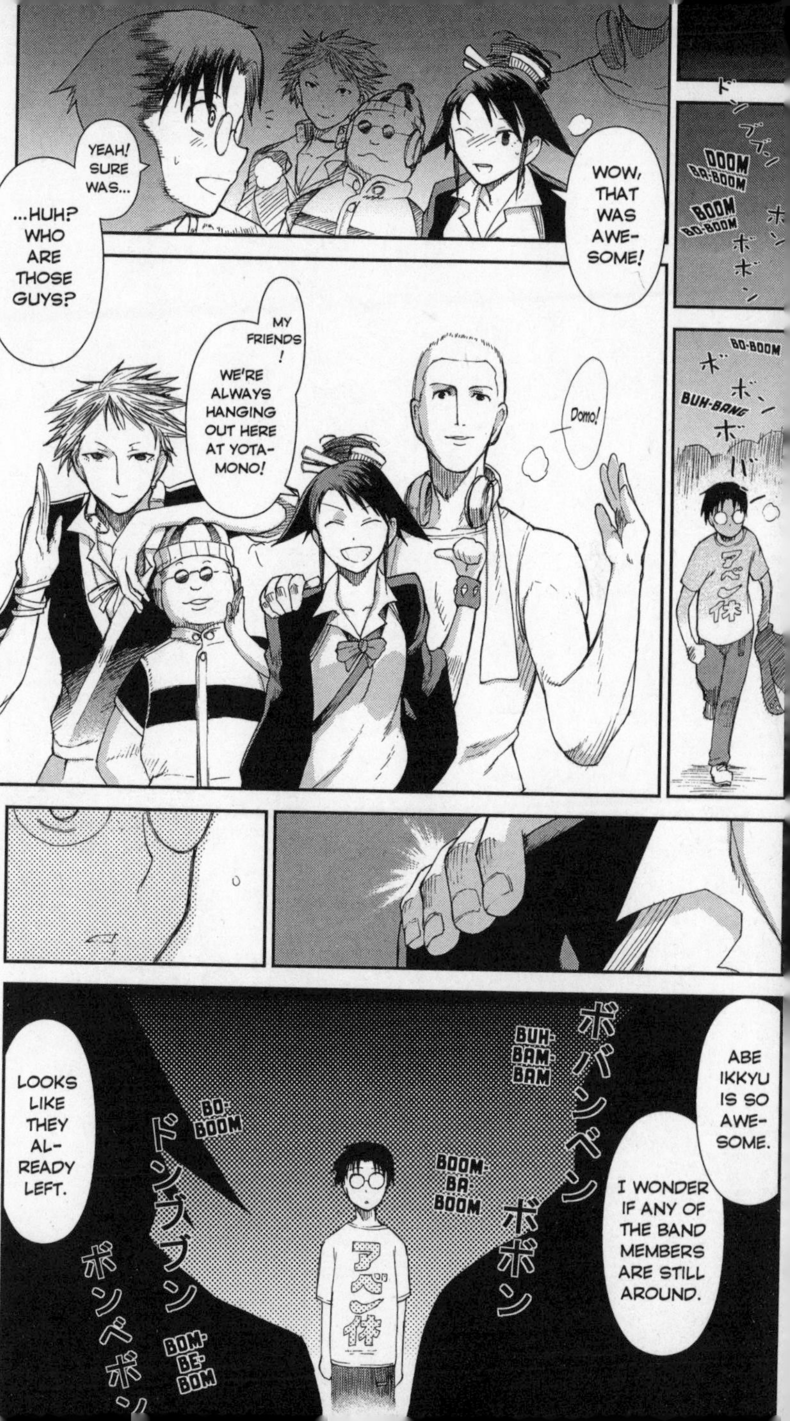

DOOM BA-BOOM
BOOM BO-BOOM
BO-BOOM
BUH-BANG
WOW, THAT WAS AWE-SOME!
YEAH! SURE WAS...
...HUH? WHO ARE THOSE GUYS?
Domo!
MY FRIENDS! WE'RE ALWAYS HANGING OUT HERE AT YOTA-MONO!
ABE IKKYU IS SO AWE-SOME.
I WONDER IF ANY OF THE BAND MEMBERS ARE STILL AROUND.
BUH-BAM-BAM
BOOM-BA-BOOM
BO-BOOM
BOM-BE-BOM
LOOKS LIKE THEY AL-READY LEFT.

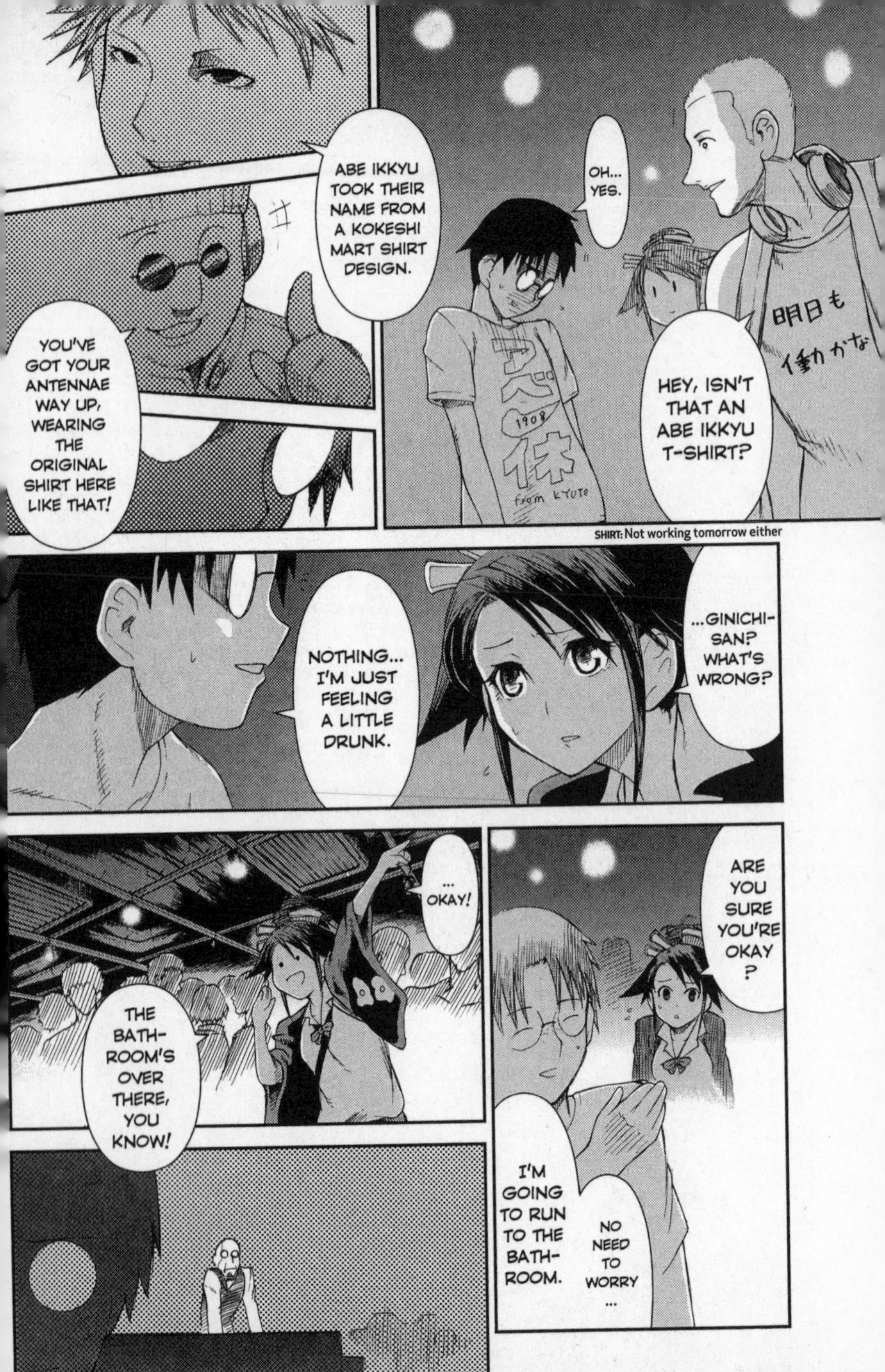
HEY, ISN'T THAT AN ABE IKKYU T-SHIRT?
OH... YES.
明日も働かな
ABE IKKYU TOOK THEIR NAME FROM A KOKESHI MART SHIRT DESIGN.
YOU'VE GOT YOUR ANTENNAE WAY UP, WEARING THE ORIGINAL SHIRT HERE LIKE THAT!
...GINICHI-SAN? WHAT'S WRONG?
NOTHING... I'M JUST FEELING A LITTLE DRUNK.
ARE YOU SURE YOU'RE OKAY?
I'M GOING TO RUN TO THE BATH-ROOM.
NO NEED TO WORRY...
...OKAY!
THE BATH-ROOM'S OVER THERE, YOU KNOW!

SHIRT: Not working tomorrow either

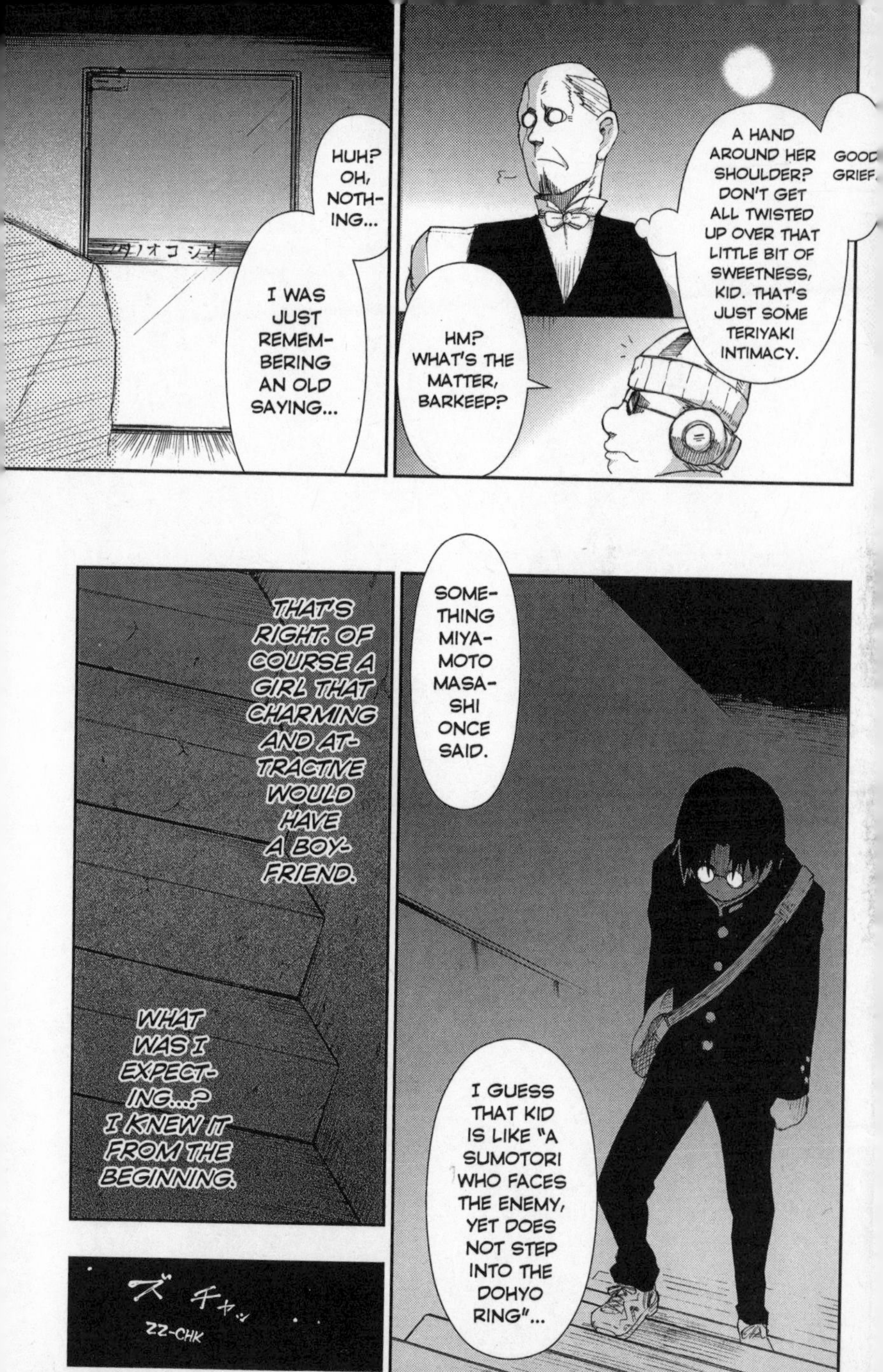
GOOD GRIEF.
A HAND AROUND HER SHOULDER? DON'T GET ALL TWISTED UP OVER THAT LITTLE BIT OF SWEETNESS, KID. THAT'S JUST SOME TERIYAKI INTIMACY.
HM? WHAT'S THE MATTER, BARKEEP?
HUH? OH, NOTHING...
I WAS JUST REMEMBERING AN OLD SAYING...
SOMETHING MIYAMOTO MASASHI ONCE SAID.
I GUESS THAT KID IS LIKE "A SUMOTORI WHO FACES THE ENEMY, YET DOES NOT STEP INTO THE DOHYO RING"...
THAT'S RIGHT. OF COURSE A GIRL THAT CHARMING AND ATTRACTIVE WOULD HAVE A BOYFRIEND.
WHAT WAS I EXPECTING...? I KNEW IT FROM THE BEGINNING.
ズチャッ
ZZ-CHK

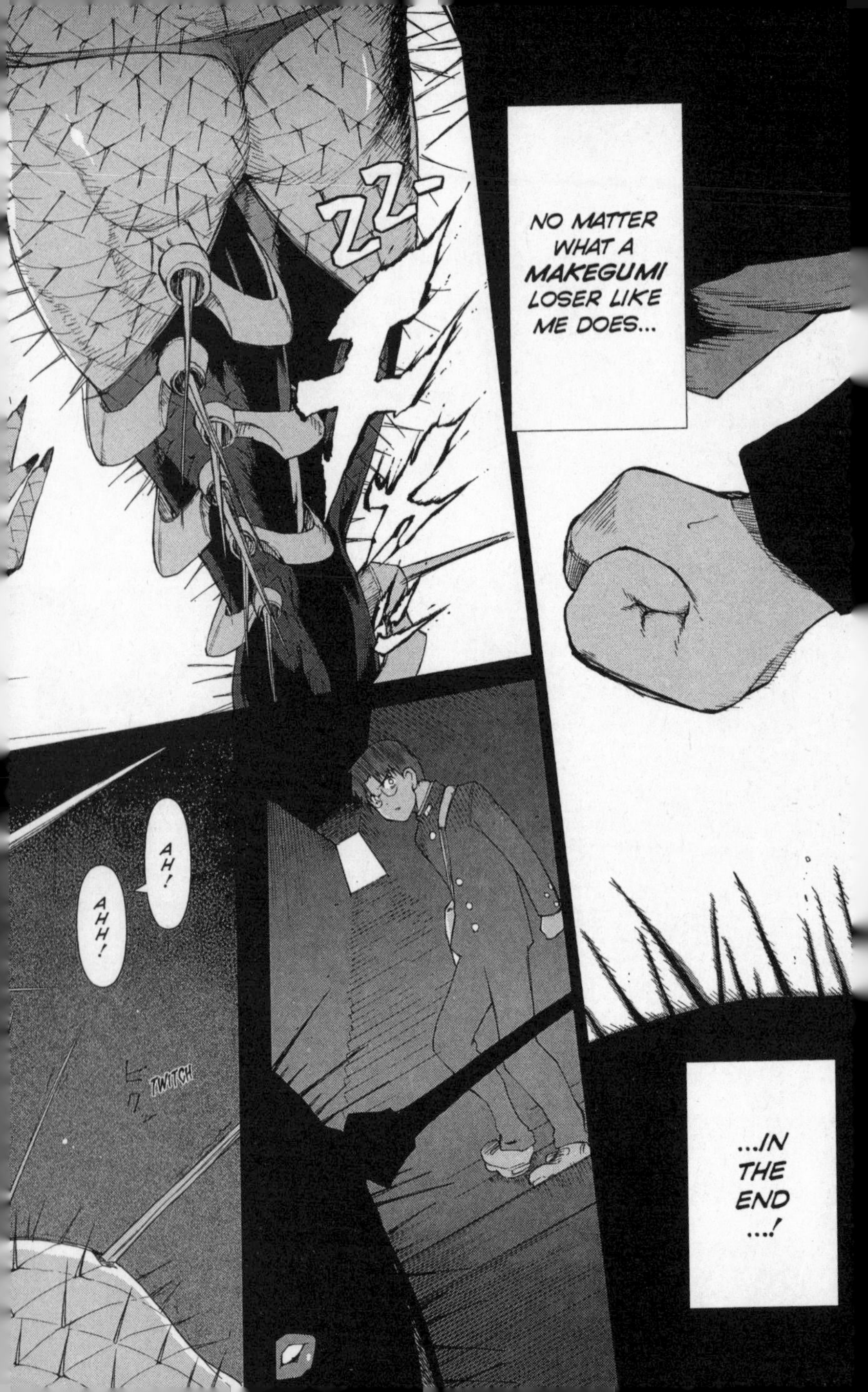
NO MATTER WHAT A MAKEGUMI LOSER LIKE ME DOES...
ZZ-
...IN THE END ...!
AH!
AHH!
TWITCH

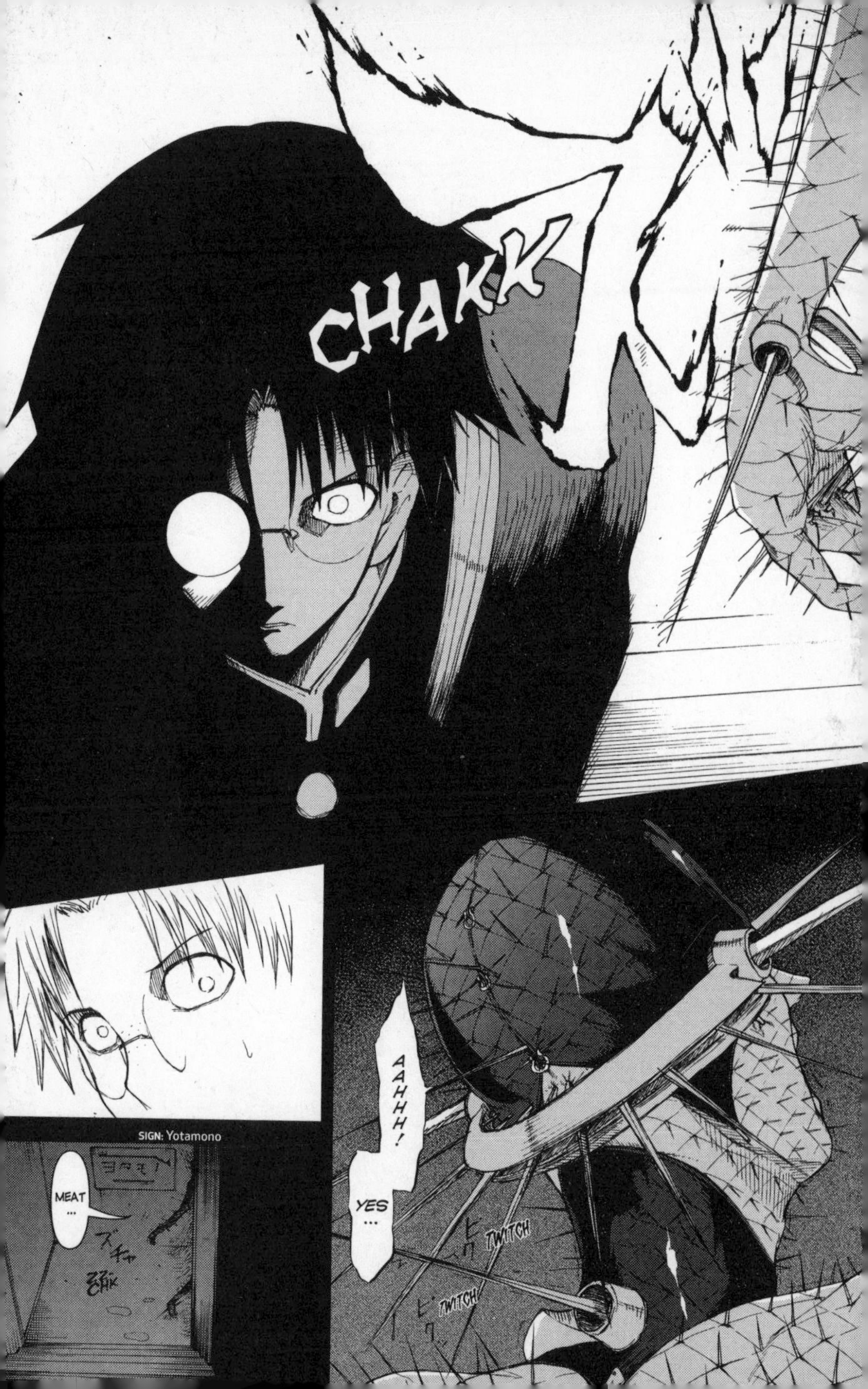
CHAKK
AAHHH!
YES...
TWITCH
TWITCH
SIGN: Yotamono
MEAT...
CHK

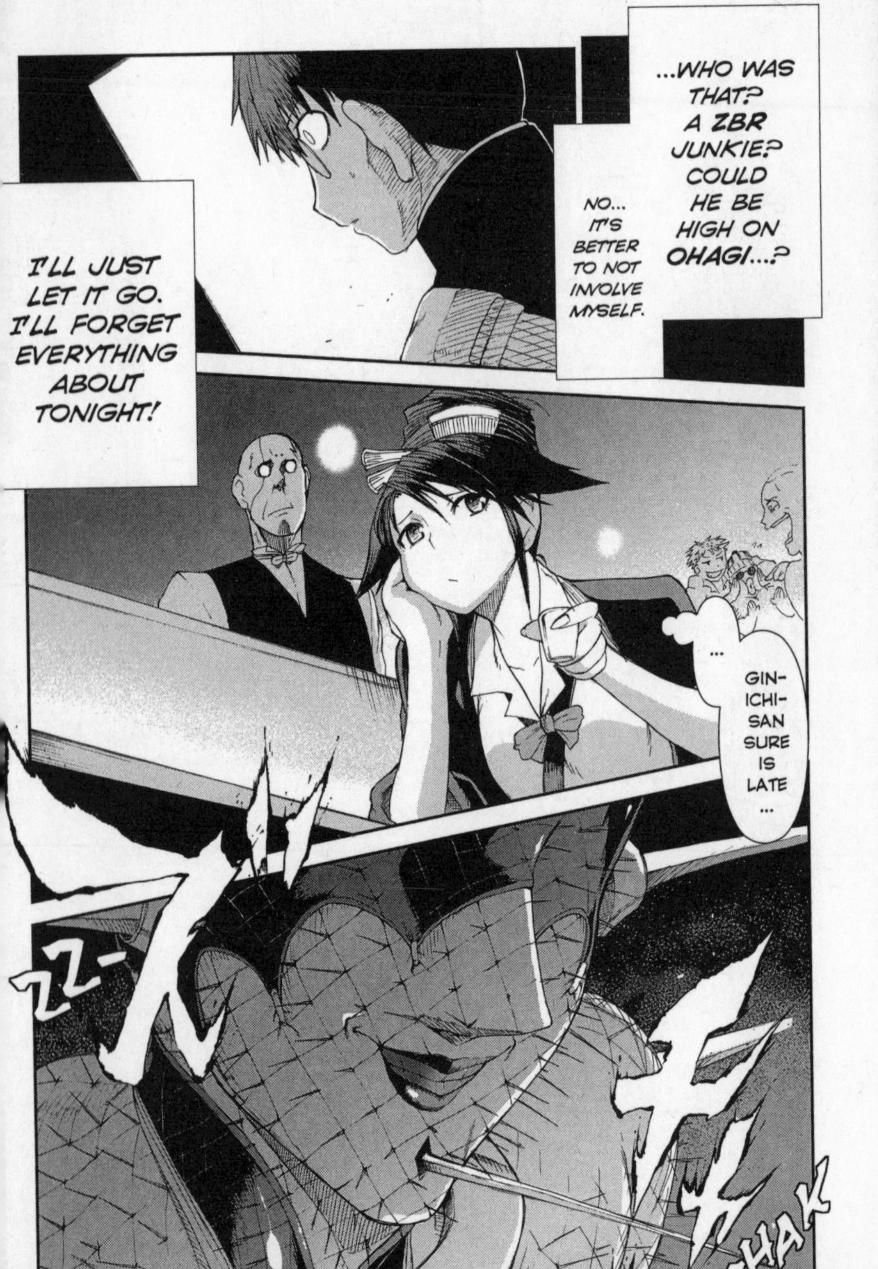
...WHO WAS THAT? A ZBR JUNKIE? COULD HE BE HIGH ON OHAGI...?
NO... IT'S BETTER TO NOT INVOLVE MYSELF.
I'LL JUST LET IT GO. I'LL FORGET EVERYTHING ABOUT TONIGHT!
...
GIN-ICHI-SAN SURE IS LATE...
CHAK
ZZ-

[KICK OUT THE NINJA MOTHERFUCKER PART 1] • END

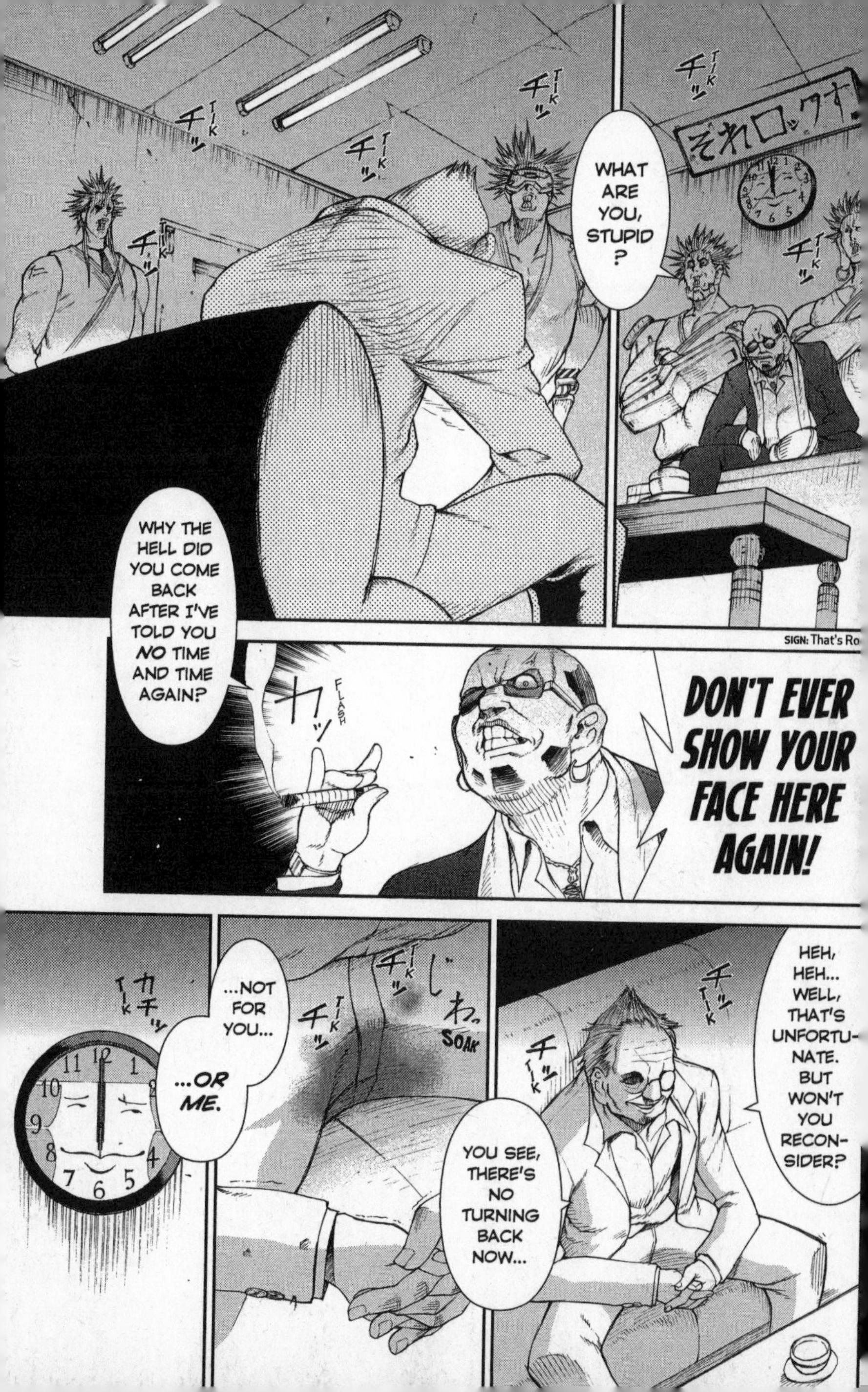
それロックす。
TIK
WHAT ARE YOU, STUPID?
TIK
SIGN: That's Ro
WHY THE HELL DID YOU COME BACK AFTER I'VE TOLD YOU *NO* TIME AND TIME AGAIN?
FLASH
DON'T EVER SHOW YOUR FACE HERE AGAIN!
TIK
HEH, HEH... WELL, THAT'S UNFORTU-NATE. BUT WON'T YOU RECON-SIDER?
YOU SEE, THERE'S NO TURNING BACK NOW...
TIK
SOAK
...NOT FOR YOU...
...OR ME.
TIK

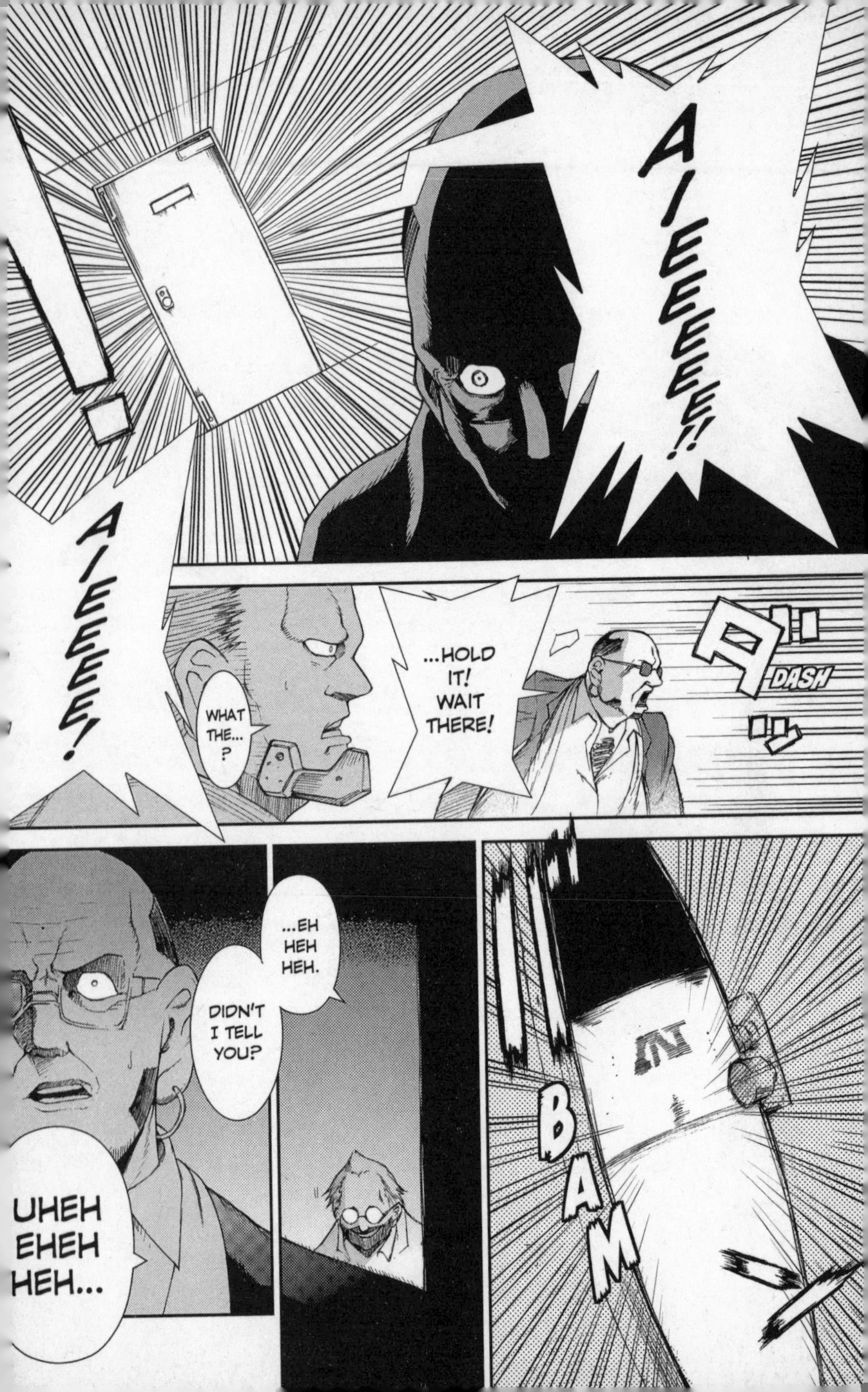
AIEEEEE!!
DASH
...HOLD IT! WAIT THERE!
WHAT THE... ?
AIEEEEE!
BAM
...EH HEH HEH.
DIDN'T I TELL YOU?
UHEH EHEH HEH...

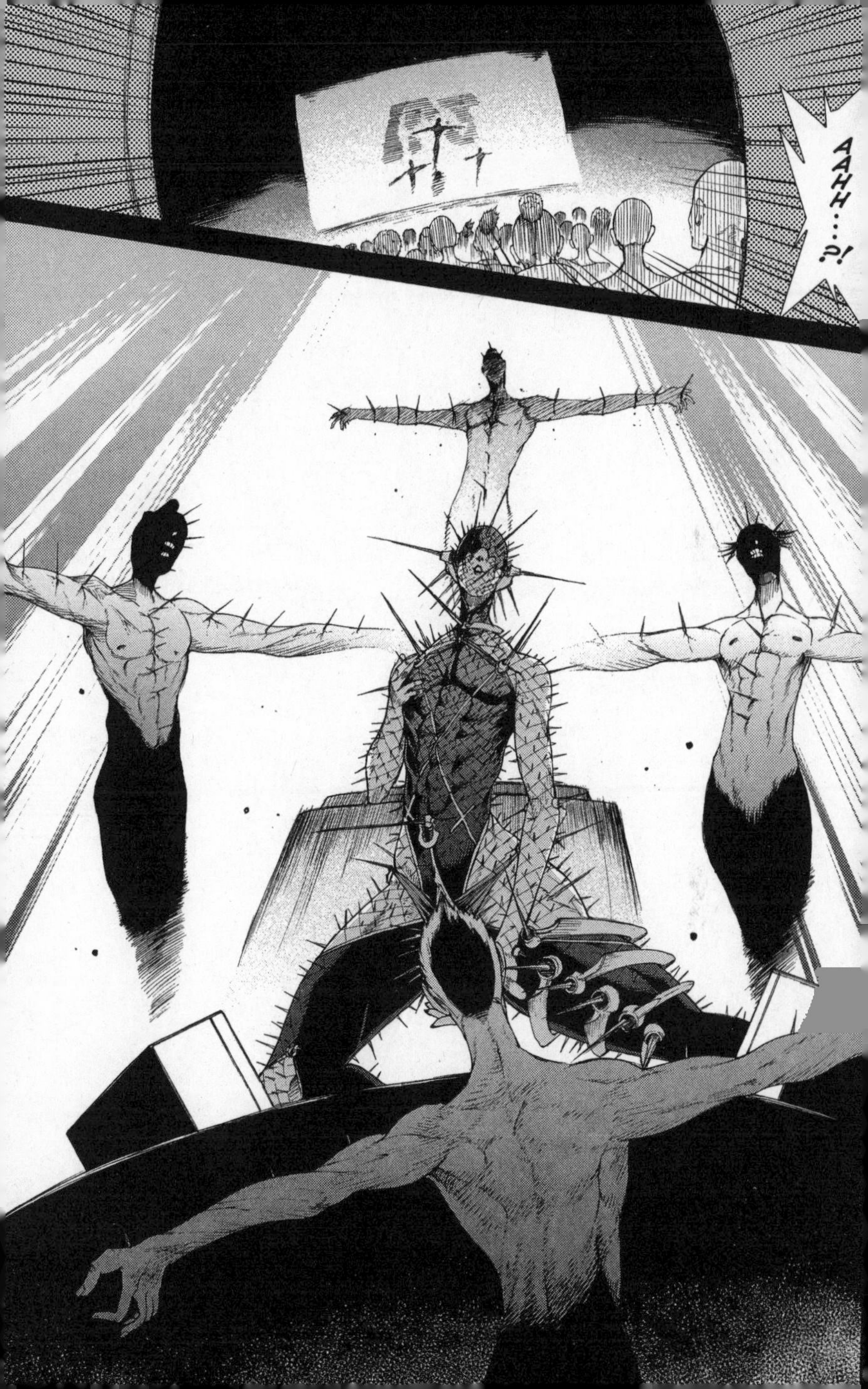
AAHH...?!

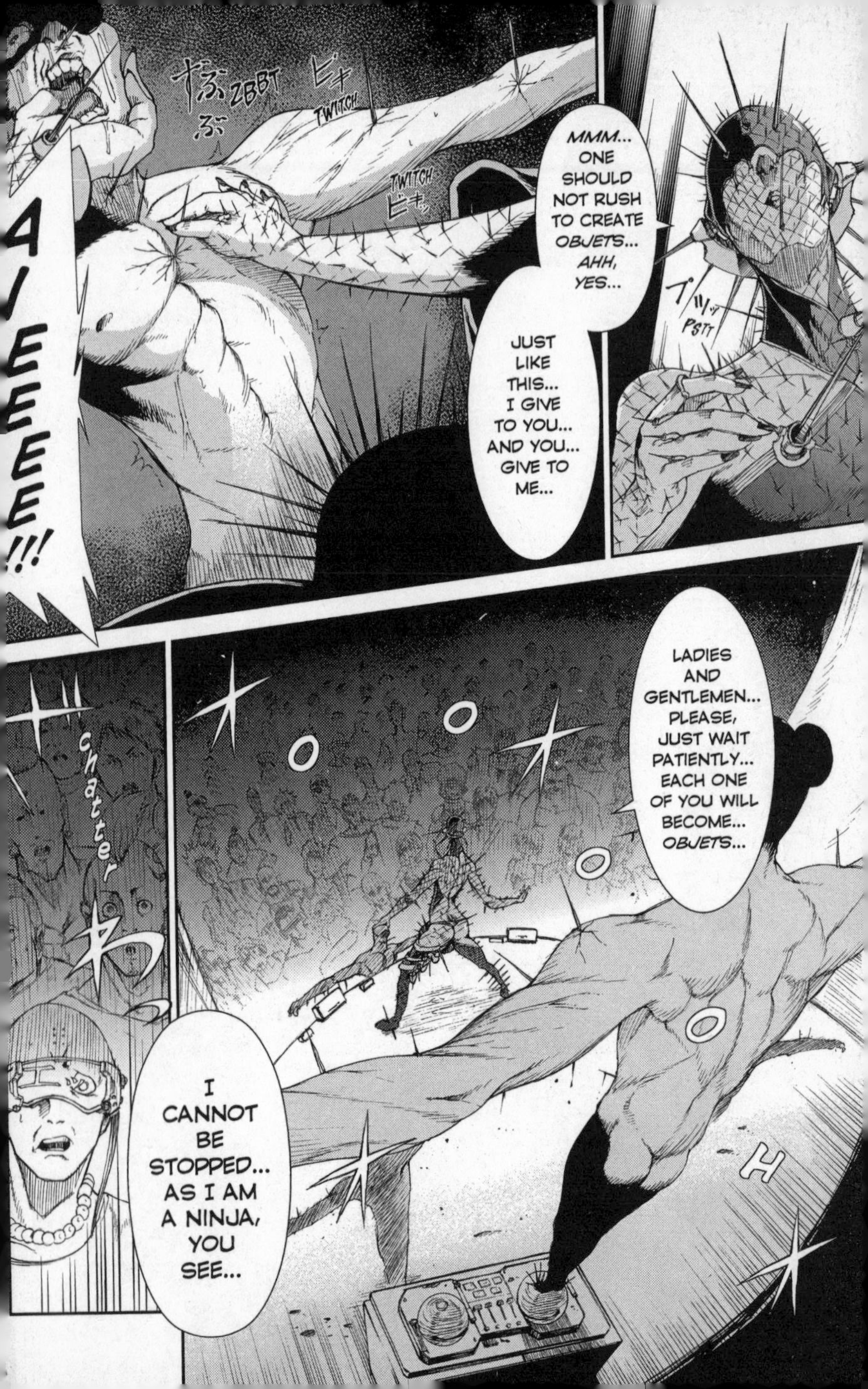
MMM... ONE SHOULD NOT RUSH TO CREATE *OBJETS*... AHH, YES...
JUST LIKE THIS... I GIVE TO YOU... AND YOU... GIVE TO ME...
PSTT
ZBBT
TWITCH
TWITCH
AIEEEEE!!!
LADIES AND GENTLEMEN... PLEASE, JUST WAIT PATIENTLY... EACH ONE OF YOU WILL BECOME... *OBJETS*...
OOOOH
chatter
I CANNOT BE STOPPED... AS I AM A NINJA, YOU SEE...

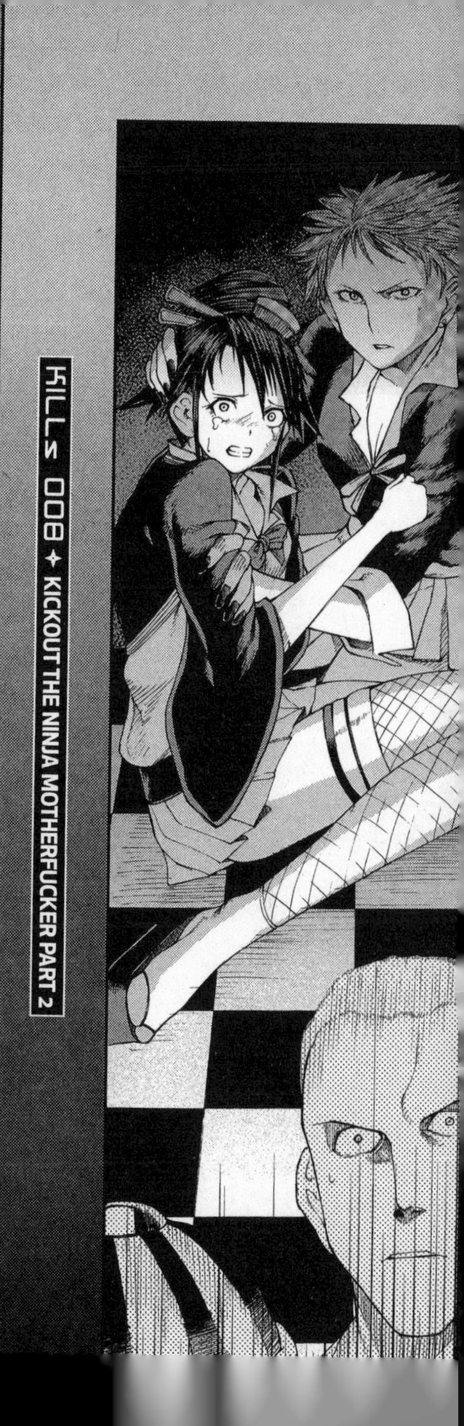

KILLs 008 ✦ KICKOUT THE NINJA MOTHERFUCKER PART 2

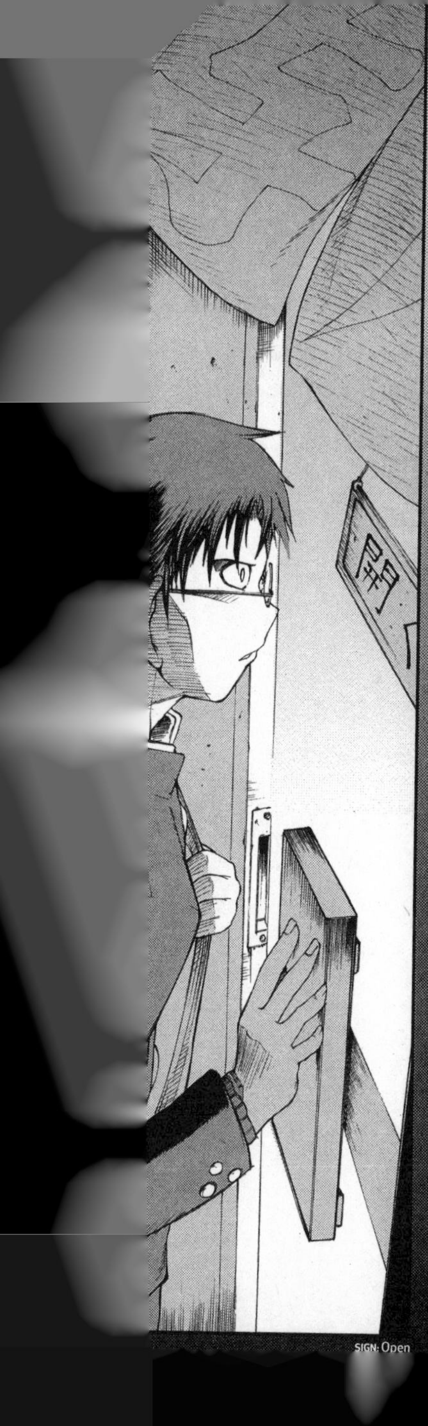

SIGN: Open

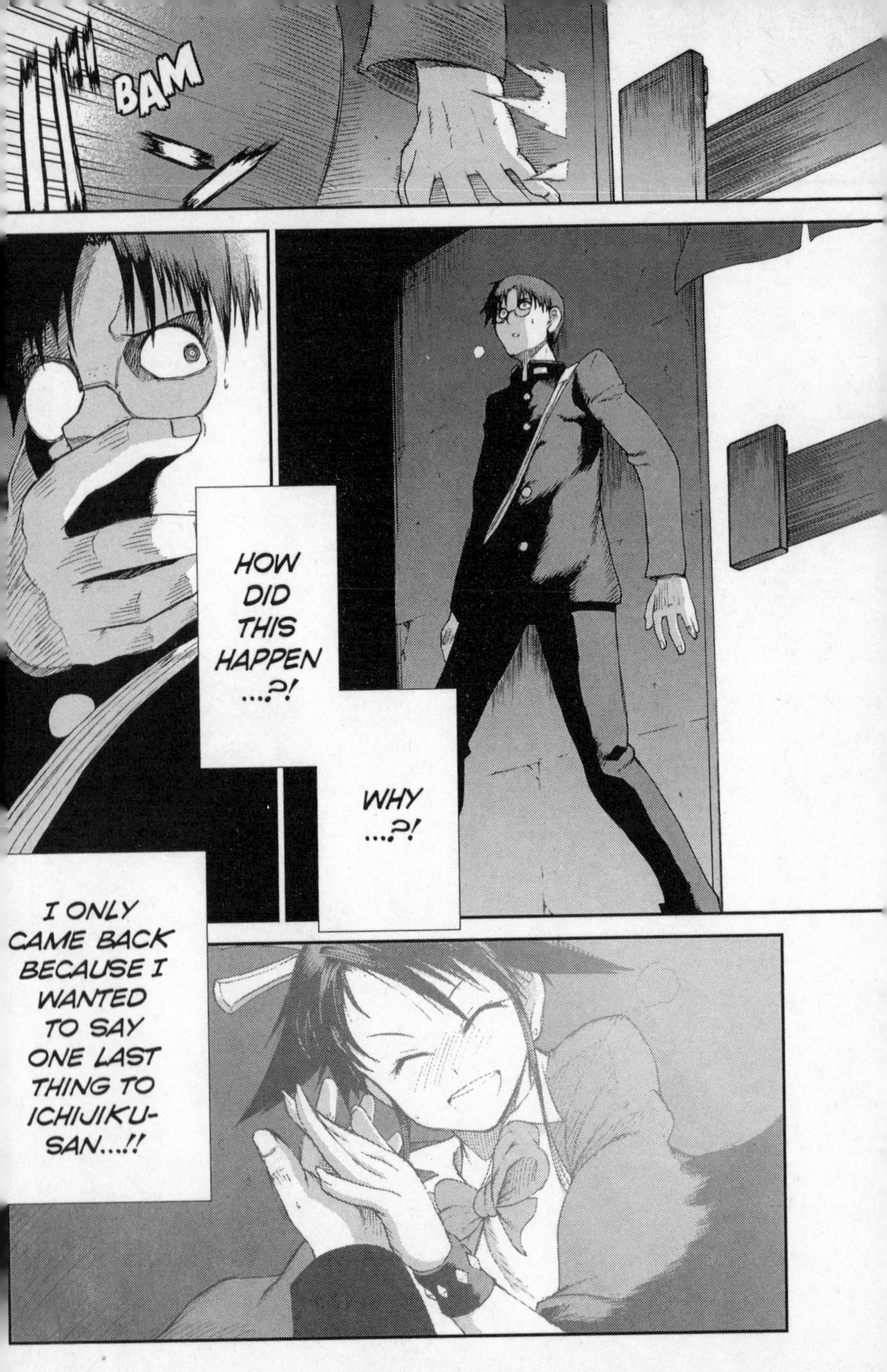
BAM
HOW DID THIS HAPPEN ...?!
WHY ...?!
I ONLY CAME BACK BECAUSE I WANTED TO SAY ONE LAST THING TO ICHIJIKU-SAN...!!

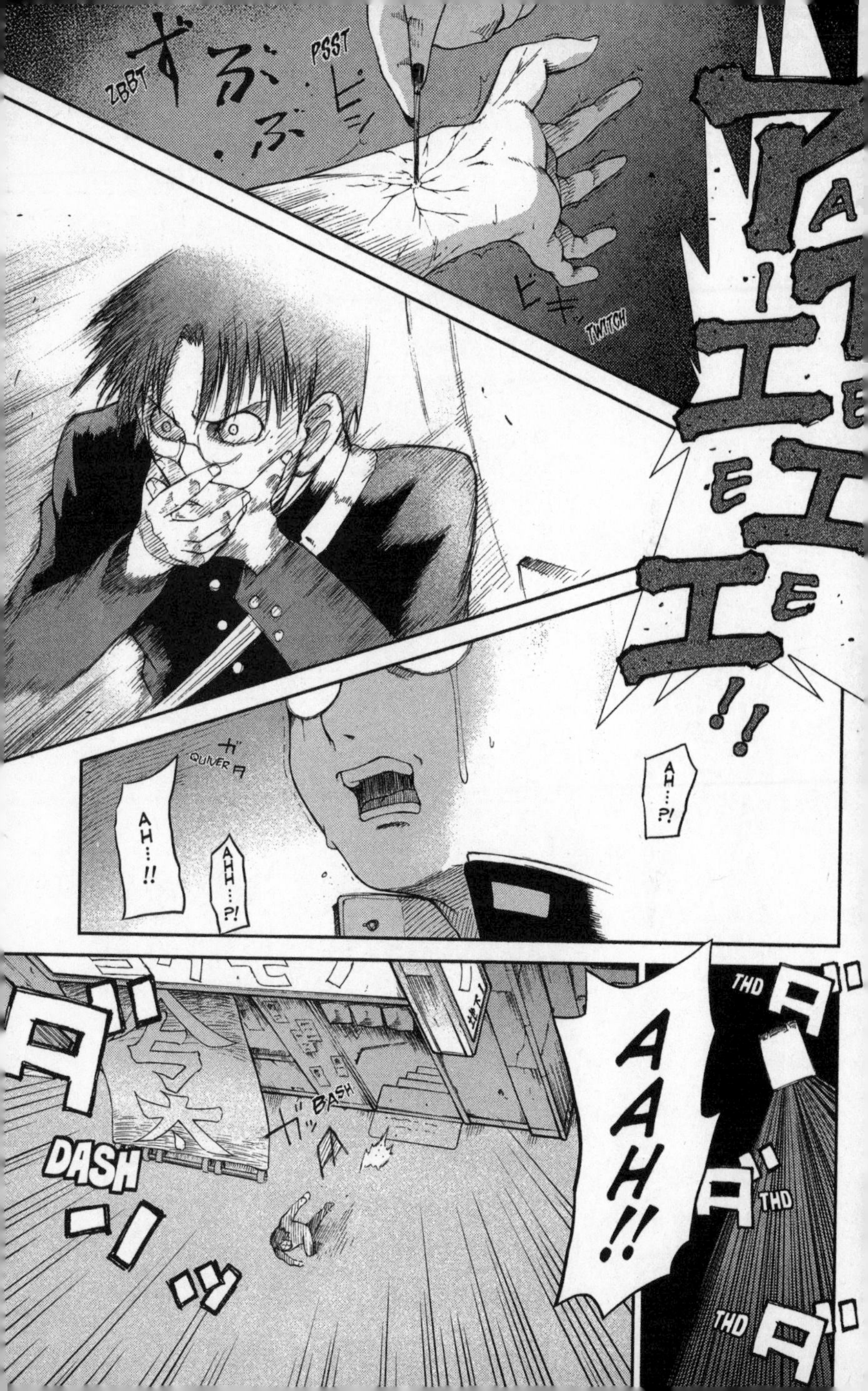

AIEEE!!
TWITCH
PSST
ZBBT
AH...?!
AHH...?!
QUIVER
AH...!!
THD
AAAH!!
THD
THD
BASH
DASH

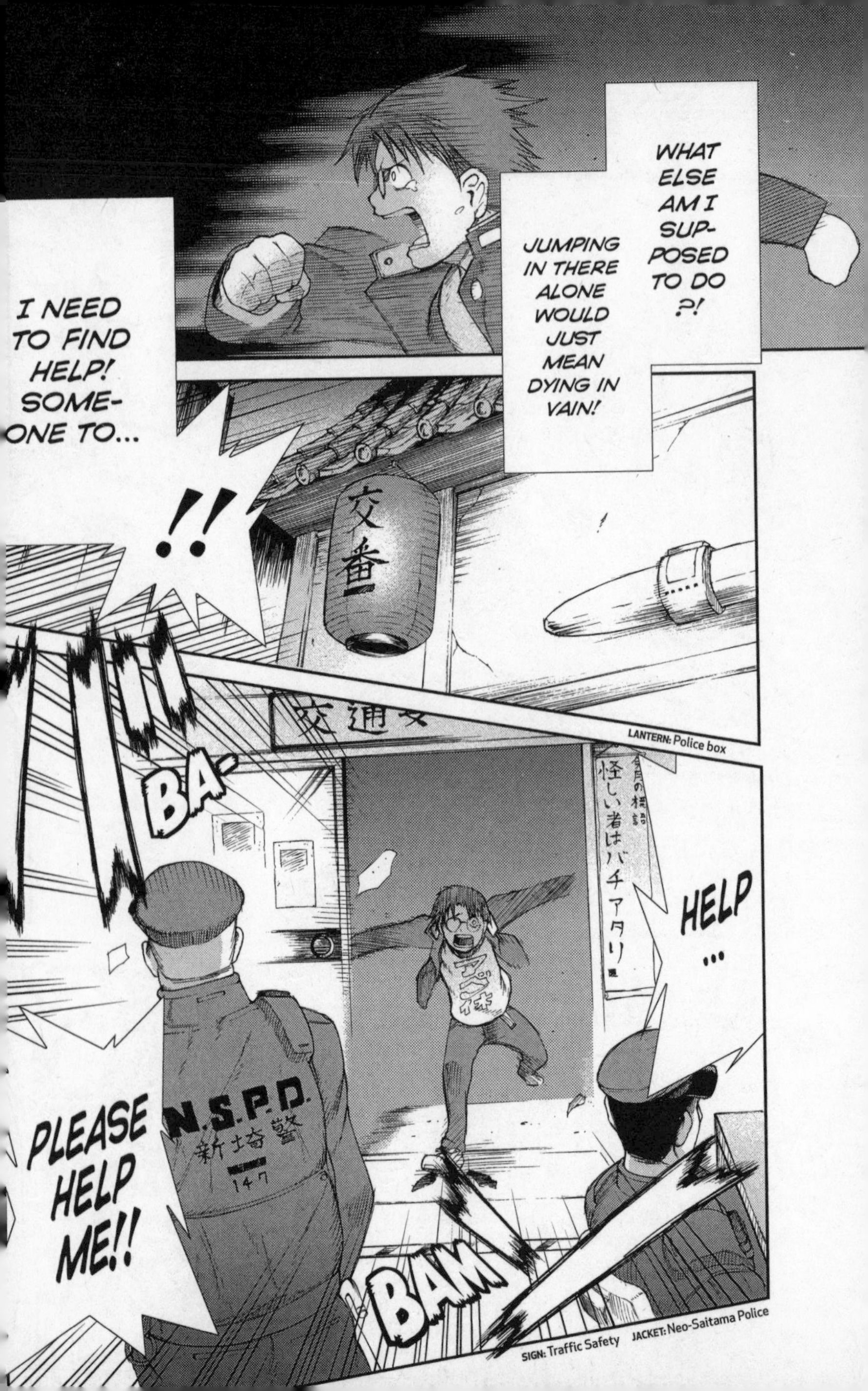
WHAT ELSE AM I SUP-POSED TO DO ?!
JUMPING IN THERE ALONE WOULD JUST MEAN DYING IN VAIN!
I NEED TO FIND HELP! SOMEONE TO...
!!
交番
HELP ...
怪しい者はバチアタリ
BA-
N.S.P.D. 新埼警 147
PLEASE HELP ME!!
BAM

LANTERN: Police box

SIGN: Traffic Safety JACKET: Neo-Saitama Police

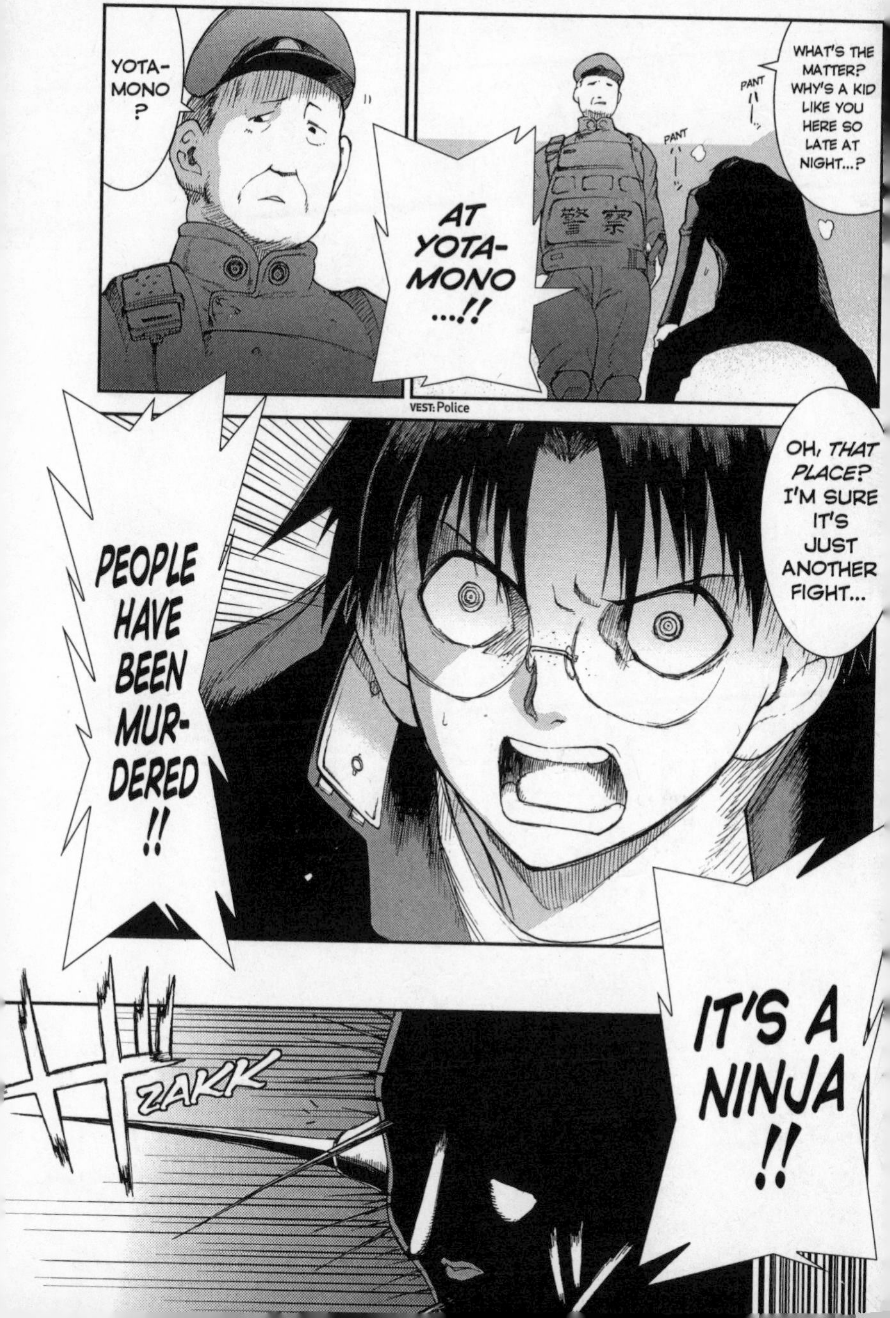
WHAT'S THE MATTER? WHY'S A KID LIKE YOU HERE SO LATE AT NIGHT...?
PANT
PANT
AT YOTA-MONO ...!!
YOTA-MONO ?
VEST: Police
OH, *THAT PLACE*? I'M SURE IT'S JUST ANOTHER FIGHT...
PEOPLE HAVE BEEN MUR-DERED !!
IT'S A NINJA !!
ZAKK

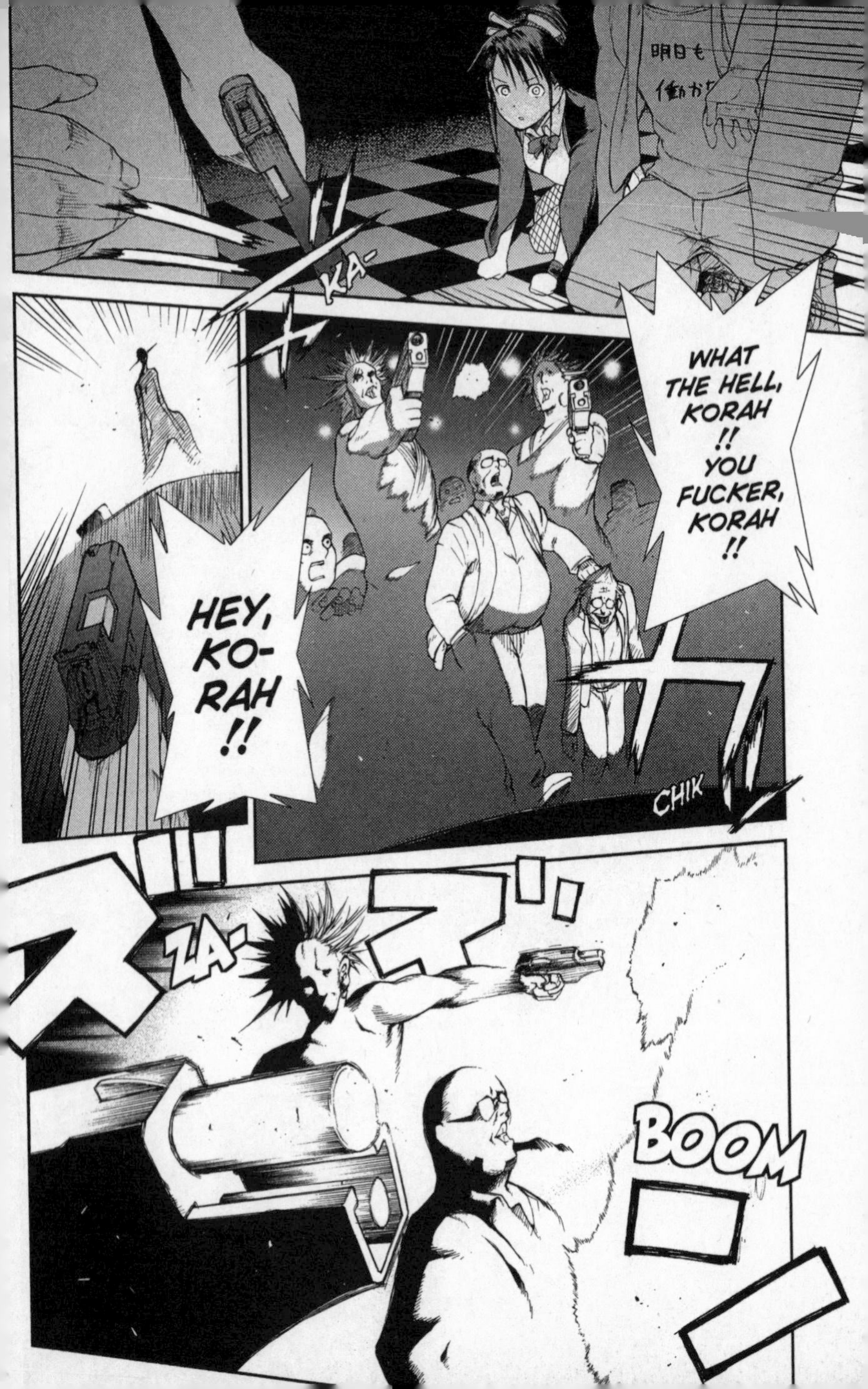
明日も
KA-
WHAT THE HELL, KORAH!! YOU FUCKER, KORAH!!
CHIK
HEY, KO-RAH!!
ZA-
BOOM

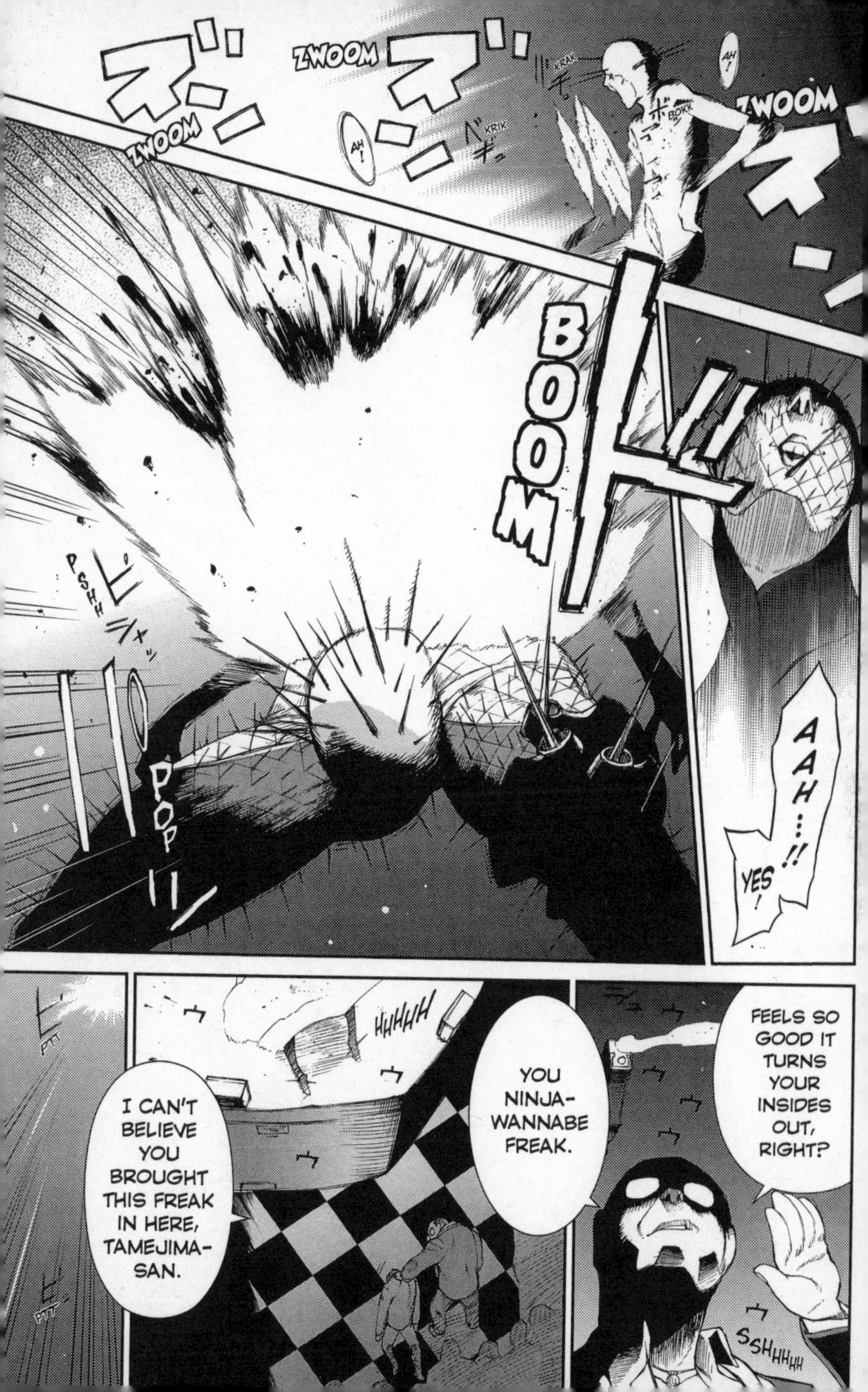
ZWOOM
AH!
KRAK
BOKK
KRIK
AH!
ZWOOM
ZWOOM
BOOM
AAH...!!
YES!
PSHH
POP
FEELS SO GOOD IT TURNS YOUR INSIDES OUT, RIGHT?
SSHHHHH
YOU NINJA-WANNABE FREAK.
HHHHH
I CAN'T BELIEVE YOU BROUGHT THIS FREAK IN HERE, TAMEJIMA-SAN.
PTT
PTT

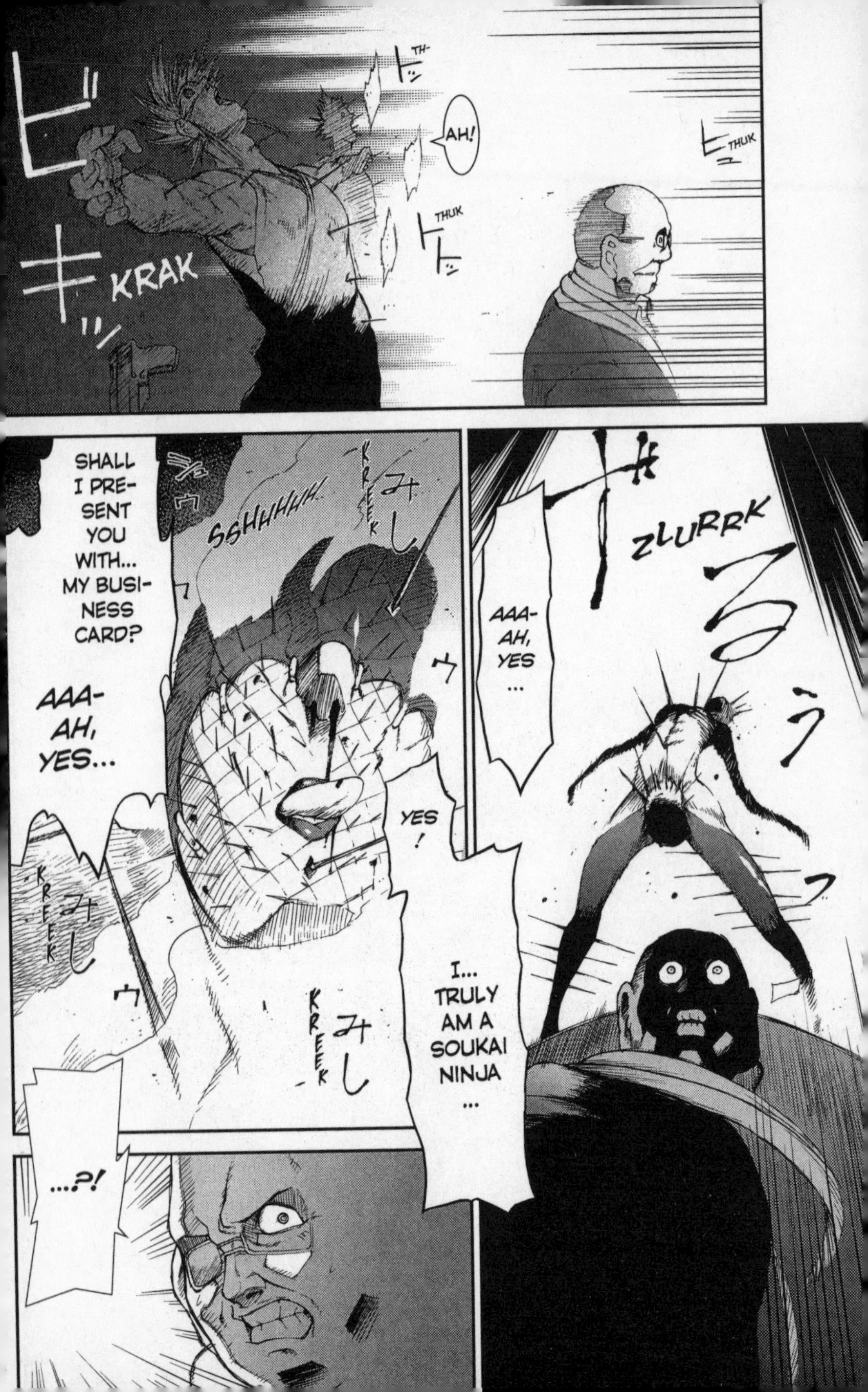
THUK
TH-
AH!
THUK
KRAK
ZLURRK
AAA-AH, YES ...
I... TRULY AM A SOUKAI NINJA ...
SHALL I PRESENT YOU WITH... MY BUSINESS CARD?
KREEK
SSHHHHH
YES!
AAA-AH, YES...
KREEK
KREEK
...?!

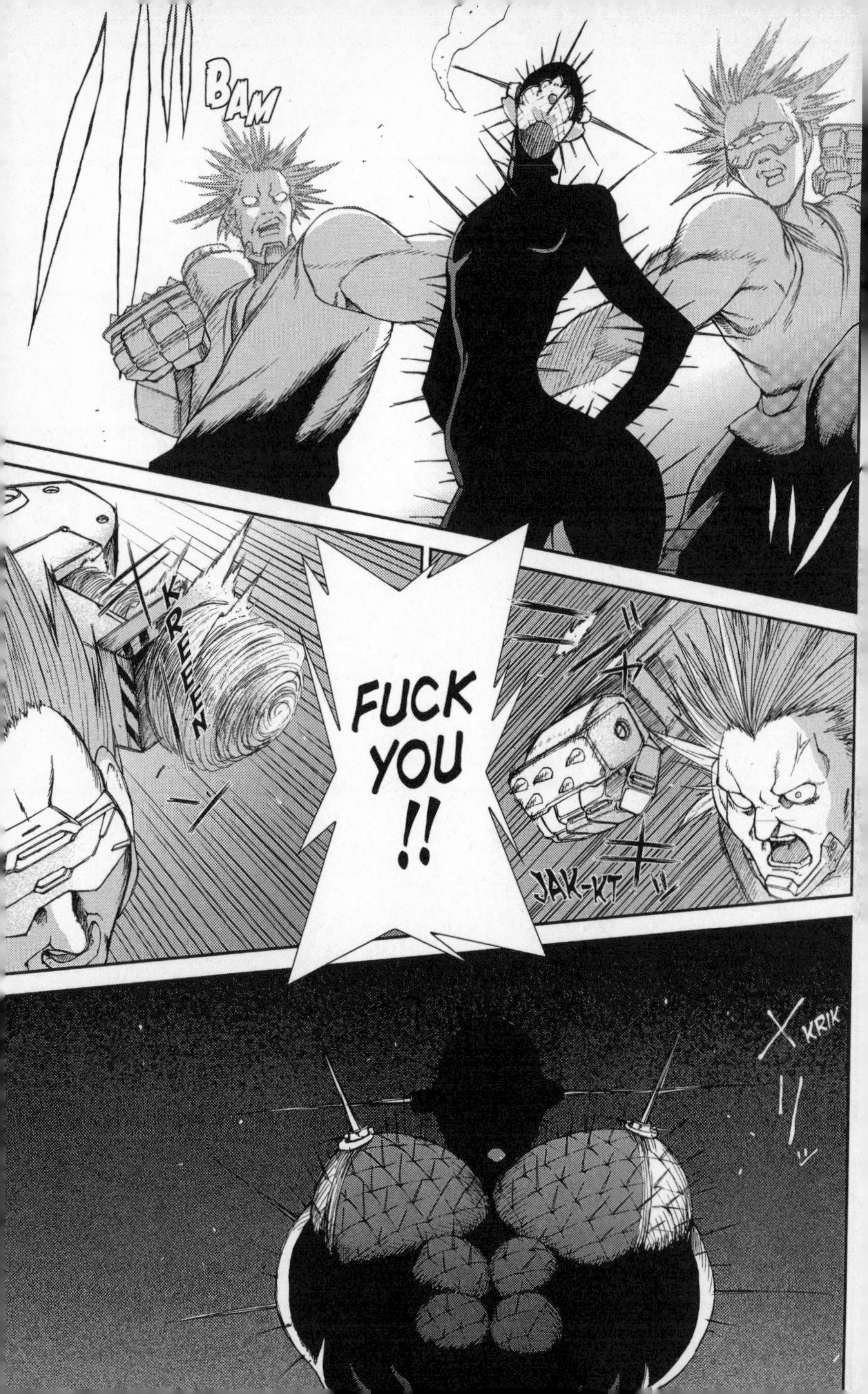
BAM
JAK-KT
FUCK YOU!!
KREEEN
KRIK

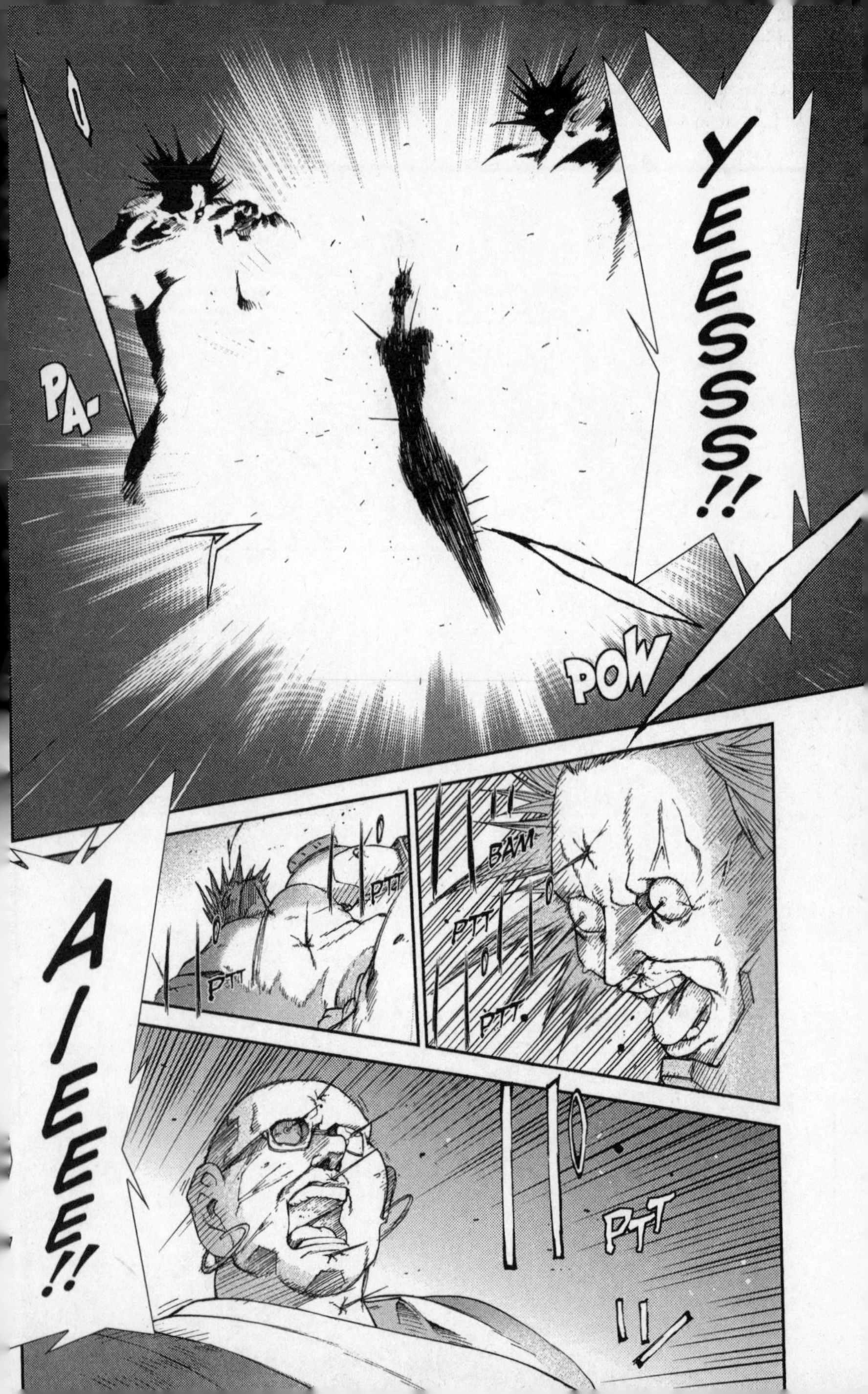
YEESSSS!!
POW
PA-
BAM
PTT
PTT
PTT
PTT
AIEEEE!!
PTT

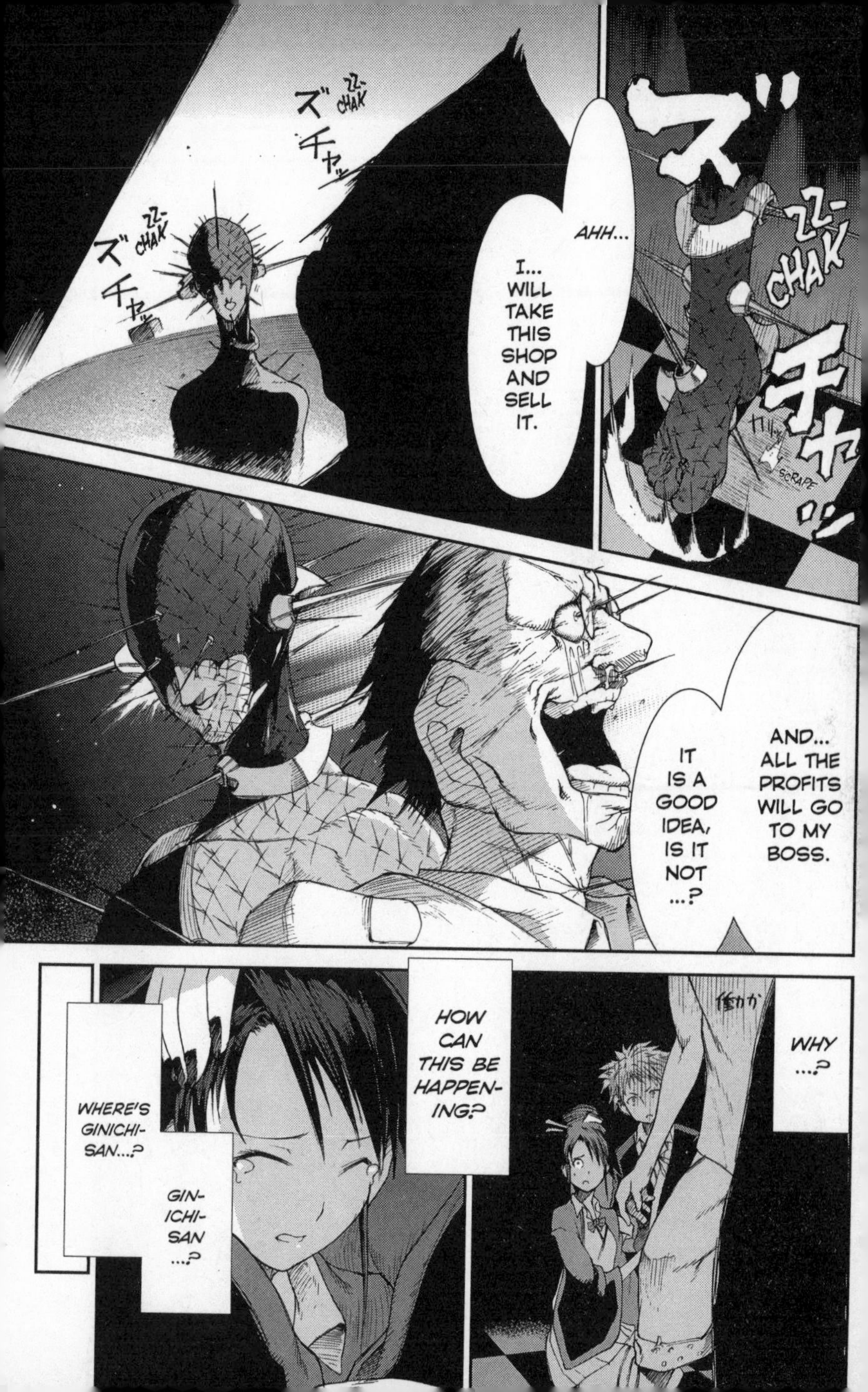
ズ
ZZ-CHAK
チャッ
SCRAPE
AHH...
I... WILL TAKE THIS SHOP AND SELL IT.
ZZ-CHAK
ズチャッ
ZZ-CHAK
ズチャッ
AND... ALL THE PROFITS WILL GO TO MY BOSS.
IT IS A GOOD IDEA, IS IT NOT ...?
WHY ...?
HOW CAN THIS BE HAPPEN-ING?
WHERE'S GINICHI-SAN...?
GIN-ICHI-SAN ...?

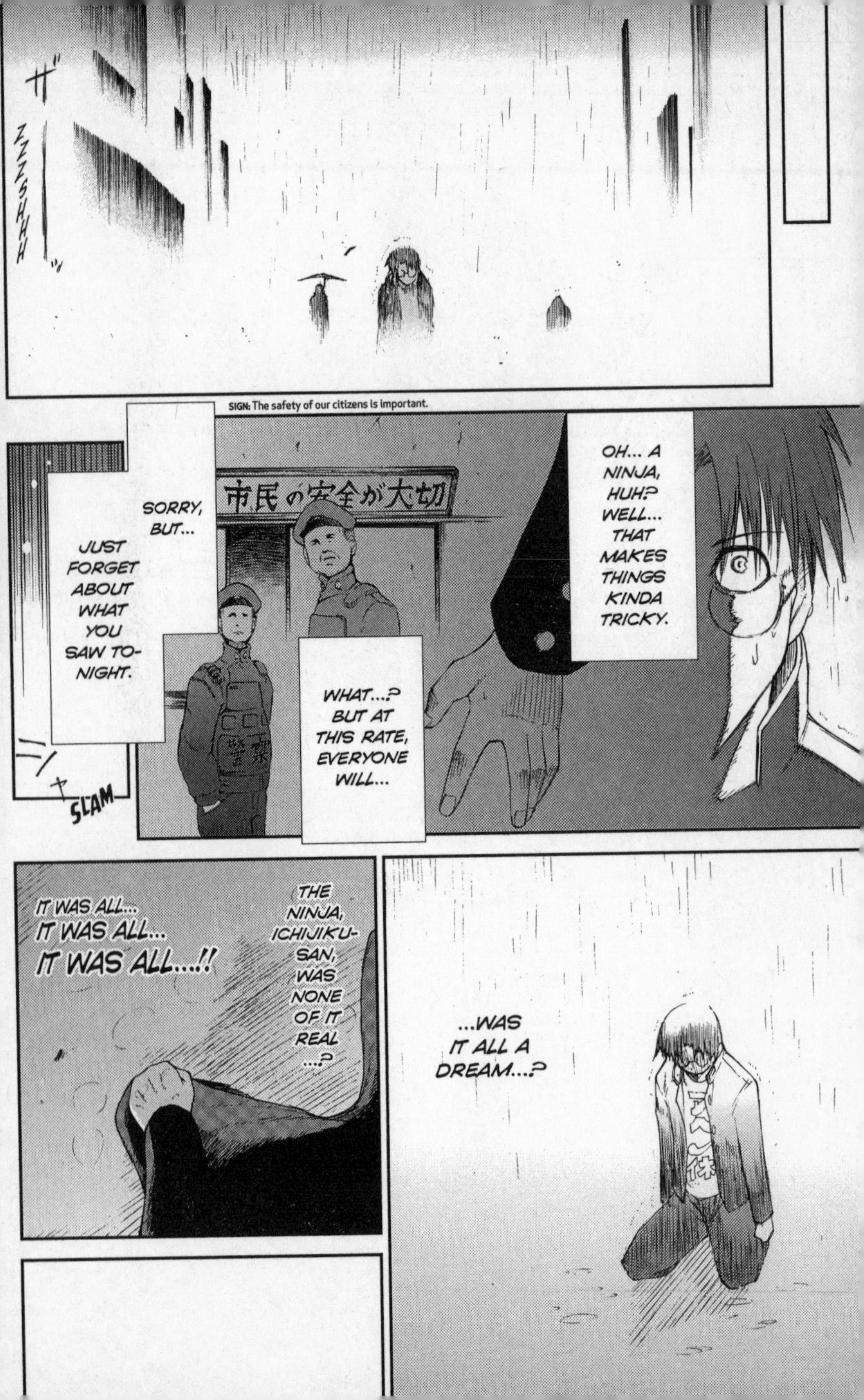
ザー
ZZZSHHH
SIGN: The safety of our citizens is important.
市民の安全が大切
OH... A NINJA, HUH? WELL... THAT MAKES THINGS KINDA TRICKY.
SORRY, BUT...
JUST FORGET ABOUT WHAT YOU SAW TO-NIGHT.
WHAT...? BUT AT THIS RATE, EVERYONE WILL...
ピシャ
SLAM
...WAS IT ALL A DREAM...?
THE NINJA, ICHIJIKU-SAN, WAS NONE OF IT REAL...?
IT WAS ALL...
IT WAS ALL...
IT WAS ALL...!!

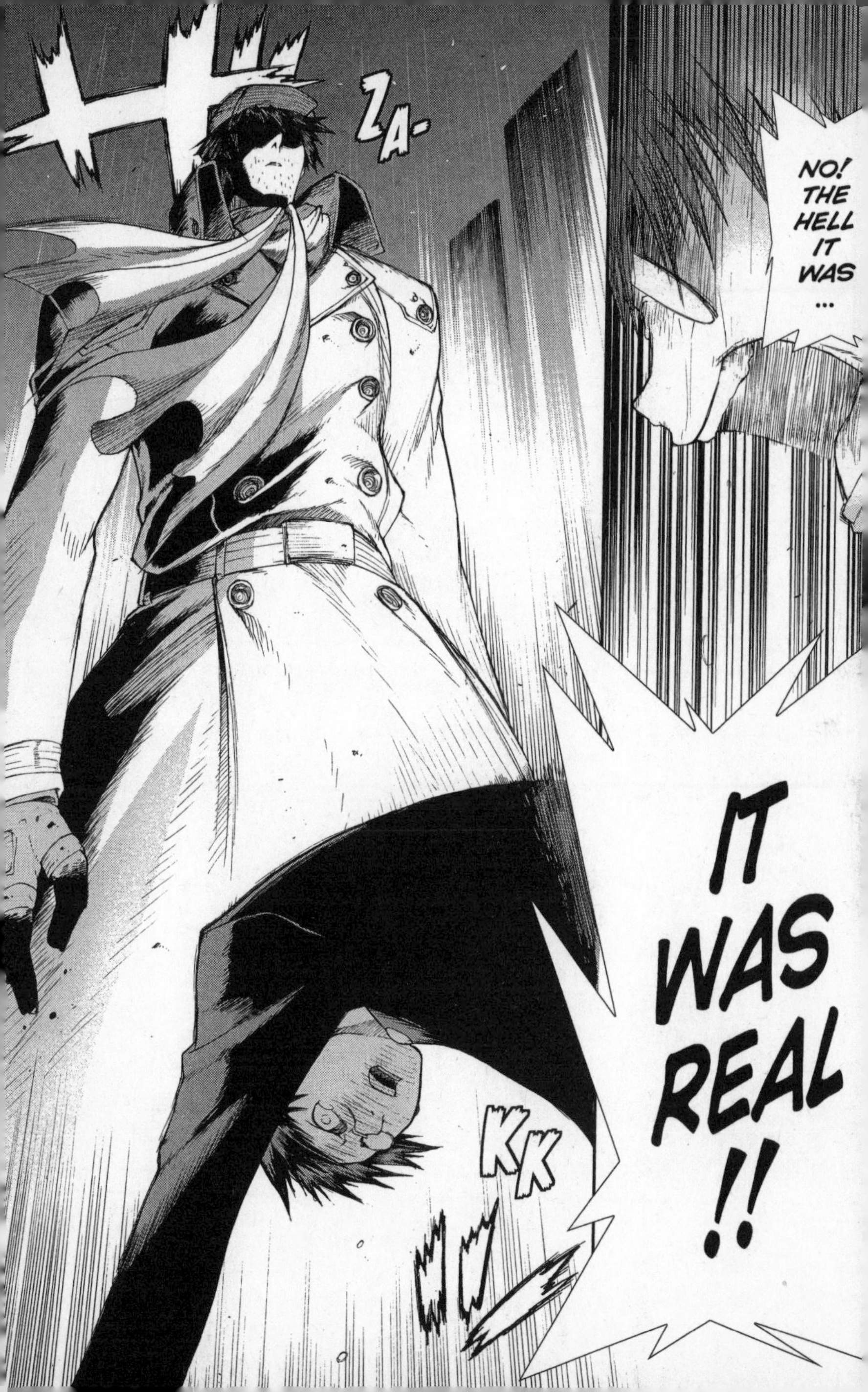
NO! THE HELL IT WAS ...
ZA-
IT WAS REAL!!
KK

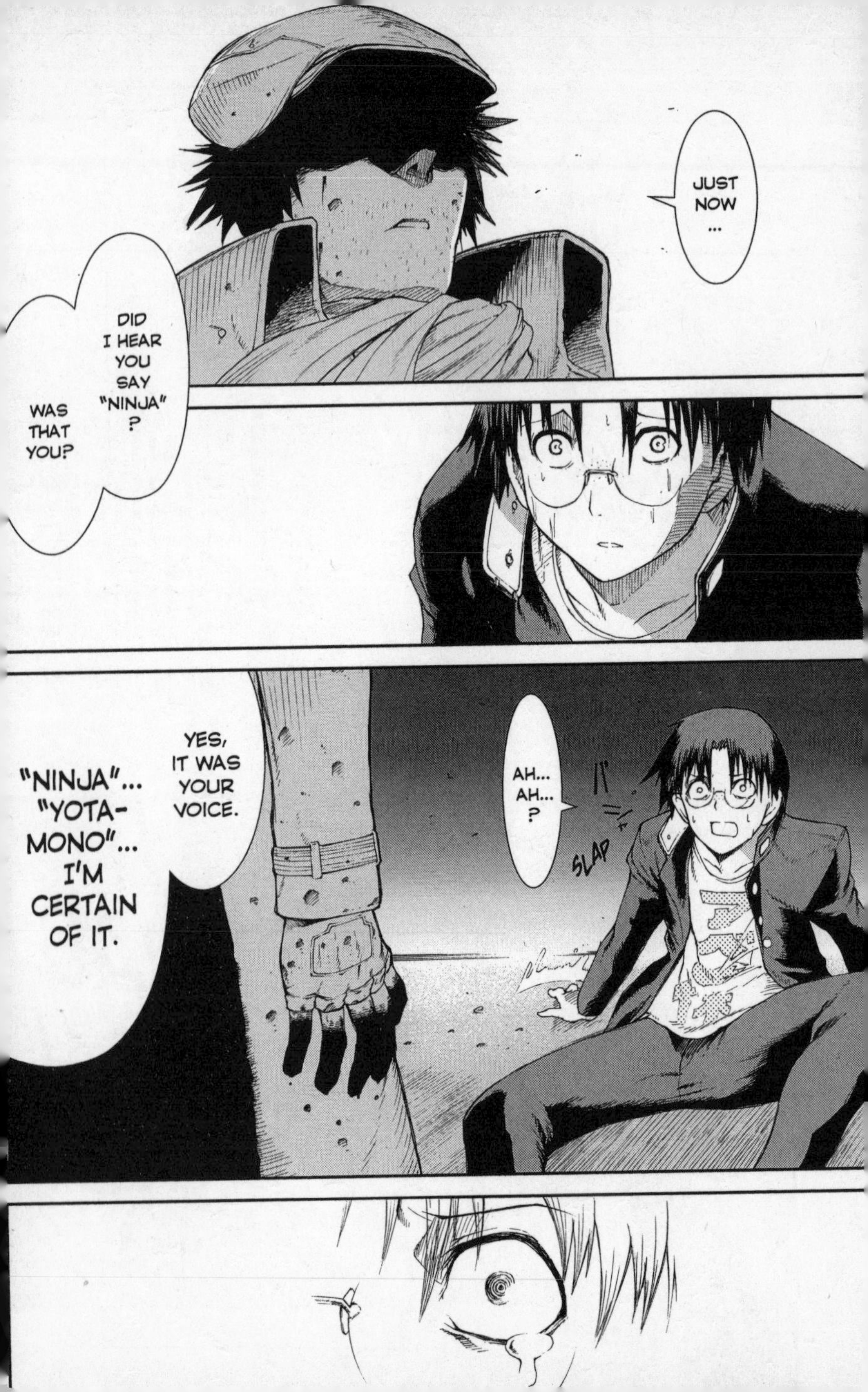
JUST NOW ...
DID I HEAR YOU SAY "NINJA" ?
WAS THAT YOU?
AH... AH... ?
SLAP
YES, IT WAS YOUR VOICE.
"NINJA"... "YOTA-MONO"... I'M CERTAIN OF IT.

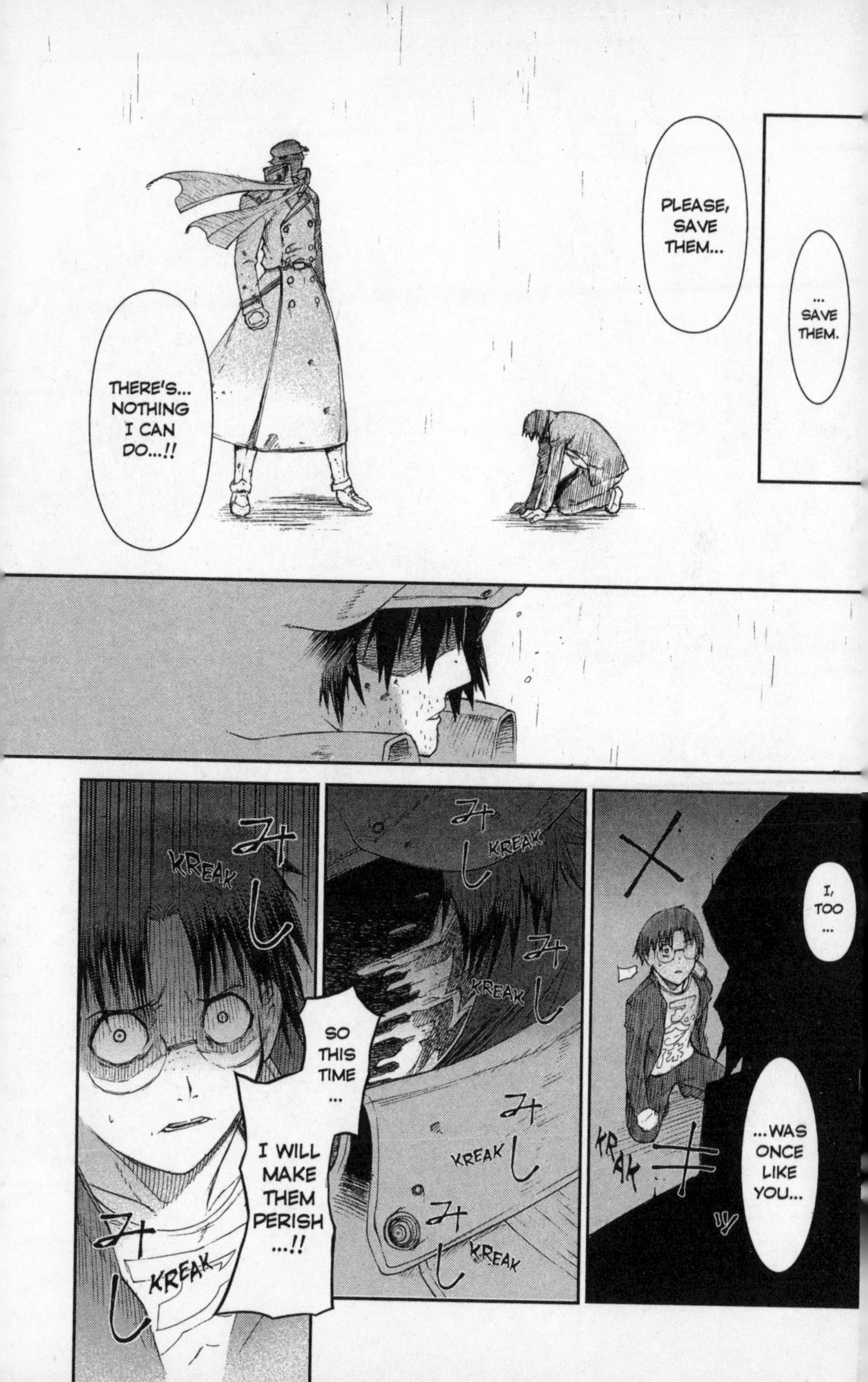

... SAVE THEM.
PLEASE, SAVE THEM...
THERE'S... NOTHING I CAN DO...!!
I, TOO ...
...WAS ONCE LIKE YOU...
KRAK
ッ
みし
KREAK
みし
KREAK
みし
KREAK
みし
KREAK
SO THIS TIME ...
I WILL MAKE THEM PERISH ...!!
みし
KREAK
みし
KREAK

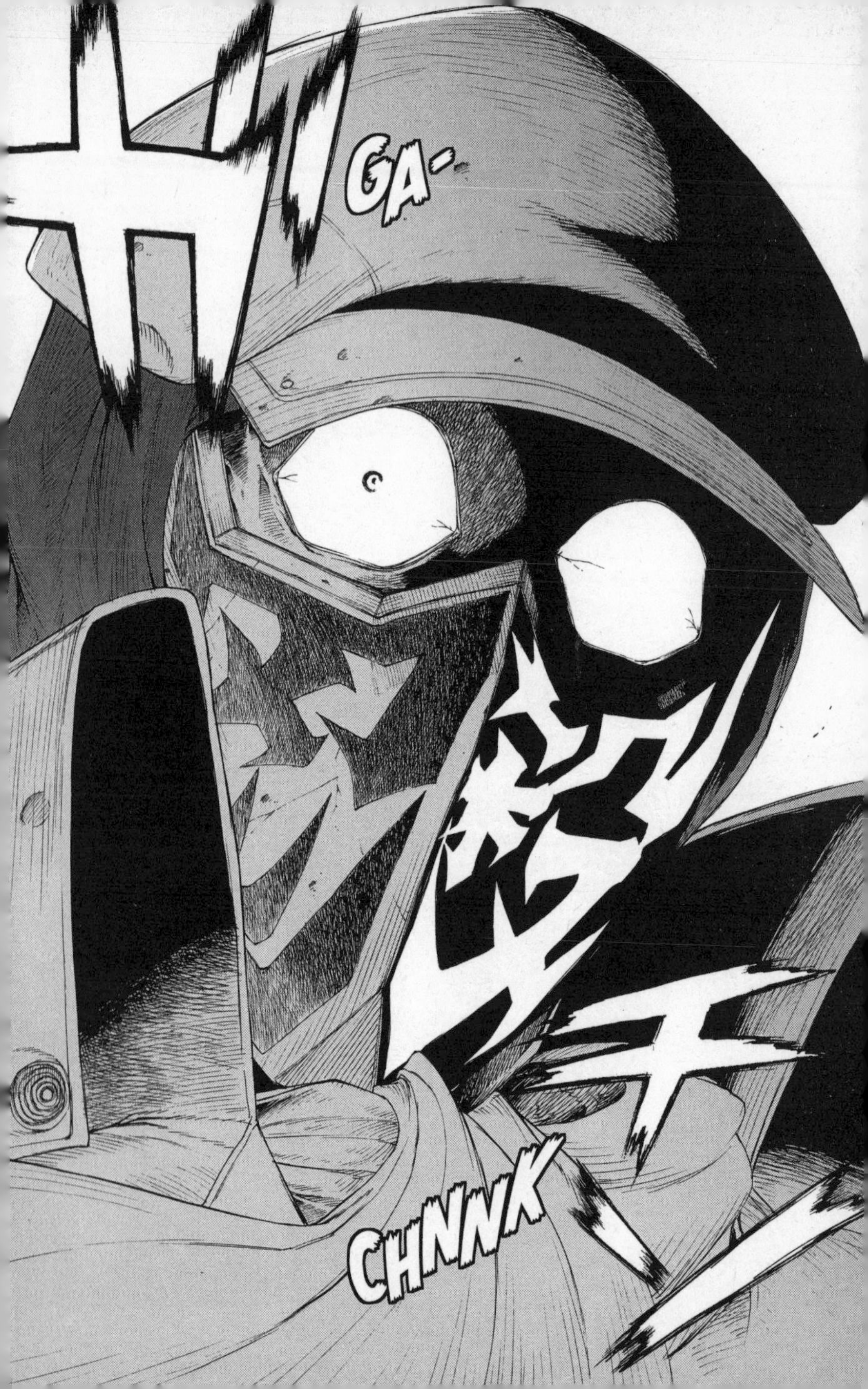
GA-
CHNNK

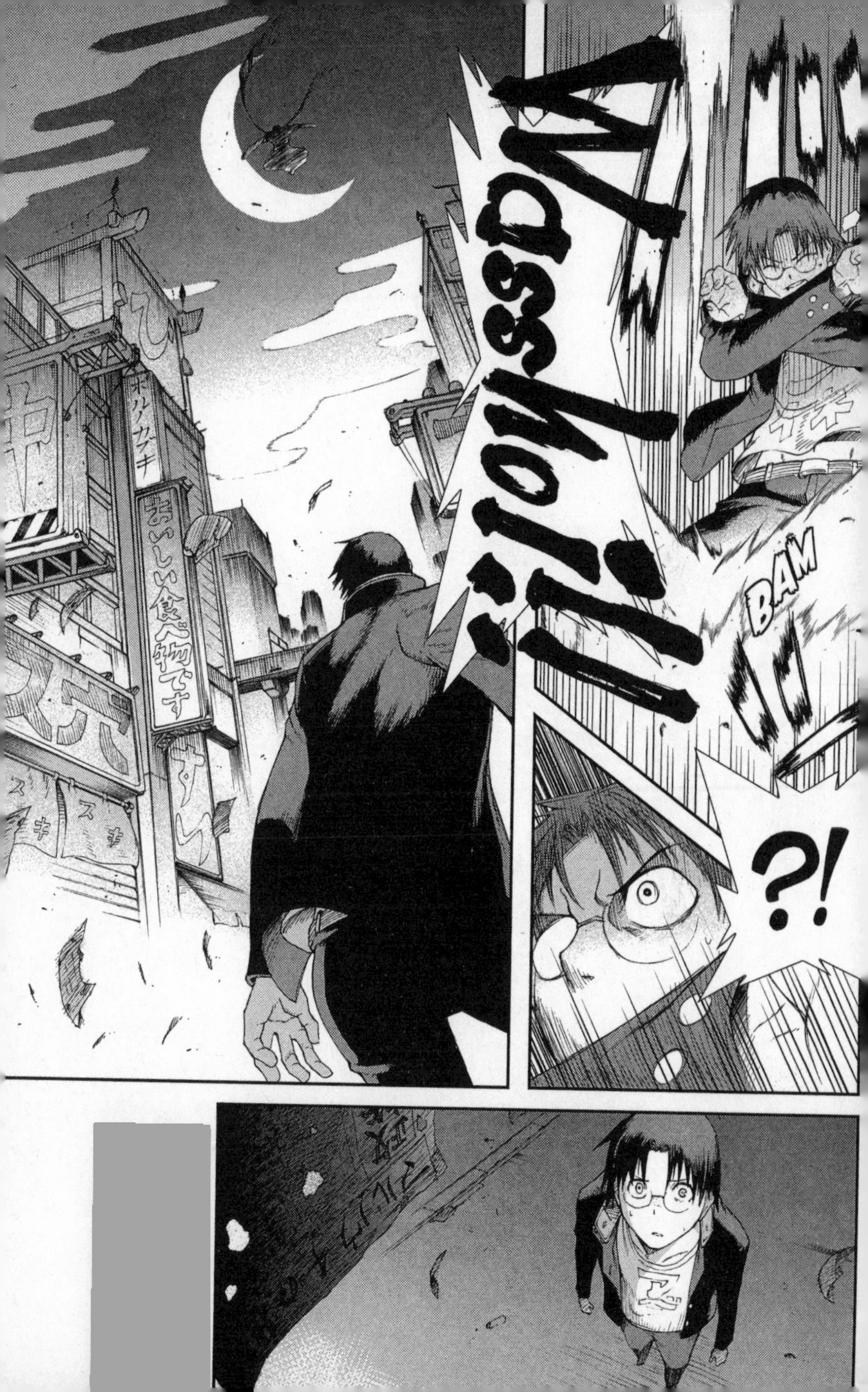
WASSHOI!!
BAM
?!
おいしい食べ物です

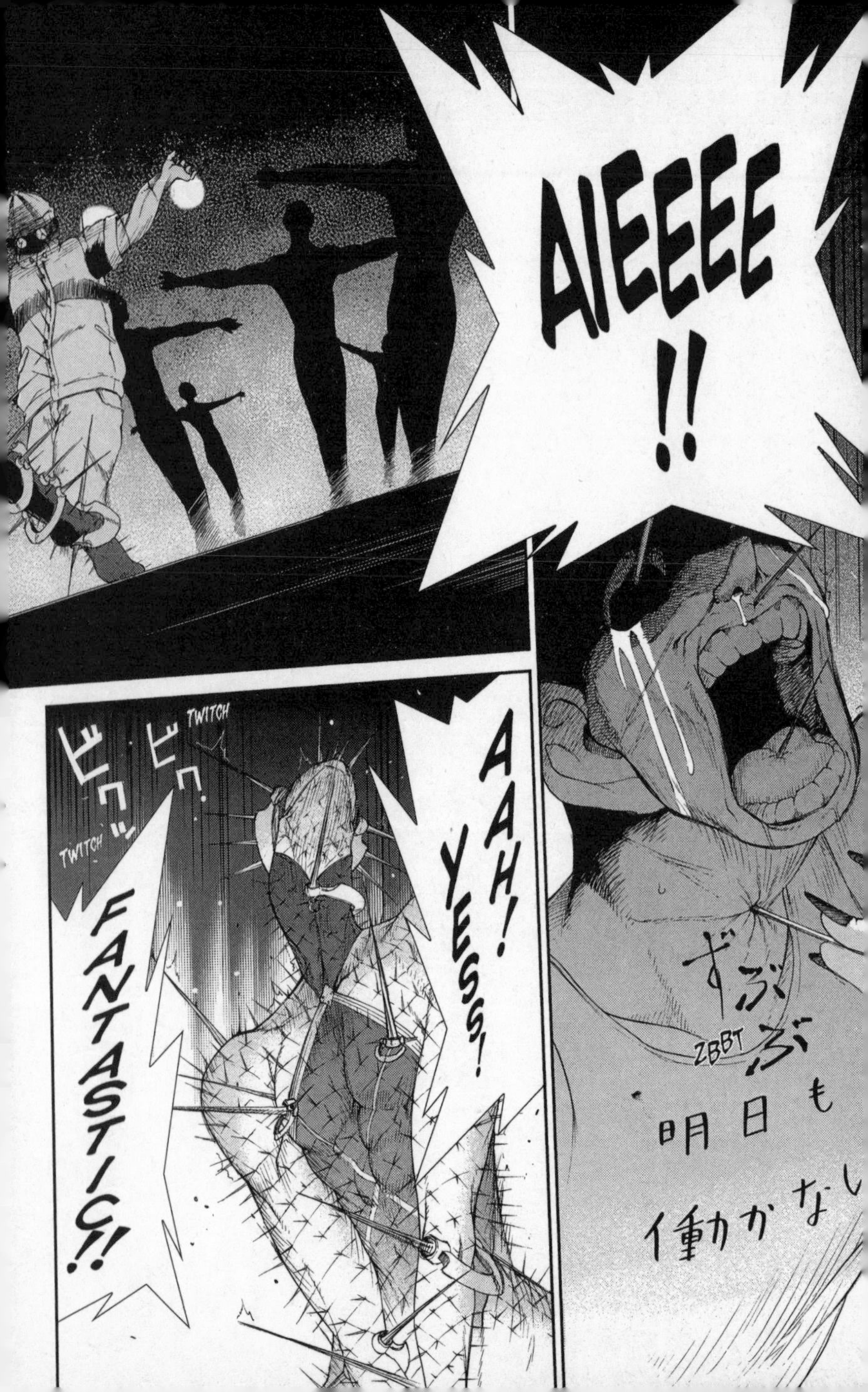
AIEEEE!!
ずぶ ぶ
ZBBT
明日も
働かなし
AAH! YESS!
ビクッ ビクッ
TWITCH
TWITCH
FANTASTIC!!

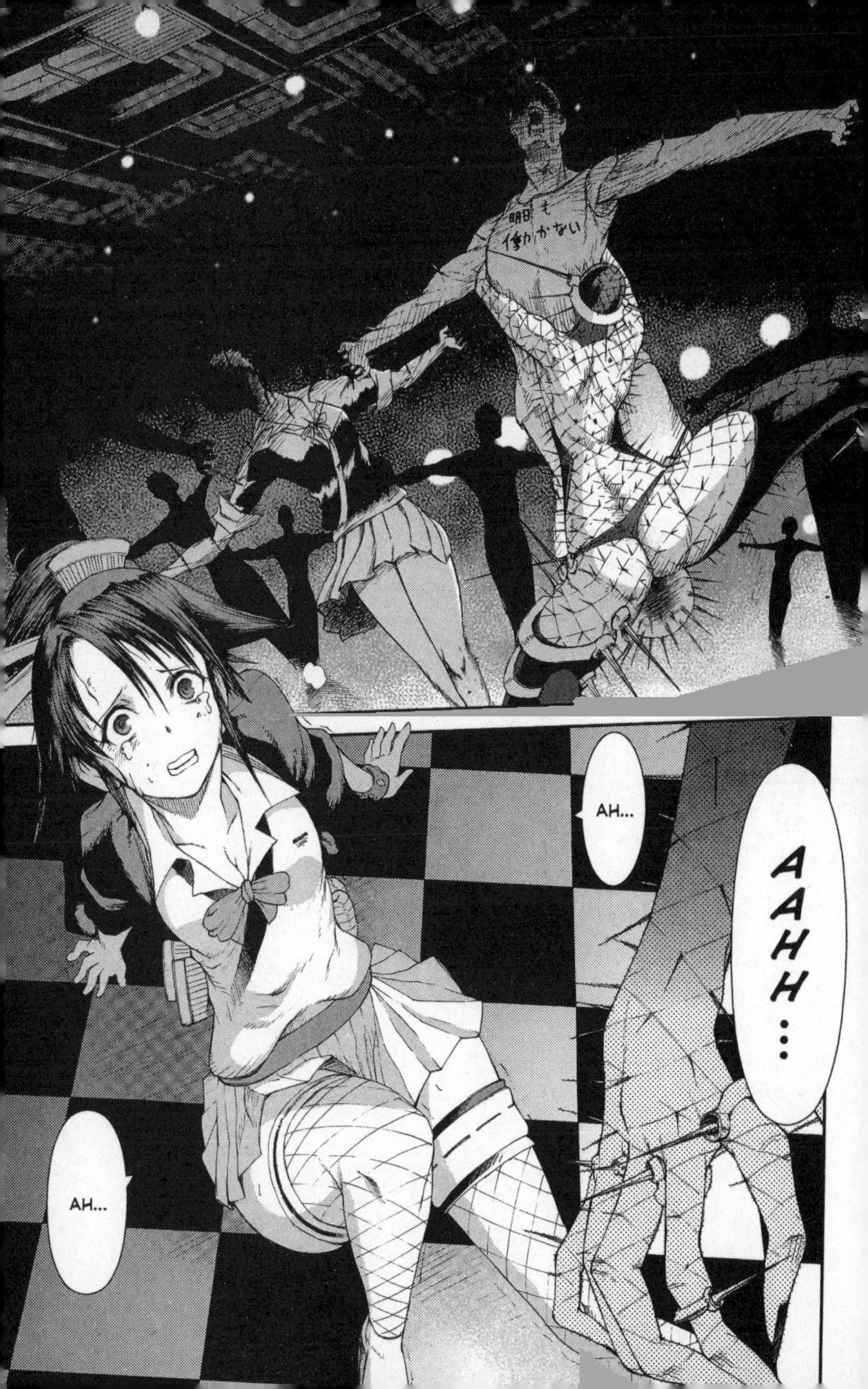
明日も
働かない
AAHH...
AH...
AH...

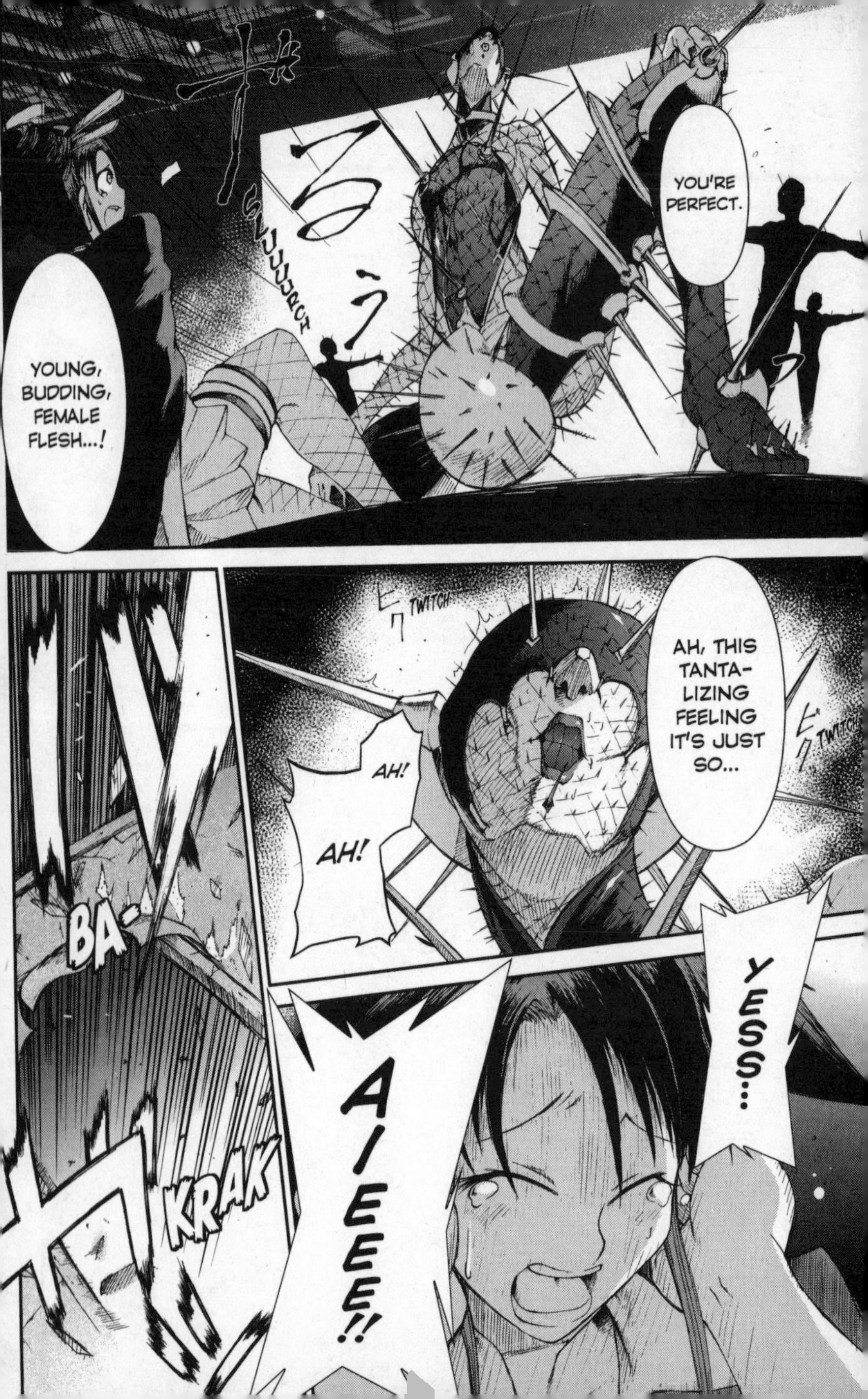
YOU'RE PERFECT.
SLUUUURCH
YOUNG, BUDDING, FEMALE FLESH...!
TWITCH
AH, THIS TANTA-LIZING FEELING IT'S JUST SO...
TWITCH
AH!
AH!
YESS...
AIEEEE!!
BA-
KRAK

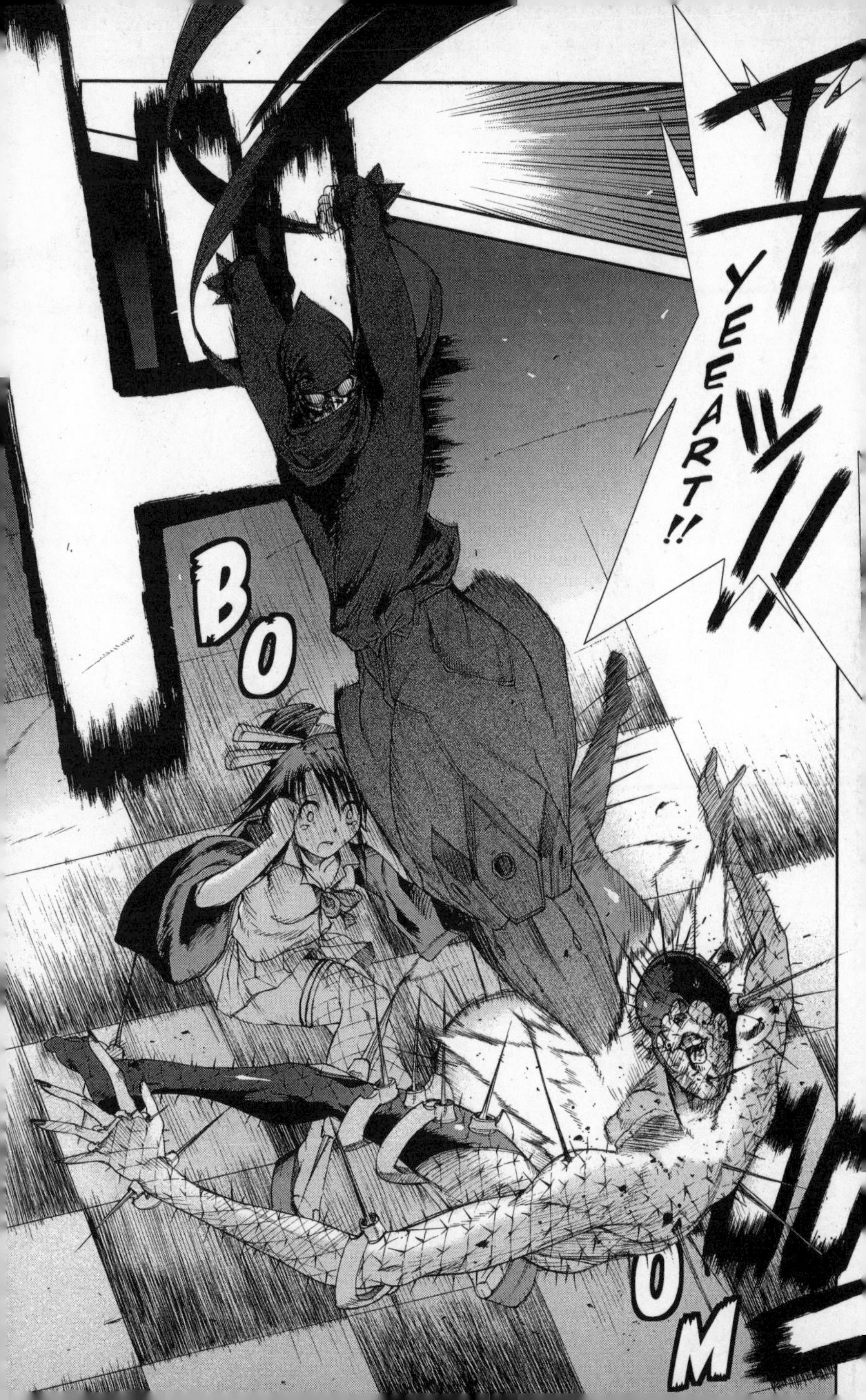
YEEEART!!
BOOM

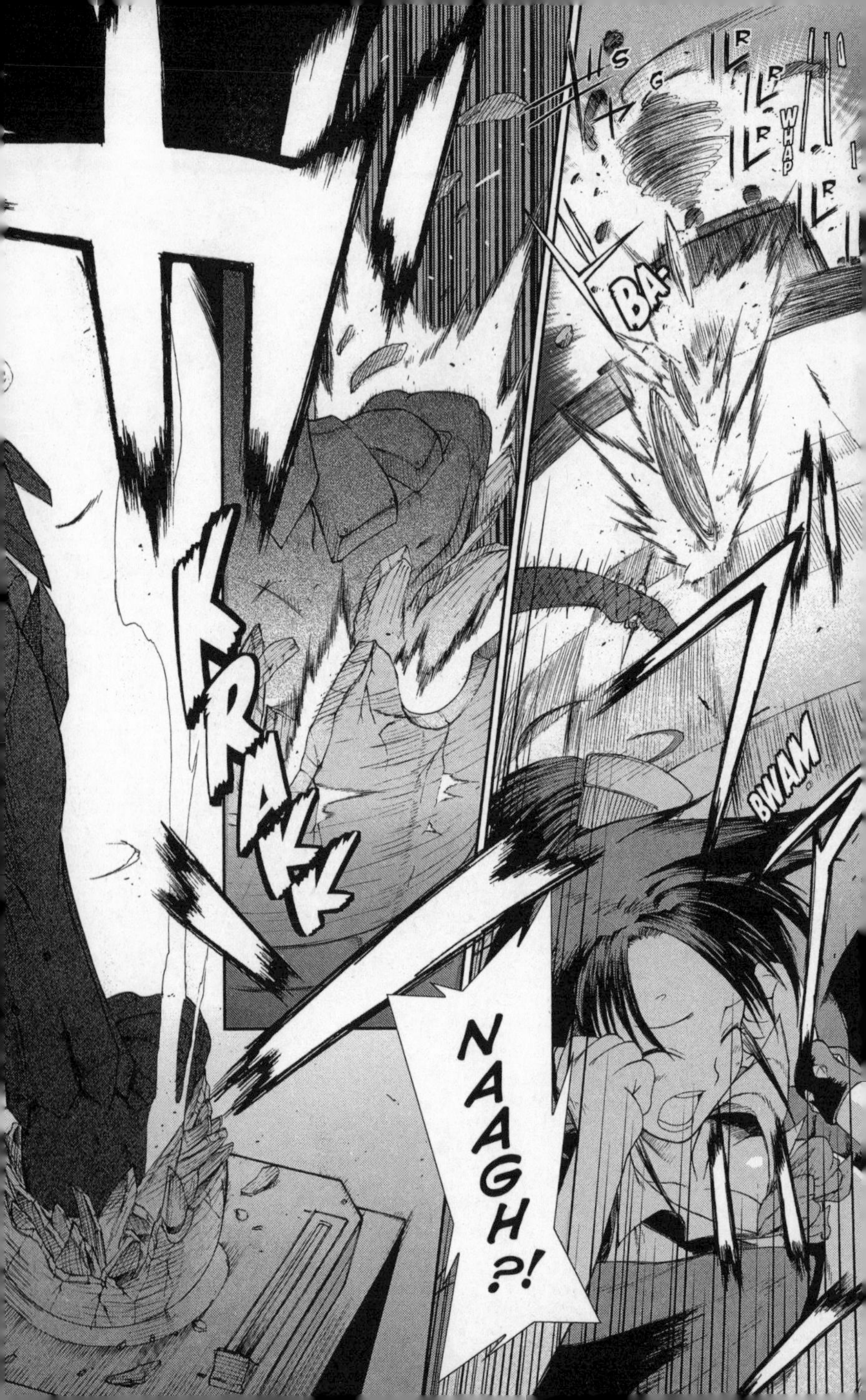
SGLLRRRRRRRRRRRRRIIIIIP
WHAP
BA-
KRAKK
BWAM
NAAGH?!

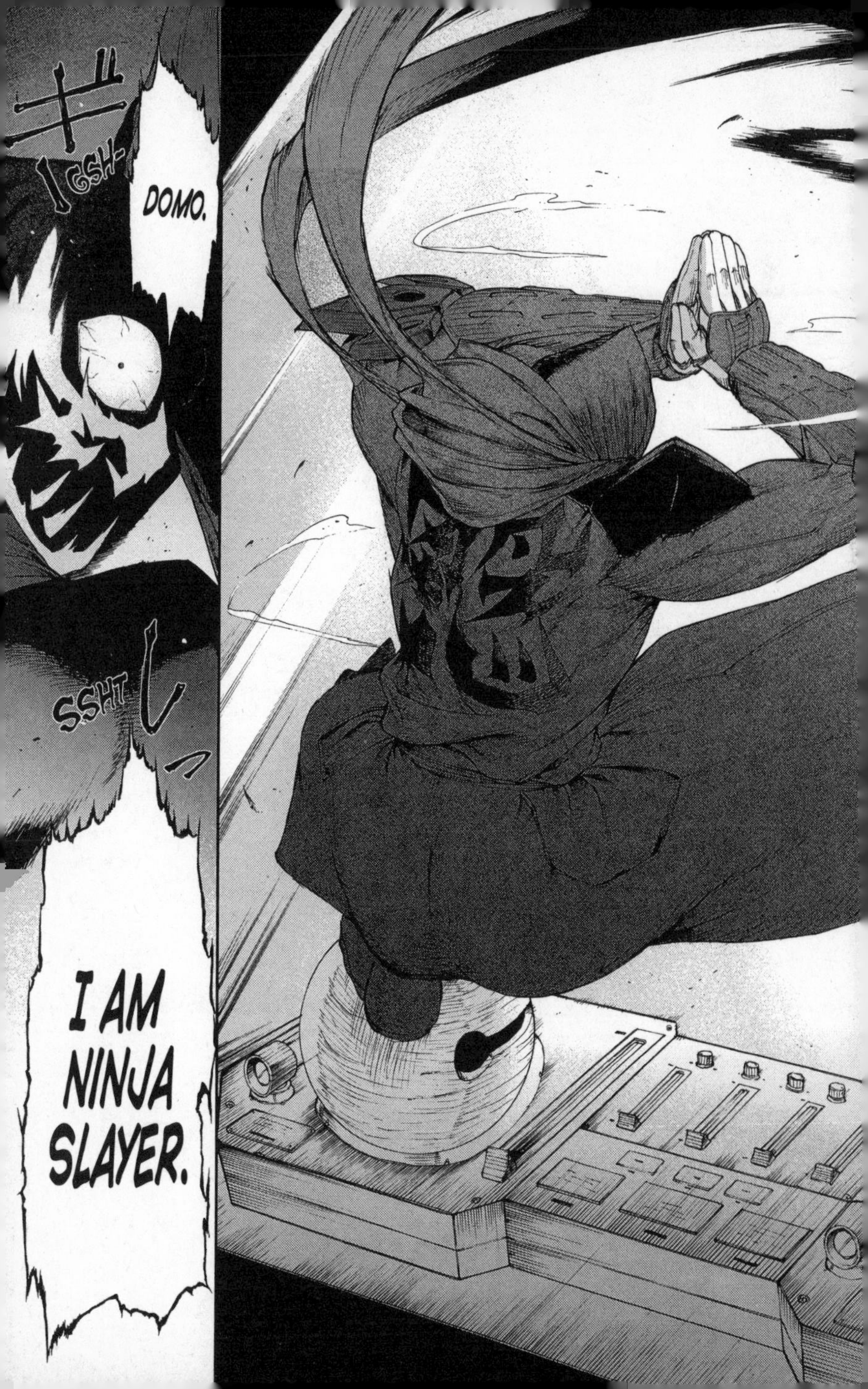

ギュッ
GSH-
DOMO.
SSHT
しっ
I AM NINJA SLAYER.

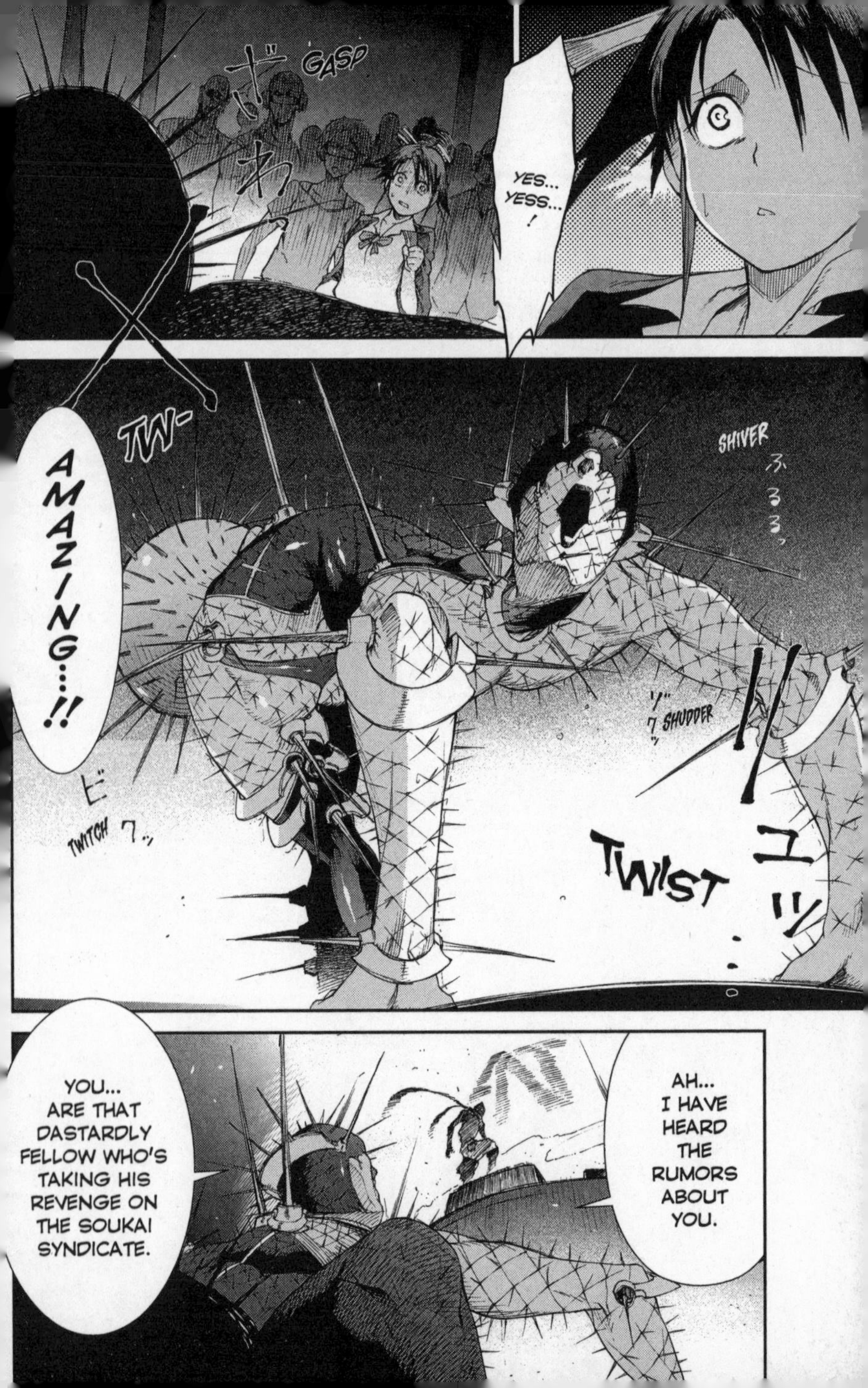
YES... YESS...!
ざわ
GASP
AMAZING...!!
TW-
SHIVER
ふるるっ
ゾワッ
SHUDDER
ユッ
TWIST
ビクッ
TWITCH
AH... I HAVE HEARD THE RUMORS ABOUT YOU.
YOU... ARE THAT DASTARDLY FELLOW WHO'S TAKING HIS REVENGE ON THE SOUKAI SYNDICATE.

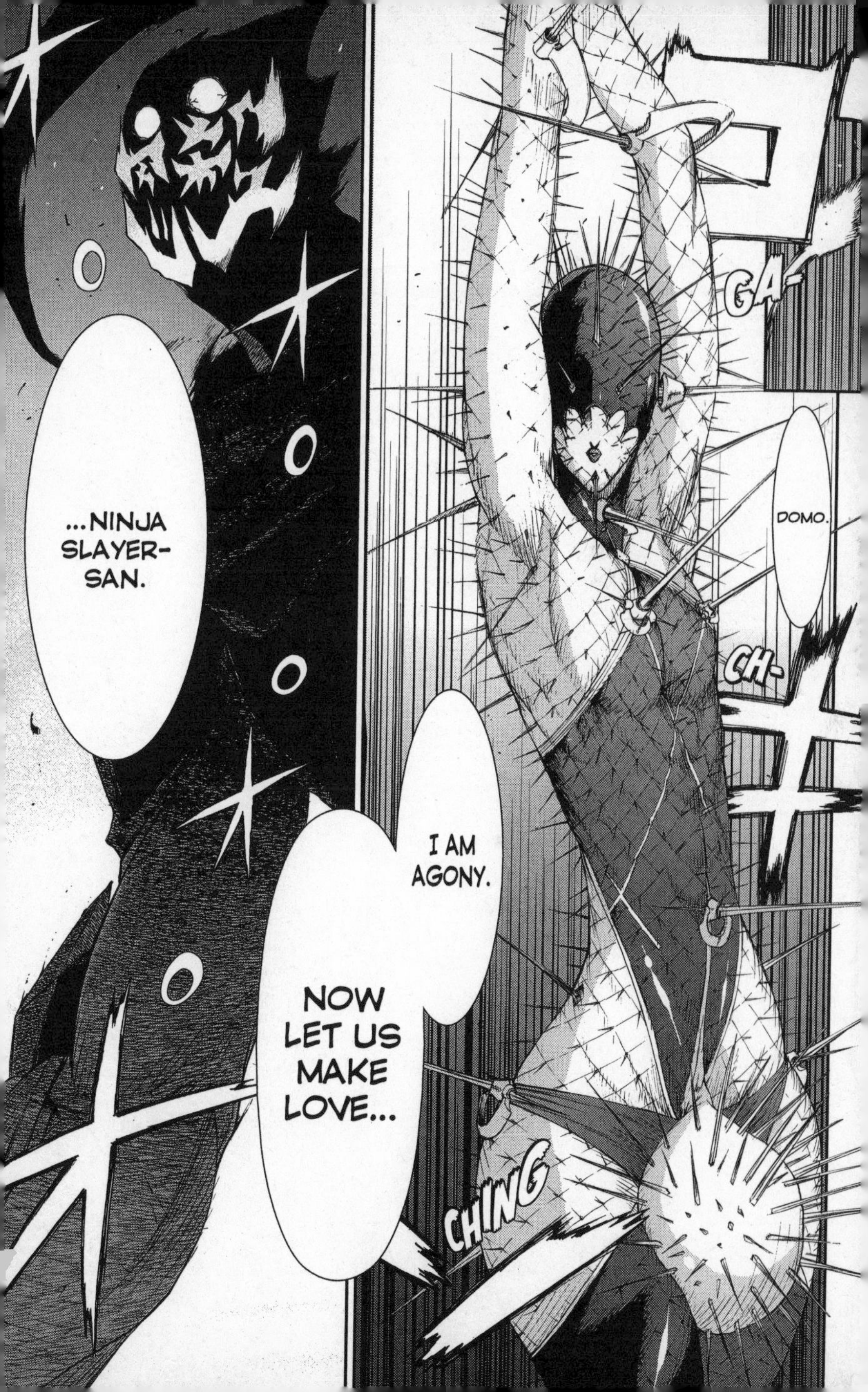
GA-
DOMO.
CH-
I AM AGONY.
NOW LET US MAKE LOVE...
CHING
...NINJA SLAYER-SAN.

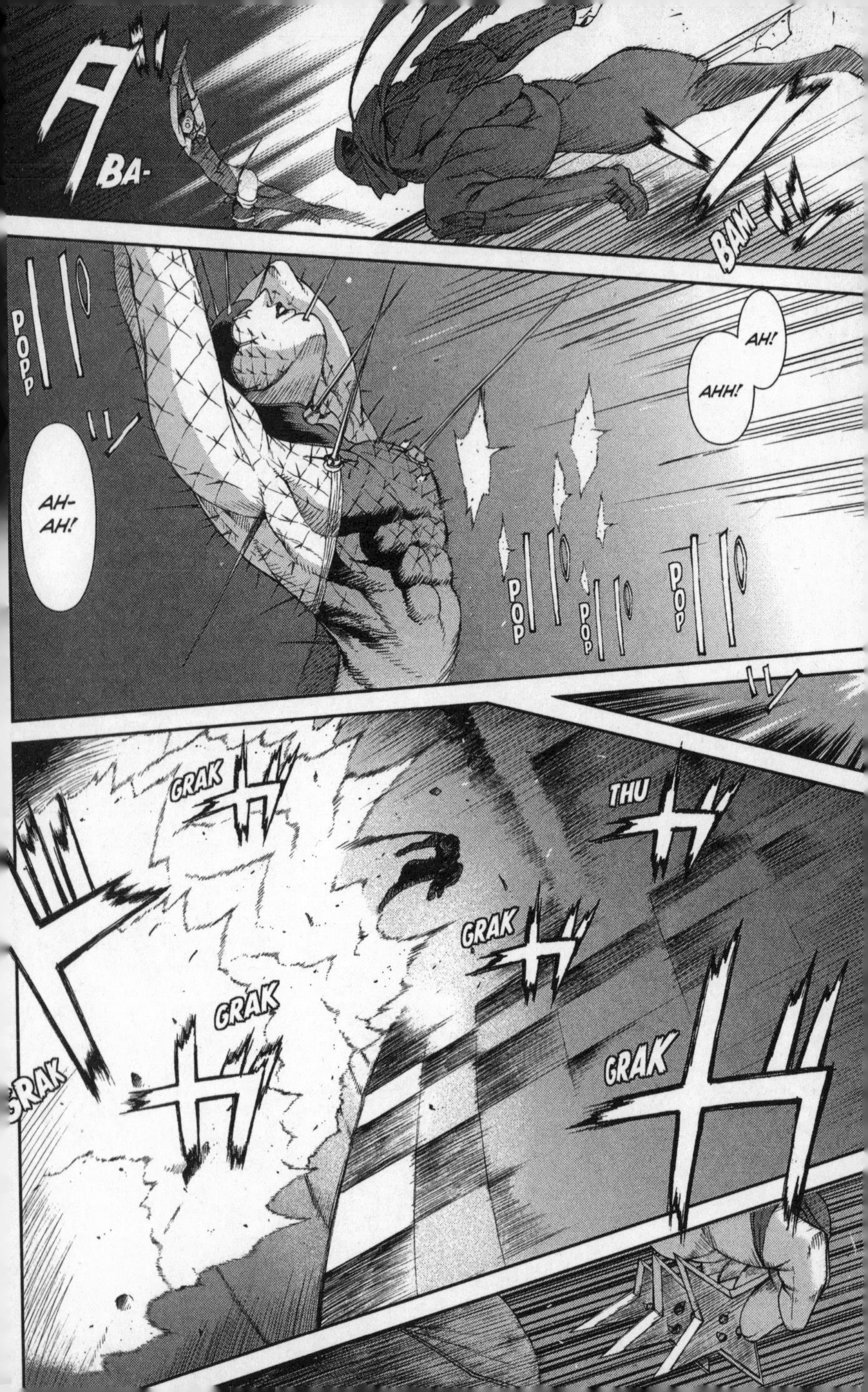
BAM
BA-
AH!
AHH!
POP
POP
POP
AH-
AH!
POPP
THU
GRAK
GRAK
GRAK
GRAK
GRAK

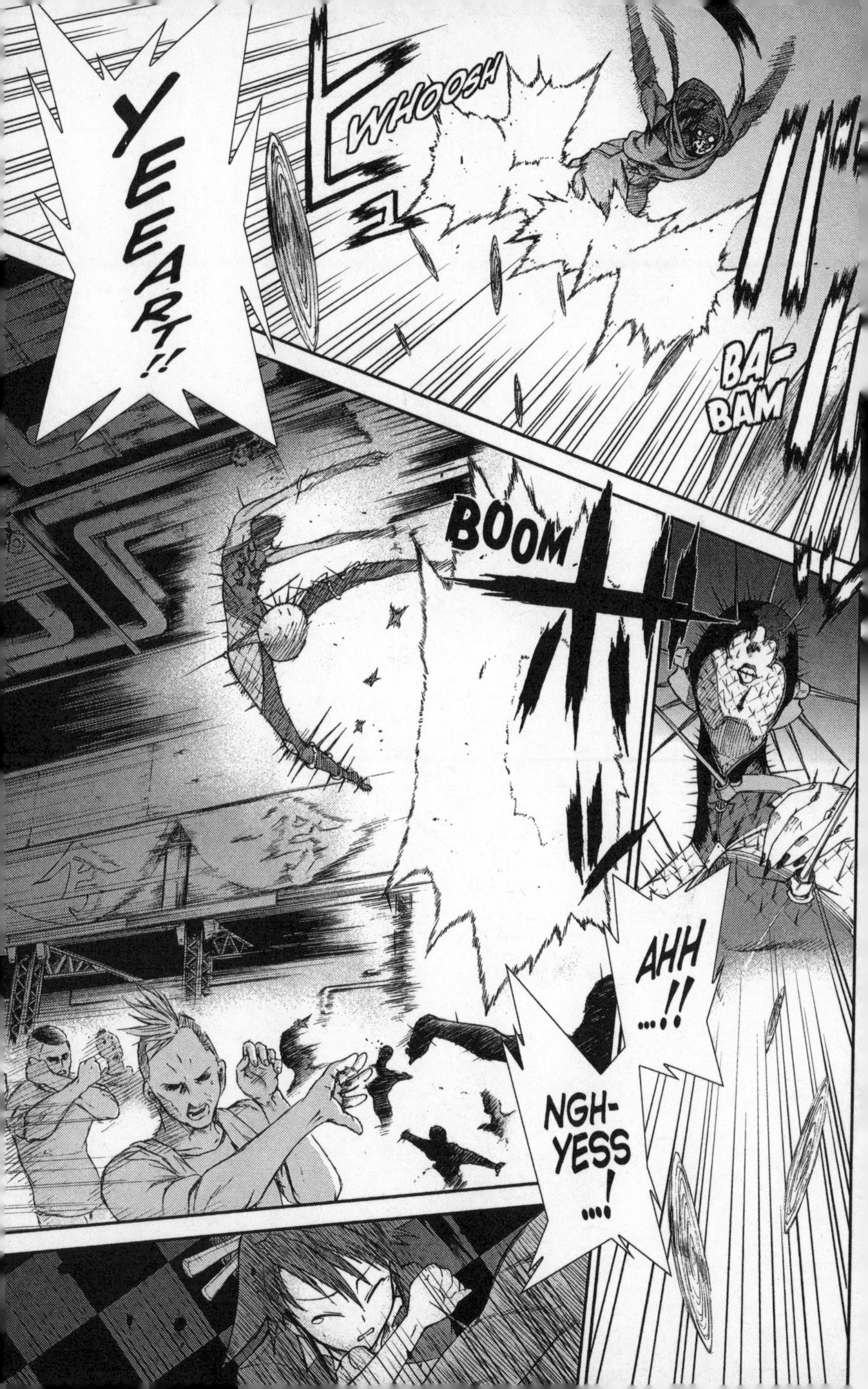
WHOOSH
YEEART!!
BA-BAM
BOOM
AHH ...!!
NGH-YESS ...!

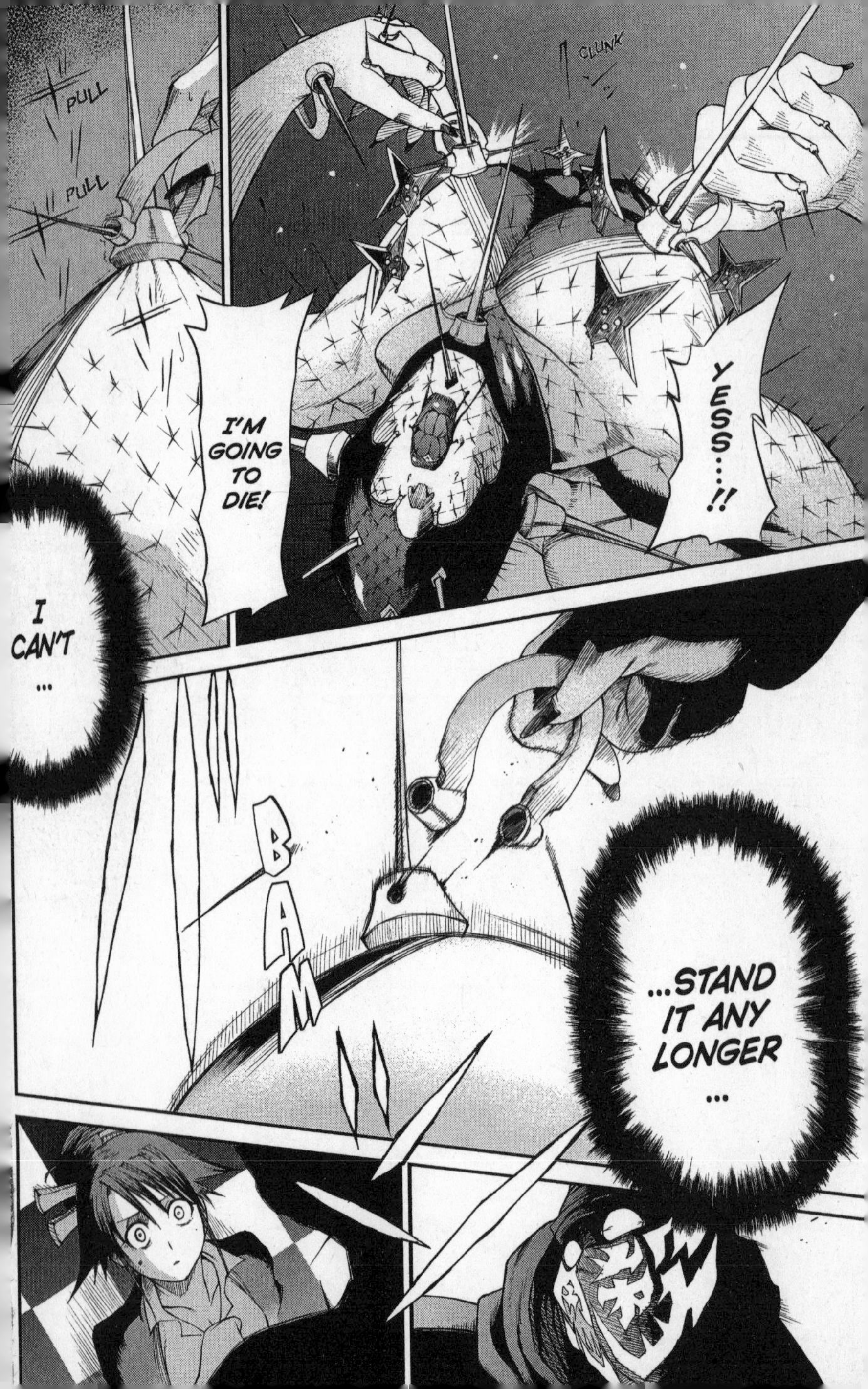
CLUNK
YESS...!!
PULL
PULL
I'M GOING TO DIE!
I CAN'T ...
BAM
...STAND IT ANY LONGER ...

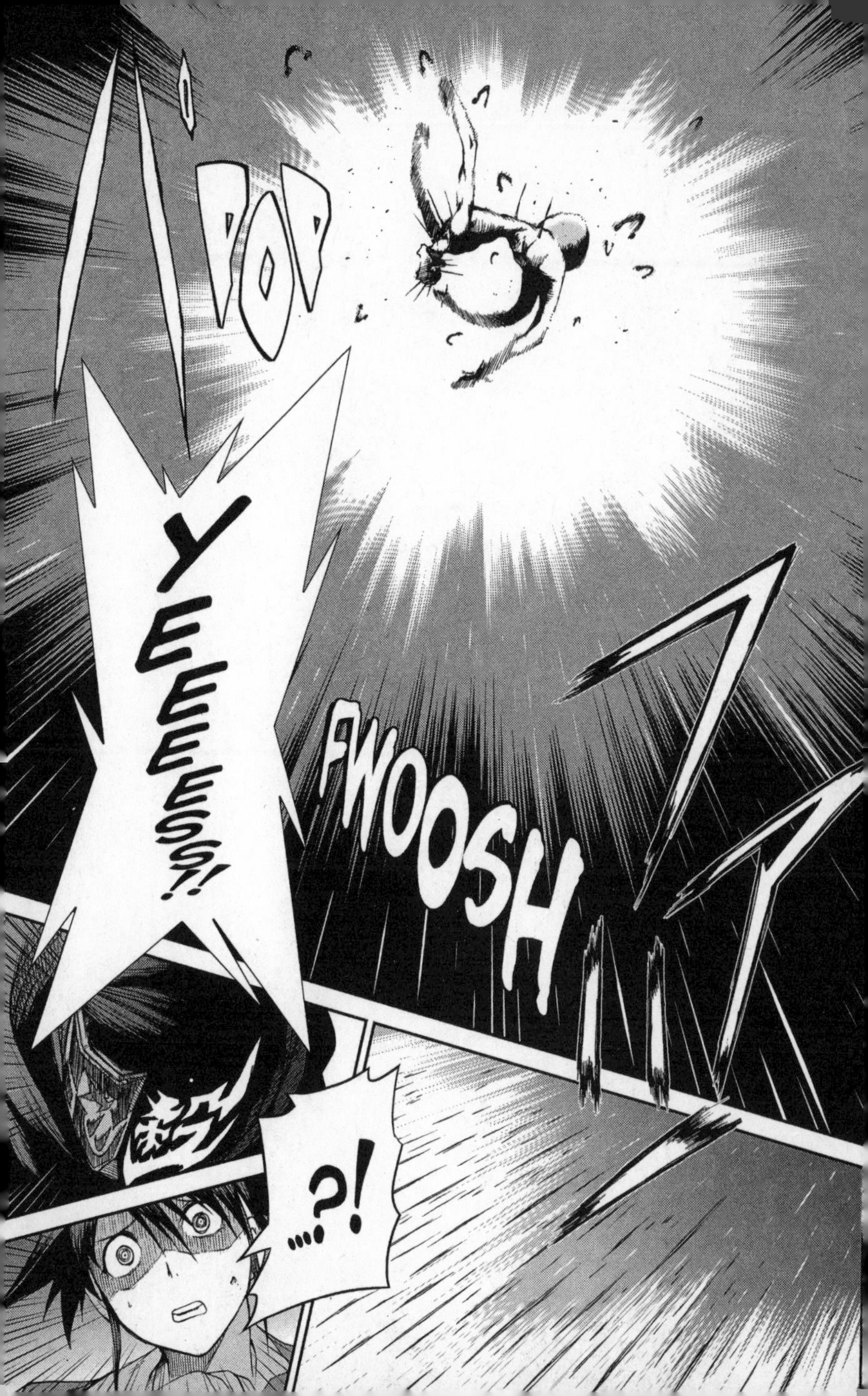
POP
YEEEEESS?!
FWOOSH
...?!

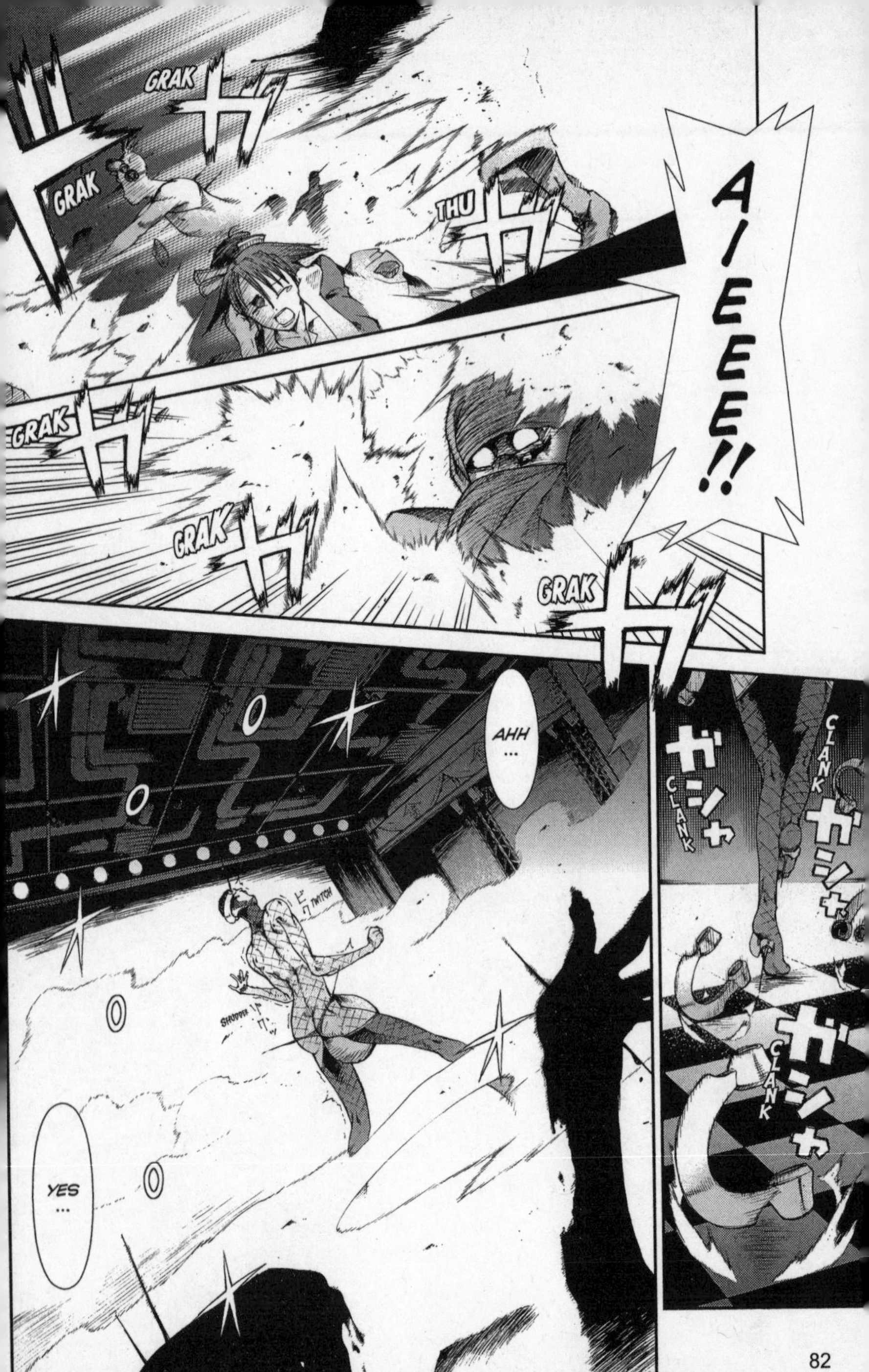
AIEEE!!
THU
GRAK
GRAK
GRAK
GRAK
GRAK
CLANK
CLANK
CLANK
AHH ...
TWITCH
SHUDDER
YES ...

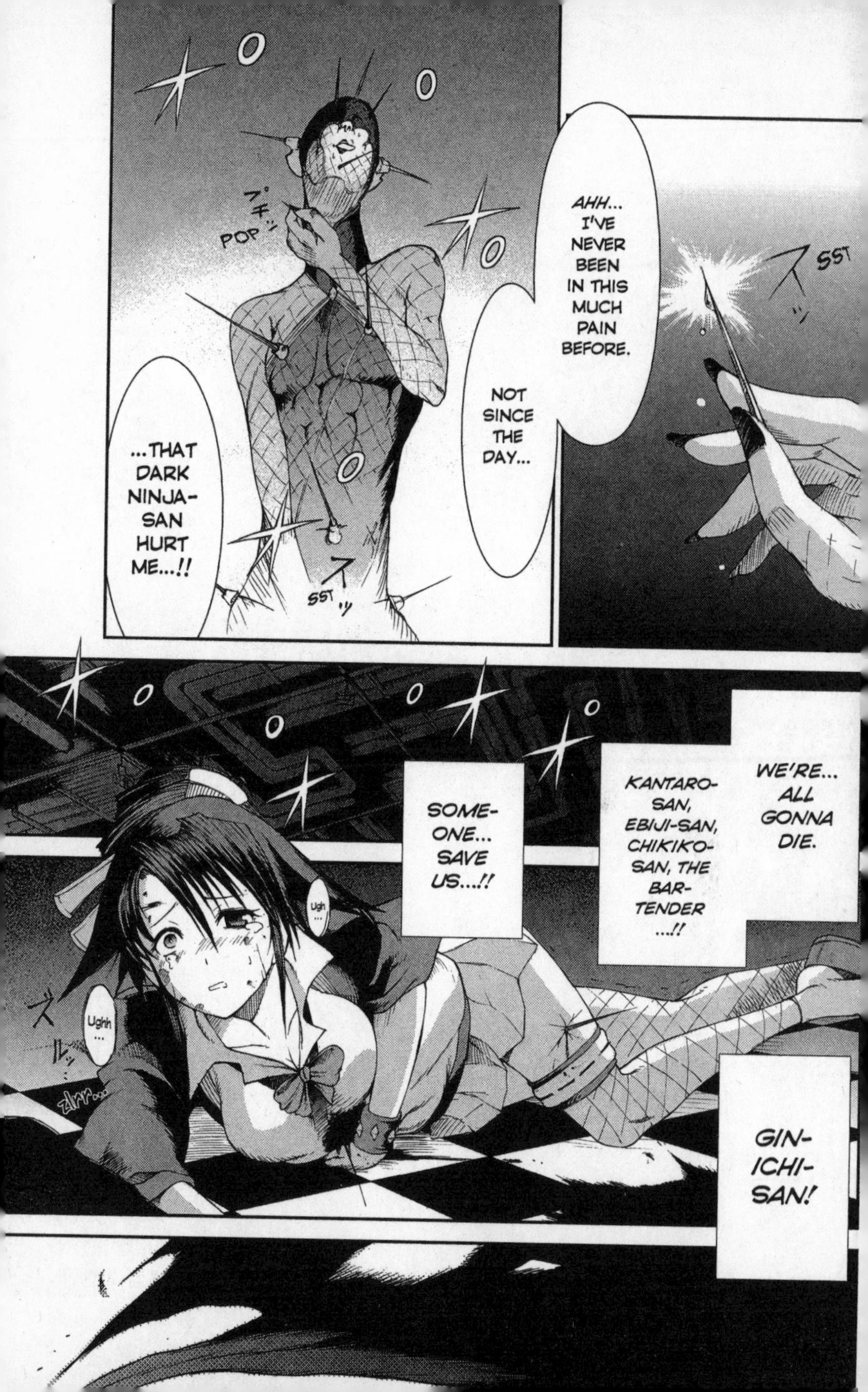
SST
AHH... I'VE NEVER BEEN IN THIS MUCH PAIN BEFORE.
POP
NOT SINCE THE DAY...
...THAT DARK NINJA-SAN HURT ME...!!
SST
WE'RE... ALL GONNA DIE.
KANTARO-SAN, EBIJI-SAN, CHIKIKO-SAN, THE BAR-TENDER ...!!
SOME-ONE... SAVE US...!!
Ugh...
Ughh...
zlrr...
GIN-ICHI-SAN!

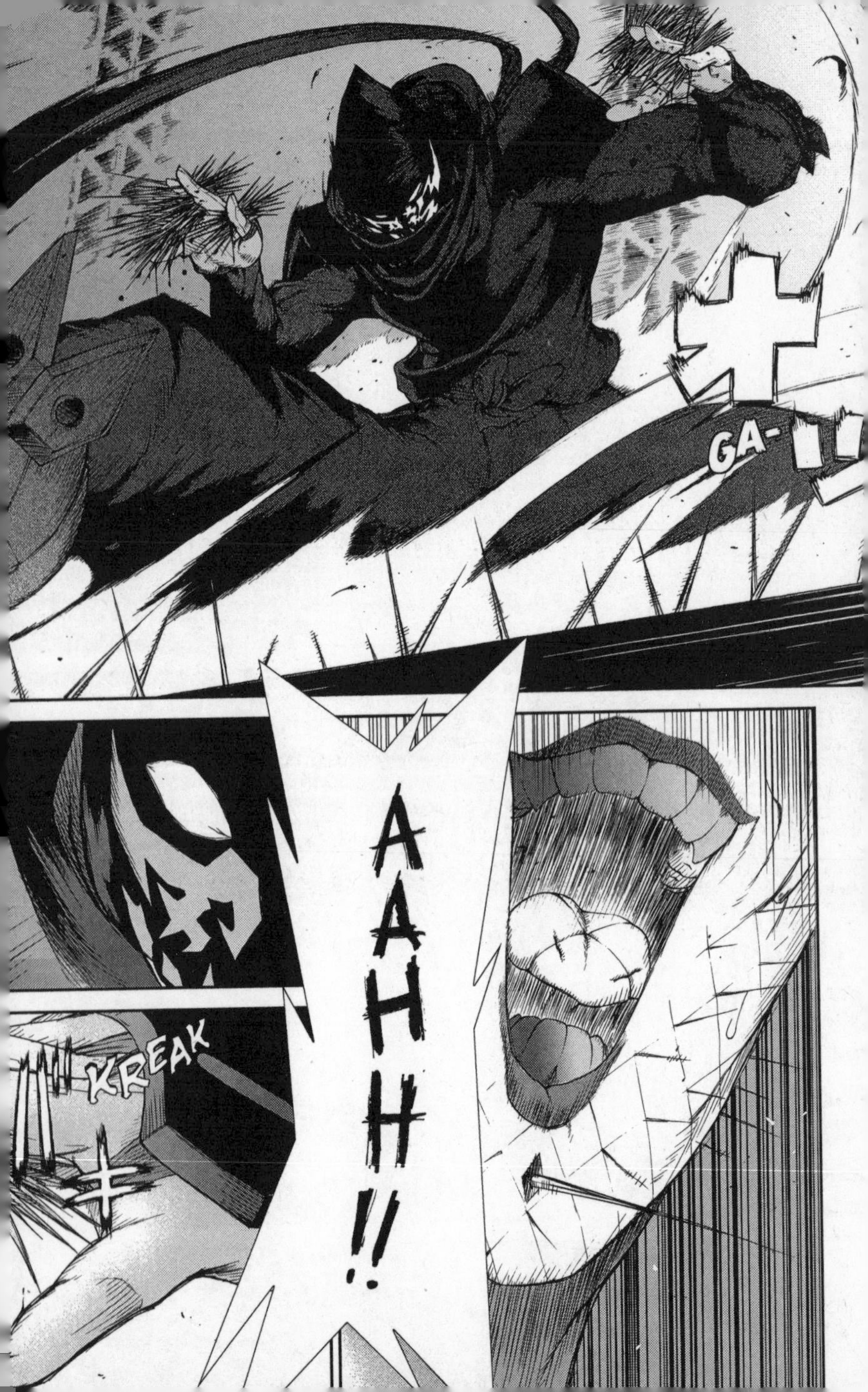
GA-
AAHH!!
KREAK

WHOOM
KRAK
KRAK
KRAK
KRAK
BA-
GRRK

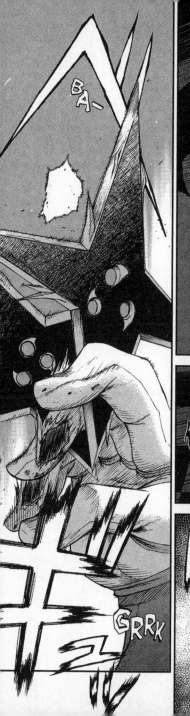

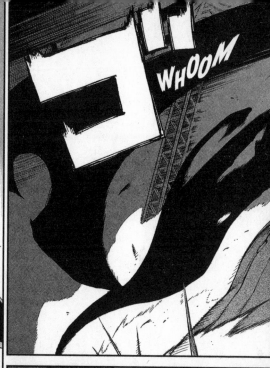

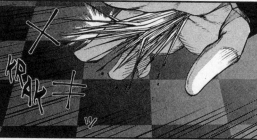

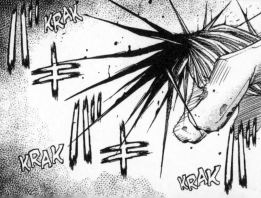

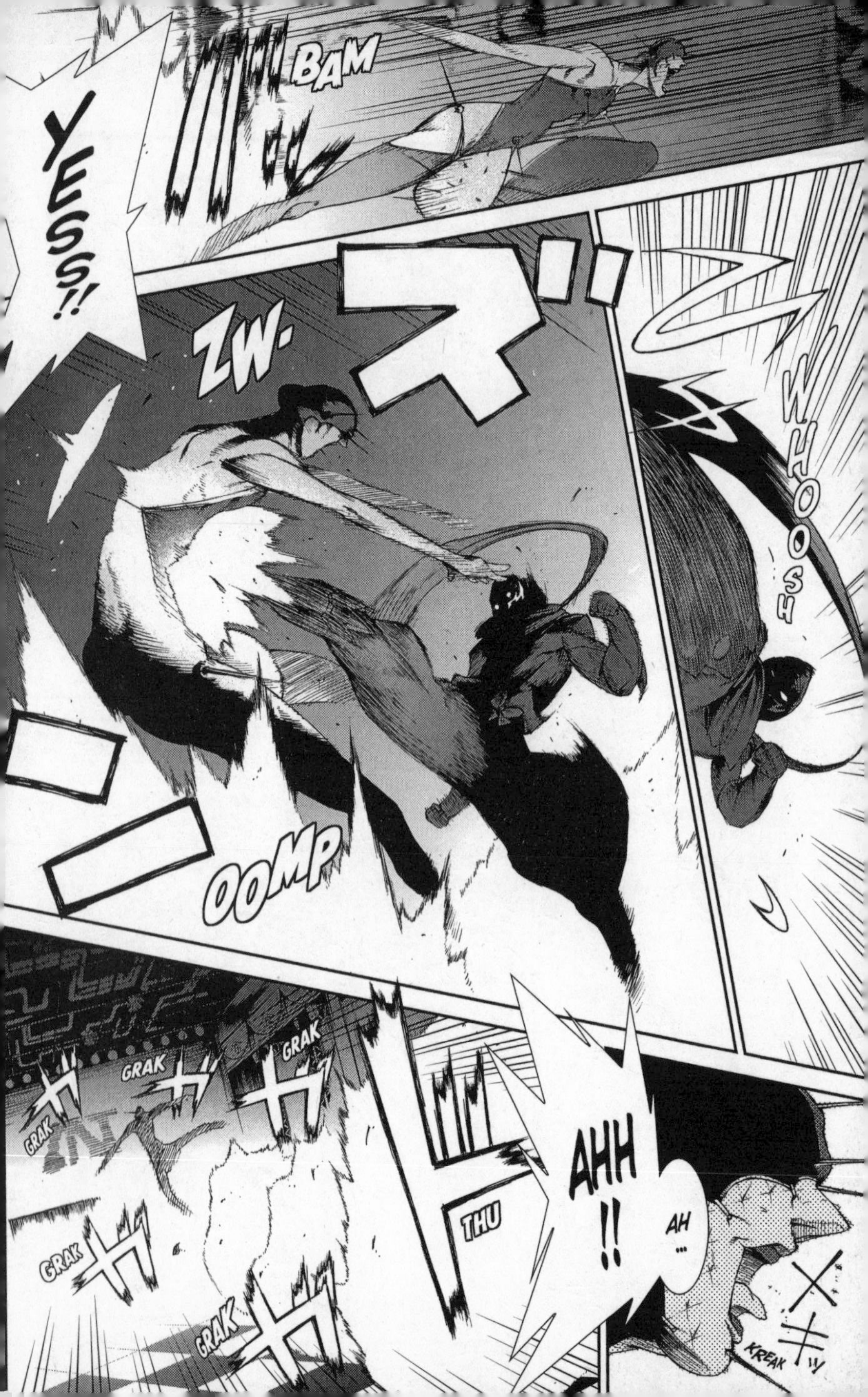
BAM
YESS!!
WHOOSH
ZW-
OOMP
GRAK
GRAK
GRAK
GRAK
GRAK
THU
AHH!!
AH ...
KREAK

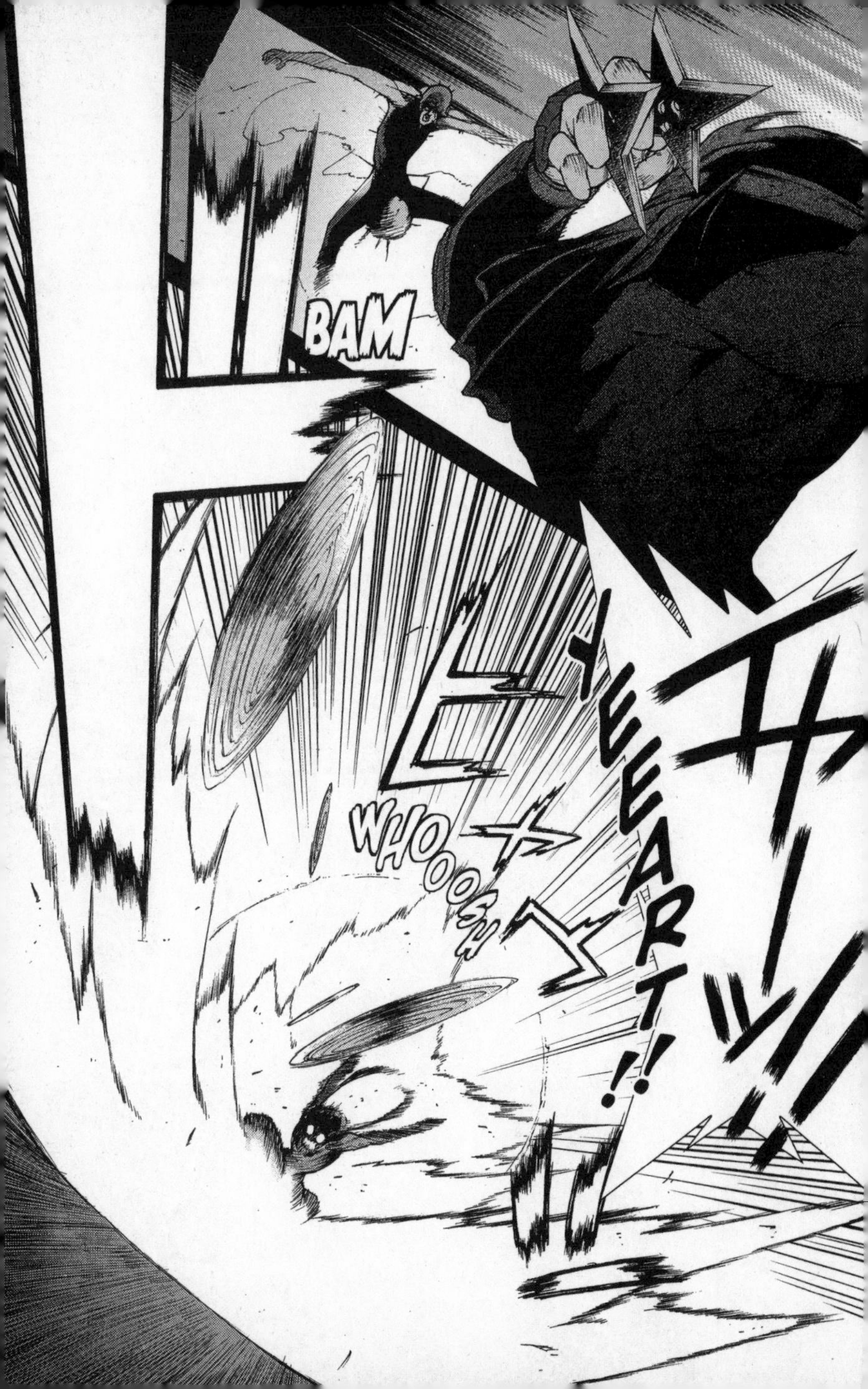
BAM
YEEEART!!
WHOOOSH

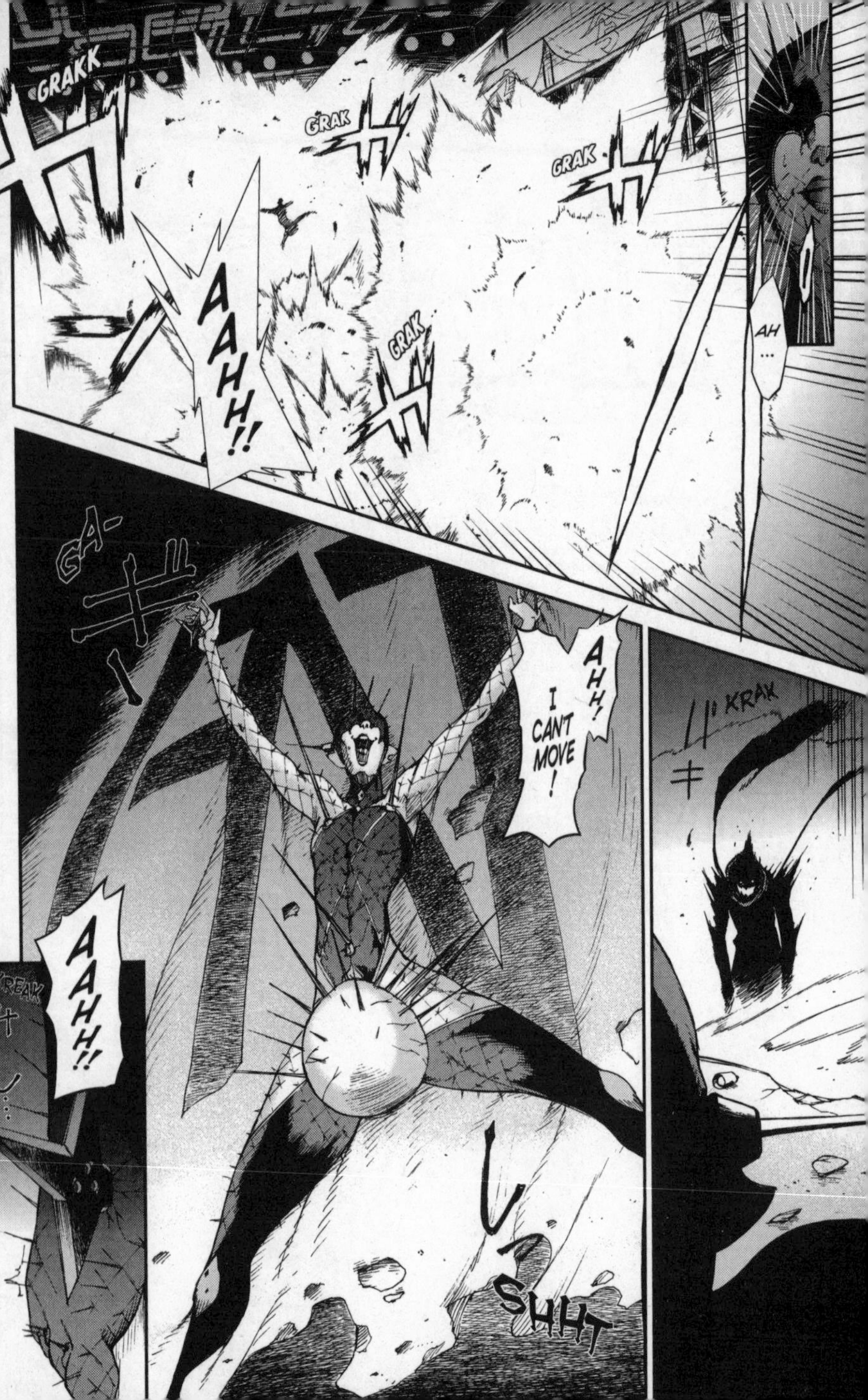
AH ...
GRAK
GRAK
GRAKK
GRAK
AAHH!!
KRAK
AHH! I CAN'T MOVE!
GA-
AAHH!!
KREAK
SHHT

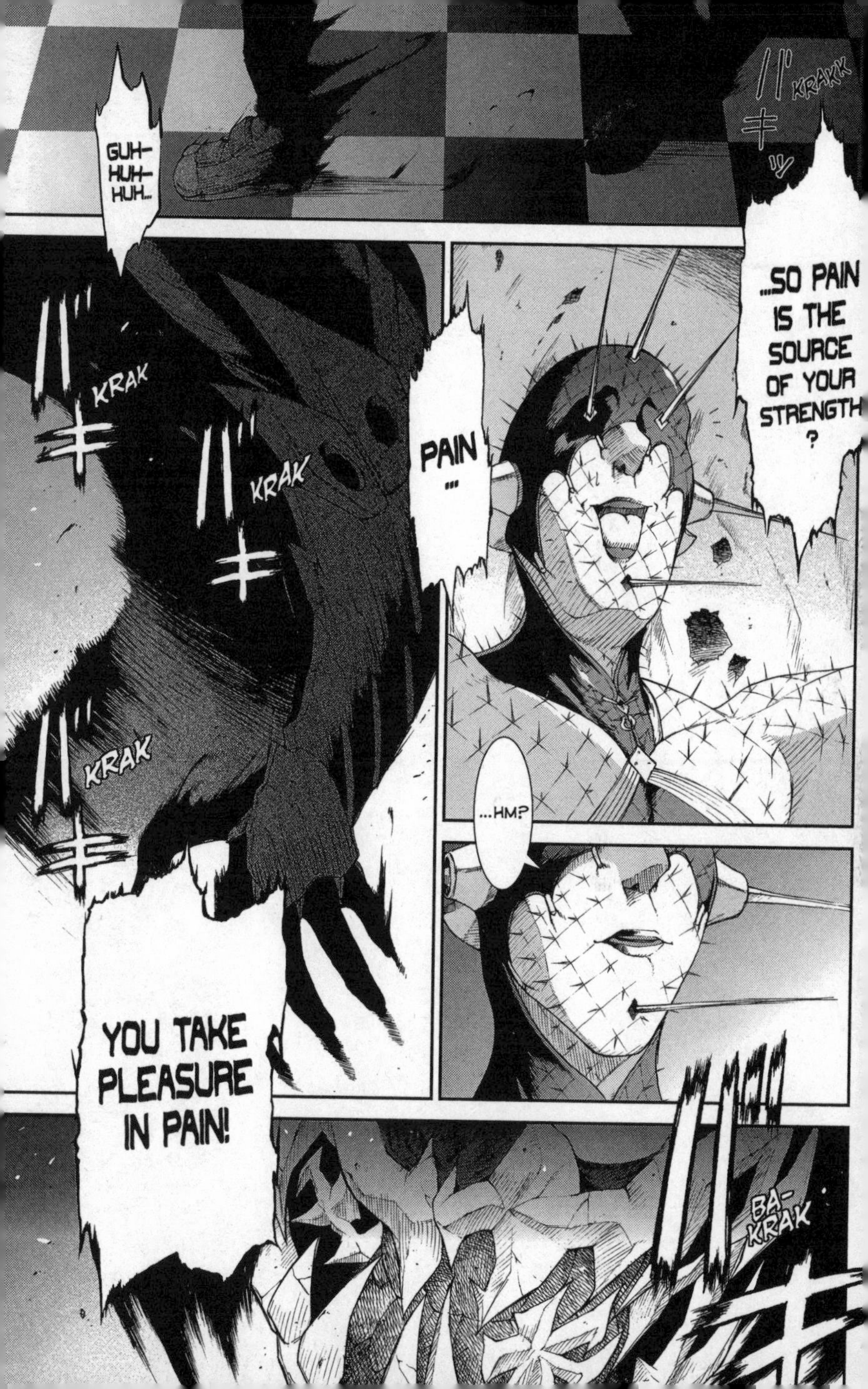
KRAKK
GUH-HUH-HUH...
...SO PAIN IS THE SOURCE OF YOUR STRENGTH?
PAIN...
...HM?
KRAK
KRAK
KRAK
YOU TAKE PLEASURE IN PAIN!
BA-KRAK

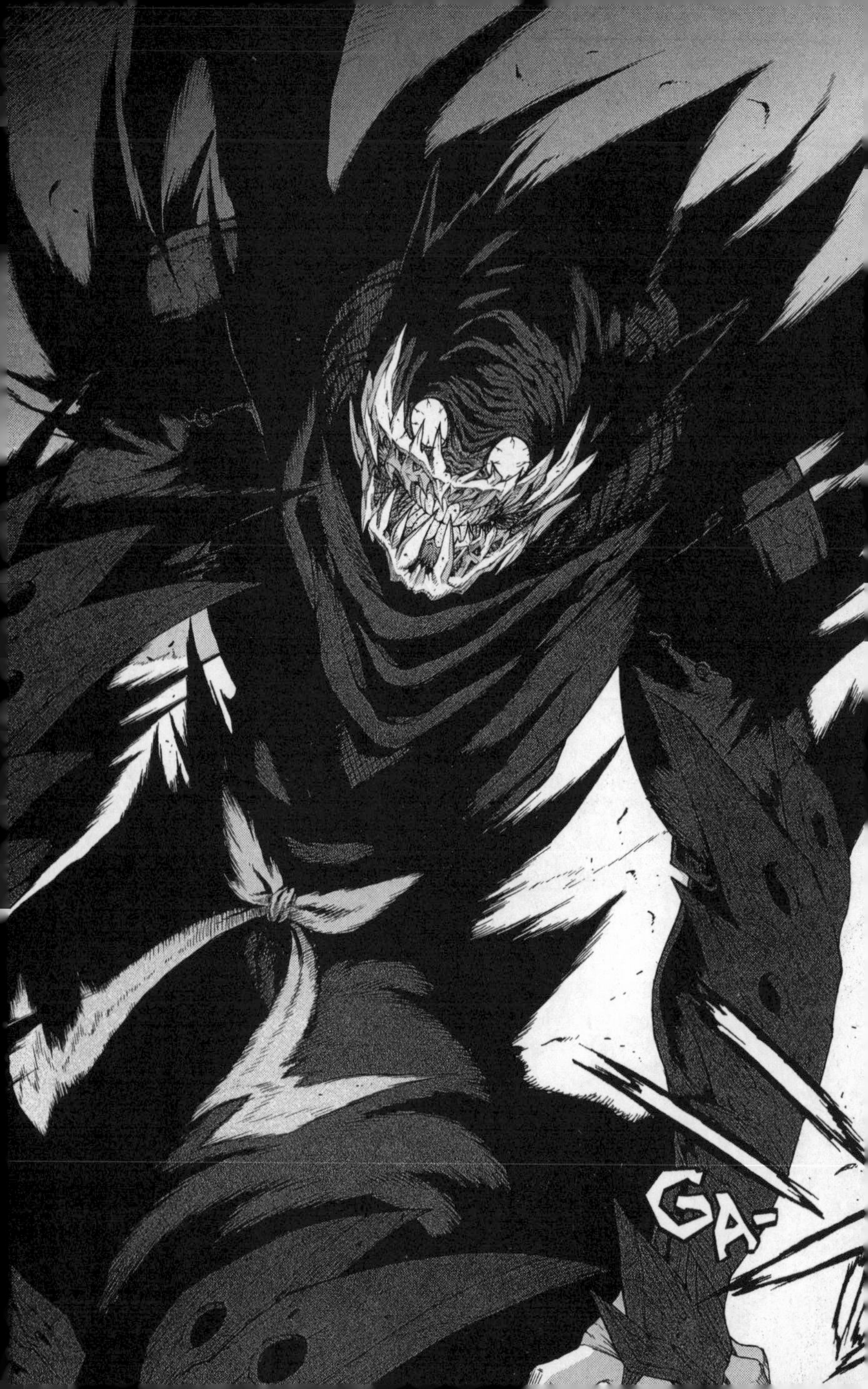
GA-

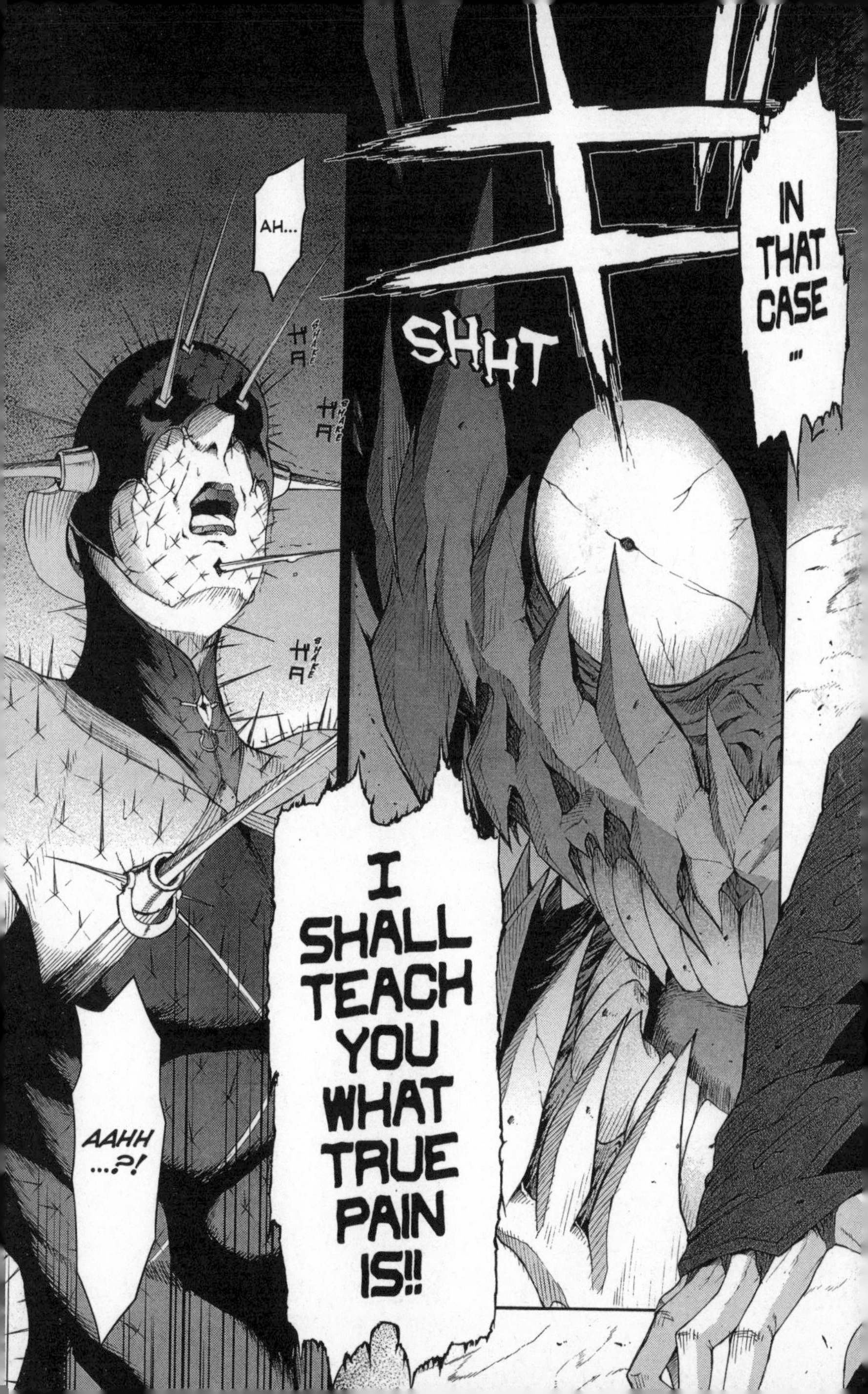
IN THAT CASE ...
SHHT
I SHALL TEACH YOU WHAT TRUE PAIN IS!!
AH...
HA SHAKE
HA SHAKE
HA SHAKE
AAHH ...?!

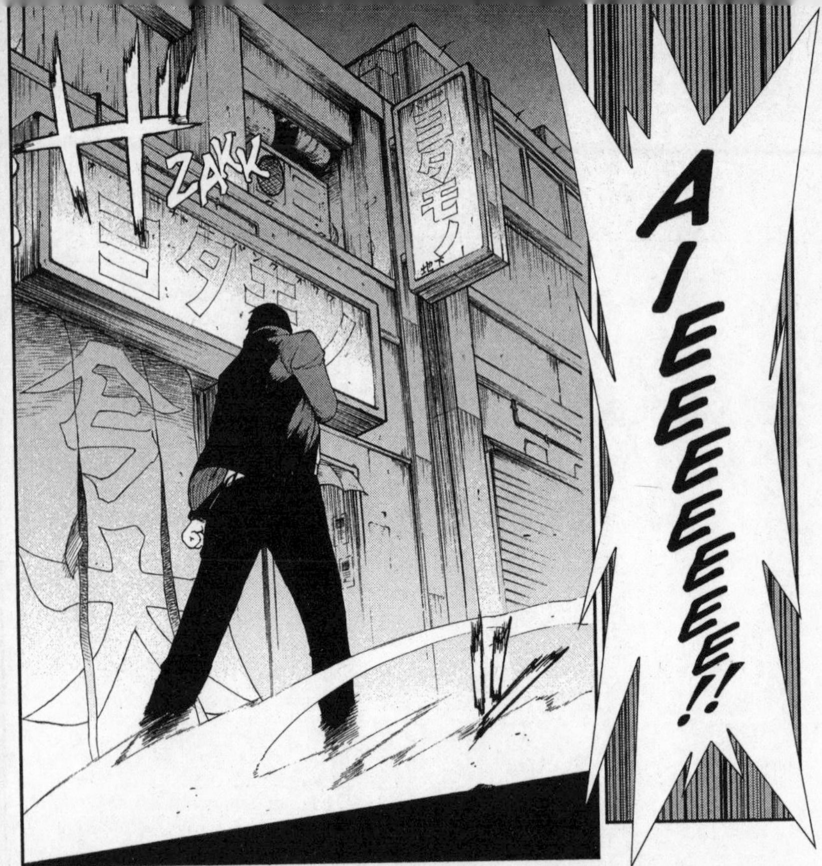
ZAKK
ヨタモノ
地下
AIEEEEEEEE!!
SIGNS: Yotamono

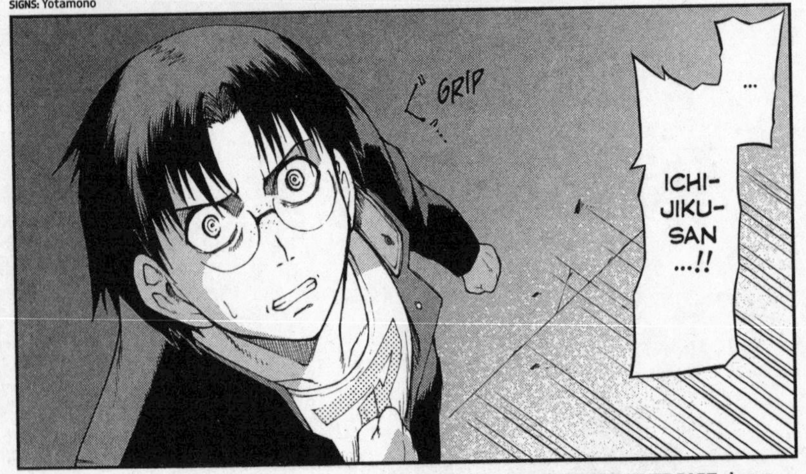
...
ICHI-JIKU-SAN ...!!
GRIP

[KICK OUT THE NINJA MOTHERFUCKER PART 2] • END

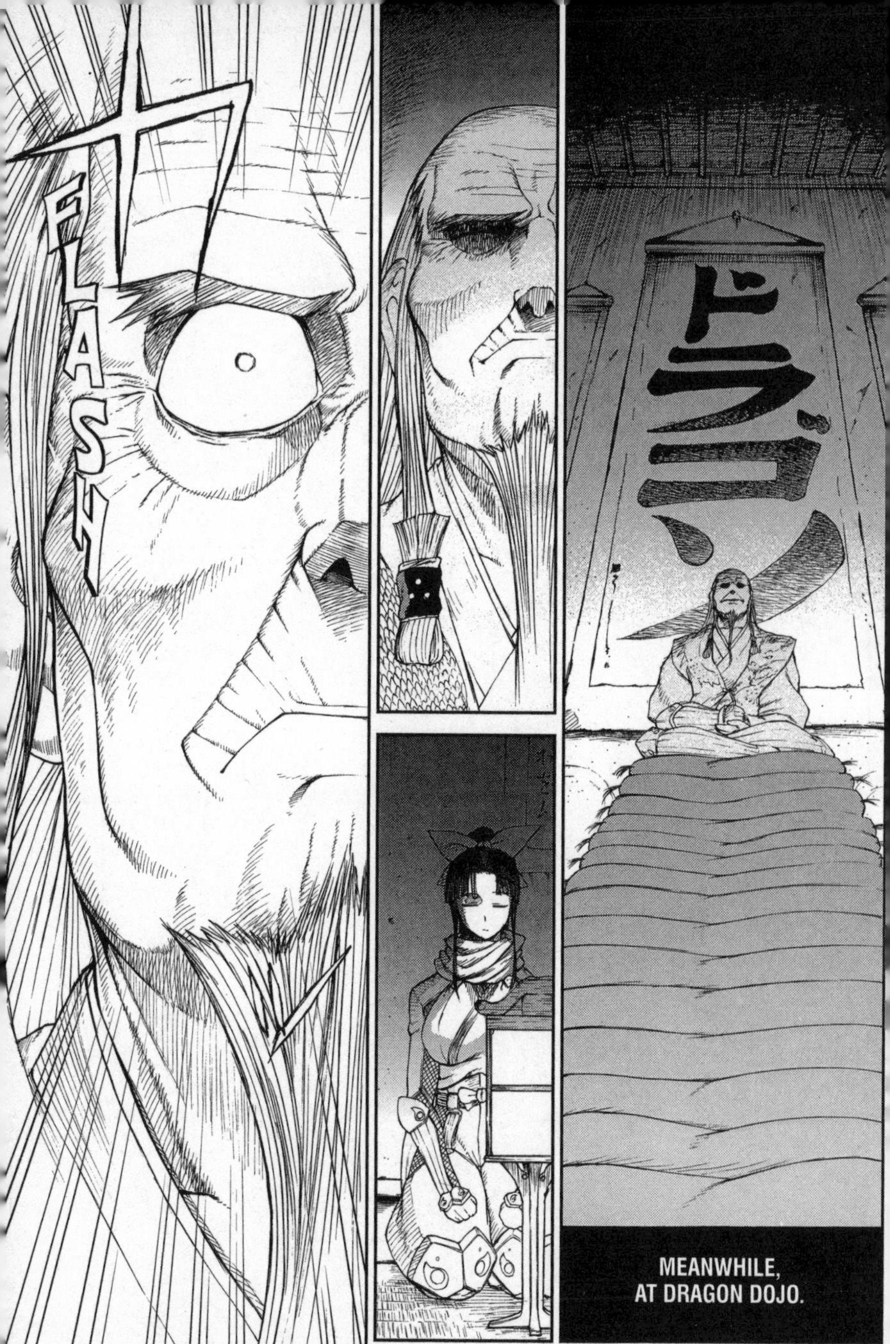
ドラゴン
MEANWHILE,
AT DRAGON DOJO.
FLASH
SIGN: DRAGON

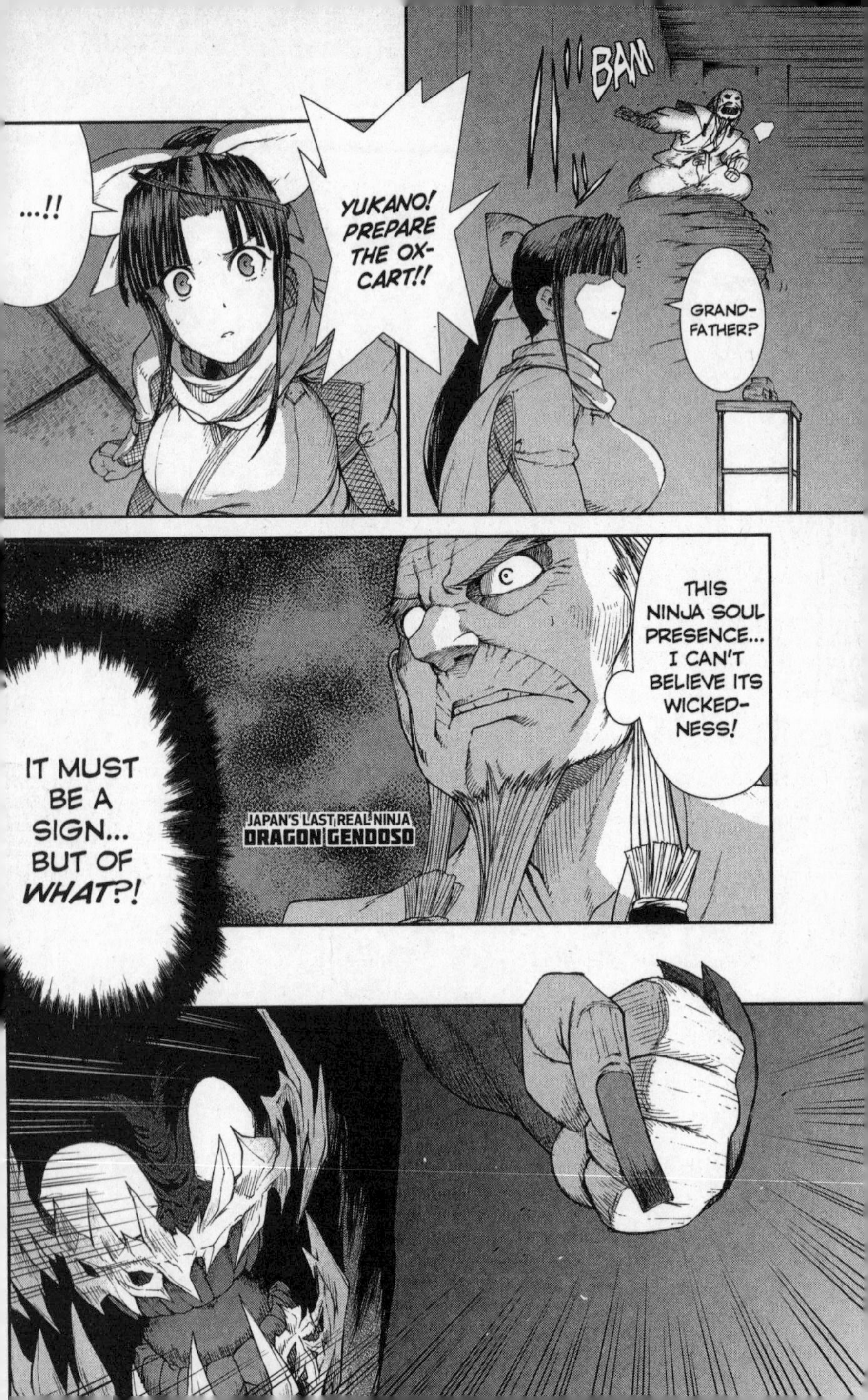
BAM
GRAND-FATHER?
YUKANO! PREPARE THE OX-CART!!
...!!
THIS NINJA SOUL PRESENCE... I CAN'T BELIEVE ITS WICKED-NESS!
JAPAN'S LAST REAL NINJA
DRAGON GENDOSO
IT MUST BE A SIGN... BUT OF *WHAT*?!

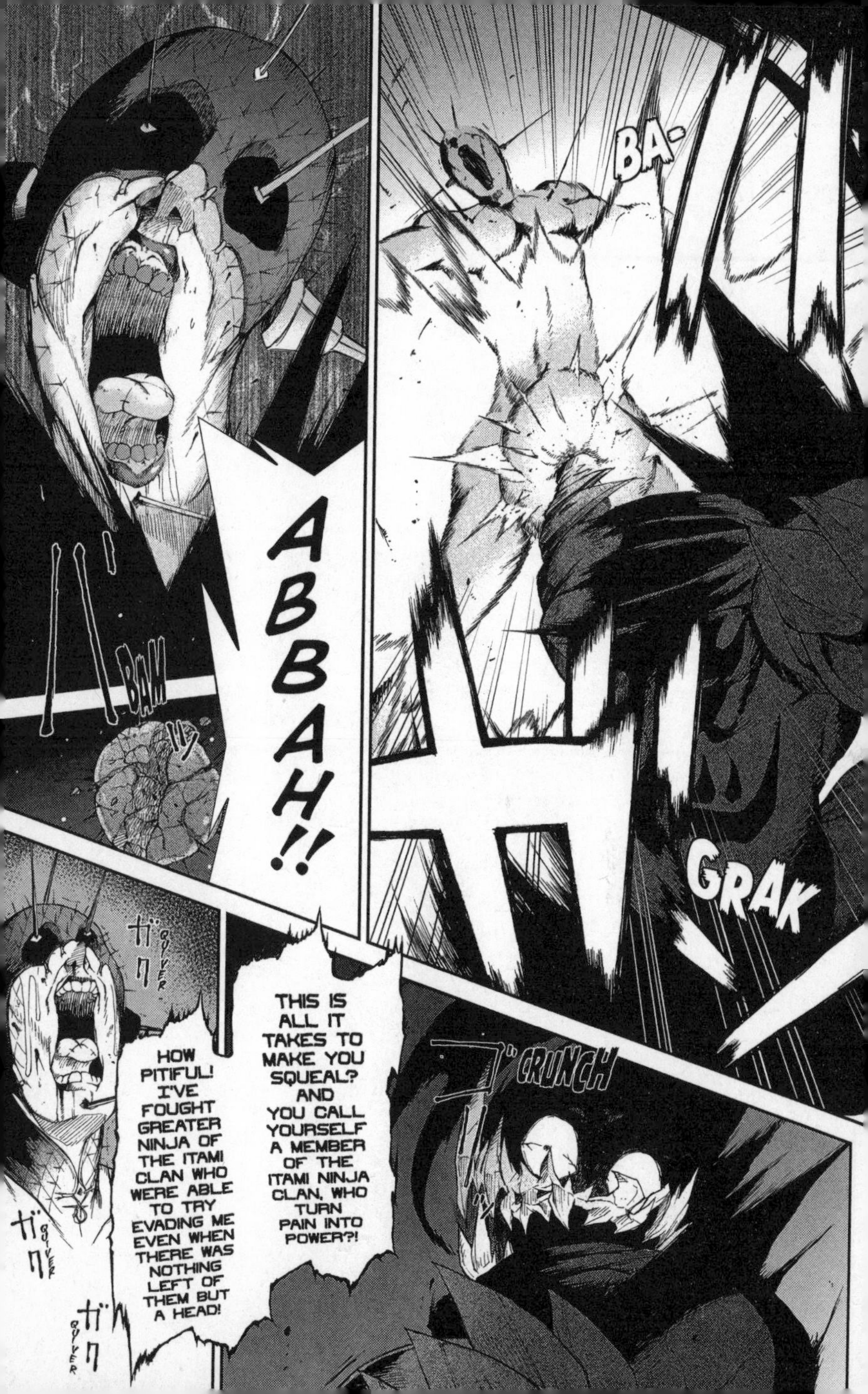
BA-
GRAK
ABBAH!!
BAM
CRUNCH
THIS IS ALL IT TAKES TO MAKE YOU SQUEAL? AND YOU CALL YOURSELF A MEMBER OF THE ITAMI NINJA CLAN, WHO TURN PAIN INTO POWER?!
HOW PITIFUL! I'VE FOUGHT GREATER NINJA OF THE ITAMI CLAN WHO WERE ABLE TO TRY EVADING ME EVEN WHEN THERE WAS NOTHING LEFT OF THEM BUT A HEAD!
QUIVER
QUIVER
QUIVER

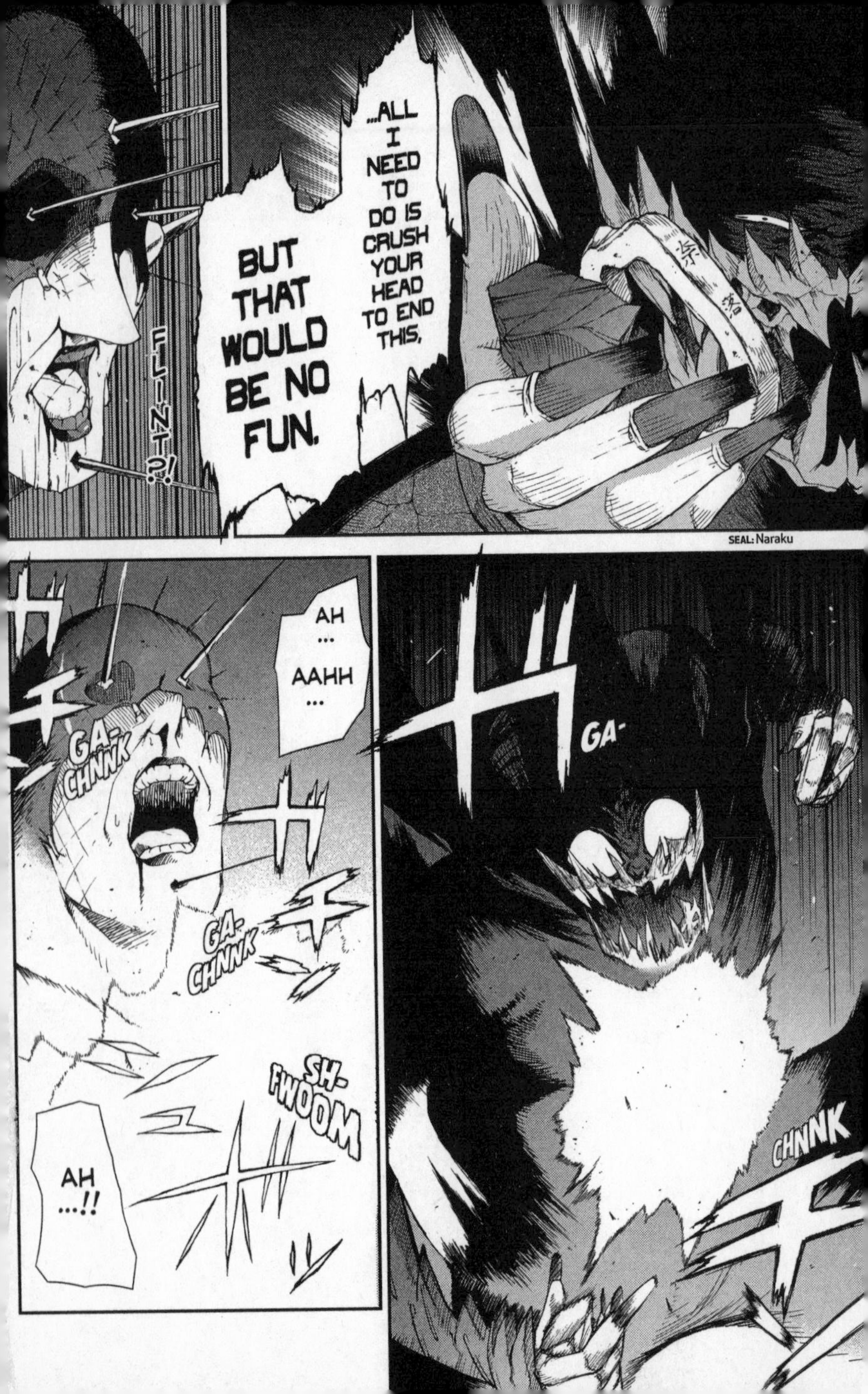
...ALL I NEED TO DO IS CRUSH YOUR HEAD TO END THIS,
BUT THAT WOULD BE NO FUN.
FLINT ?!
SEAL: Naraku
GA-
CHNNK
AH ... AAHH ...
GA-CHNNK
GA-CHNNK
SH-FWOOM
AH ...!!

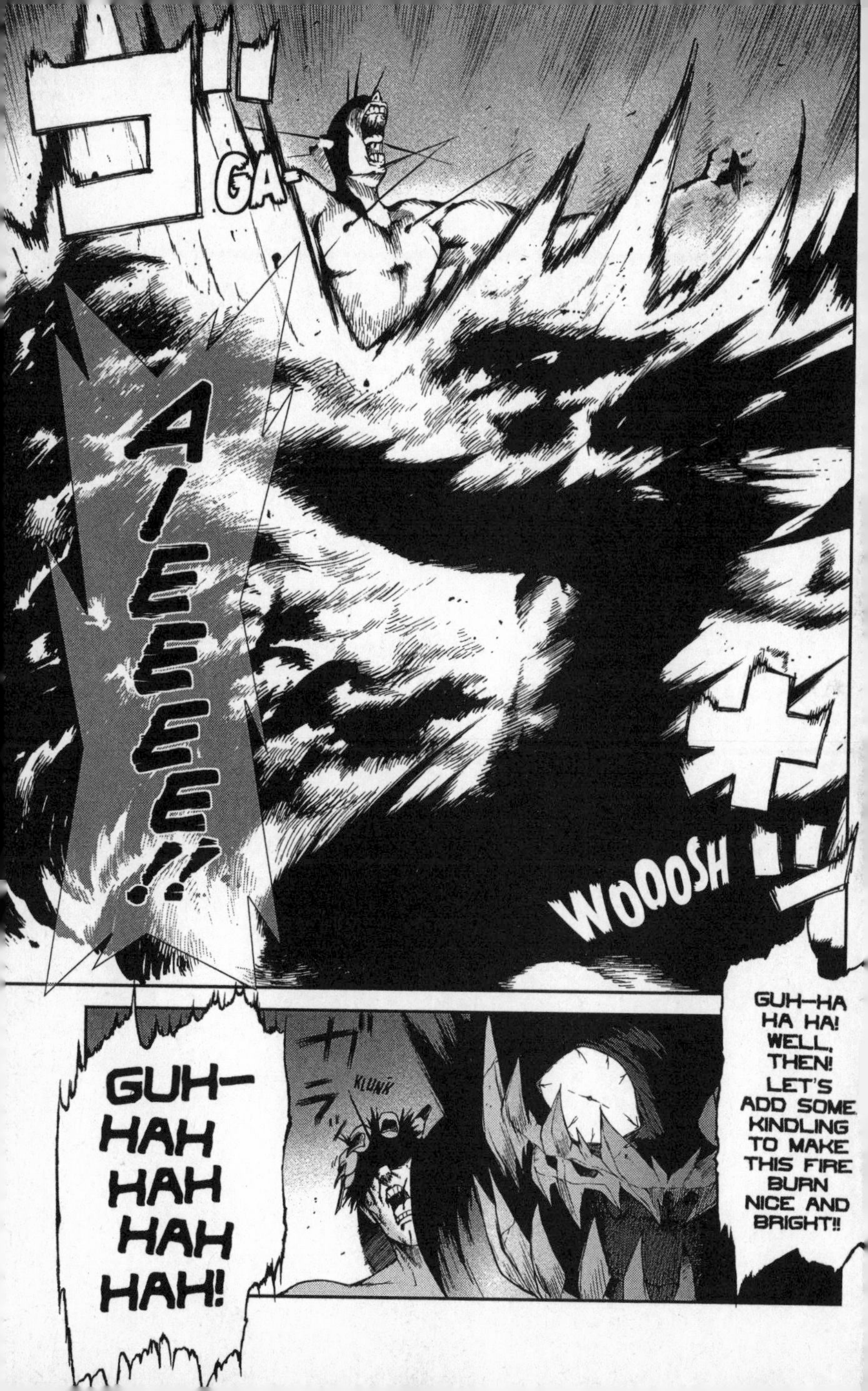
GA-
AIEEEE!!
WOOOSH
GUH-HA HA HA! WELL, THEN! LET'S ADD SOME KINDLING TO MAKE THIS FIRE BURN NICE AND BRIGHT!!
KLUNK
GUH-HAH HAH HAH HAH!

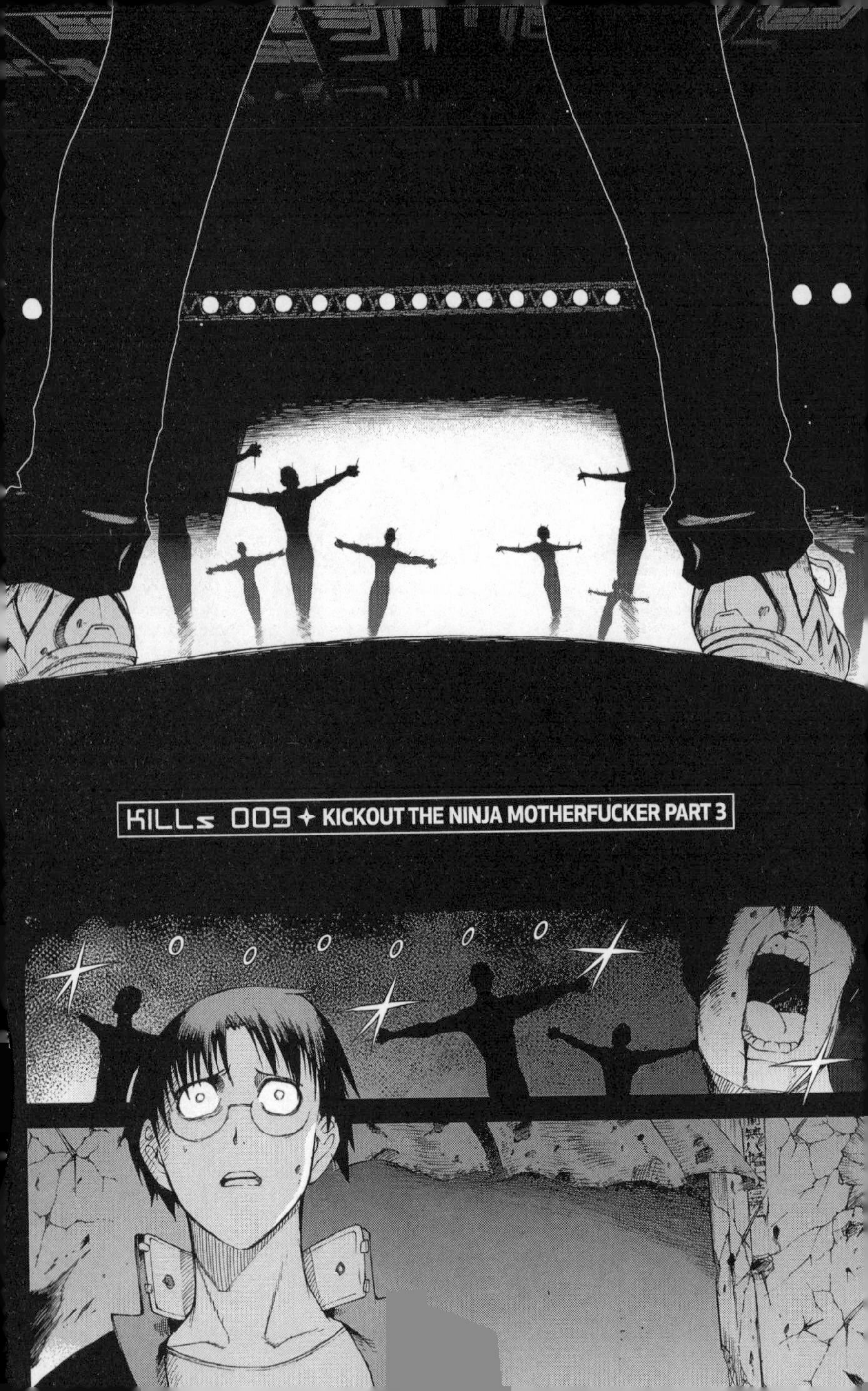
KILLs 009 ✦ KICKOUT THE NINJA MOTHERFUCKER PART 3

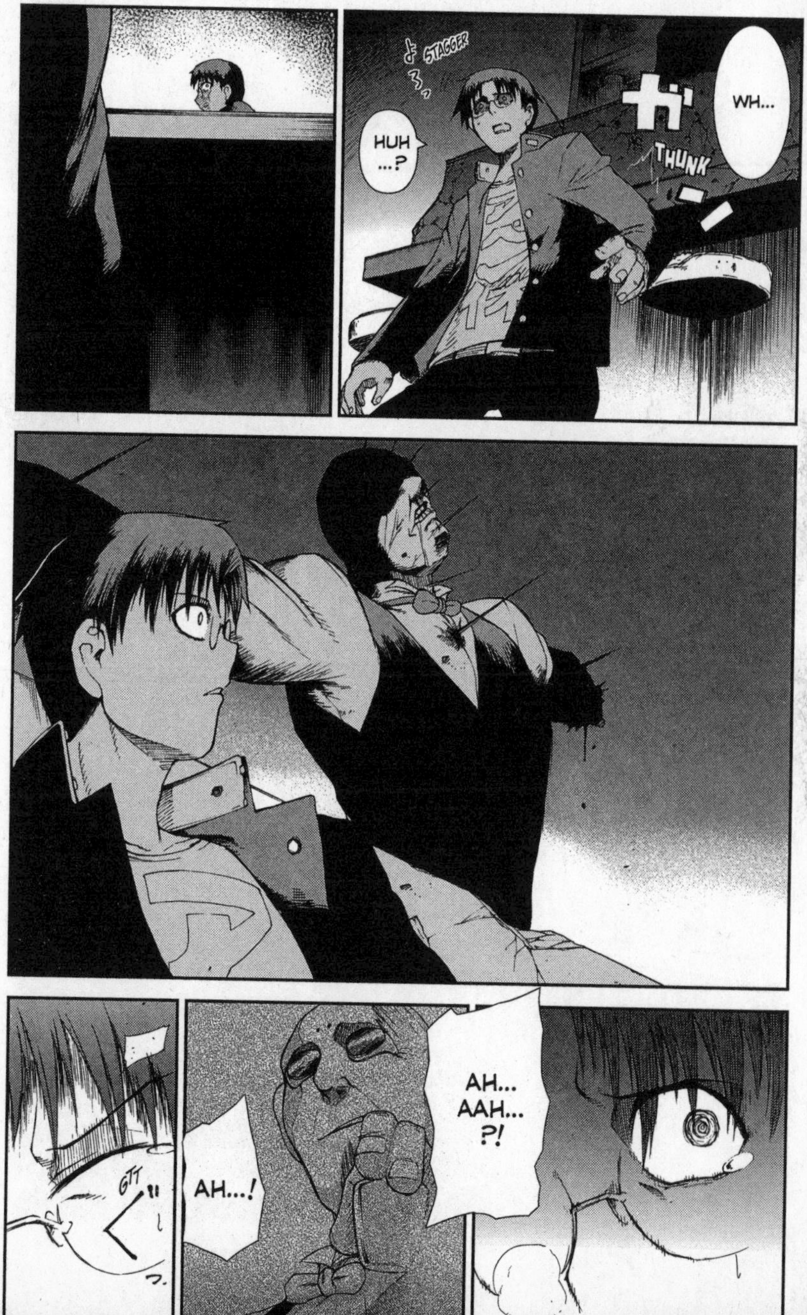
WH...
ガ
THUNK
よろ
STAGGER
HUH ...?
AH... AAH... ?!
AH...!
GTT

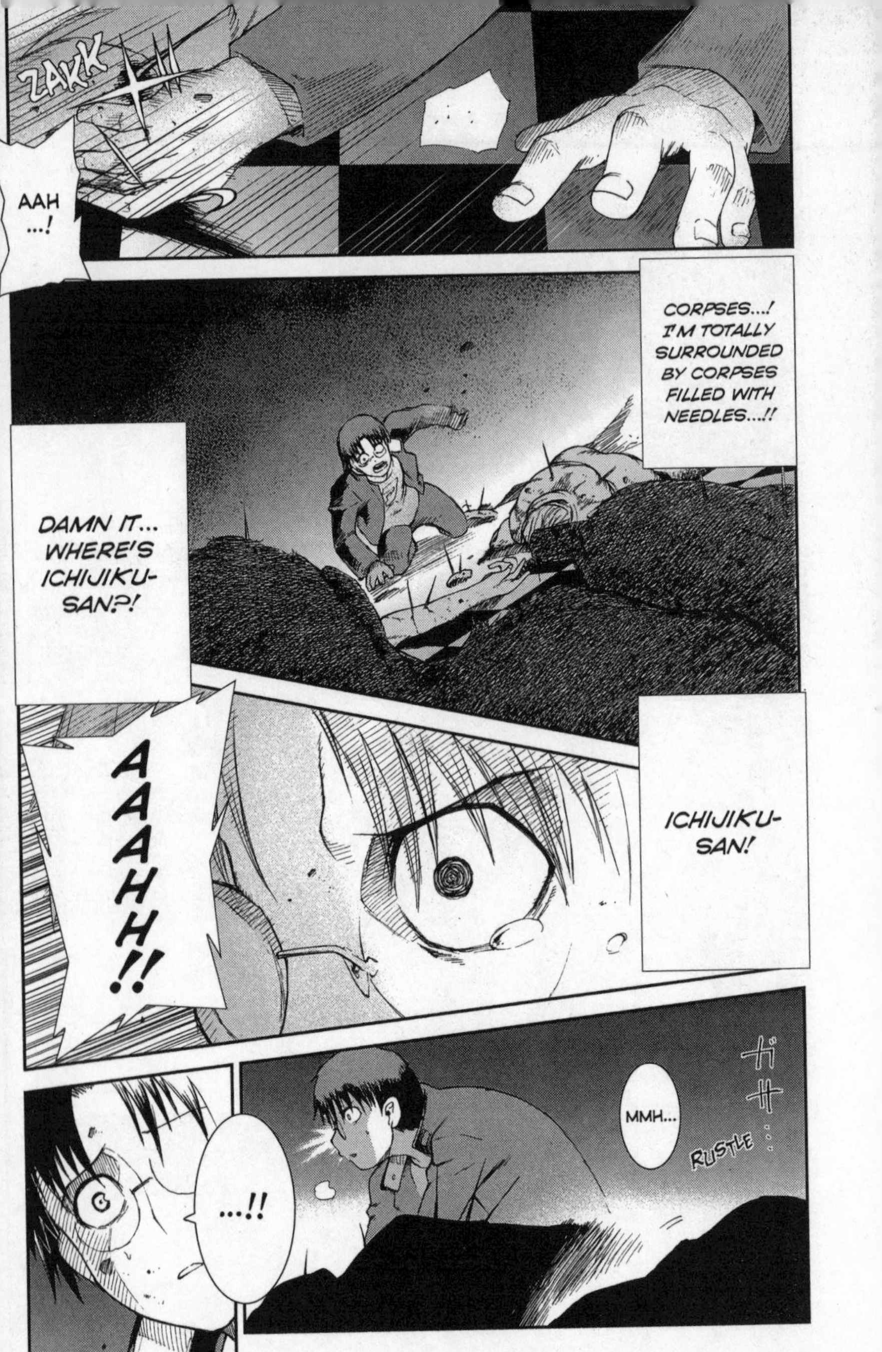
ZAKK
AAH ...!
CORPSES...! I'M TOTALLY SURROUNDED BY CORPSES FILLED WITH NEEDLES...!!
DAMN IT... WHERE'S ICHIJIKU-SAN?!
ICHIJIKU-SAN!
AAAAHH!!
MMH...
ガサ
RUSTLE
...!!

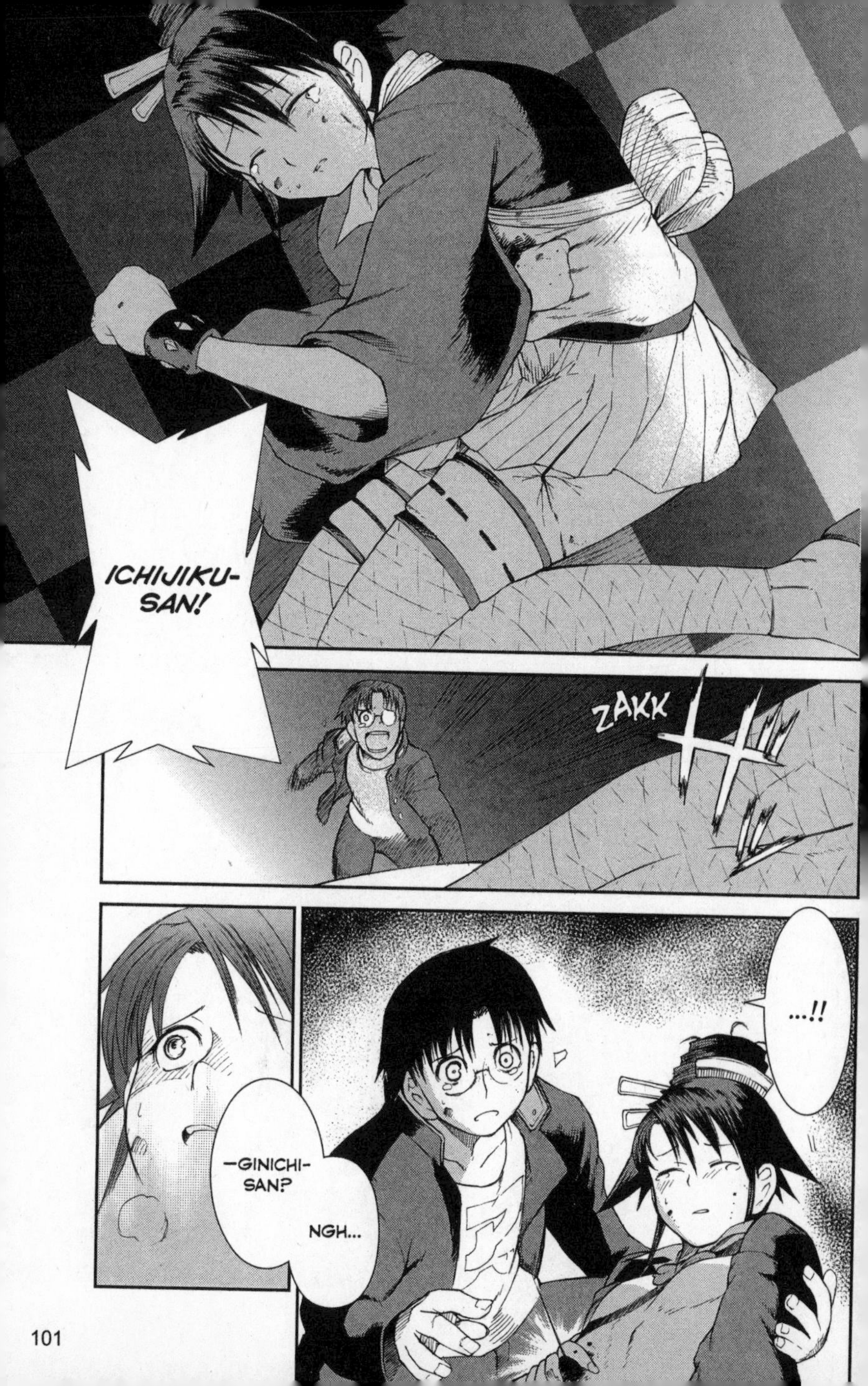
ICHIJIKU-SAN!
ZAKK
...!!
NGH...
—GINICHI-SAN?

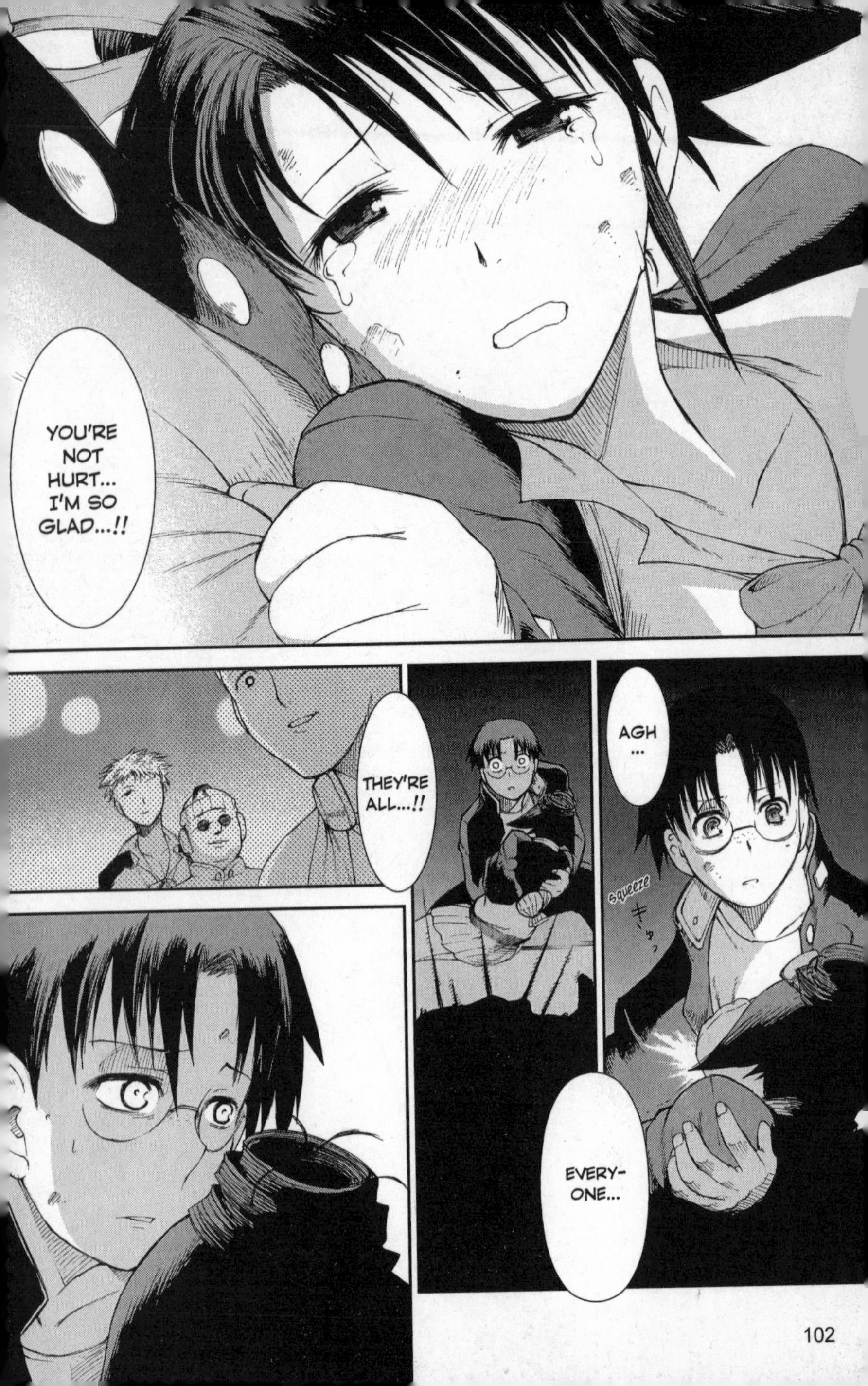
YOU'RE NOT HURT... I'M SO GLAD...!!
AGH ...
squeeze
EVERY-ONE...
THEY'RE ALL...!!

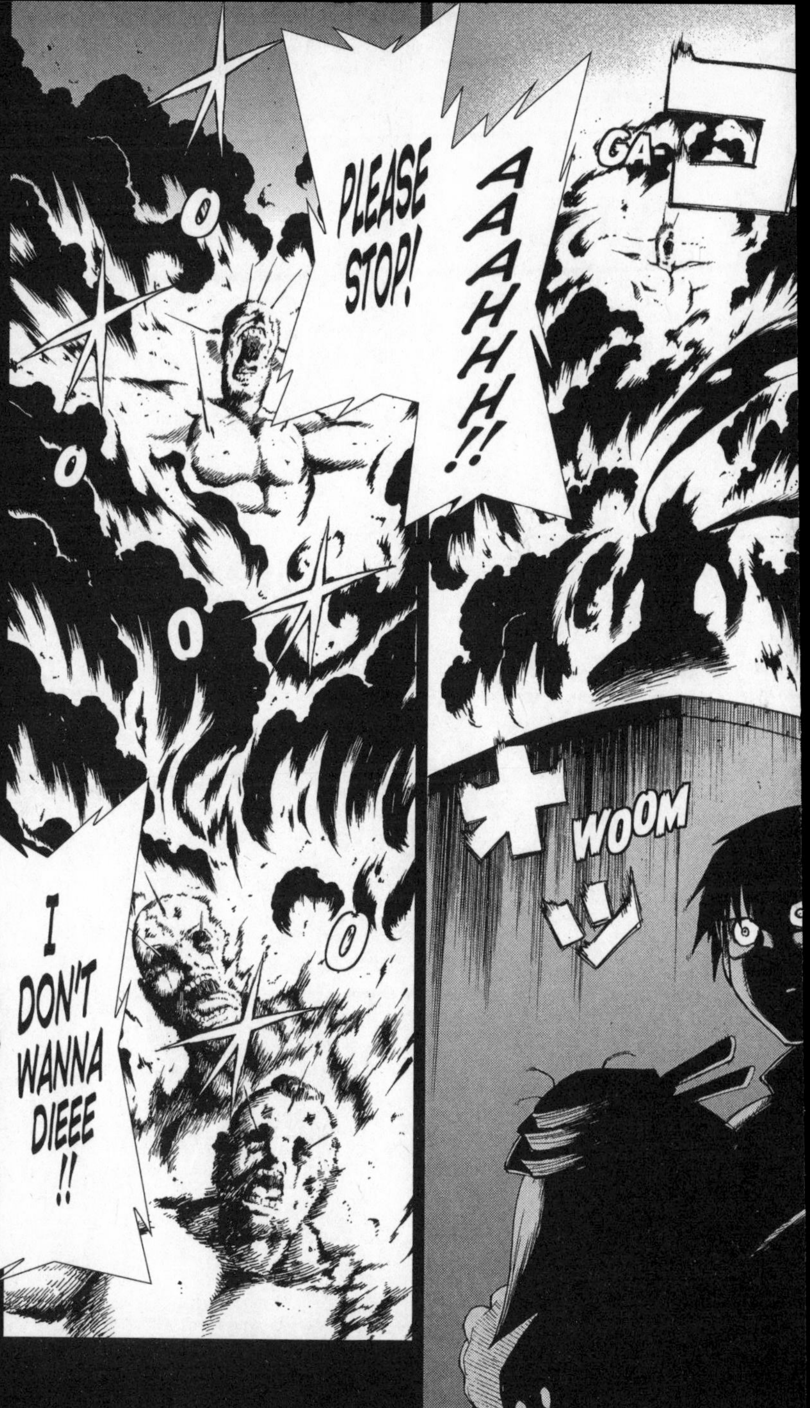
GA-
AAAHHHH!!
WOOM
PLEASE STOP!
O
O
O
O
I DON'T WANNA DIEEE!!

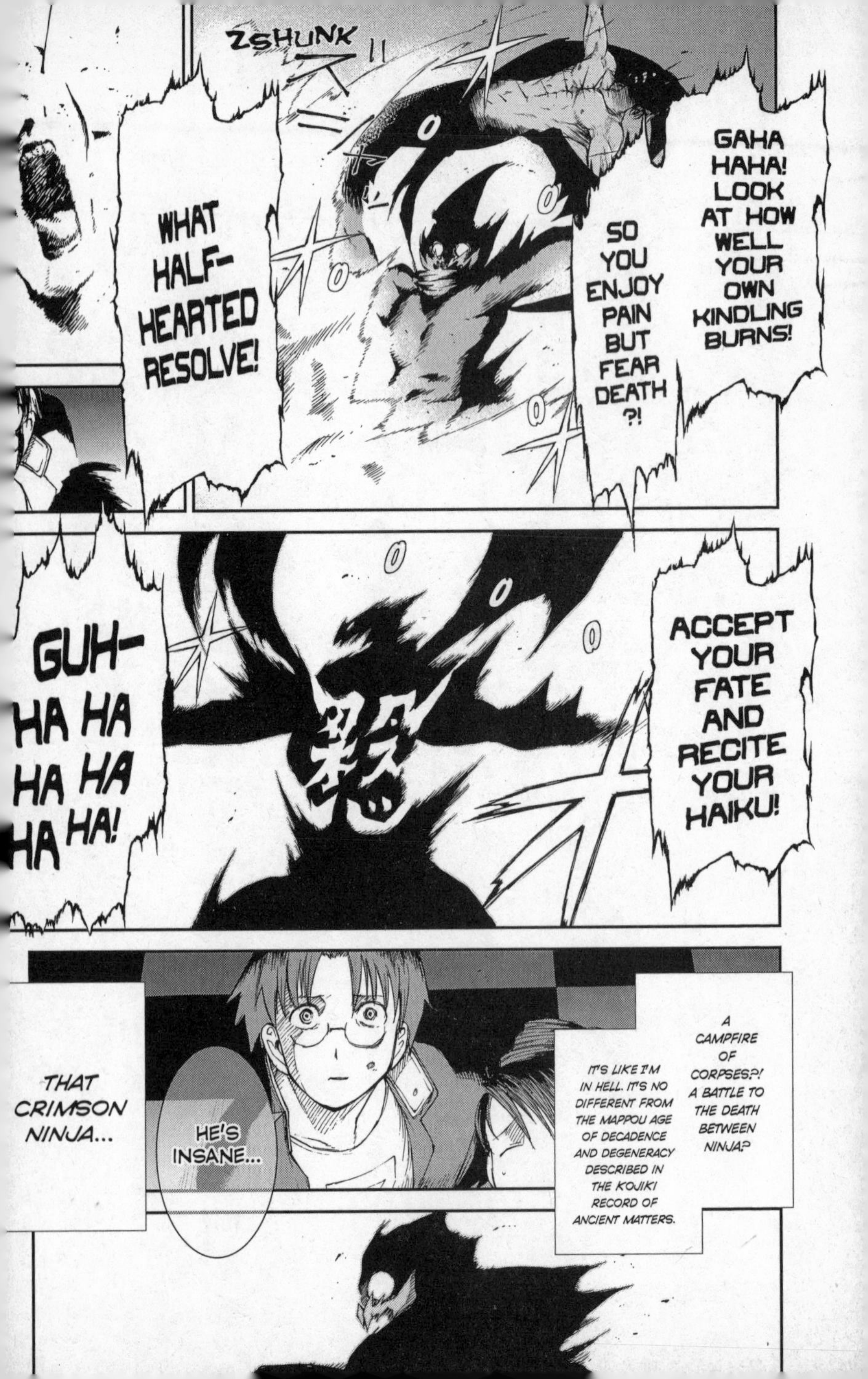
ZSHUNK
GAHA HAHA! LOOK AT HOW WELL YOUR OWN KINDLING BURNS!
SO YOU ENJOY PAIN BUT FEAR DEATH?!
WHAT HALF-HEARTED RESOLVE!
ACCEPT YOUR FATE AND RECITE YOUR HAIKU!
殺
GUH-HA HA HA HA HA HA HA HA!
A CAMPFIRE OF CORPSES?! A BATTLE TO THE DEATH BETWEEN NINJA?
IT'S LIKE I'M IN HELL. IT'S NO DIFFERENT FROM THE MAPPOU AGE OF DECADENCE AND DEGENERACY DESCRIBED IN THE KOJIKI RECORD OF ANCIENT MATTERS.
HE'S INSANE...
THAT CRIMSON NINJA...

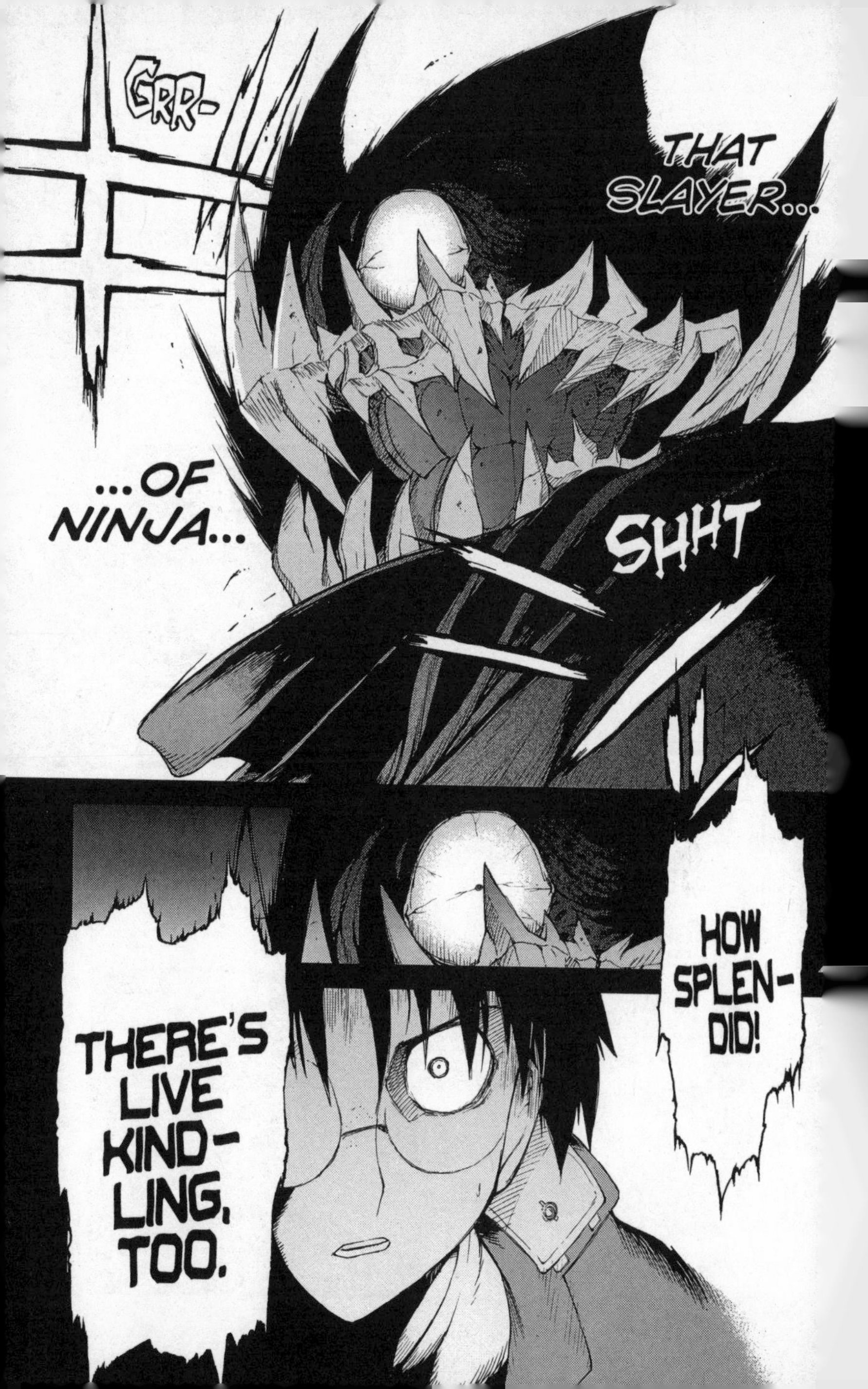
THAT SLAYER...
GRR-
...OF NINJA...
SHHT
HOW SPLEN-DID!
THERE'S LIVE KIND-LING, TOO.

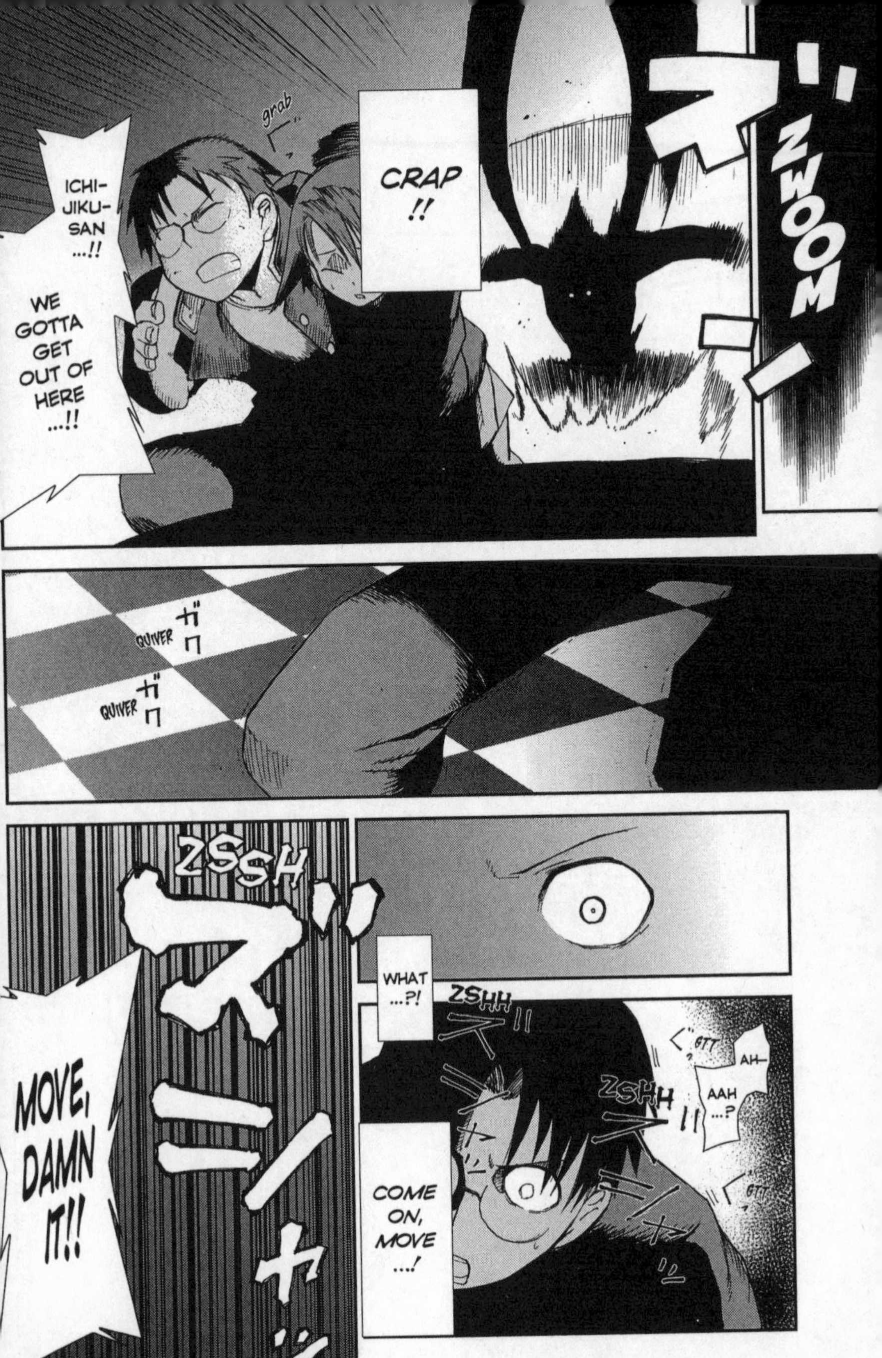
ZWOOM
CRAP!!
grab
ICHI-JIKU-SAN...!!
WE GOTTA GET OUT OF HERE...!!
QUIVER
QUIVER
WHAT...?!
ZSHH!!
GTT
AH— AAH...?
ZSHH!!
GTT
COME ON, MOVE...!
ZSSH
MOVE, DAMN IT!!

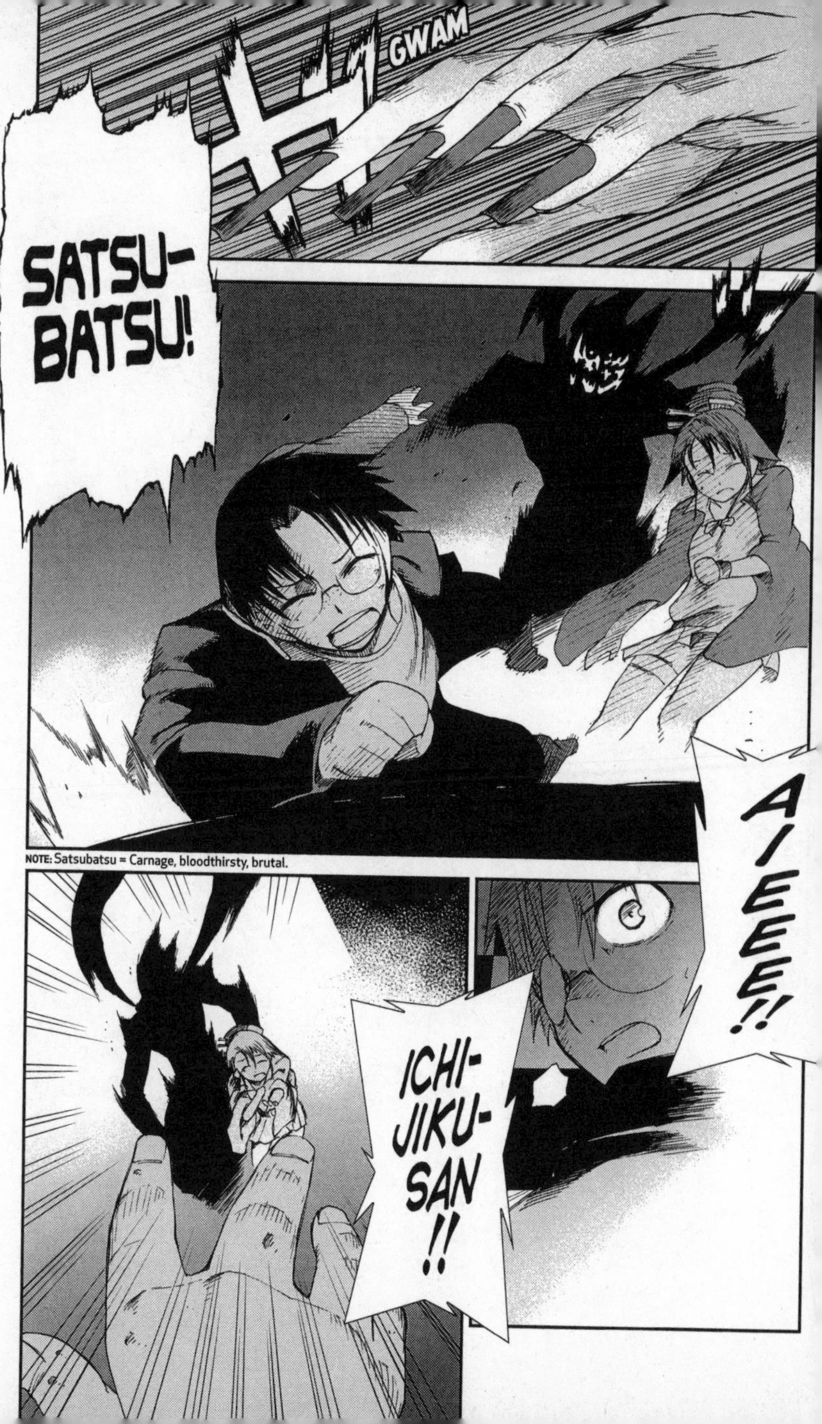
GWAM
SATSU-BATSU!
AIEEEE!!
ICHI-JIKU-SAN!!
NOTE: Satsubatsu = Carnage, bloodthirsty, brutal.

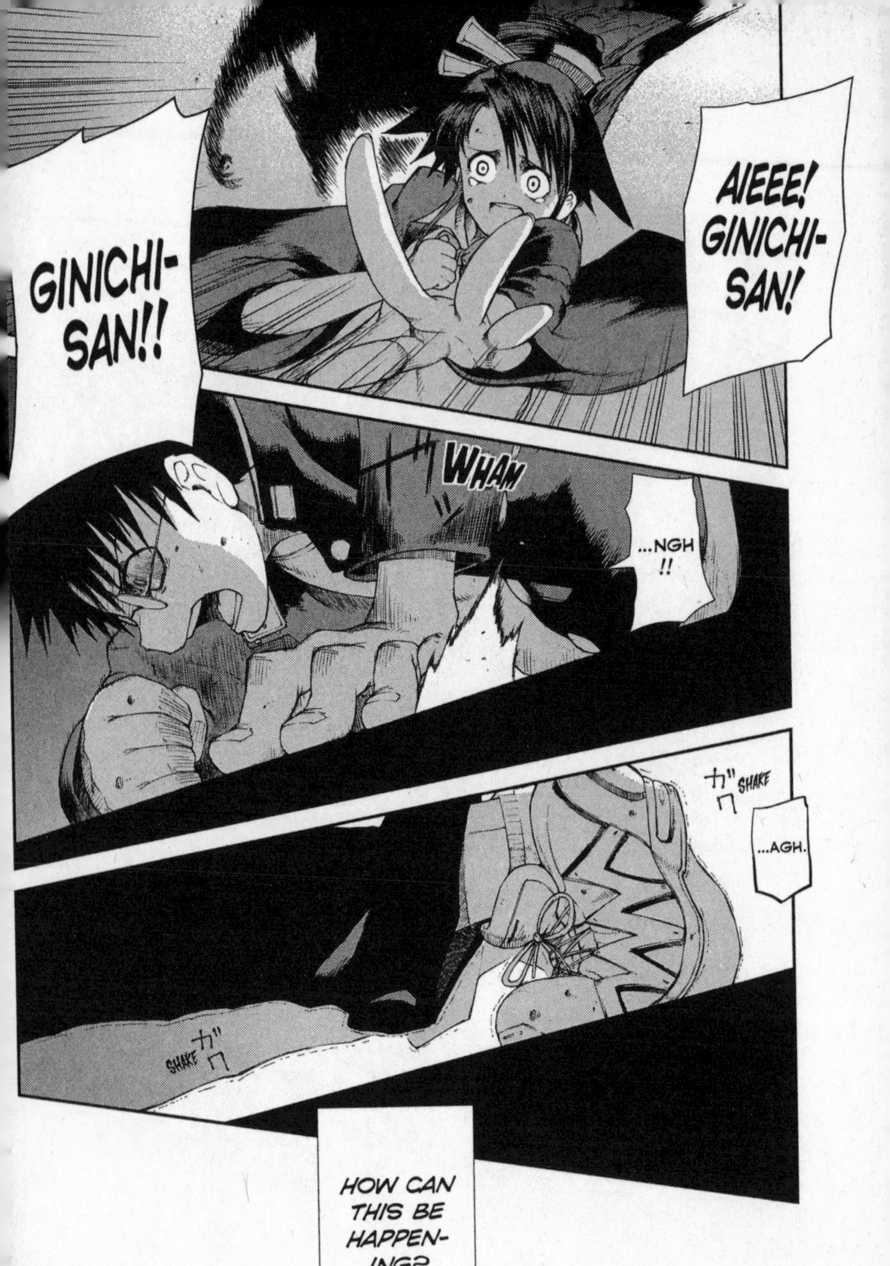
AIEEE! GINICHI-SAN!
GINICHI-SAN!!
WHAM
...NGH!!
ガク SHAKE
...AGH.
SHAKE ガク
HOW CAN THIS BE HAPPEN-ING?

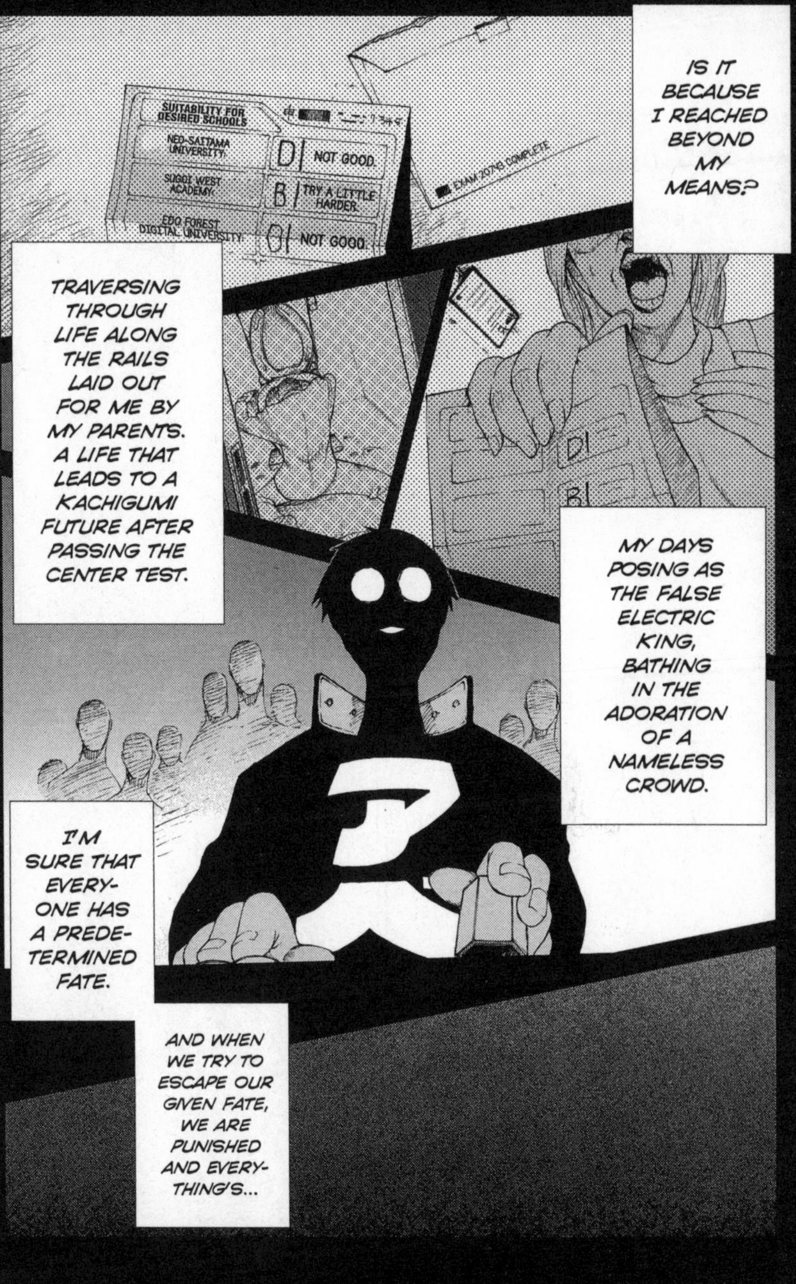
IS IT BECAUSE I REACHED BEYOND MY MEANS?
SUITABILITY FOR DESIRED SCHOOLS
NEO-SAITAMA UNIVERSITY: D NOT GOOD.
SUGOI WEST ACADEMY: B TRY A LITTLE HARDER.
EDO FOREST DIGITAL UNIVERSITY: D NOT GOOD.
EXAM 20743 COMPLETE
TRAVERSING THROUGH LIFE ALONG THE RAILS LAID OUT FOR ME BY MY PARENTS. A LIFE THAT LEADS TO A KACHIGUMI FUTURE AFTER PASSING THE CENTER TEST.
MY DAYS POSING AS THE FALSE ELECTRIC KING, BATHING IN THE ADORATION OF A NAMELESS CROWD.
I'M SURE THAT EVERY-ONE HAS A PREDE-TERMINED FATE.
AND WHEN WE TRY TO ESCAPE OUR GIVEN FATE, WE ARE PUNISHED AND EVERY-THING'S...

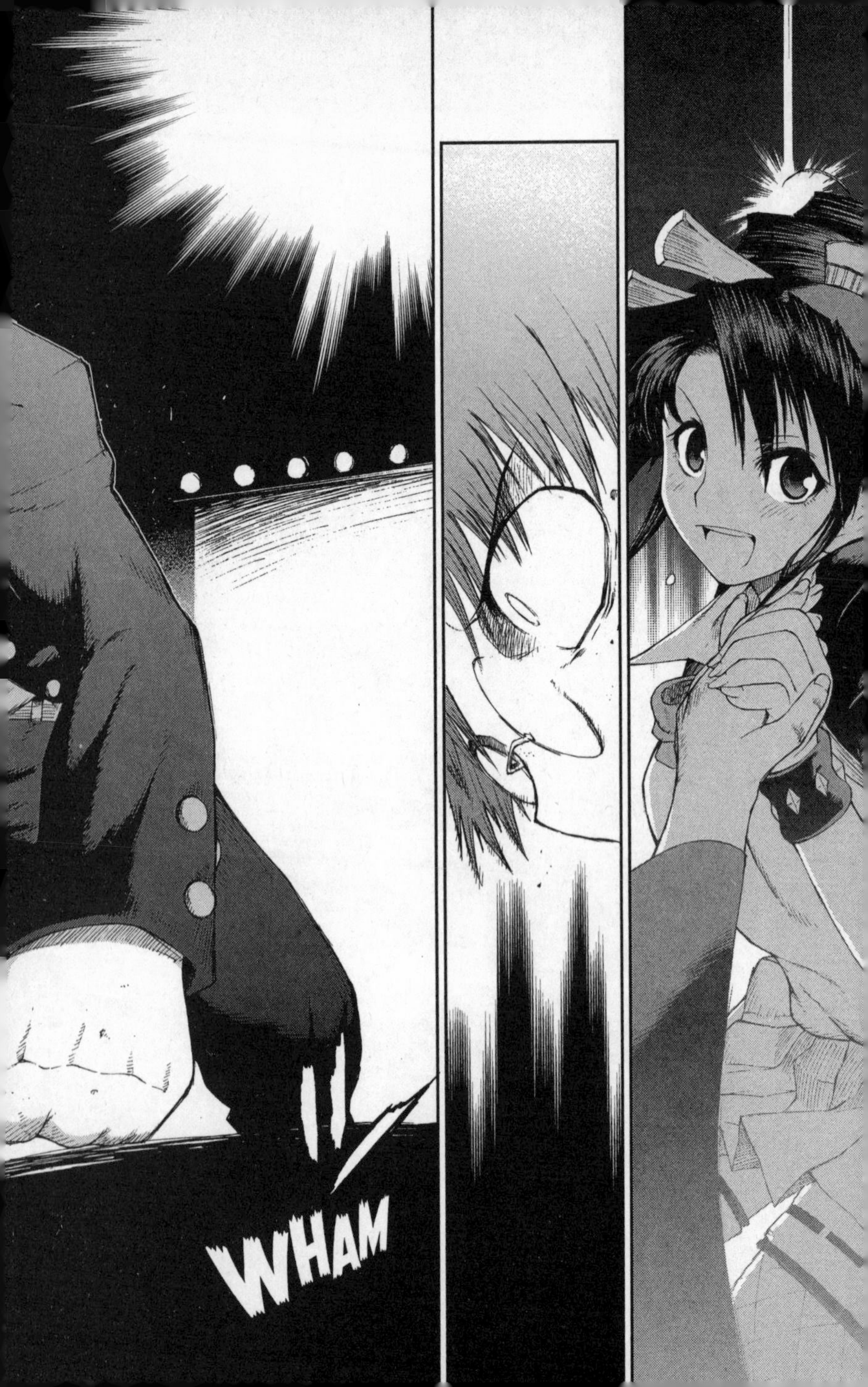
WHAM

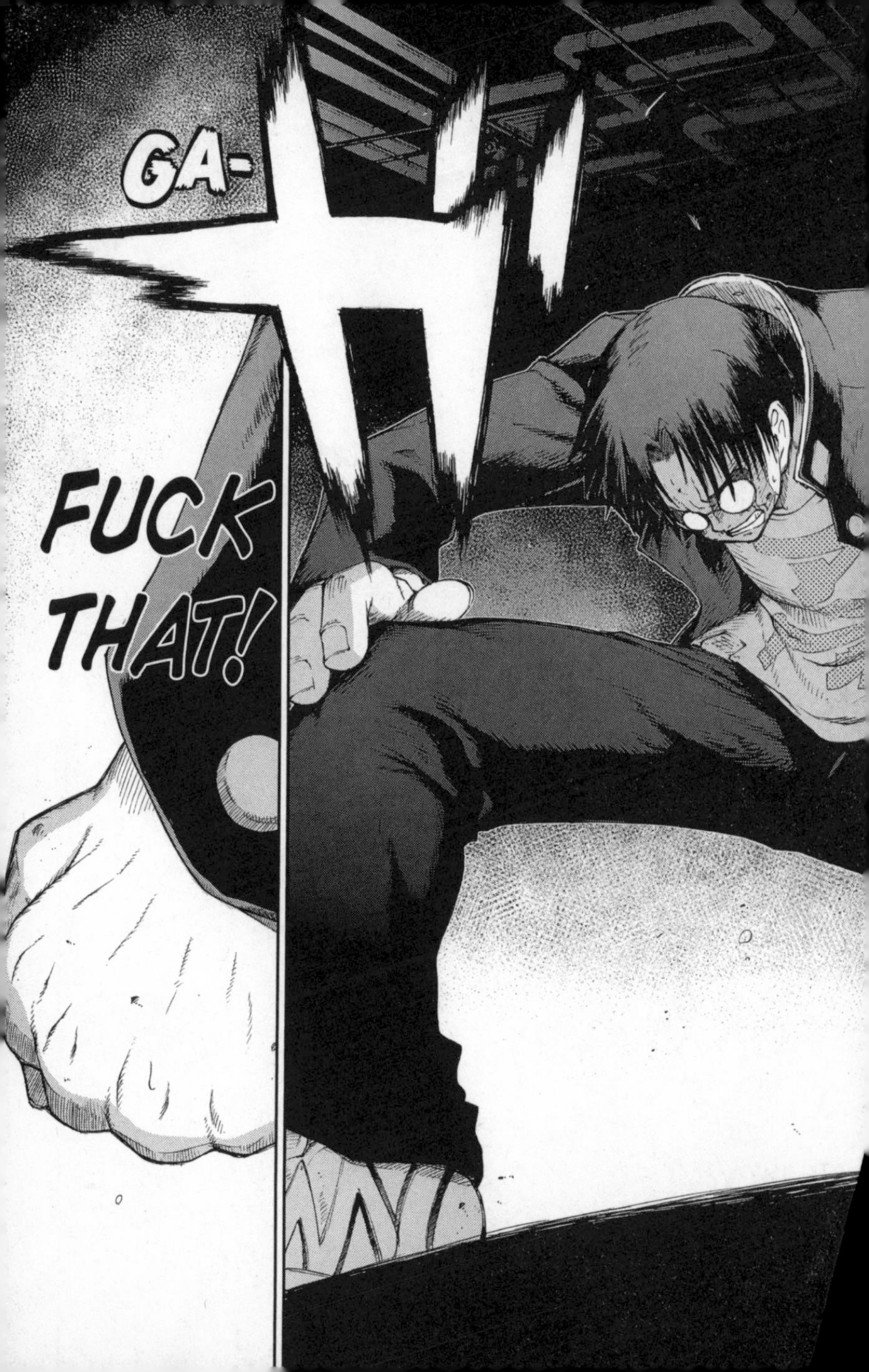
GA-
FUCK THAT!

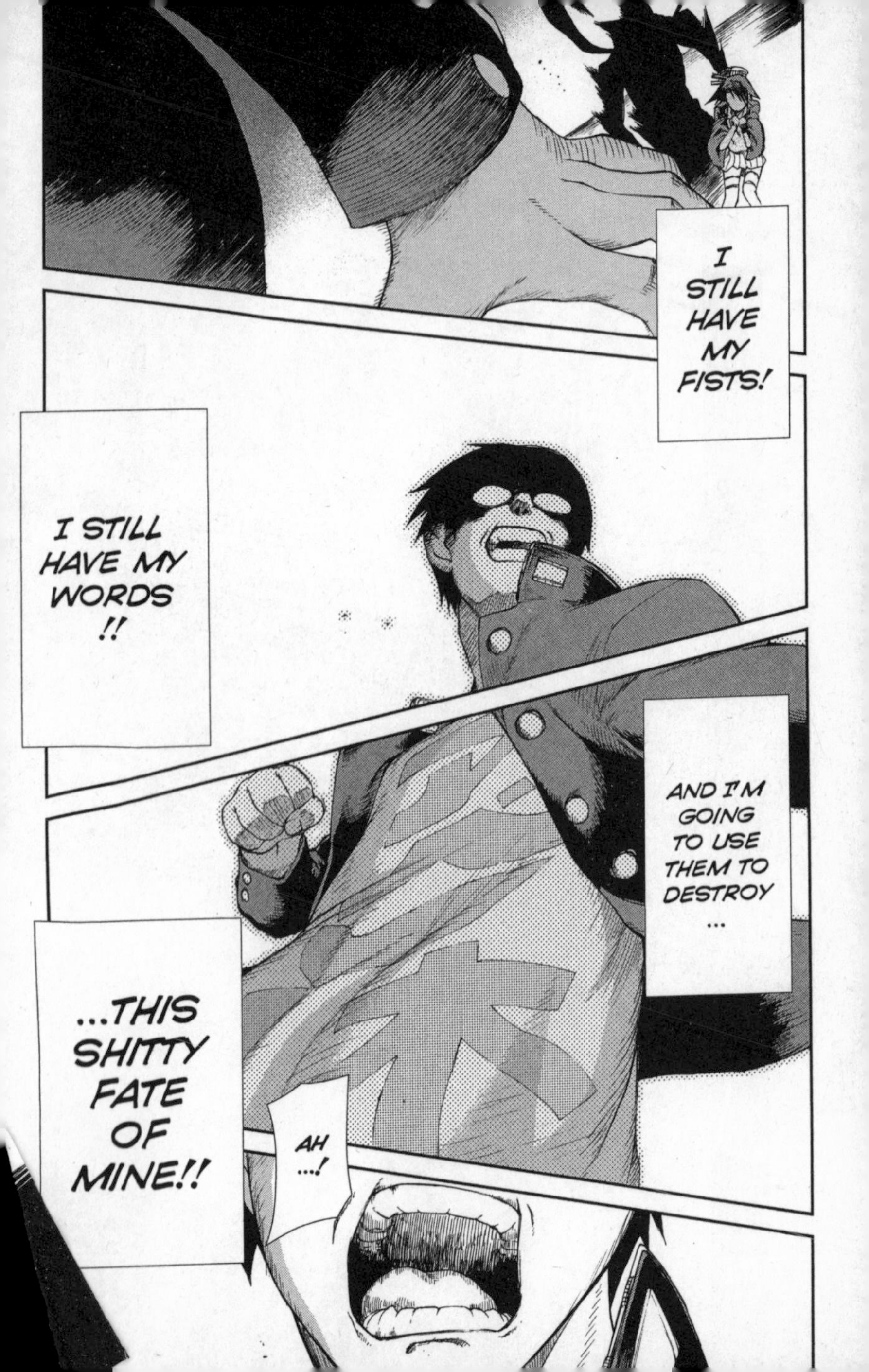
I STILL HAVE MY FISTS!
I STILL HAVE MY WORDS !!
AND I'M GOING TO USE THEM TO DESTROY ...
...THIS SHITTY FATE OF MINE!!
AH ...!

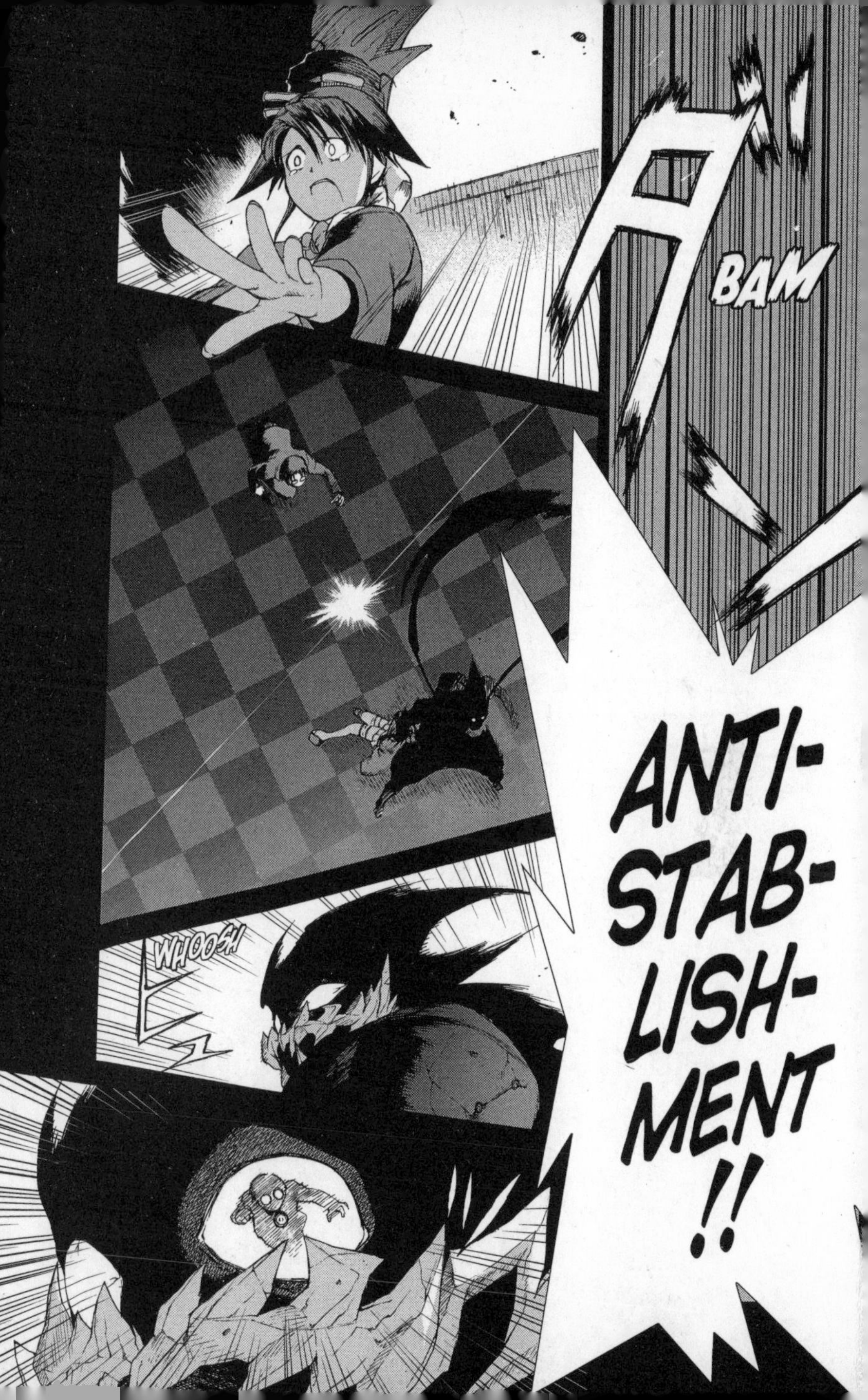
BAM
WHOOSH
ANTI-STAB-LISH-MENT!!

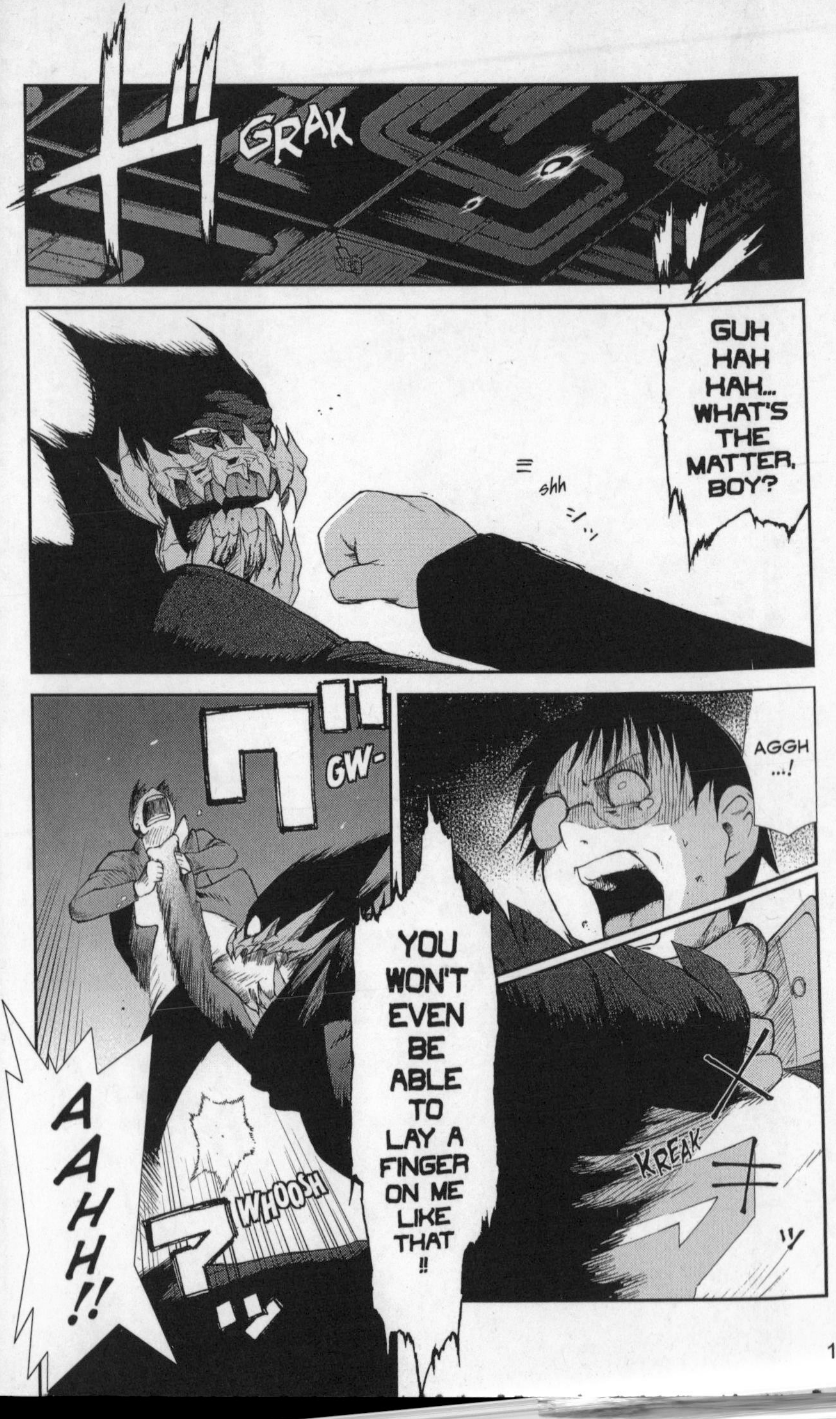
GRAK
GUH HAH HAH... WHAT'S THE MATTER, BOY?
shh
AGGH ...!
GW-
YOU WON'T EVEN BE ABLE TO LAY A FINGER ON ME LIKE THAT !!
KREAK
WHOOSH
AAHH!!

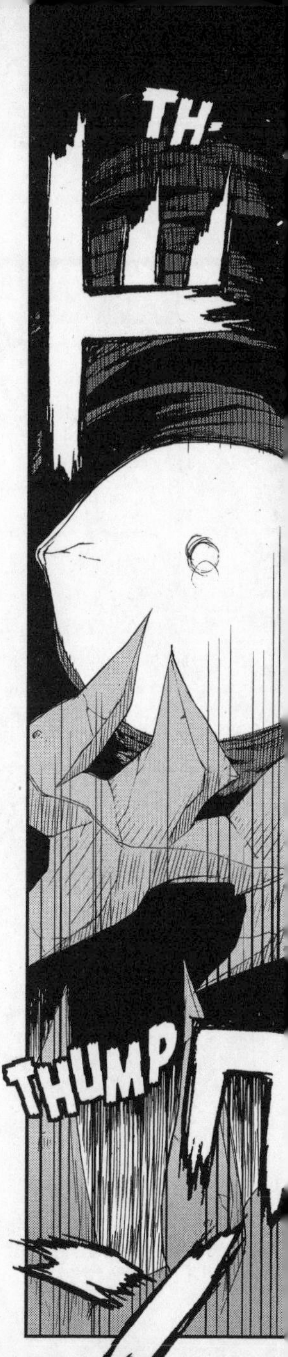
TH-
THUMP

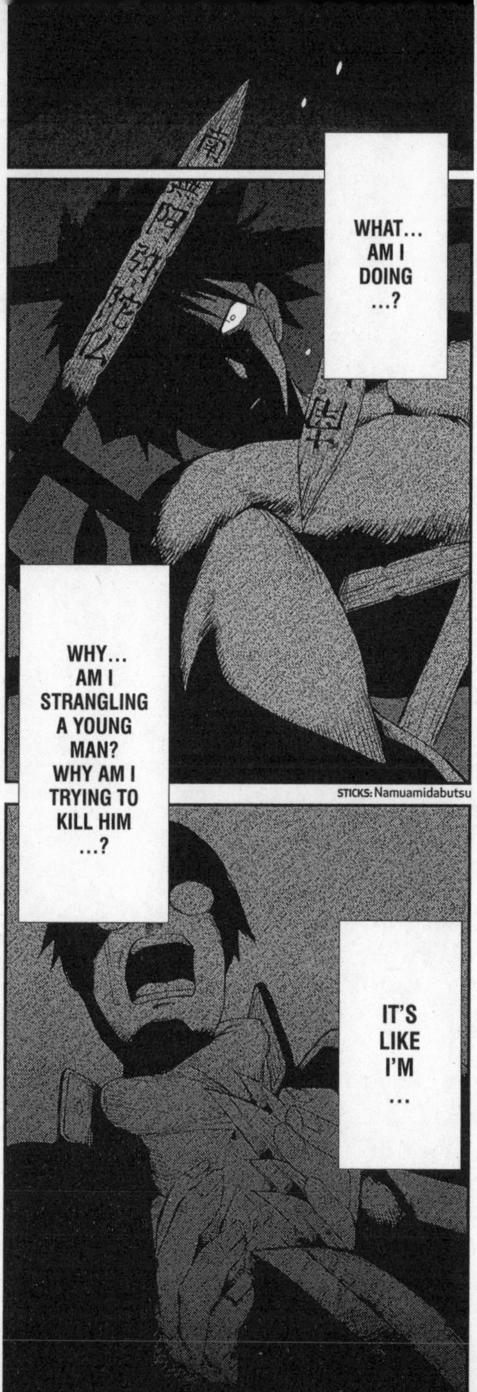
南無阿弥陀仏
WHAT… AM I DOING …?
STICKS: Namuamidabutsu
WHY… AM I STRANGLING A YOUNG MAN? WHY AM I TRYING TO KILL HIM …?
IT'S LIKE I'M …

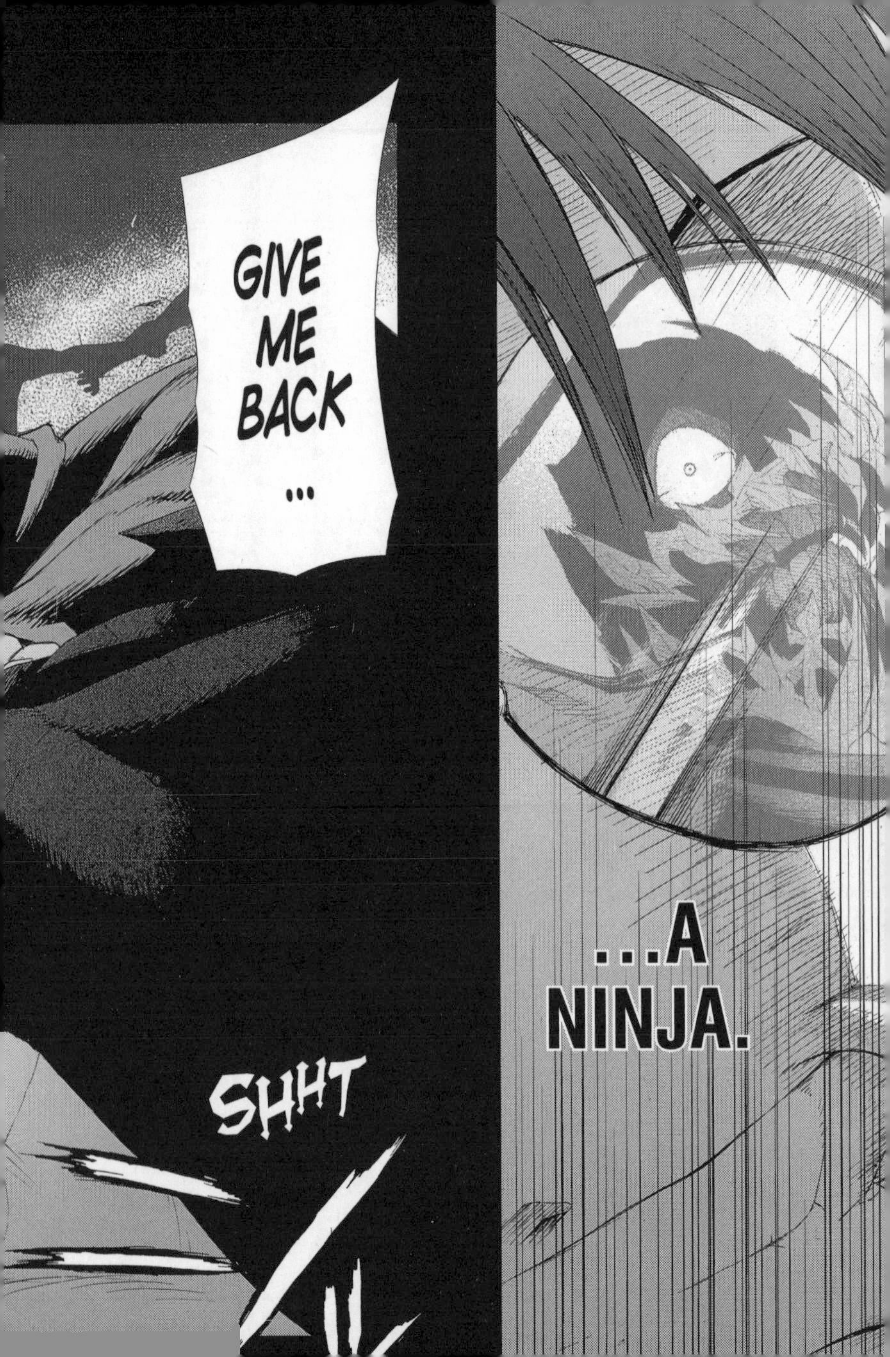
...A NINJA.
GIVE ME BACK ...
SHHT

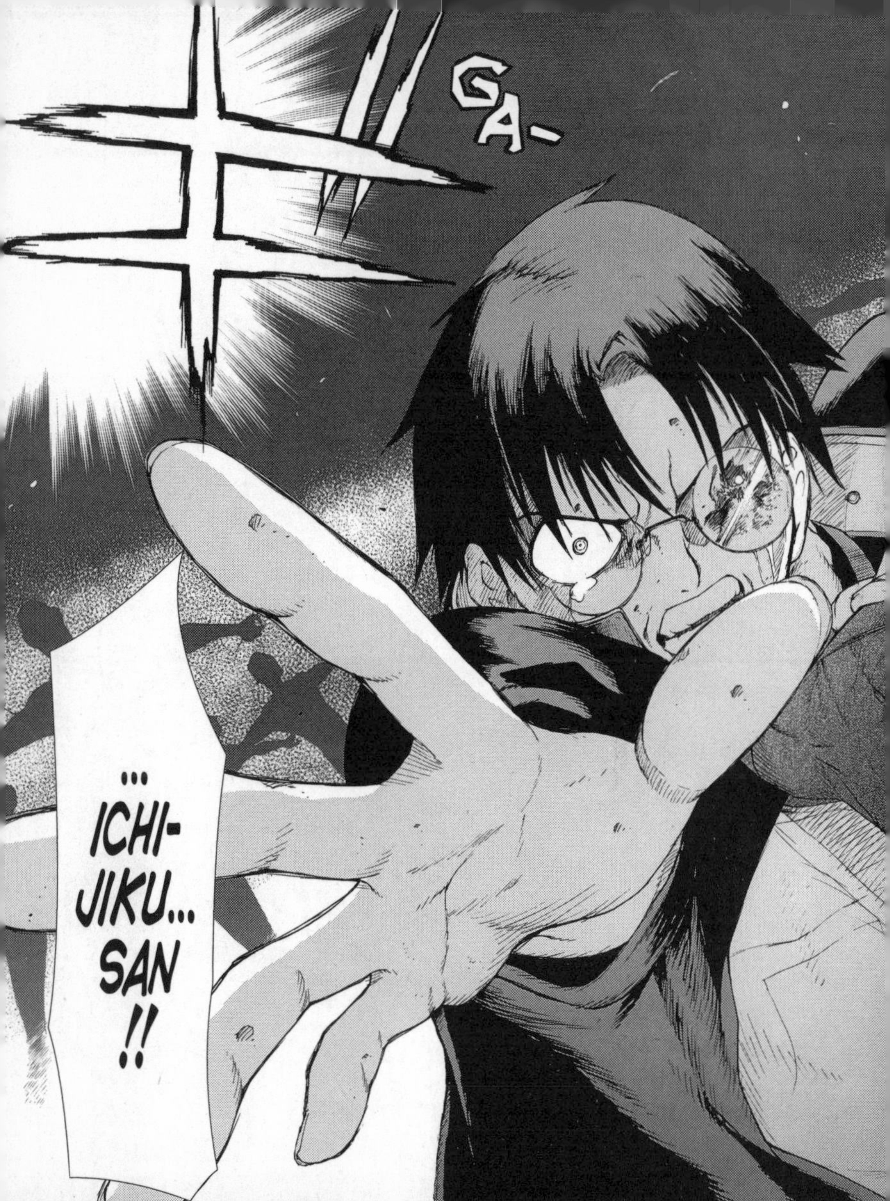
GA-
... ICHI-JIKU... SAN !!

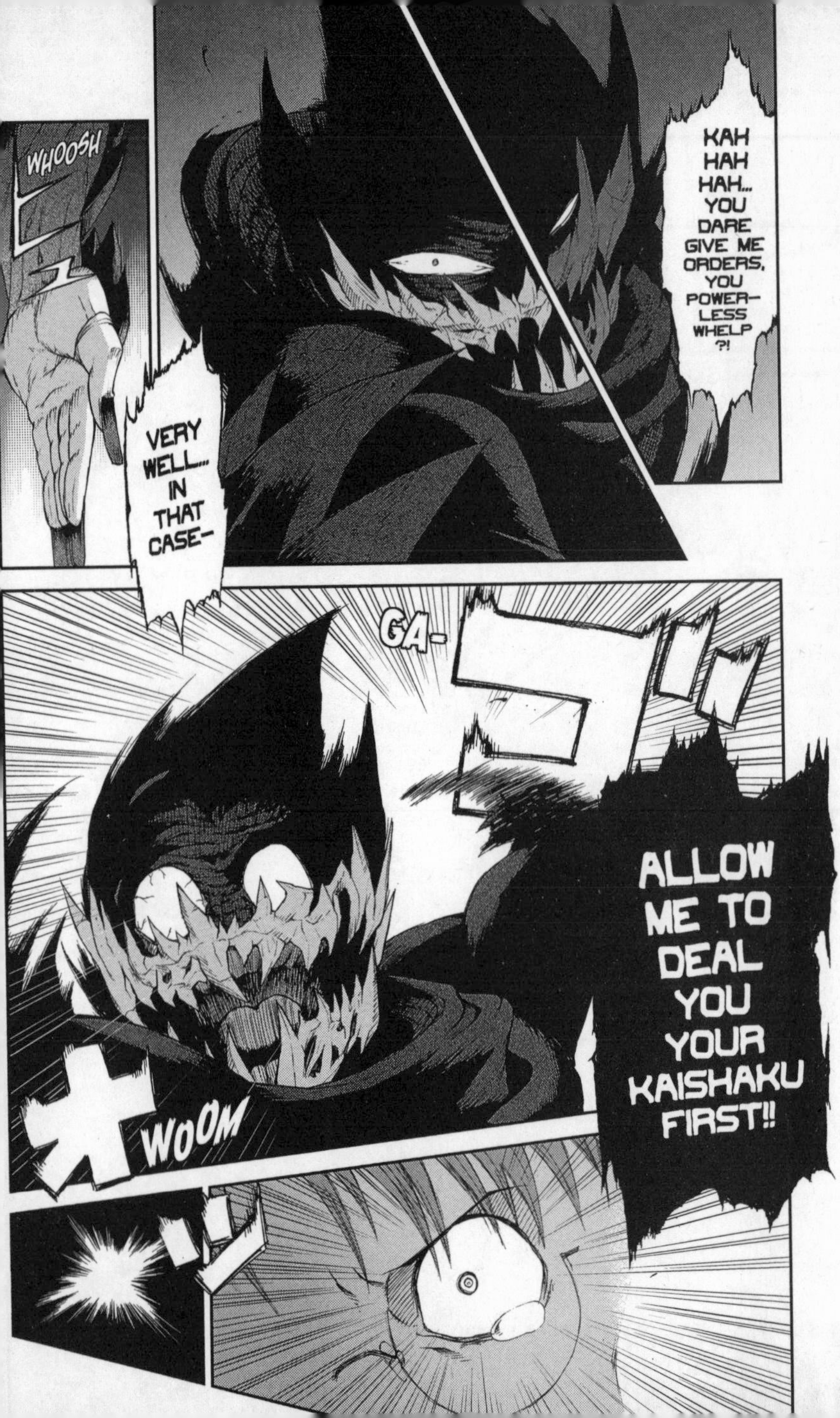
KAH HAH HAH... YOU DARE GIVE ME ORDERS, YOU POWER-LESS WHELP?!
VERY WELL... IN THAT CASE-
WHOOSH
GA-
ALLOW ME TO DEAL YOU YOUR KAISHAKU FIRST!!
WOOM

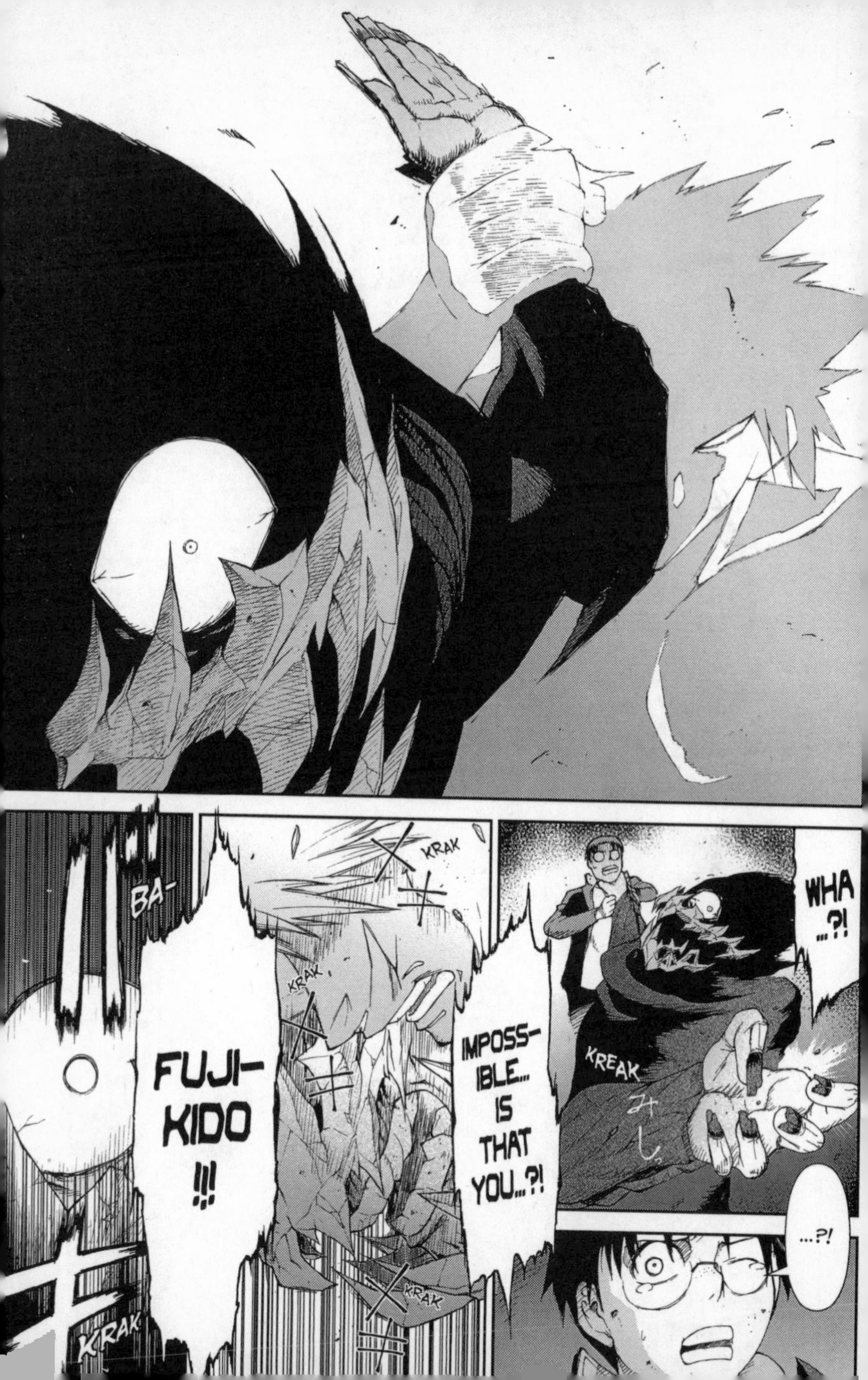
WHA ...?!
KREAK
みし
...?!
KRAK
KRAK
IMPOSS-IBLE... IS THAT YOU...?!
KRAK
BA-
FUJI-KIDO !!!
KRAK

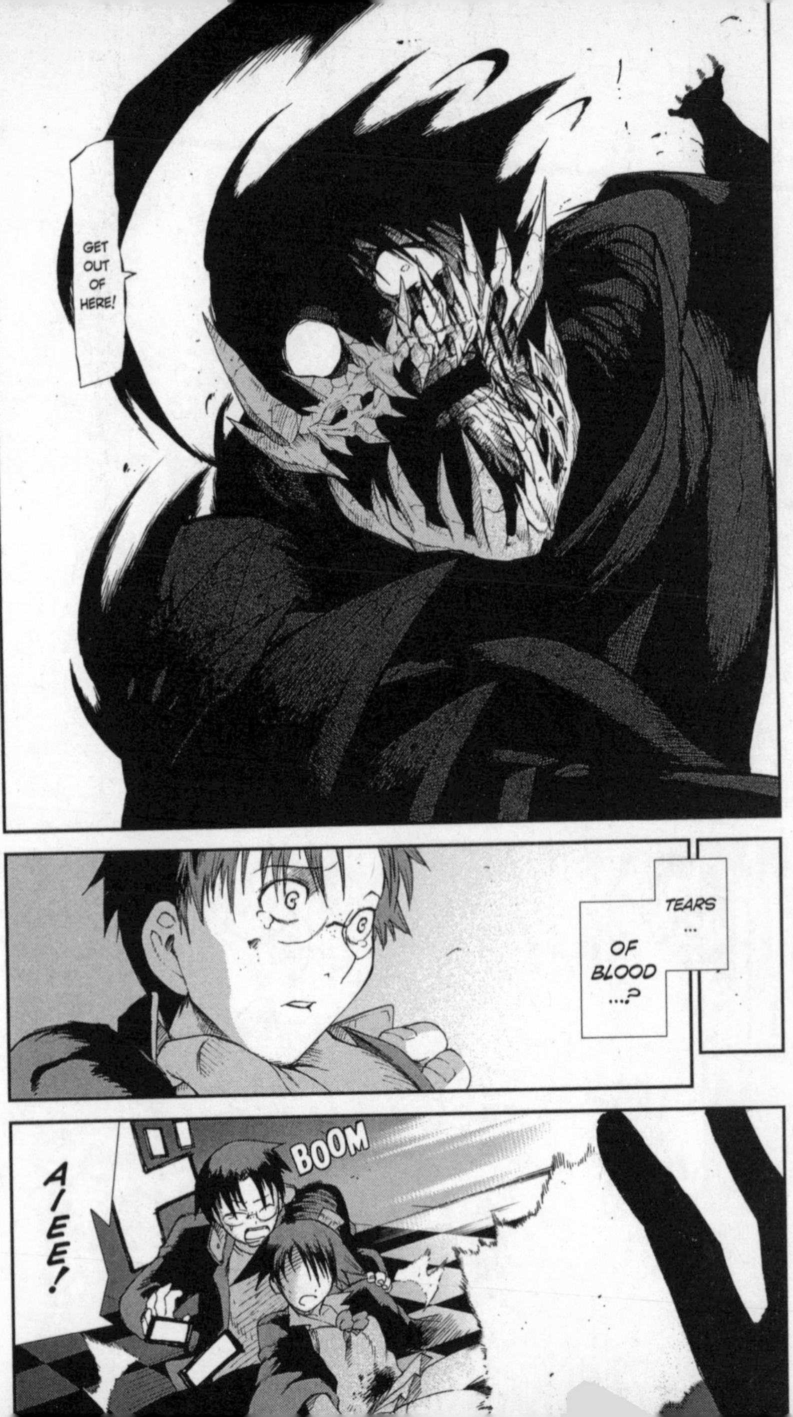
GET OUT OF HERE!
TEARS ... OF BLOOD ...?
BOOM
AIEEE!

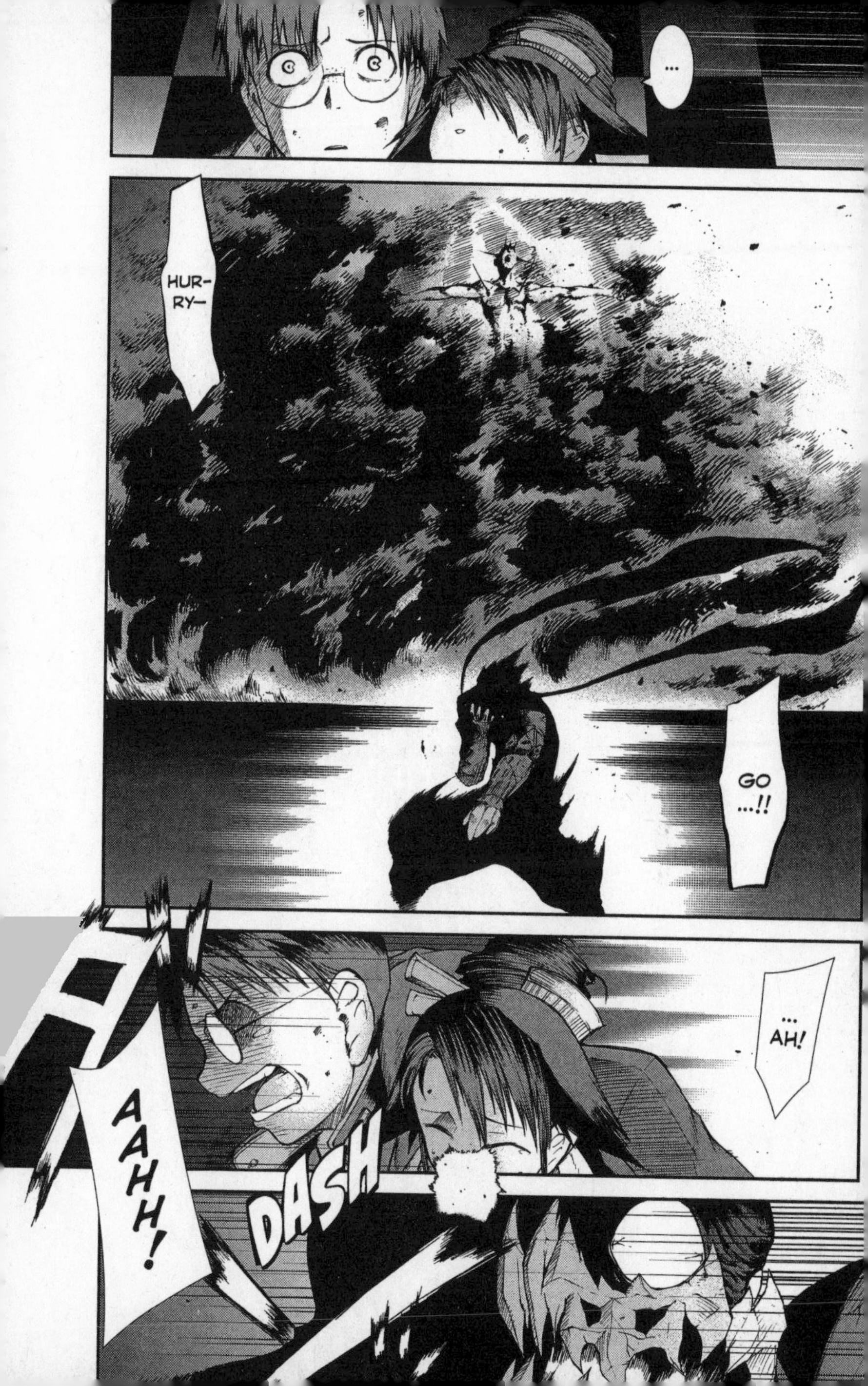
...
HUR-RY—
GO ...!!
... AH!
AAHH!
DASH

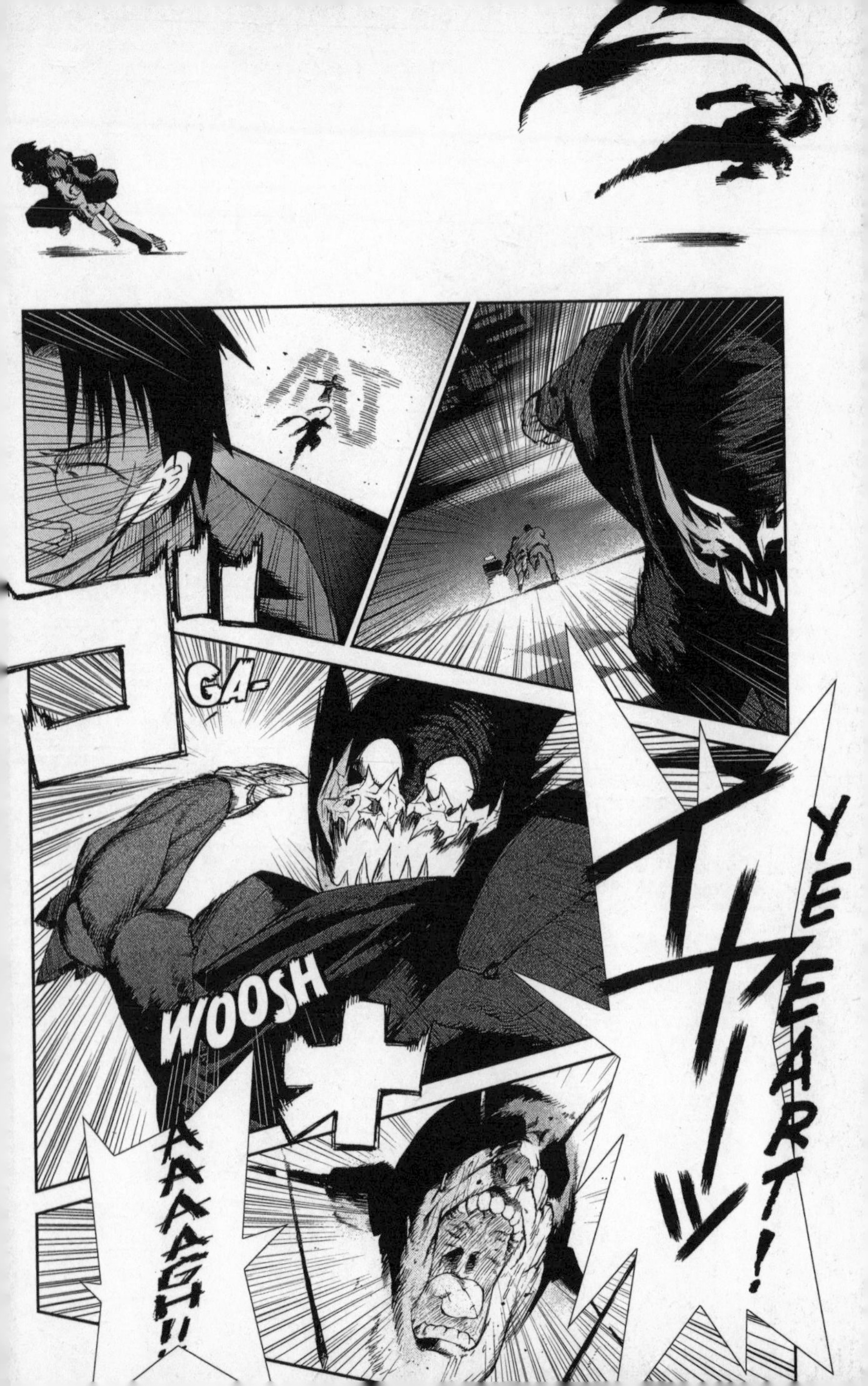
YEEART!!
GA-
WOOSH
AAAAGH!!

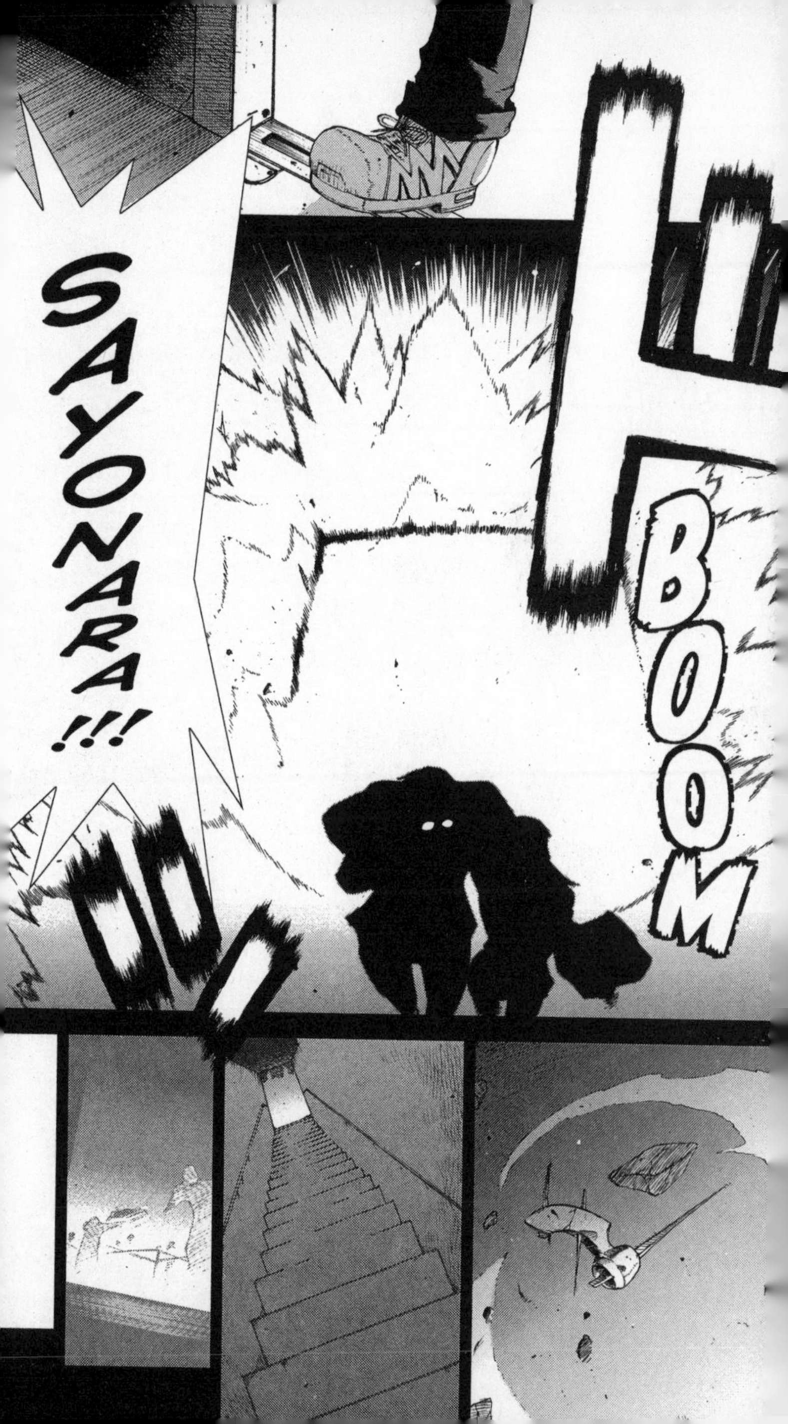
SAYONARA!!!
BOOM

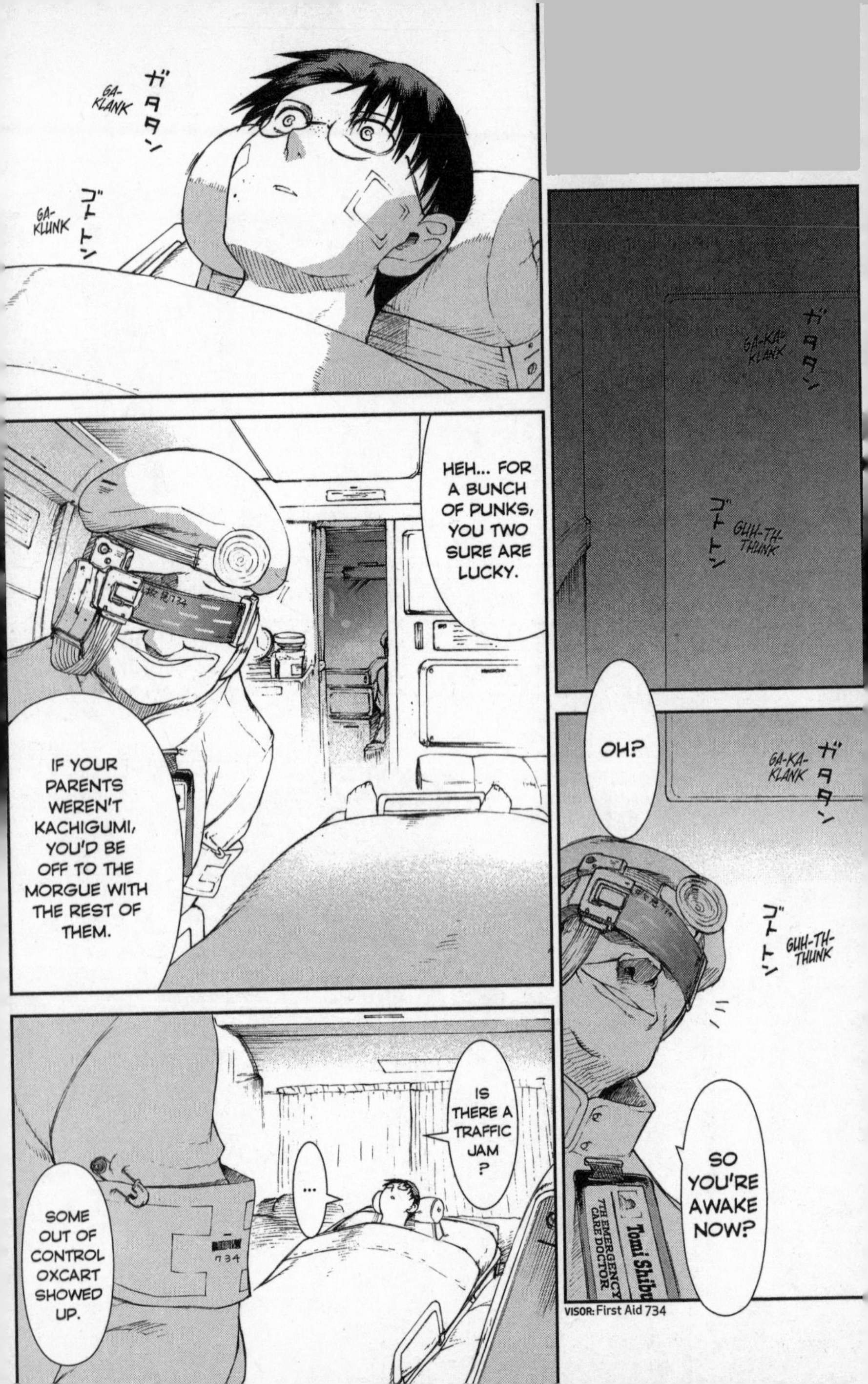

ガタタン
GA-KA-KLANX
ゴトトン
GUH-TH-THUNK
OH?
ガタタン
GA-KA-KLANK
ゴトトン
GUH-TH-THUNK
SO YOU'RE AWAKE NOW?
Tomi Shiba
TH EMERGENCY CARE DOCTOR
VISOR: First Aid 734
ガタタン
GA-KLANK
ゴトトン
GA-KLUNK
HEH... FOR A BUNCH OF PUNKS, YOU TWO SURE ARE LUCKY.
IF YOUR PARENTS WEREN'T KACHIGUMI, YOU'D BE OFF TO THE MORGUE WITH THE REST OF THEM.
IS THERE A TRAFFIC JAM?
...
SOME OUT OF CONTROL OXCART SHOWED UP.

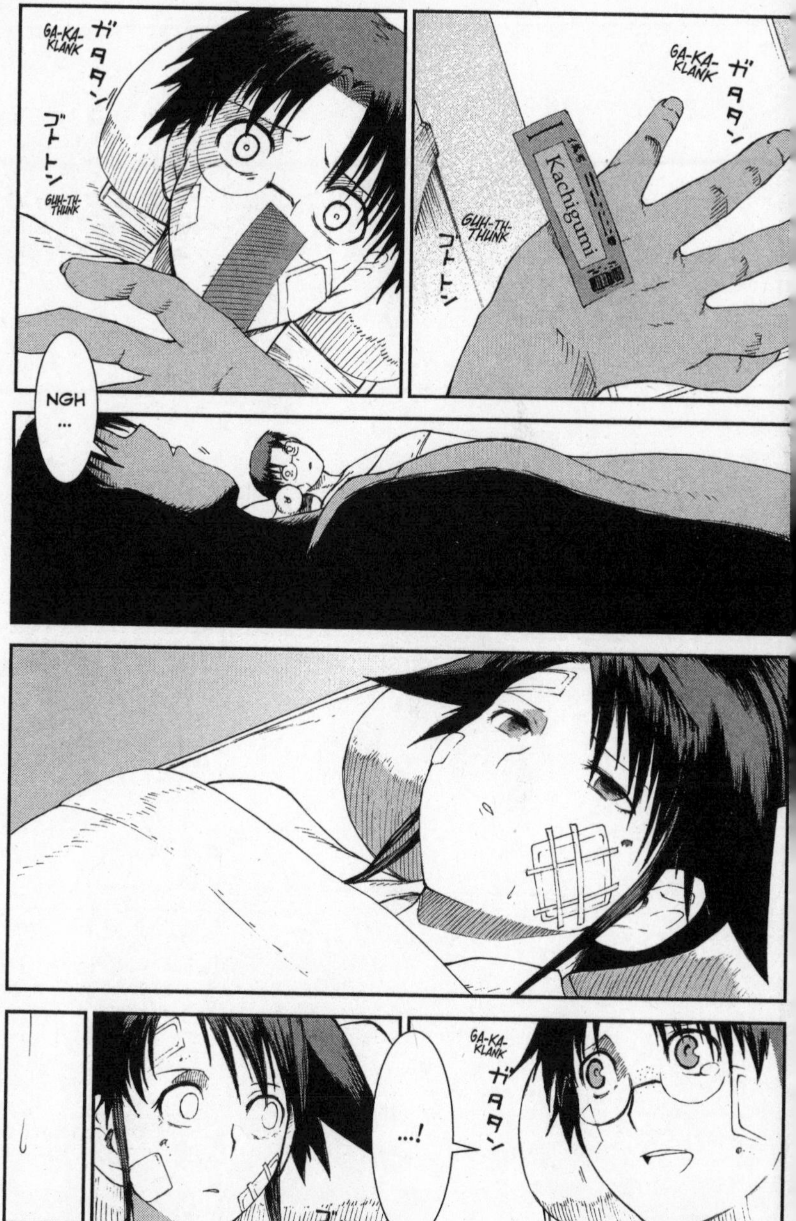
GA-KA-KLANK
ガタタン
Kachigumi
GUH-TH-THUNK
ゴトトン
GA-KA-KLANK
ガタタン
ゴトトン
GUH-TH-THUNK
NGH ...
GA-KA-KLANK
ガタタン
...!
ゴトトン
GUH-TH-THUNK

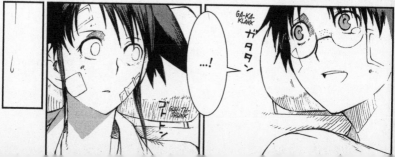

ガタタン
GA-KA
KLANK

ゴトトン
GUH-TH-
THUNK

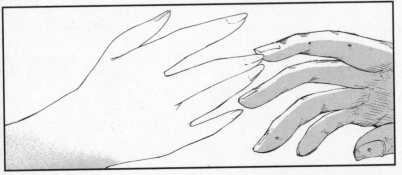

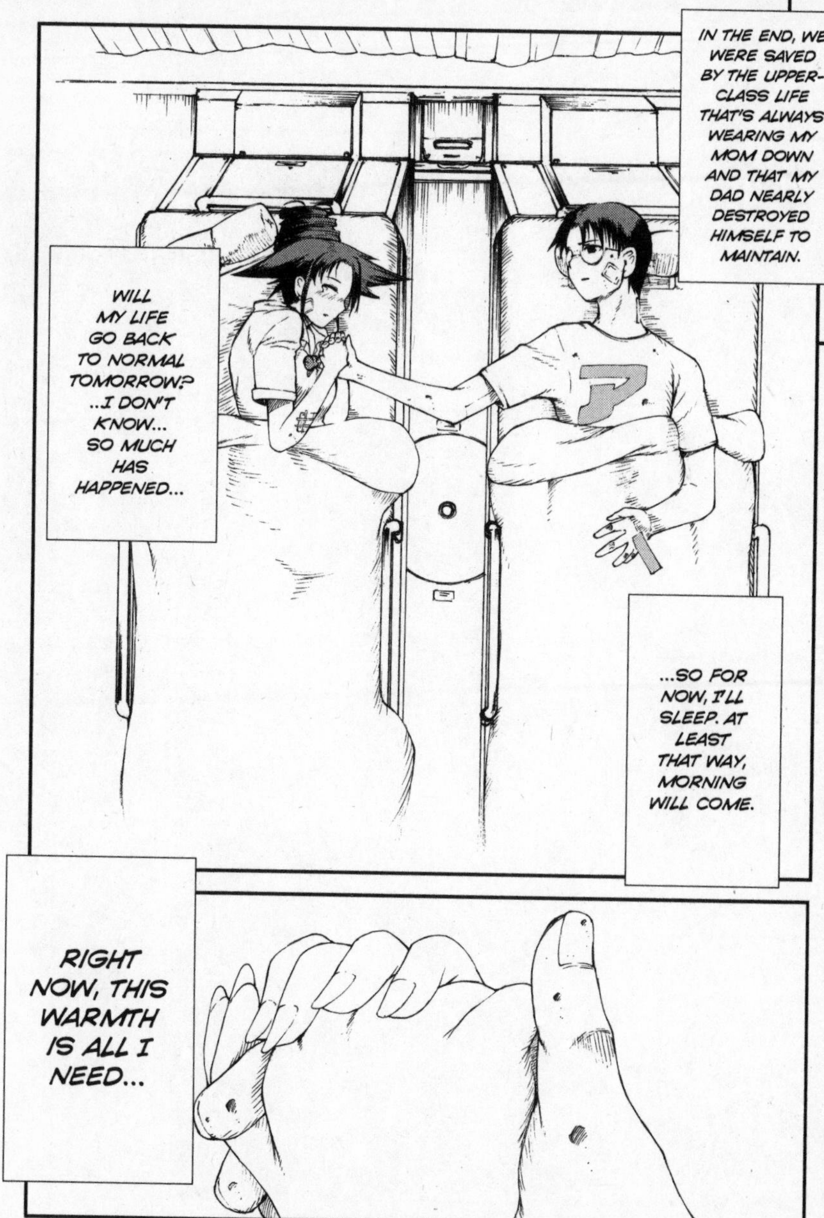
IN THE END, WE WERE SAVED BY THE UPPER-CLASS LIFE THAT'S ALWAYS WEARING MY MOM DOWN AND THAT MY DAD NEARLY DESTROYED HIMSELF TO MAINTAIN.
WILL MY LIFE GO BACK TO NORMAL TOMORROW? ...I DON'T KNOW... SO MUCH HAS HAPPENED...
...SO FOR NOW, I'LL SLEEP. AT LEAST THAT WAY, MORNING WILL COME.
RIGHT NOW, THIS WARMTH IS ALL I NEED...

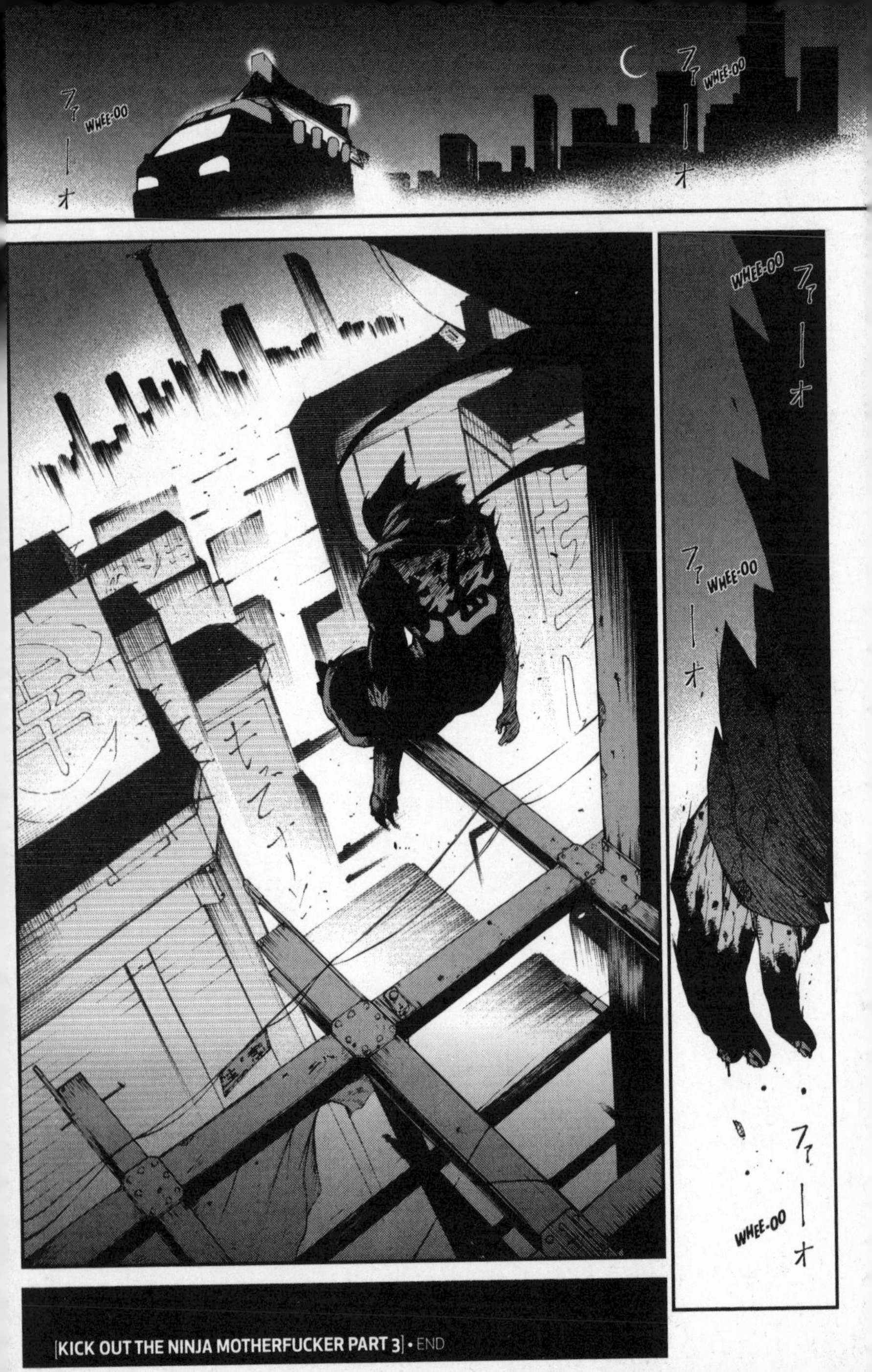
ファーオ
WHEE-OO
ファーオ
WHEE-OO
ファーオ
WHEE-OO
ファーオ
WHEE-OO
ファーオ
WHEE-OO
ファーオ
WHEE-OO

[KICK OUT THE NINJA MOTHERFUCKER PART 3] • END

NINJA SLAYER KILLs!!

NINJA SLAYER
KILLs!!

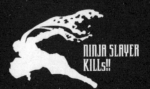

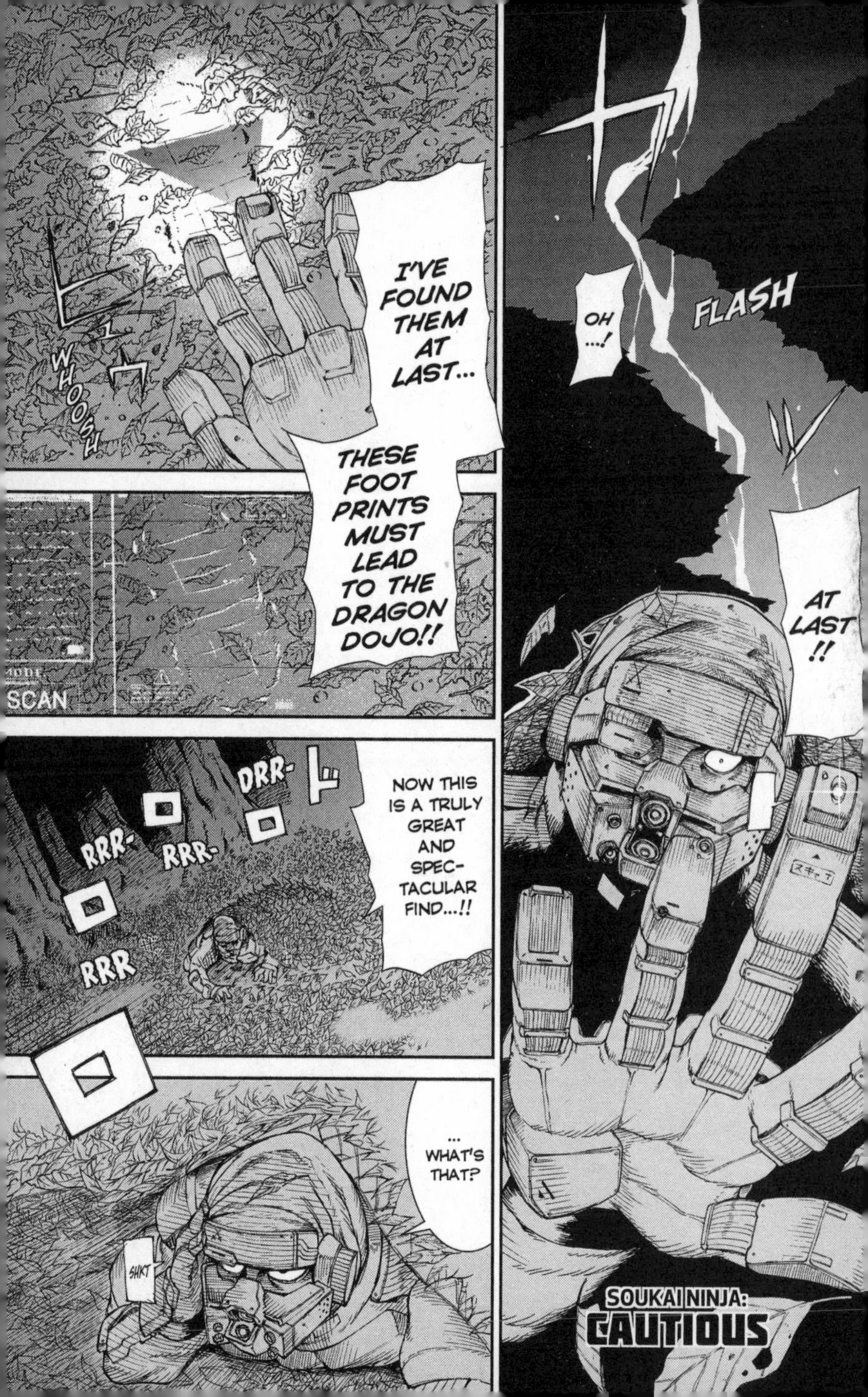
OH ...!
FLASH
AT LAST !!
SOUKAI NINJA:
CAUTIOUS
WHOOSH
I'VE FOUND THEM AT LAST...
THESE FOOT PRINTS MUST LEAD TO THE DRAGON DOJO!!
SCAN
NOW THIS IS A TRULY GREAT AND SPEC-TACULAR FIND...!!
DRR-
RRR-
RRR-
RRR
... WHAT'S THAT?
SHKT

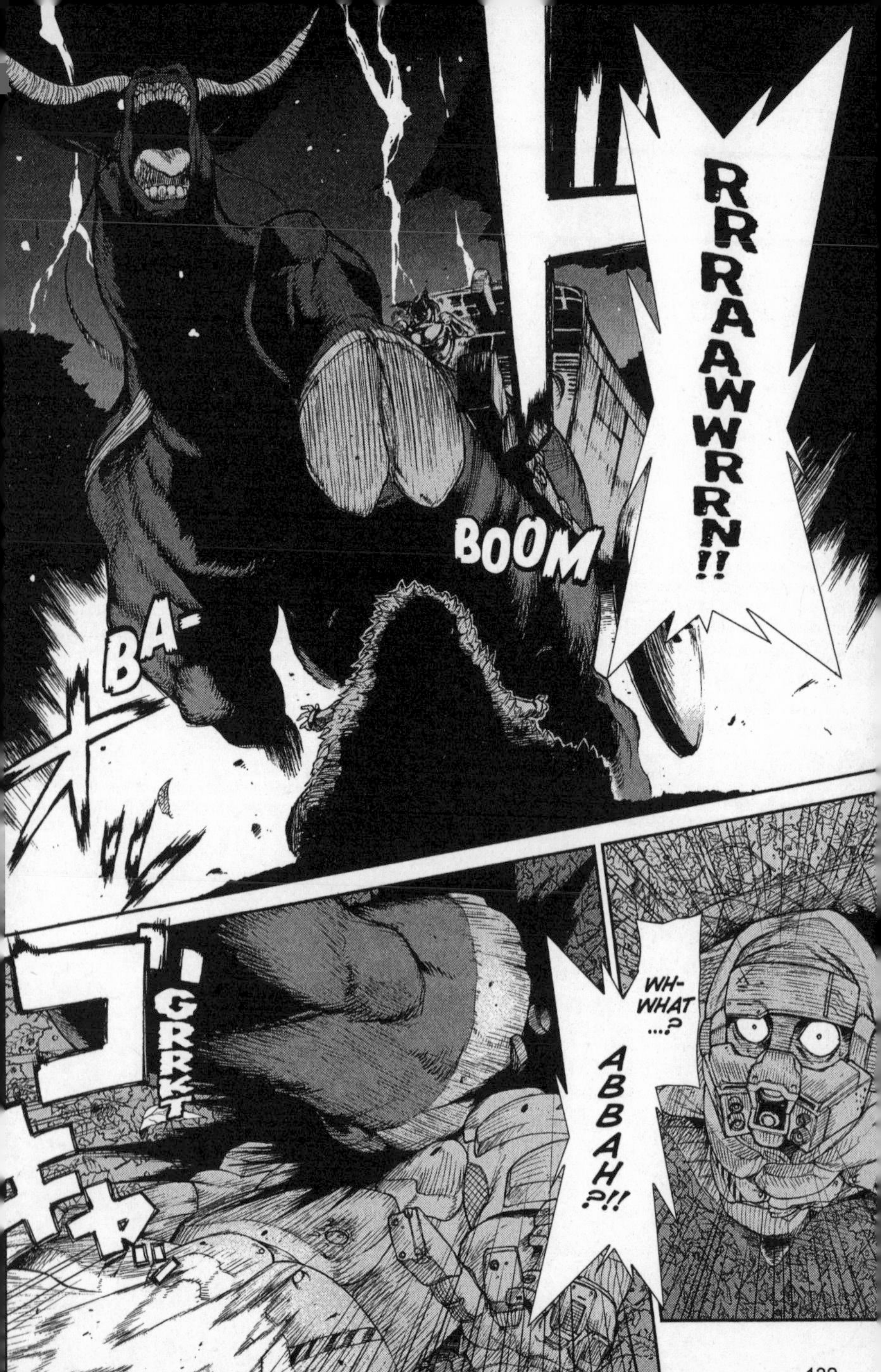
RRRAAWWRRN!!
BOOM
BA-
WH-WHAT ...?
ABBAH?!!
GRRKT

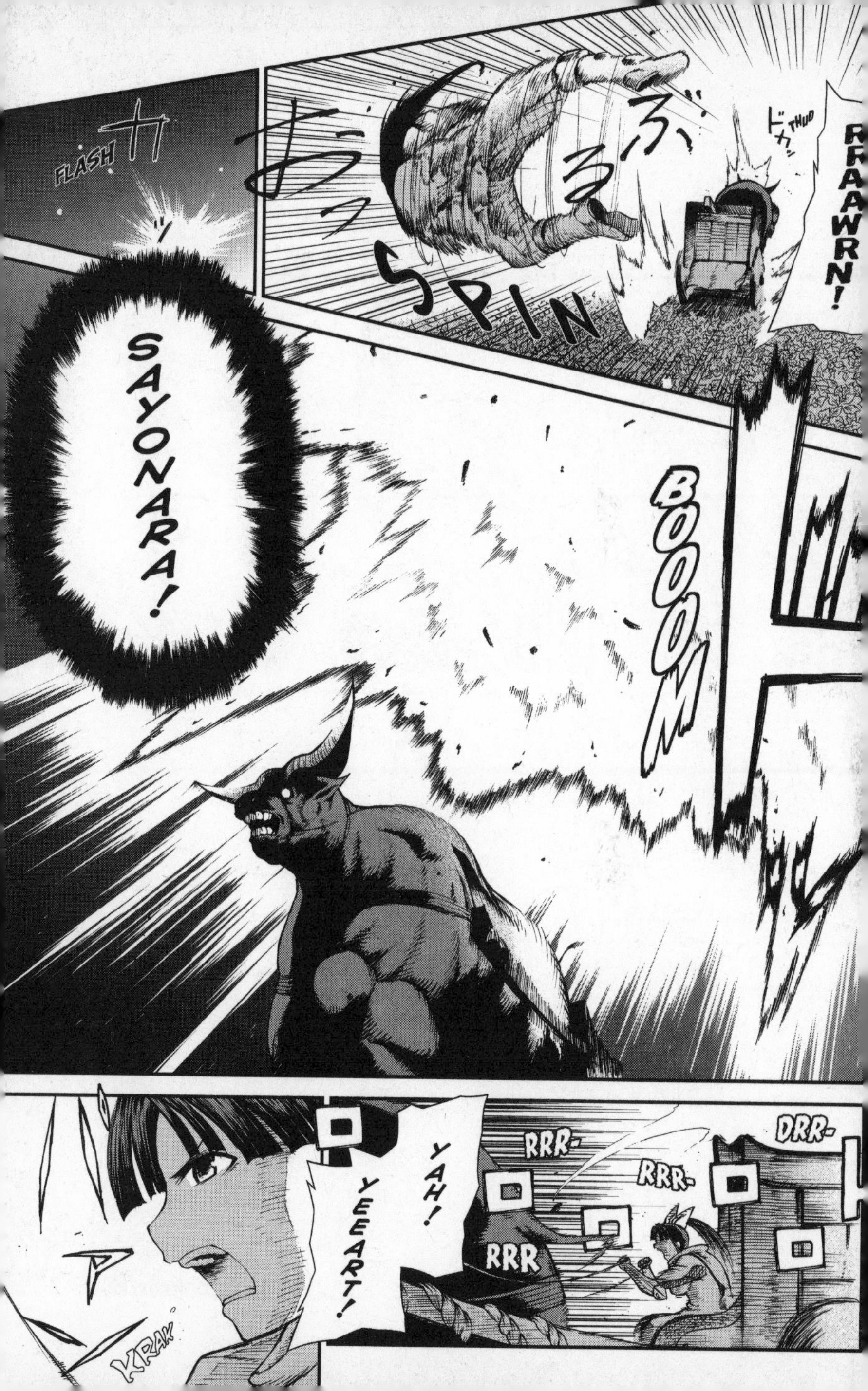
RRAAAWRN!
THUD
SPIN
FLASH
SAYONARA!
BOOOOM
DRR-
RRR-
RRR-
YAH! YEEEART!
RRR
KRAK

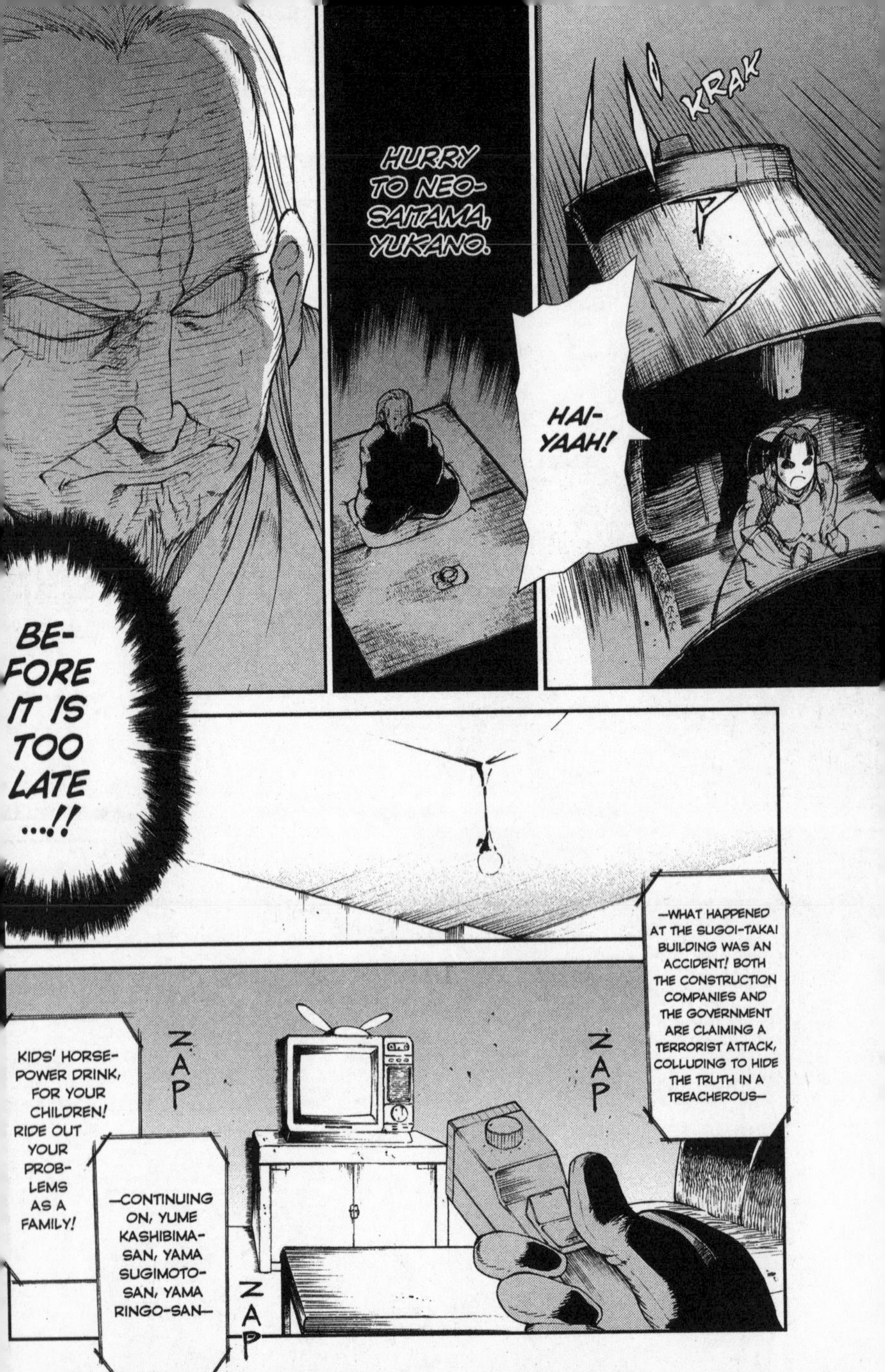
KRAK
HAI-YAAH!
HURRY TO NEO-SAITAMA, YUKANO.
BE-FORE IT IS TOO LATE ...!!
—WHAT HAPPENED AT THE SUGOI-TAKAI BUILDING WAS AN ACCIDENT! BOTH THE CONSTRUCTION COMPANIES AND THE GOVERNMENT ARE CLAIMING A TERRORIST ATTACK, COLLUDING TO HIDE THE TRUTH IN A TREACHEROUS—
ZAP
ZAP
ZAP
—CONTINUING ON, YUME KASHIBIMA-SAN, YAMA SUGIMOTO-SAN, YAMA RINGO-SAN—
KIDS' HORSE-POWER DRINK, FOR YOUR CHILDREN! RIDE OUT YOUR PROB-LEMS AS A FAMILY!

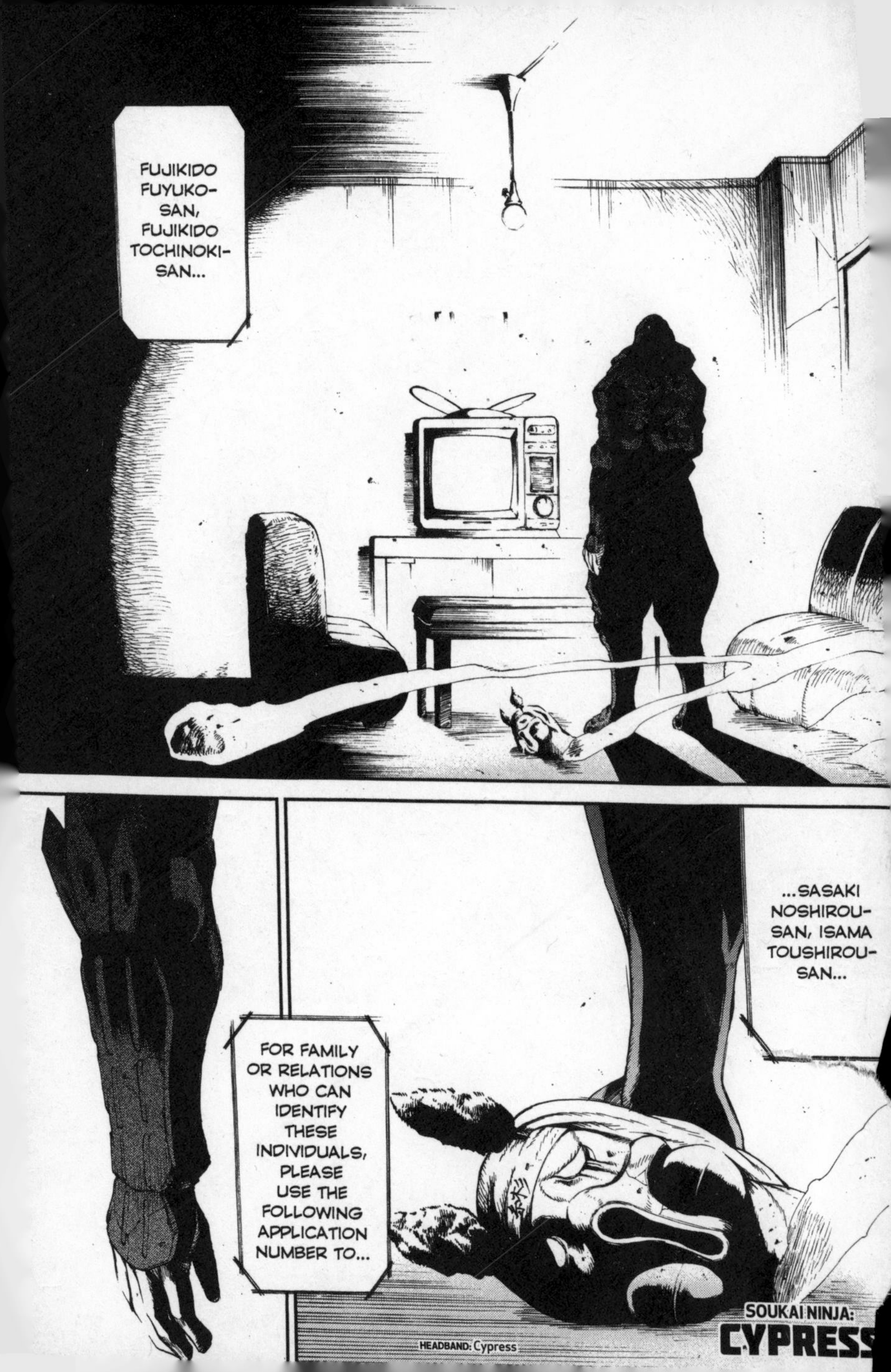
FUJIKIDO FUYUKO-SAN, FUJIKIDO TOCHINOKI-SAN...
...SASAKI NOSHIROU-SAN, ISAMA TOUSHIROU-SAN...
FOR FAMILY OR RELATIONS WHO CAN IDENTIFY THESE INDIVIDUALS, PLEASE USE THE FOLLOWING APPLICATION NUMBER TO...
SOUKAI NINJA:
CYPRESS
HEADBAND: Cypress

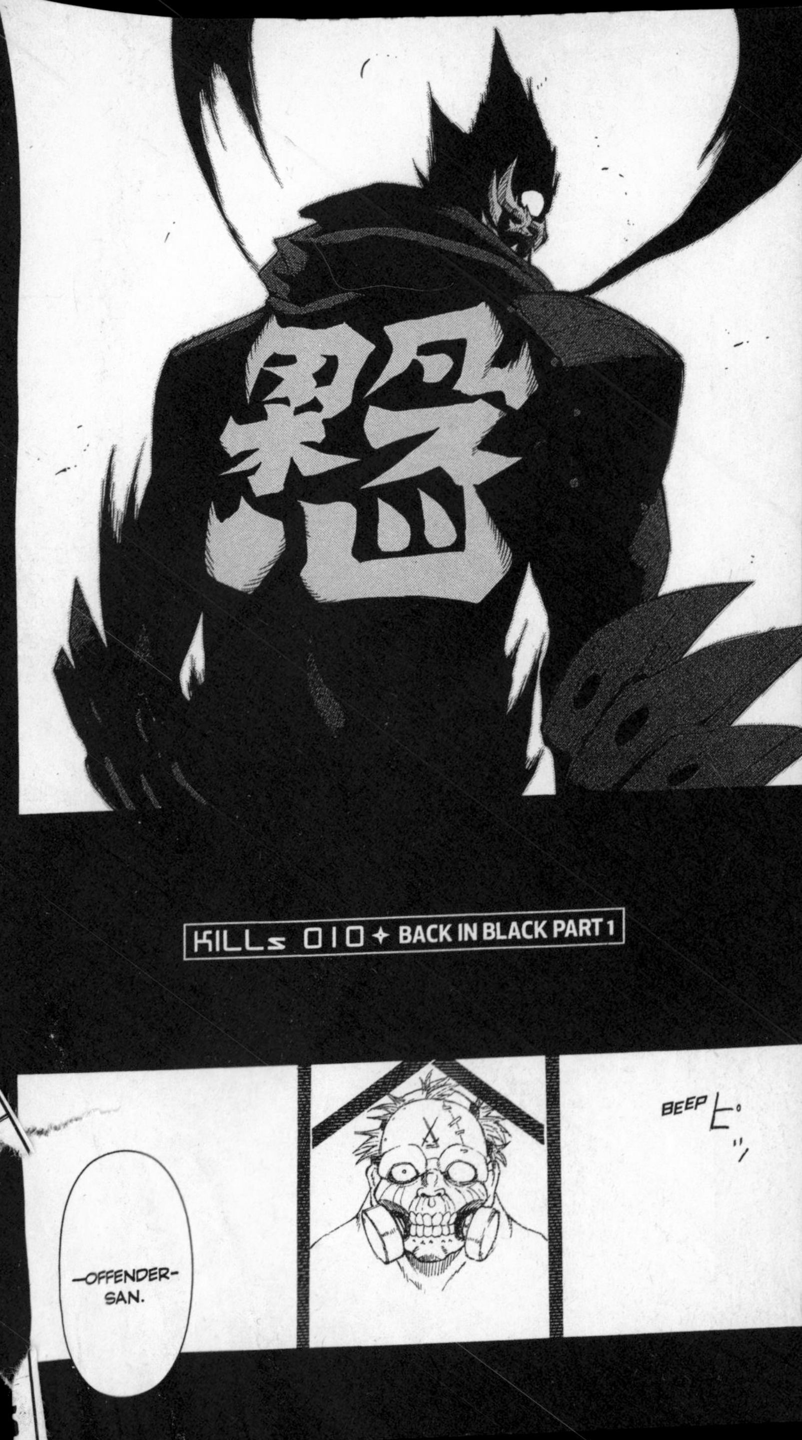
KILLs 010 ✦ BACK IN BLACK PART 1
BEEP ピッ
—OFFENDER-SAN.

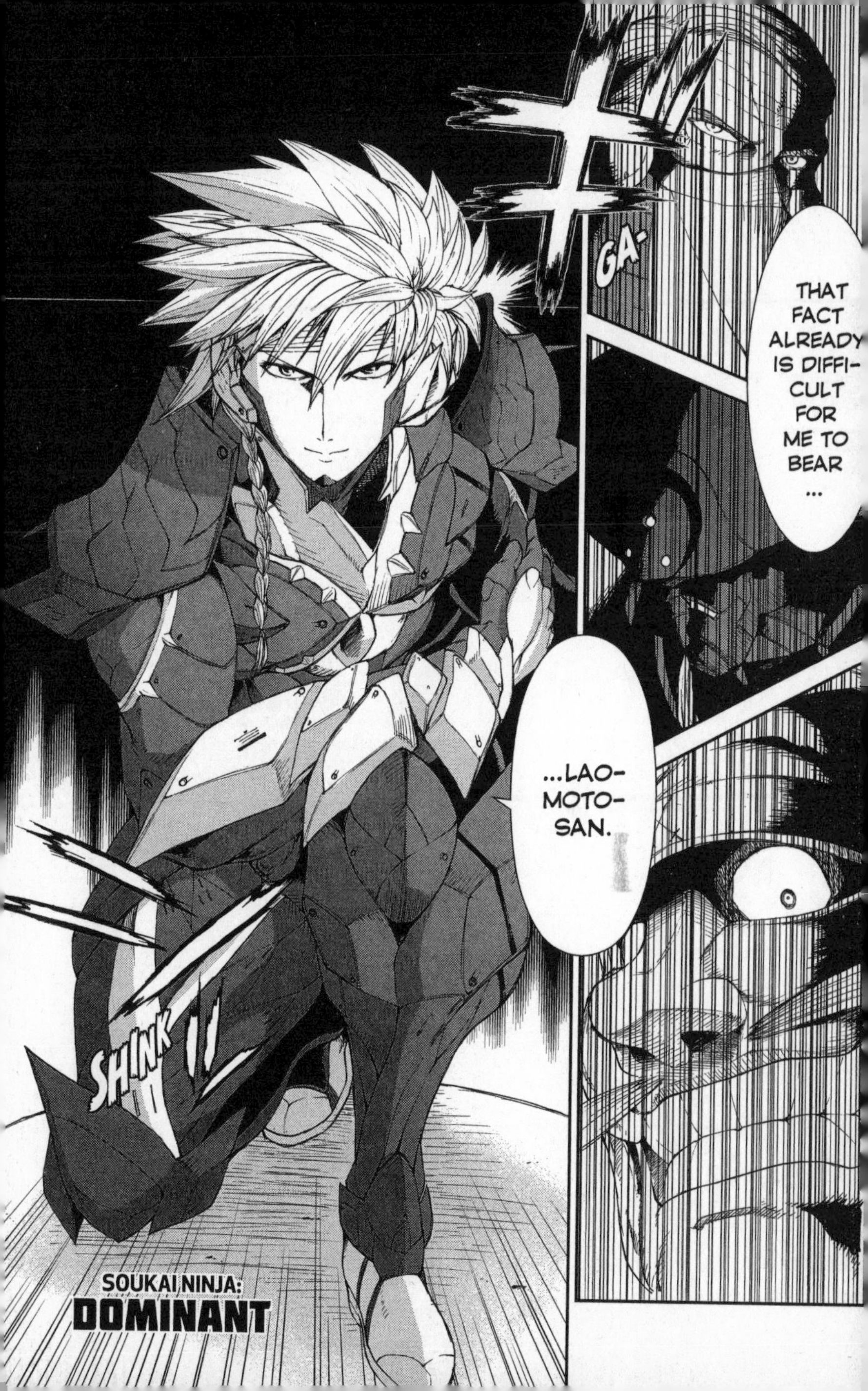
GA-
THAT FACT ALREADY IS DIFFICULT FOR ME TO BEAR ...
...LAO-MOTO-SAN.
SHINK
SOUKAI NINJA:
DOMINANT

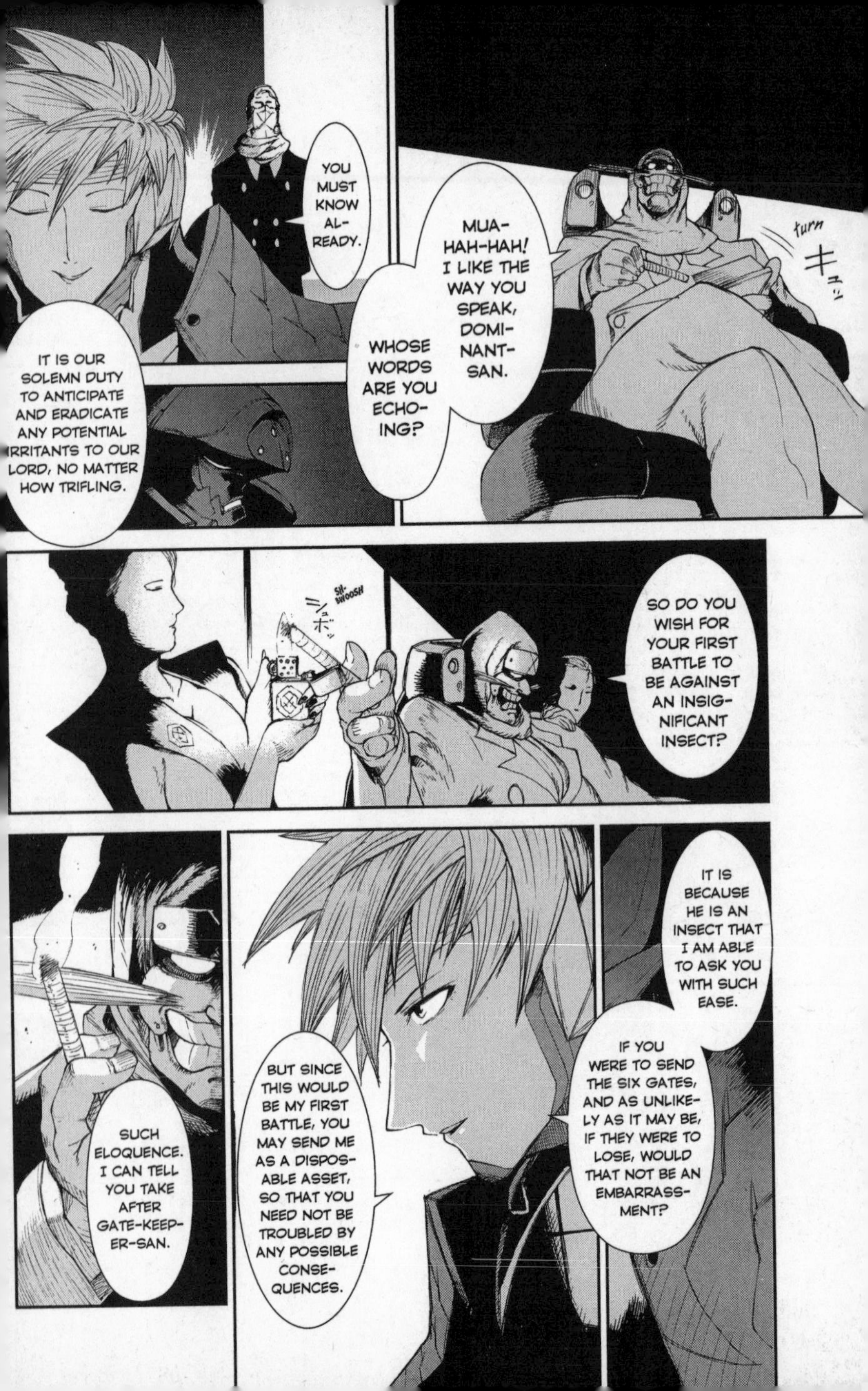
turn
MUA-HAH-HAH! I LIKE THE WAY YOU SPEAK, DOMINANT-SAN.
WHOSE WORDS ARE YOU ECHOING?
YOU MUST KNOW AL-READY.
IT IS OUR SOLEMN DUTY TO ANTICIPATE AND ERADICATE ANY POTENTIAL IRRITANTS TO OUR LORD, NO MATTER HOW TRIFLING.
SO DO YOU WISH FOR YOUR FIRST BATTLE TO BE AGAINST AN INSIG-NIFICANT INSECT?
SHWOOSH
IT IS BECAUSE HE IS AN INSECT THAT I AM ABLE TO ASK YOU WITH SUCH EASE.
IF YOU WERE TO SEND THE SIX GATES, AND AS UNLIKE-LY AS IT MAY BE, IF THEY WERE TO LOSE, WOULD THAT NOT BE AN EMBARRASS-MENT?
BUT SINCE THIS WOULD BE MY FIRST BATTLE, YOU MAY SEND ME AS A DISPOS-ABLE ASSET, SO THAT YOU NEED NOT BE TROUBLED BY ANY POSSIBLE CONSE-QUENCES.
SUCH ELOQUENCE. I CAN TELL YOU TAKE AFTER GATE-KEEP-ER-SAN.

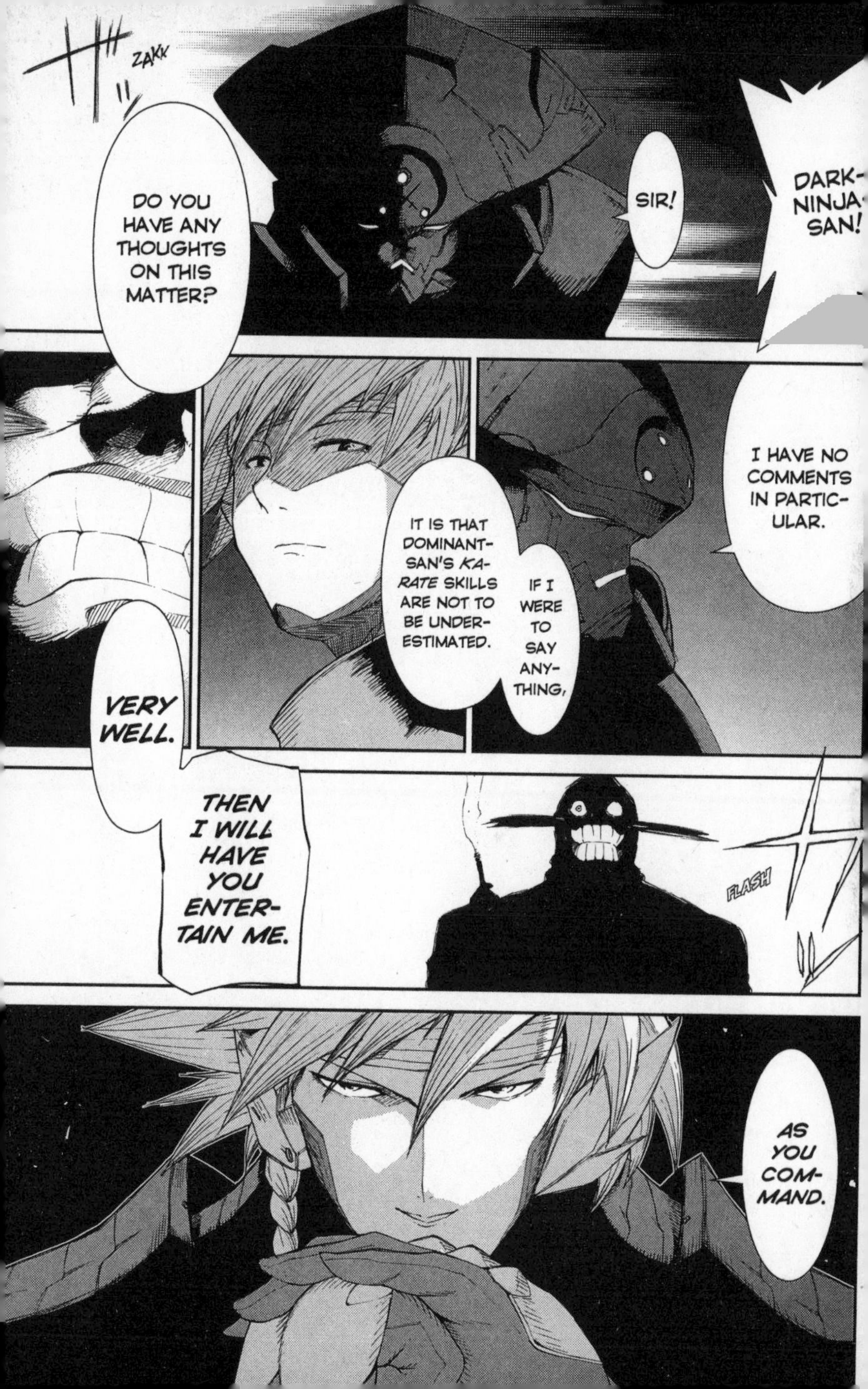
DARK-NINJA-SAN!
SIR!
ZAKK
DO YOU HAVE ANY THOUGHTS ON THIS MATTER?
I HAVE NO COMMENTS IN PARTICULAR.
IF I WERE TO SAY ANYTHING,
IT IS THAT DOMINANT-SAN'S *KARATE* SKILLS ARE NOT TO BE UNDERESTIMATED.
VERY WELL.
FLASH
THEN I WILL HAVE YOU ENTERTAIN ME.
AS YOU COMMAND.

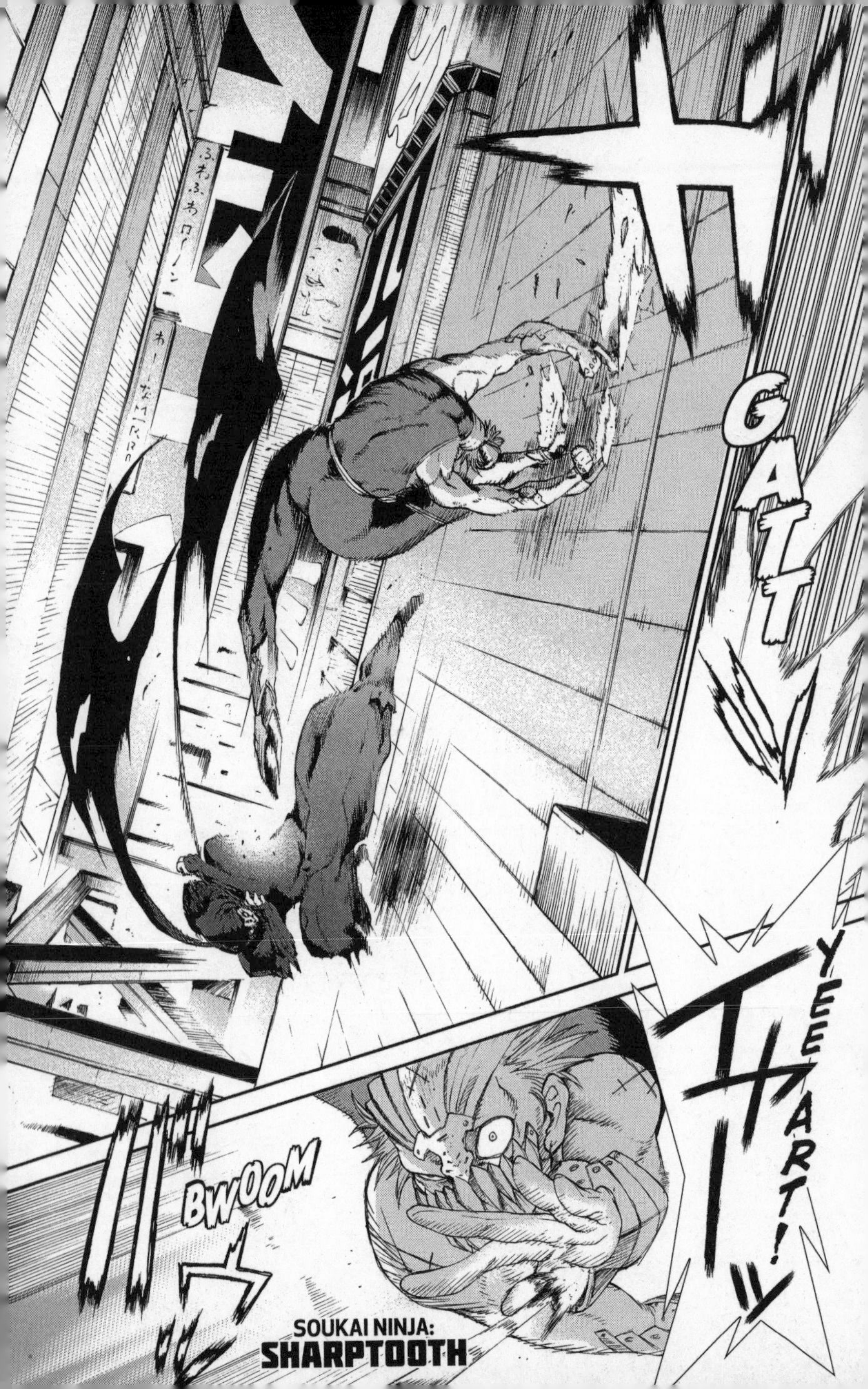
GATT
YEEART!
BWOOM
SOUKAI NINJA:
SHARPTOOTH

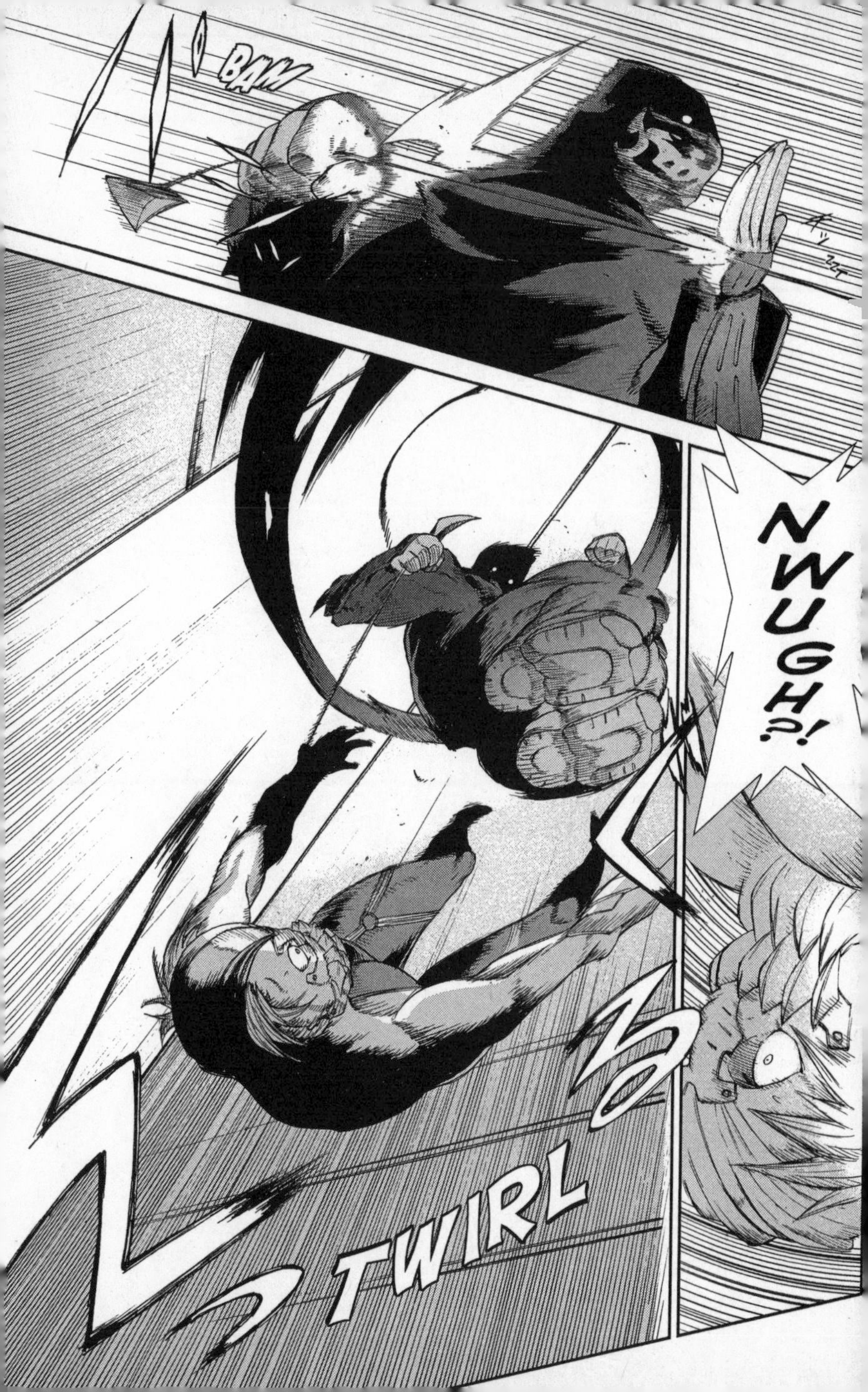
BAM
NWUGH?!
TWIRL

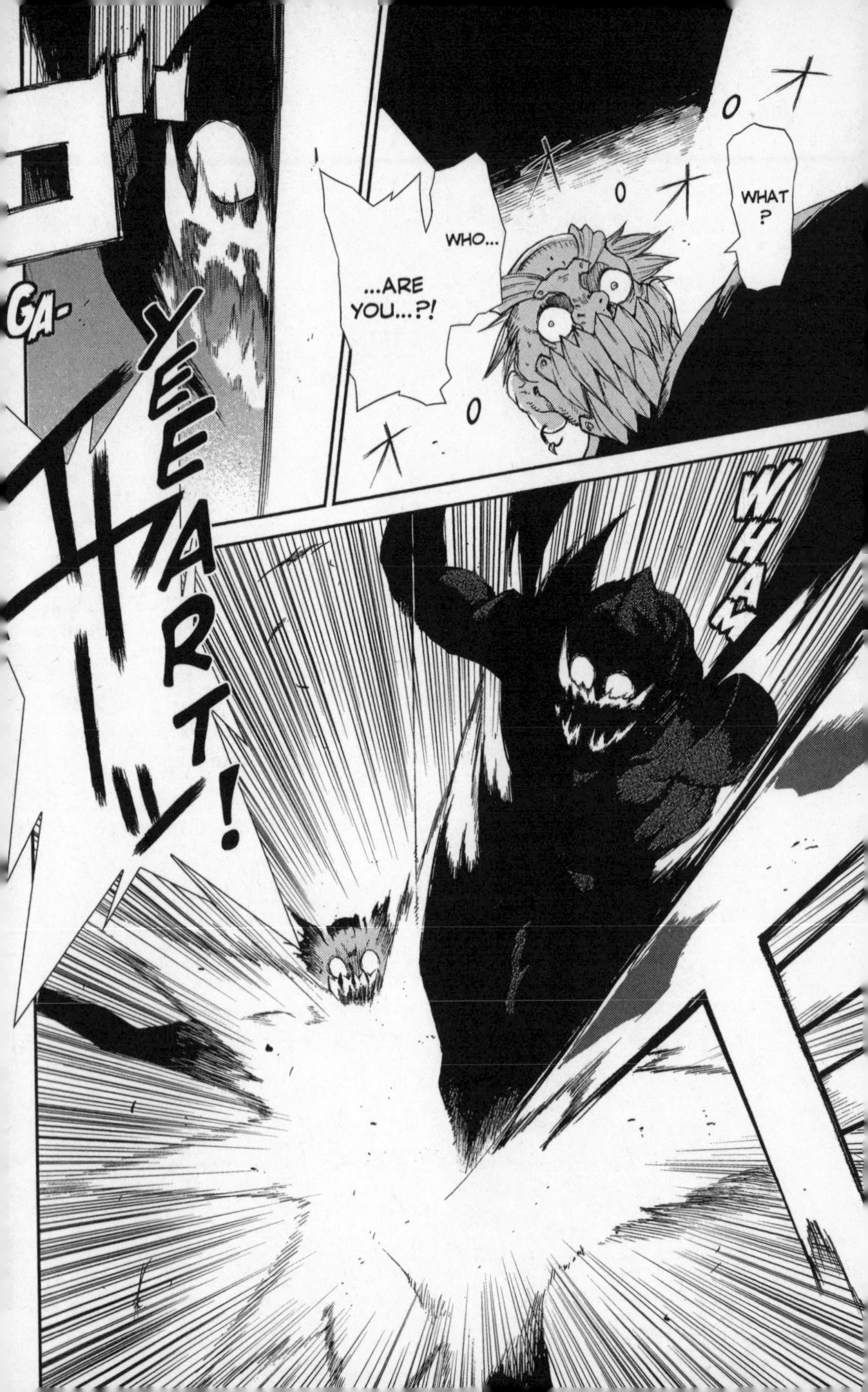
WHAT ?
WHO...
...ARE YOU...?!
GA-
YEEART!
WHAM

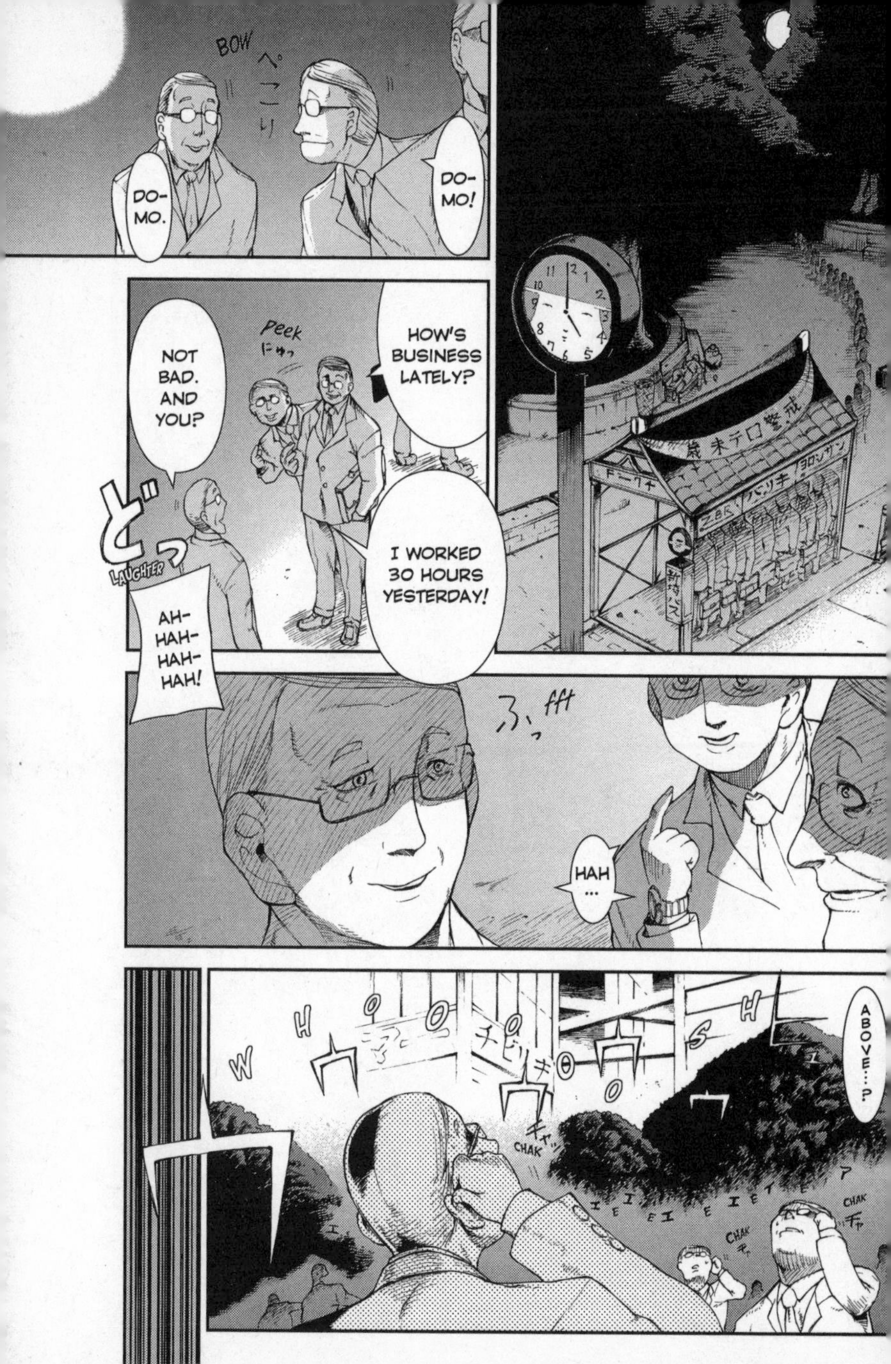
BOW
DO-MO!
DO-MO.
HOW'S BUSINESS LATELY?
Peek
NOT BAD. AND YOU?
I WORKED 30 HOURS YESTERDAY!
LAUGHTER
AH-HAH-HAH-HAH!
fft
HAH ...
ABOVE...?
WHOOOOSH
CHAK
CHAK
CHAK

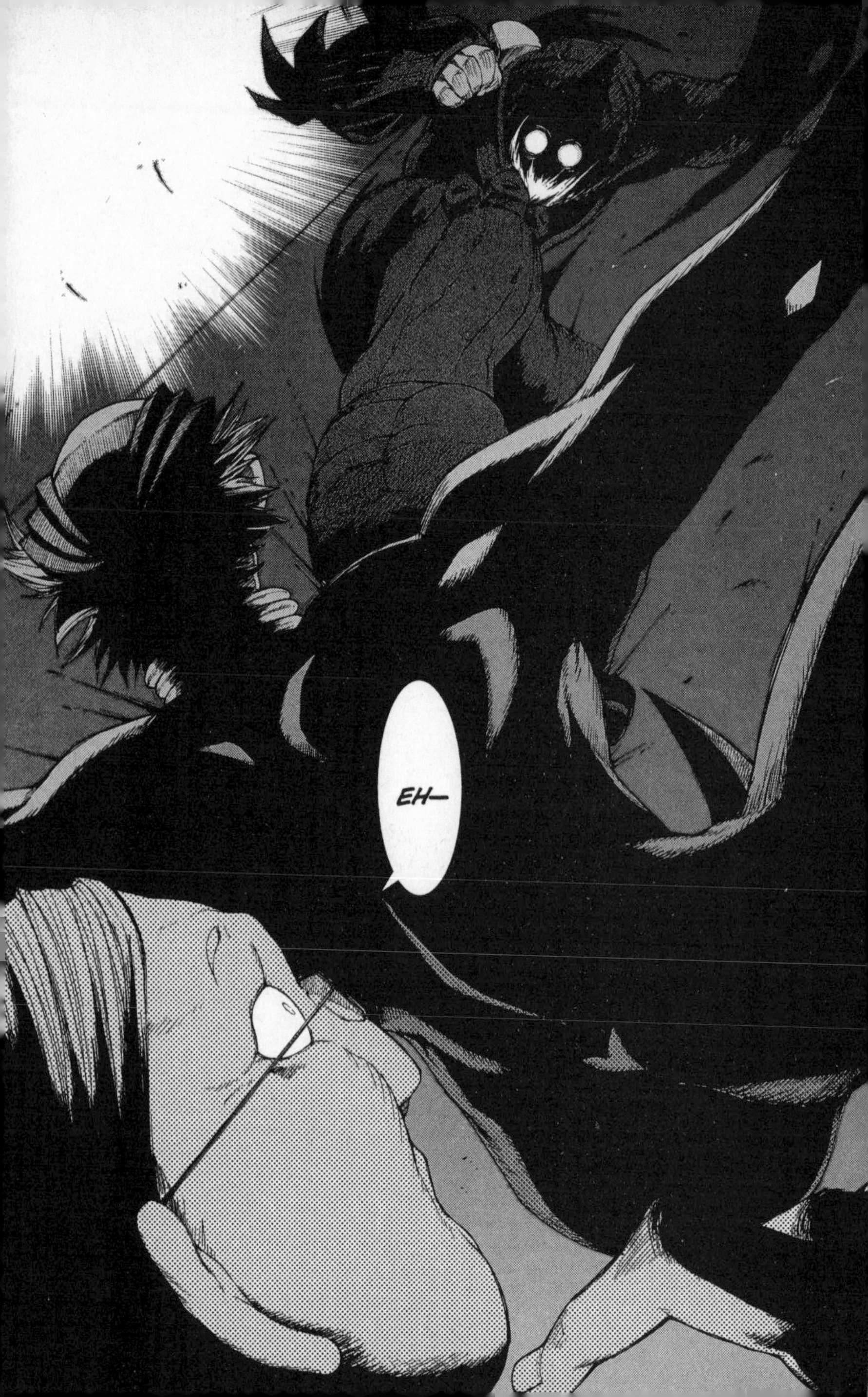
EH—

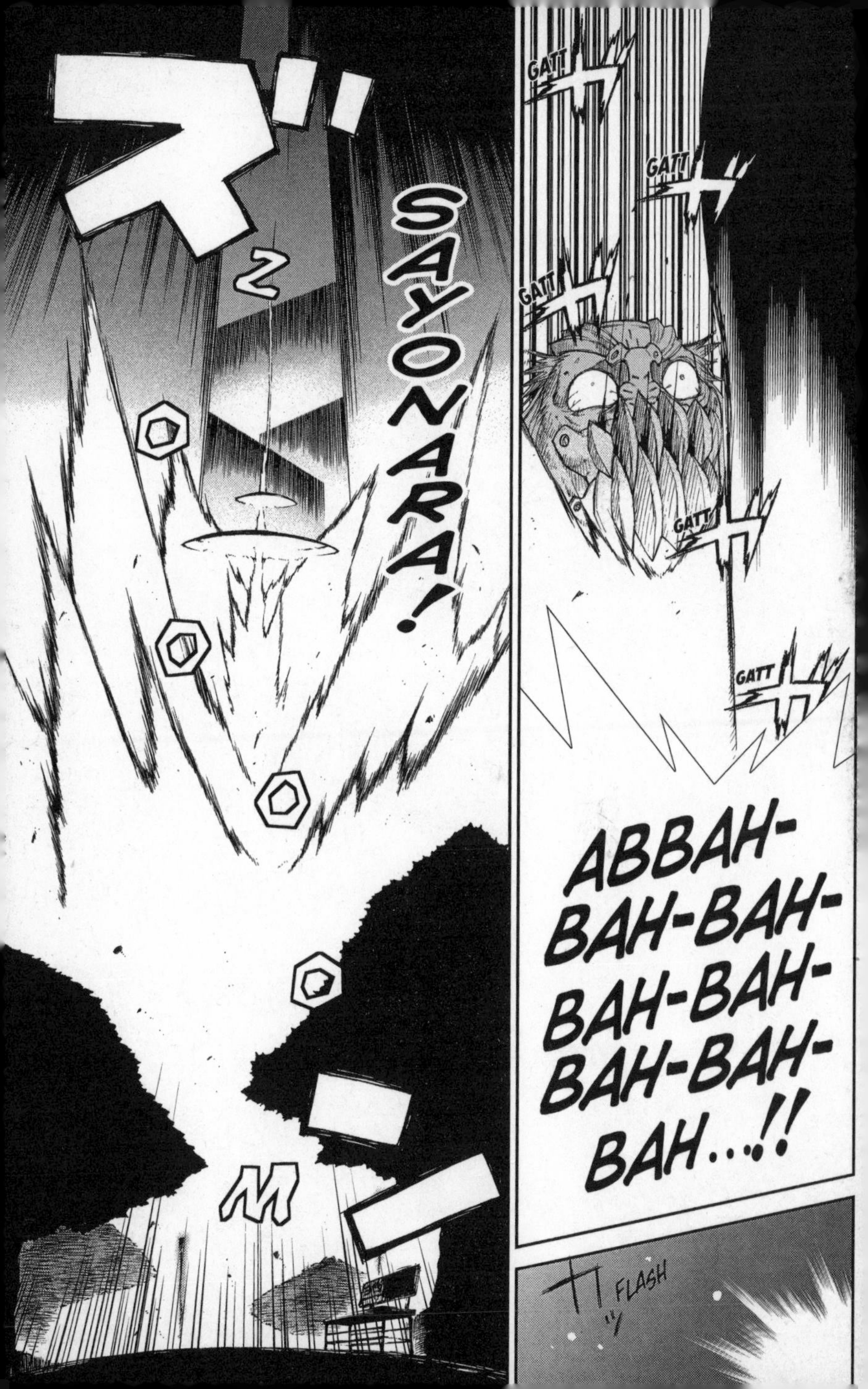
GATT
GATT
GATT
GATT
GATT
ABBAH-BAH-BAH-BAH-BAH-BAH-BAH-BAH...!!
FLASH
ズ
Z
SAYONARA!
M

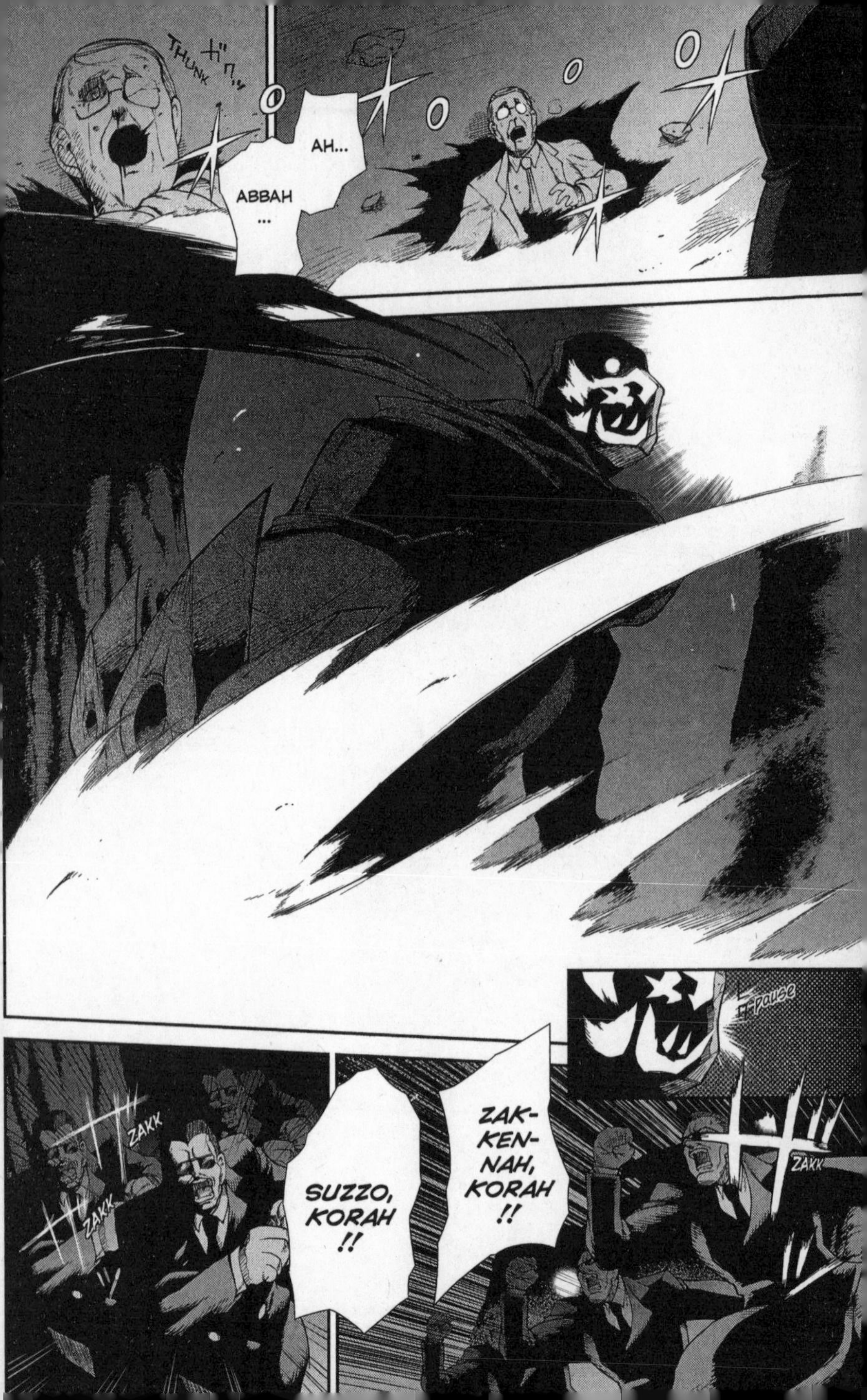
AH...
ABBAH ...
THUNK
pause
ZAKK
ZAKKEN-NAH, KORAH !!
SUZZO, KORAH !!
ZAKK
ZAKK

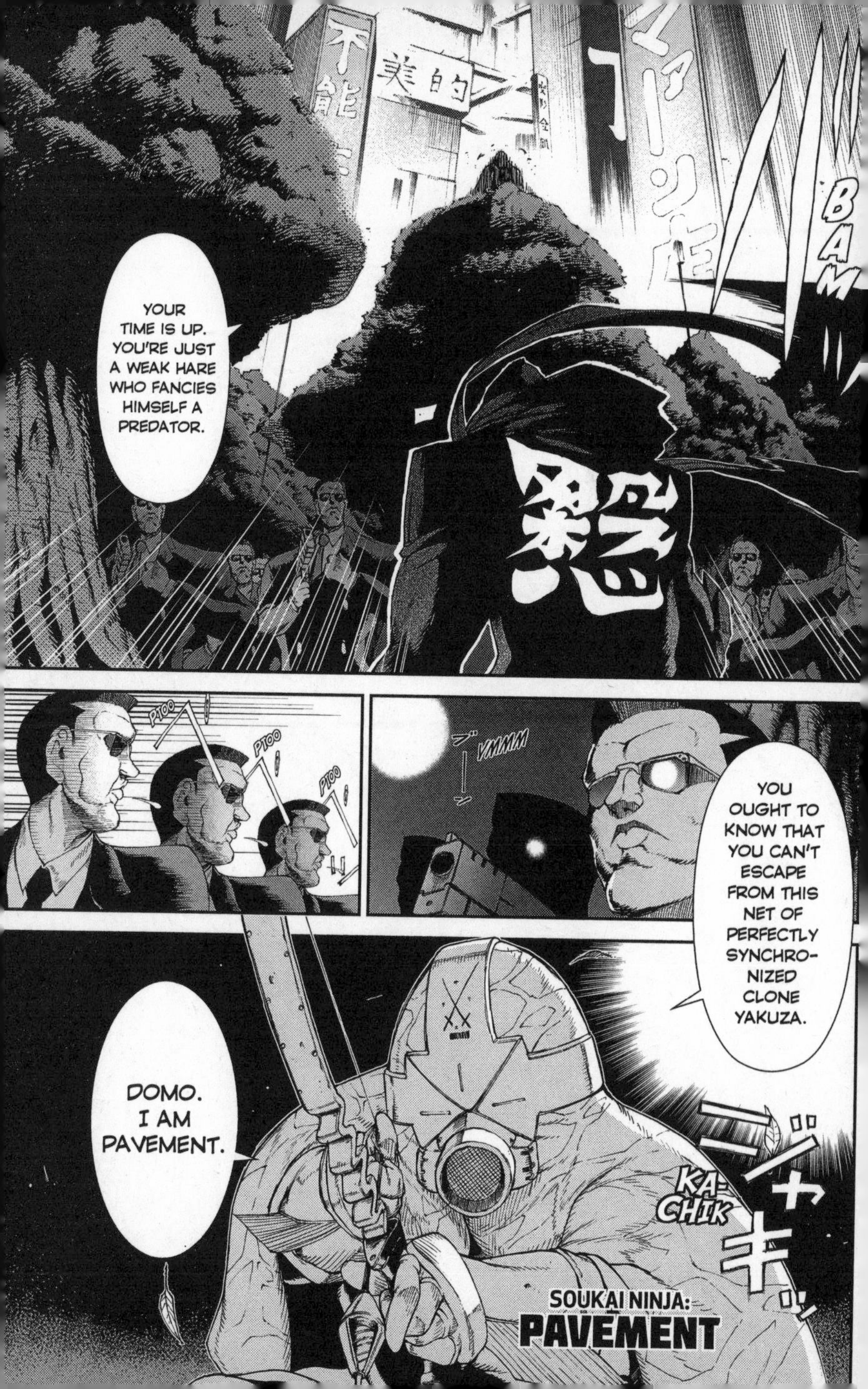
BAM
YOUR TIME IS UP. YOU'RE JUST A WEAK HARE WHO FANCIES HIMSELF A PREDATOR.
VMMM
YOU OUGHT TO KNOW THAT YOU CAN'T ESCAPE FROM THIS NET OF PERFECTLY SYNCHRO-NIZED CLONE YAKUZA.
P100
P100
P100
KA-CHIK
DOMO. I AM PAVEMENT.
SOUKAI NINJA:
PAVEMENT

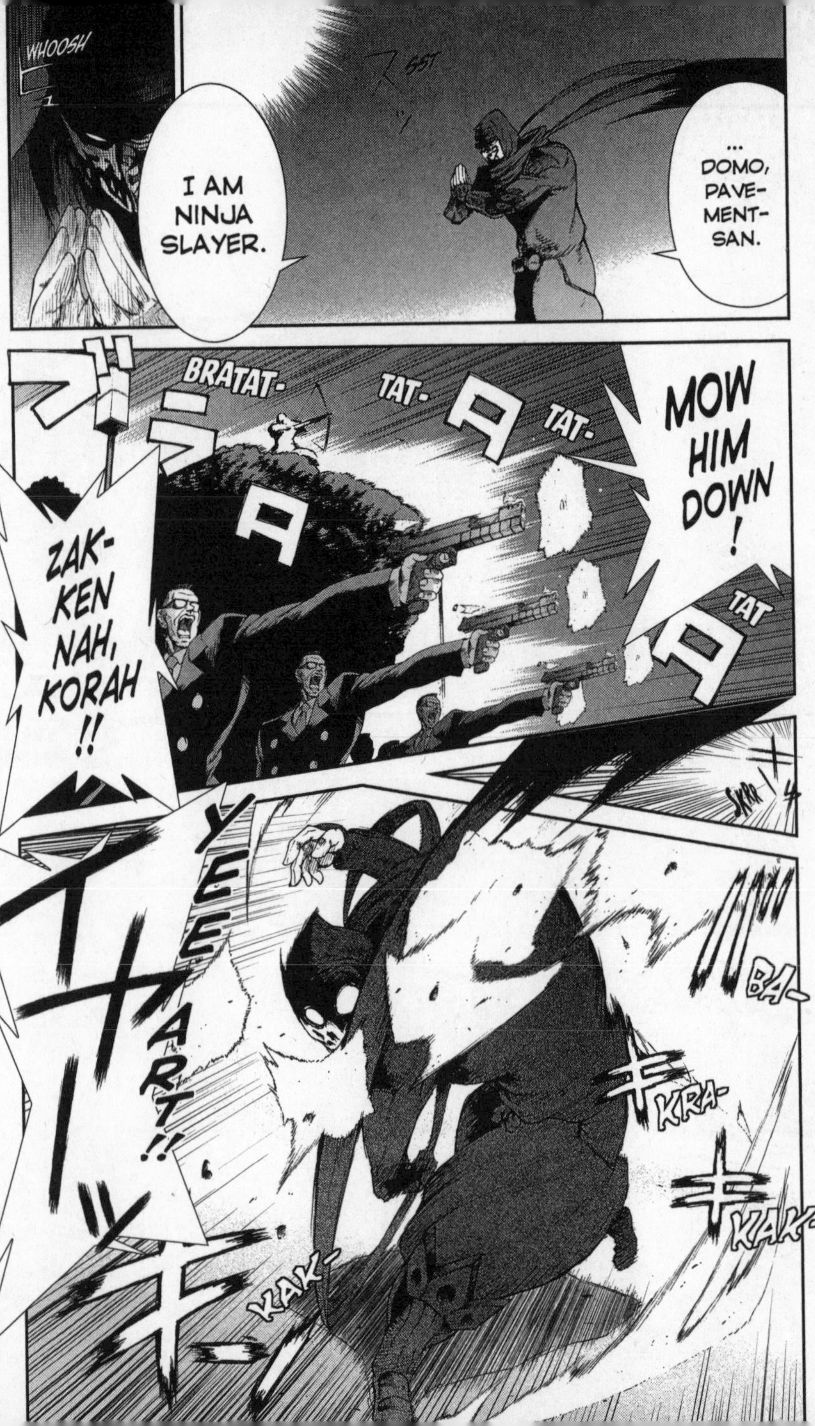
... DOMO, PAVE-MENT-SAN.
SST
WHOOSH
I AM NINJA SLAYER.
MOW HIM DOWN!
TAT-
TAT-
BRATAT-
TAT
ZAK-KEN NAH, KORAH!!
SKRA
BA-
KRA-
KAK-
YEEEART!!
KAK-

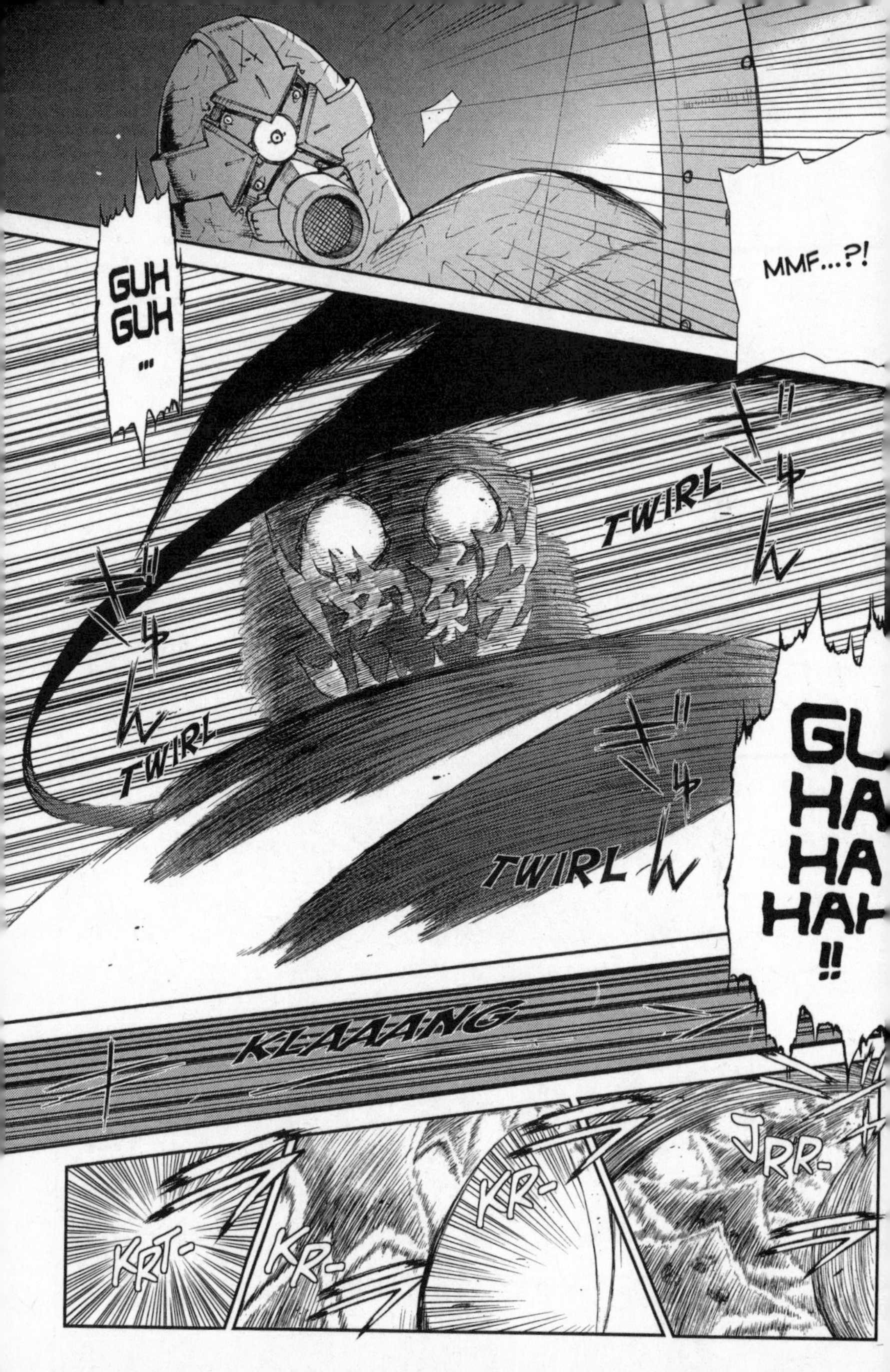
MMF...?!
GUH GUH ...
GUHAHAHAH!!
TWIRL
TWIRL
TWIRL
KLAAANG
JRR-
KR-
KR-
KRT-

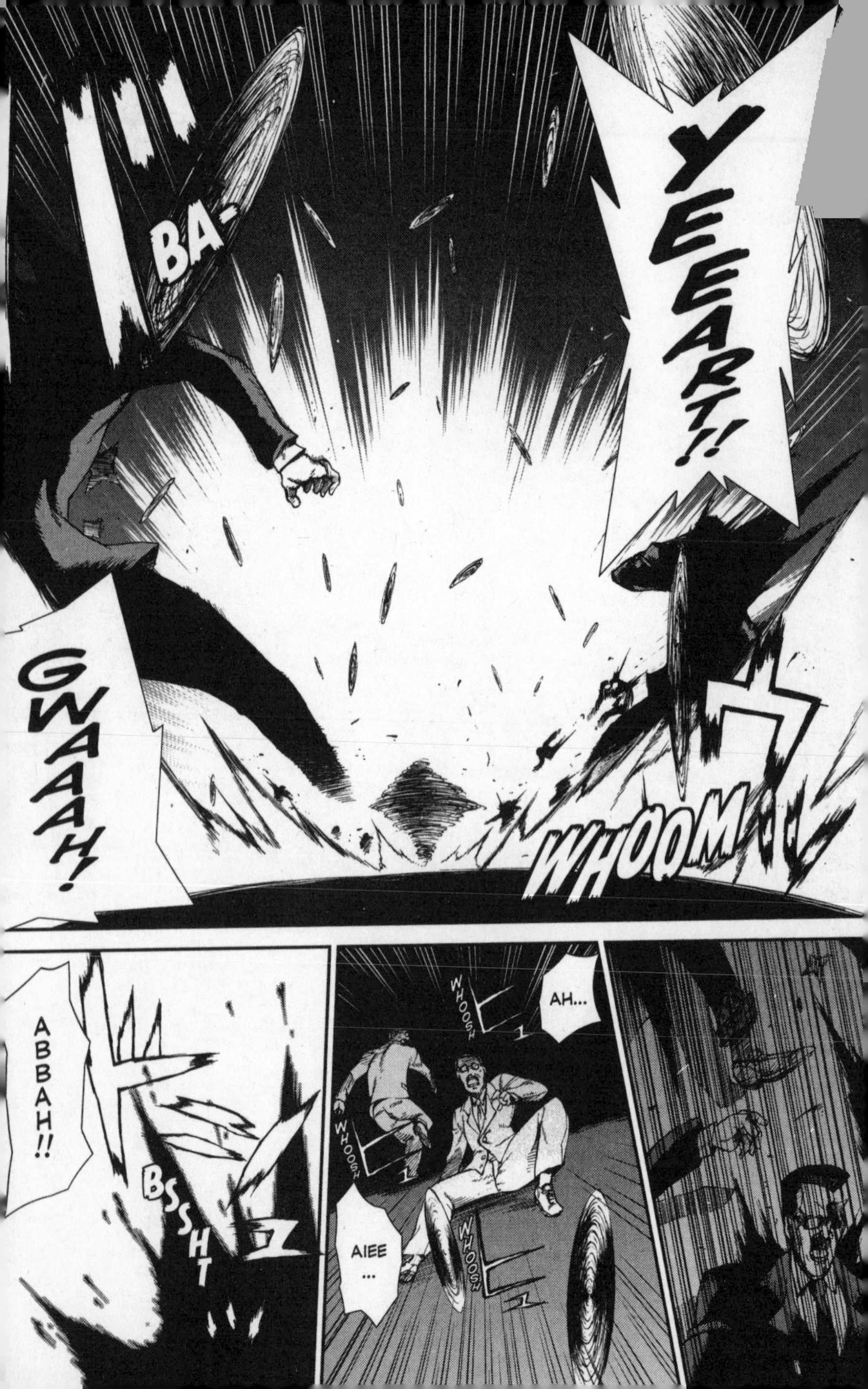

YEEART!!
BA-
WHOOM
GWAAAH!
AH...
WHOOSH
WHOOSH
WHOOSH
AIEE ...
ABBAH!!
BSSHT

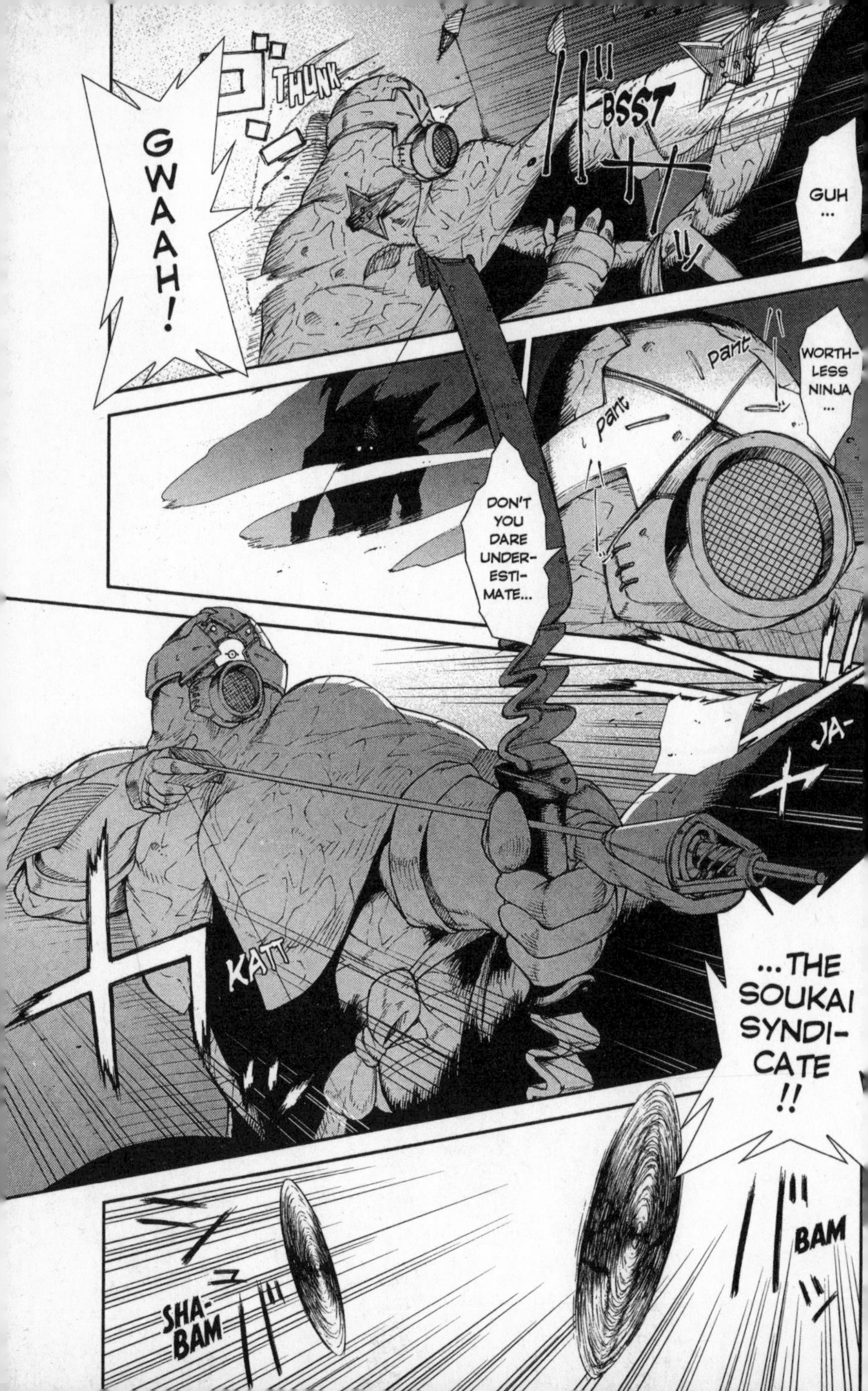
GUH ...
BSST
THUNK
GWAAH!
WORTH-LESS NINJA ...
pant
pant
DON'T YOU DARE UNDER-ESTI-MATE...
JA-
KATT
...THE SOUKAI SYNDI-CATE !!
BAM
SHA-BAM

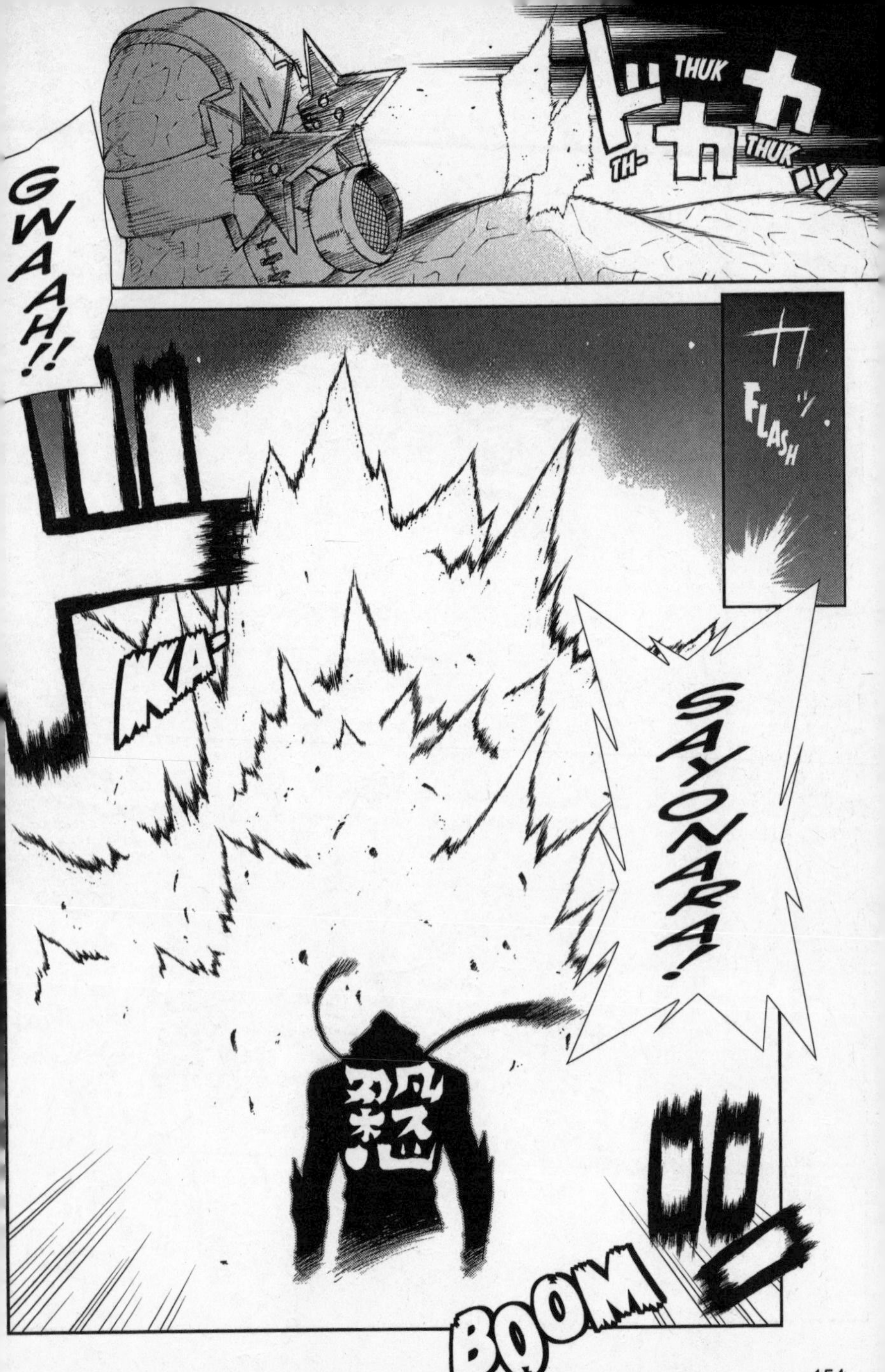
ドカカッ
THUK
TH-
THUK
GWAAH!!
カッ
FLASH
SAYONARA!
KA-
BOOM

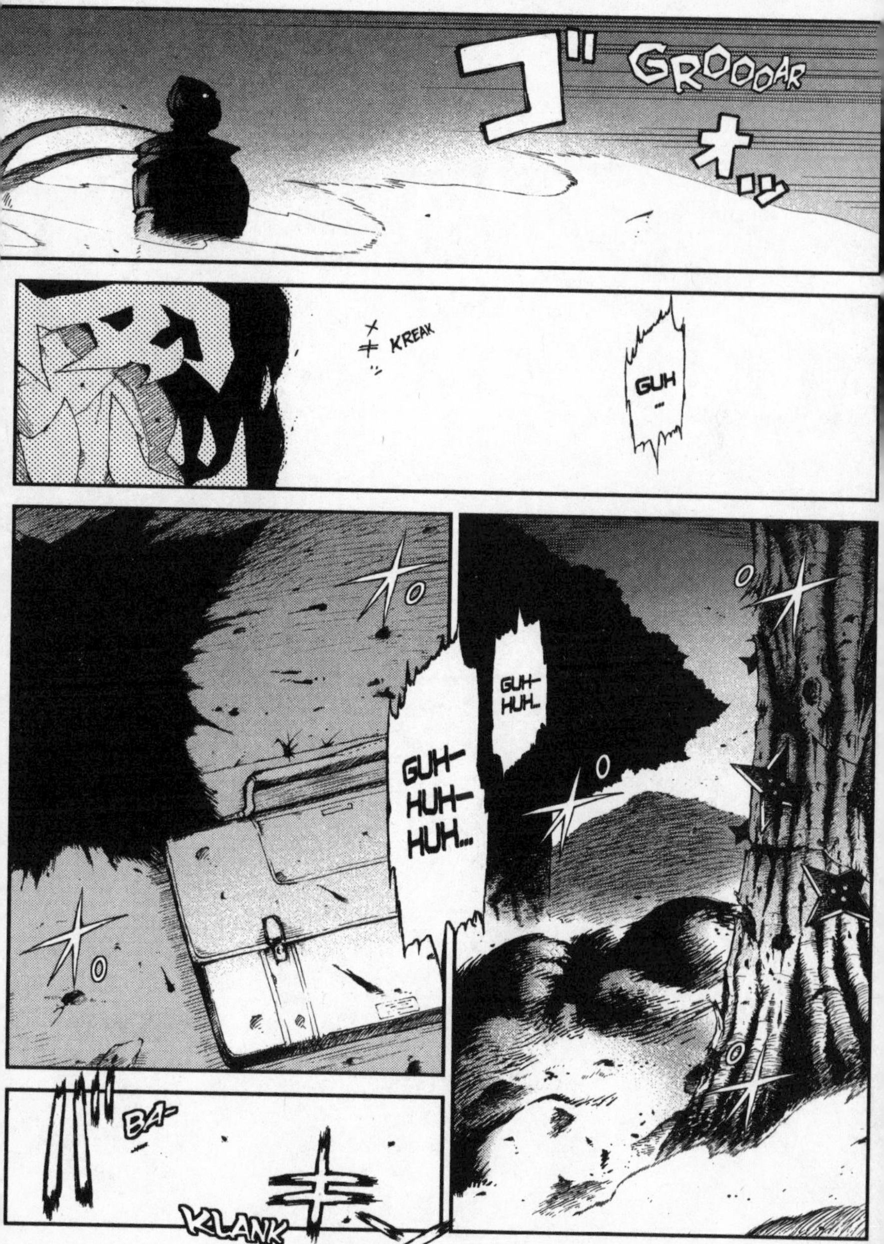
ゴオッ
GROOOAR
GUH...
KREAK
GUH-HUH...
GUH-HUH-HUH...
BA-
KLANK

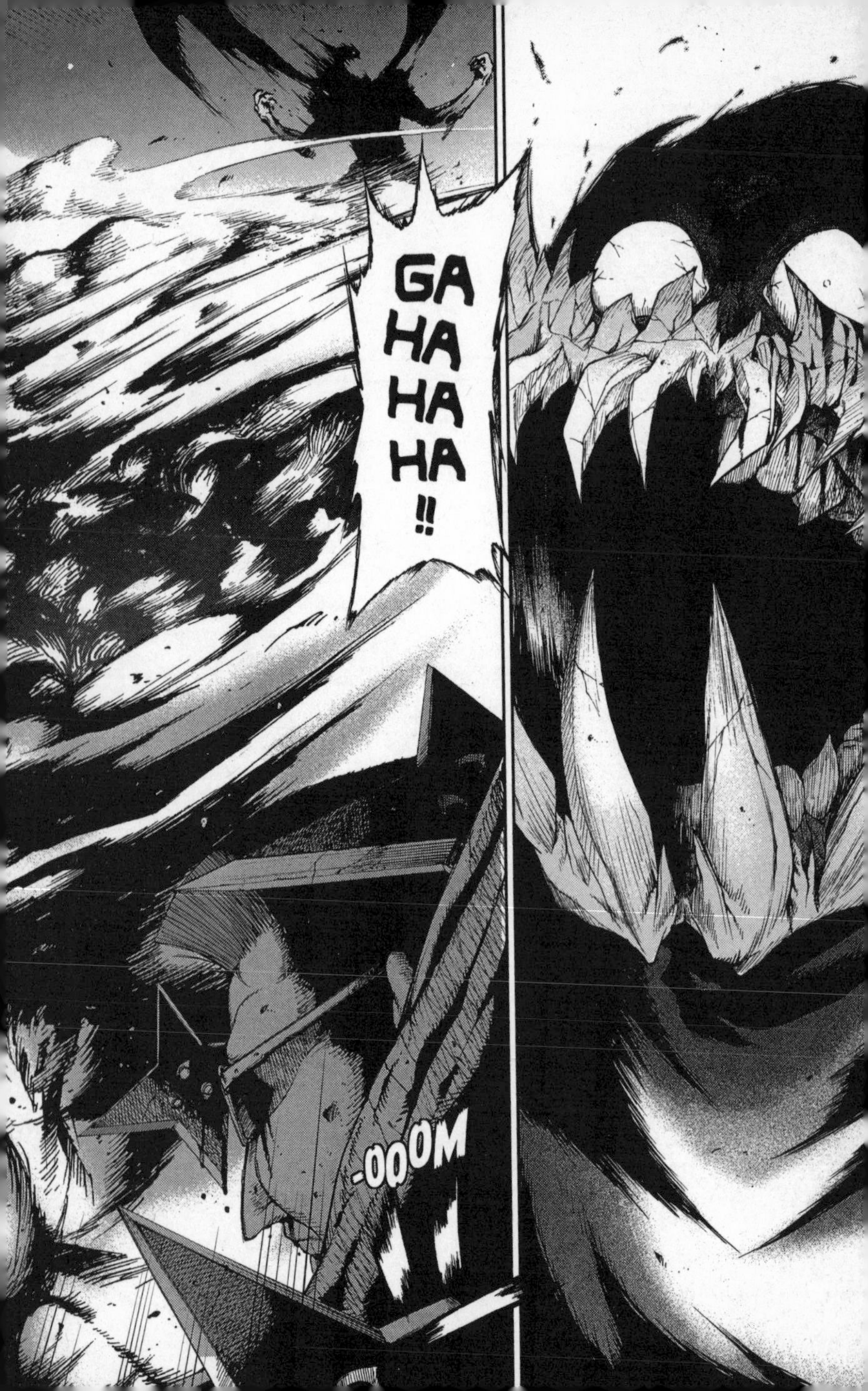
GA HA HA HA!!
-OOOM

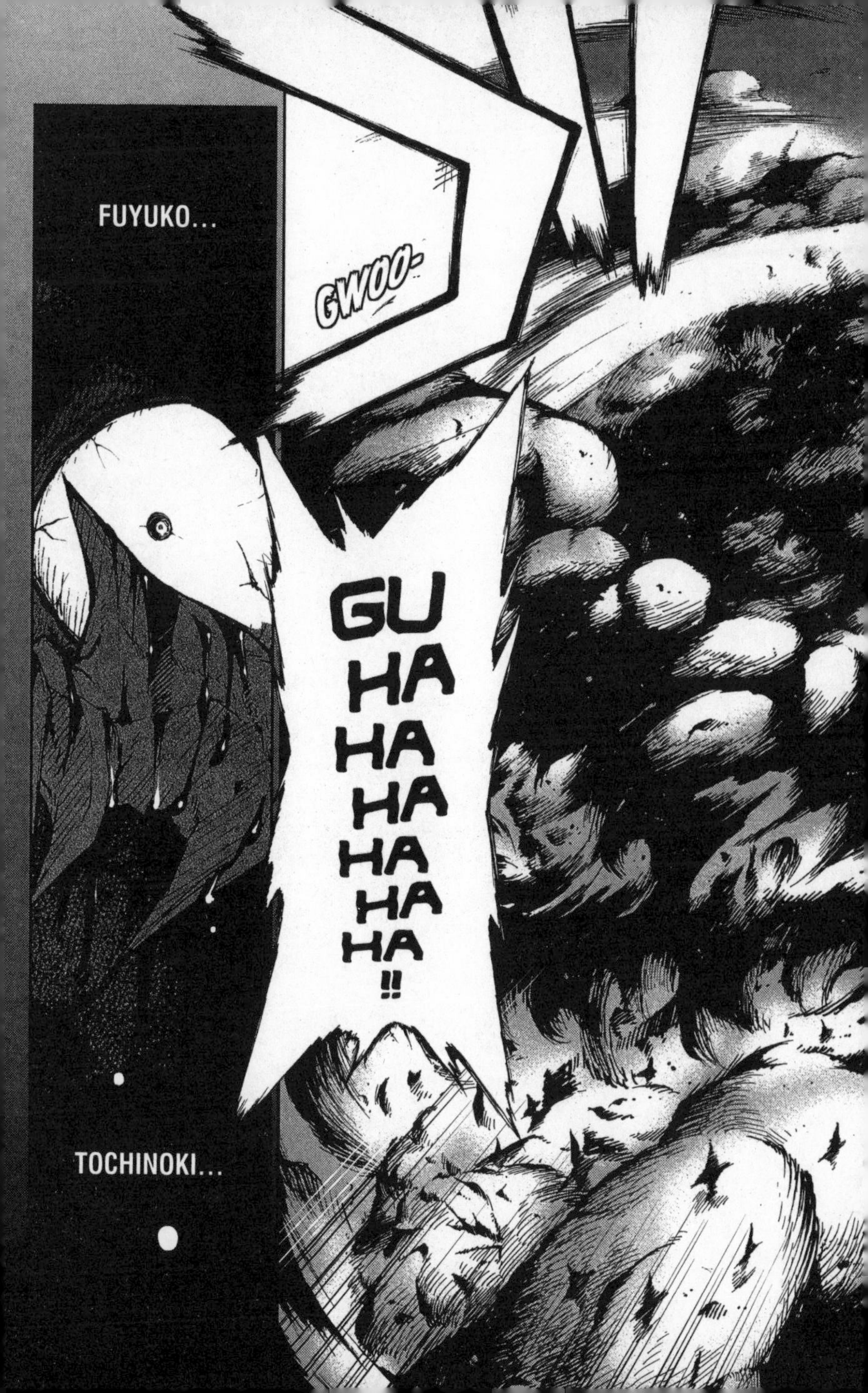
GWOO-
GU HA HA HA HA HA HA HA!!
FUYUKO...
TOCHINOKI...

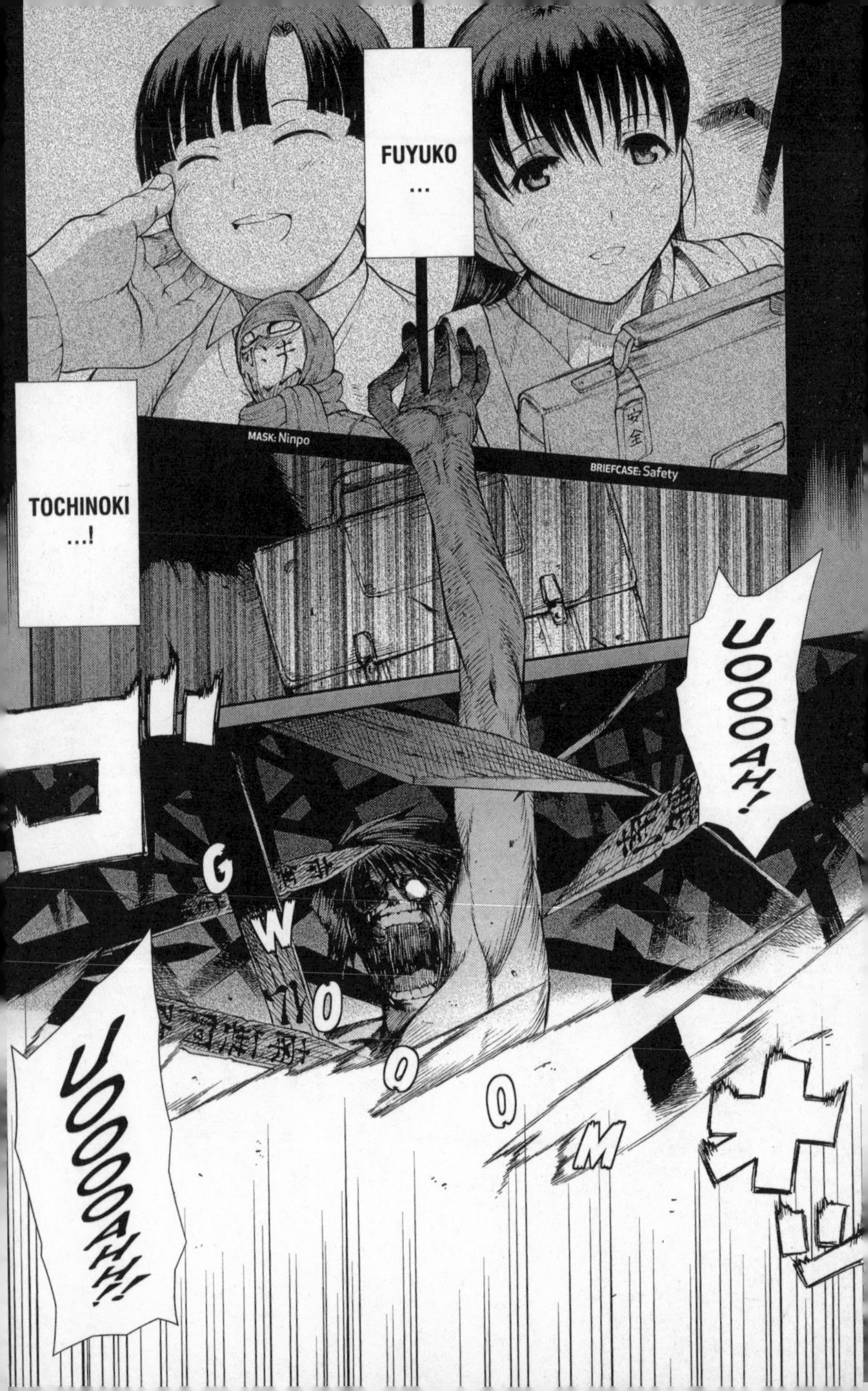
FUYUKO ...
BRIEFCASE: Safety
MASK: Ninpo
TOCHINOKI ...!
UOOOAH!
GWOOOOM
UOOOOAHH!

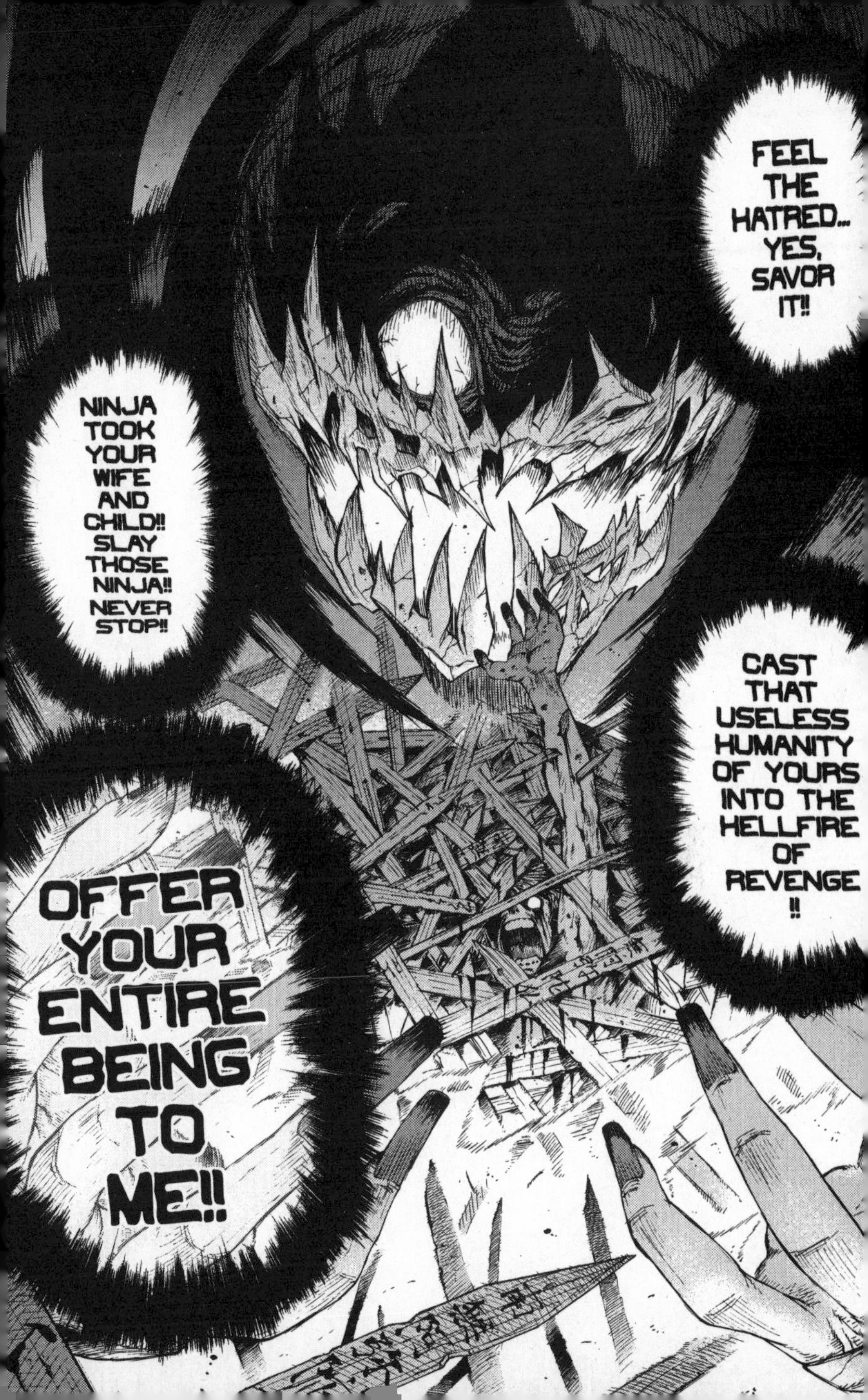
FEEL THE HATRED... YES, SAVOR IT!!
NINJA TOOK YOUR WIFE AND CHILD!! SLAY THOSE NINJA!! NEVER STOP!!
CAST THAT USELESS HUMANITY OF YOURS INTO THE HELLFIRE OF REVENGE!!
OFFER YOUR ENTIRE BEING TO ME!!

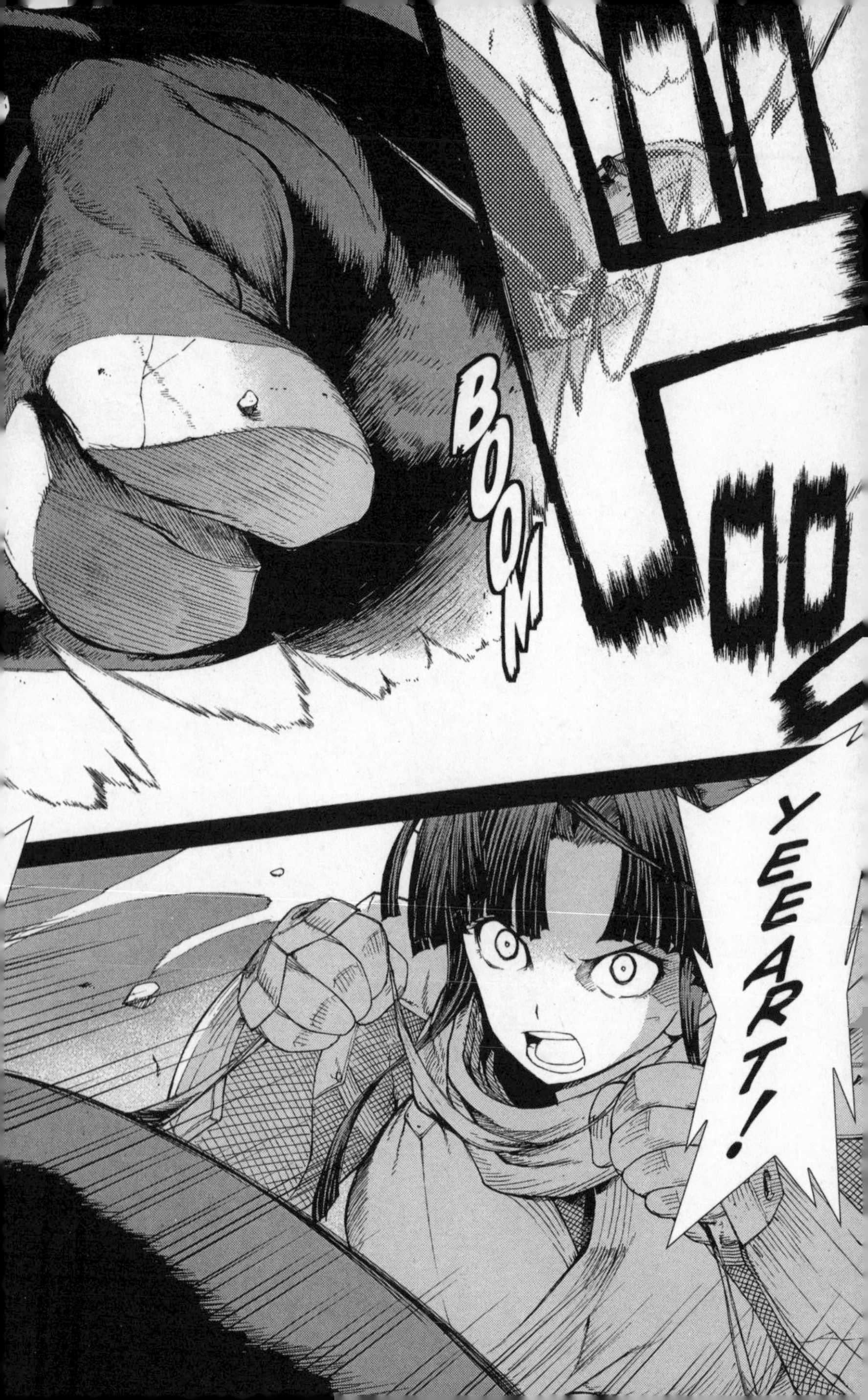
BOOM
YEEART!!

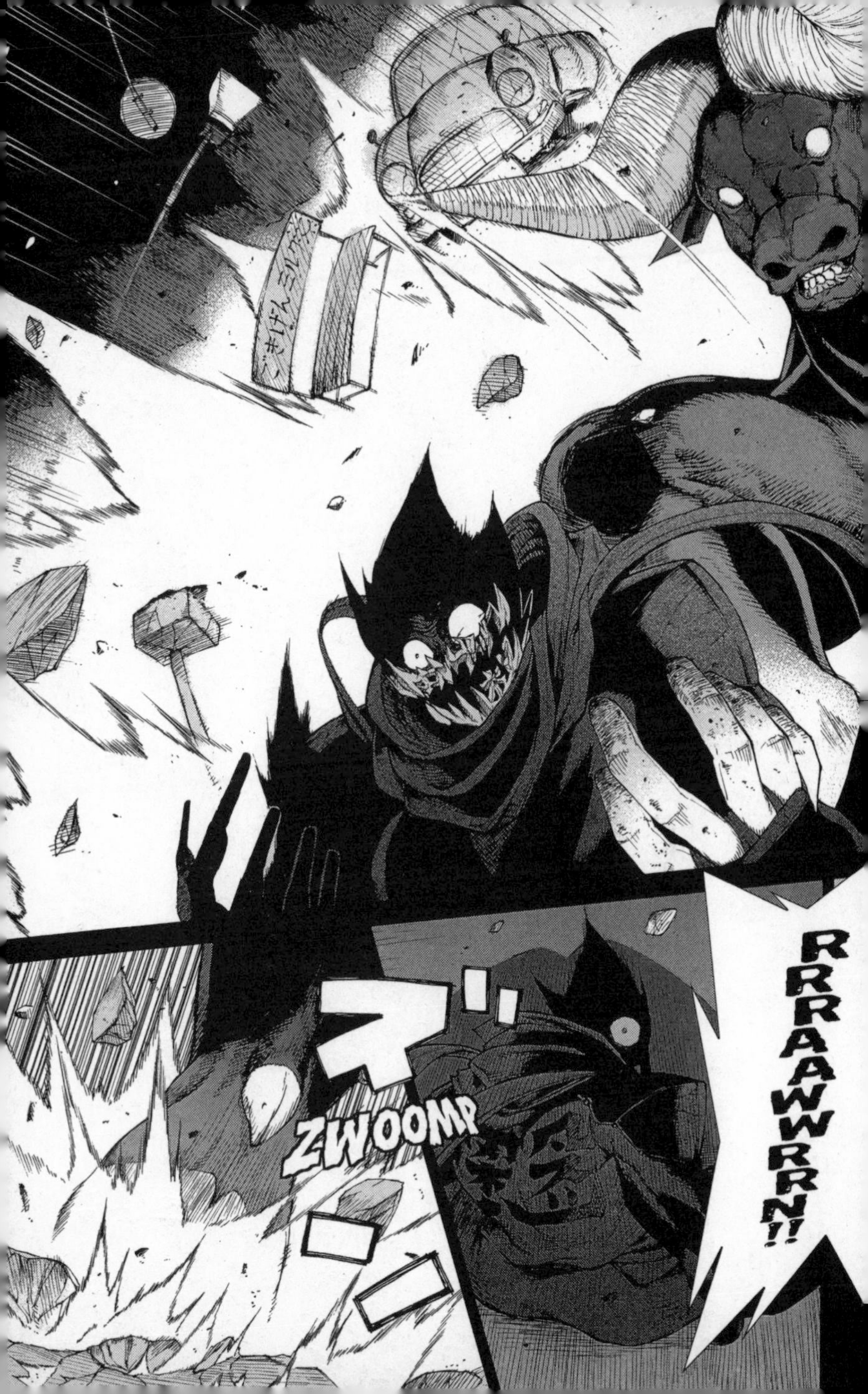
RRRAAWWRRN!!
ZWOOMP

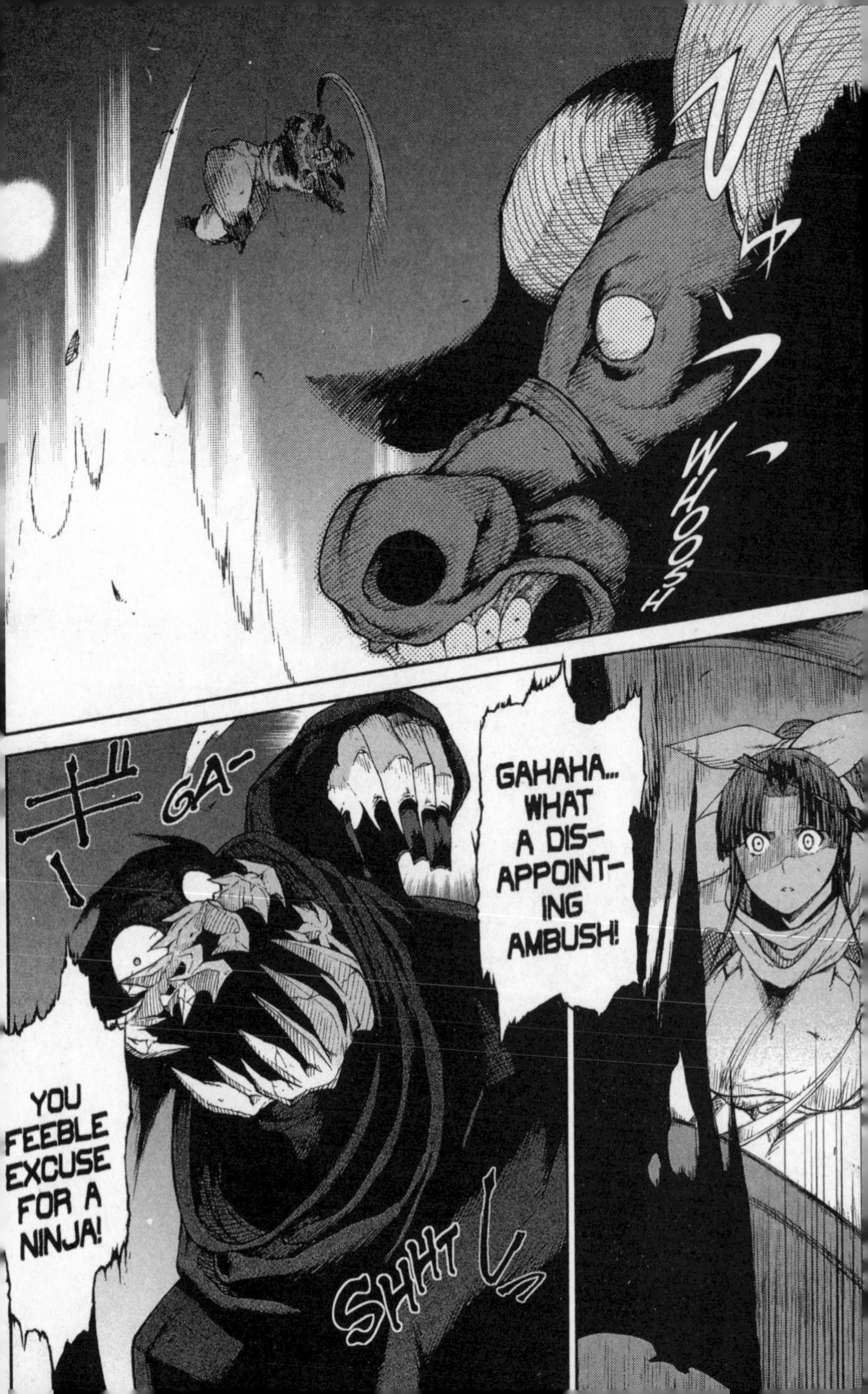
WHOOSH
GAHAHA... WHAT A DIS-APPOINTING AMBUSH!
GA-
YOU FEEBLE EXCUSE FOR A NINJA!
SHHT

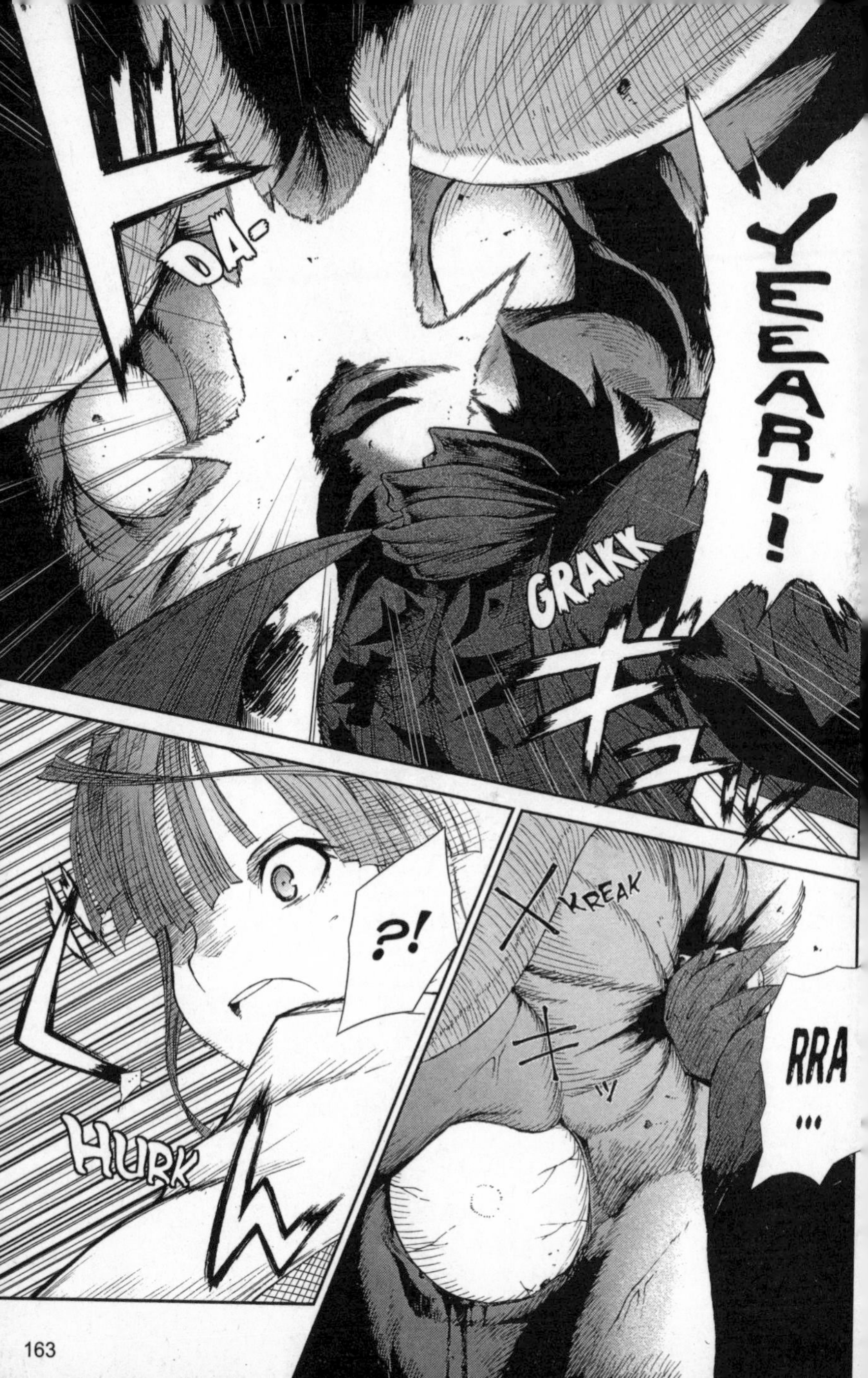

YEEART!
DA-
GRAKK
KREAK
RRA...
?!
HURK

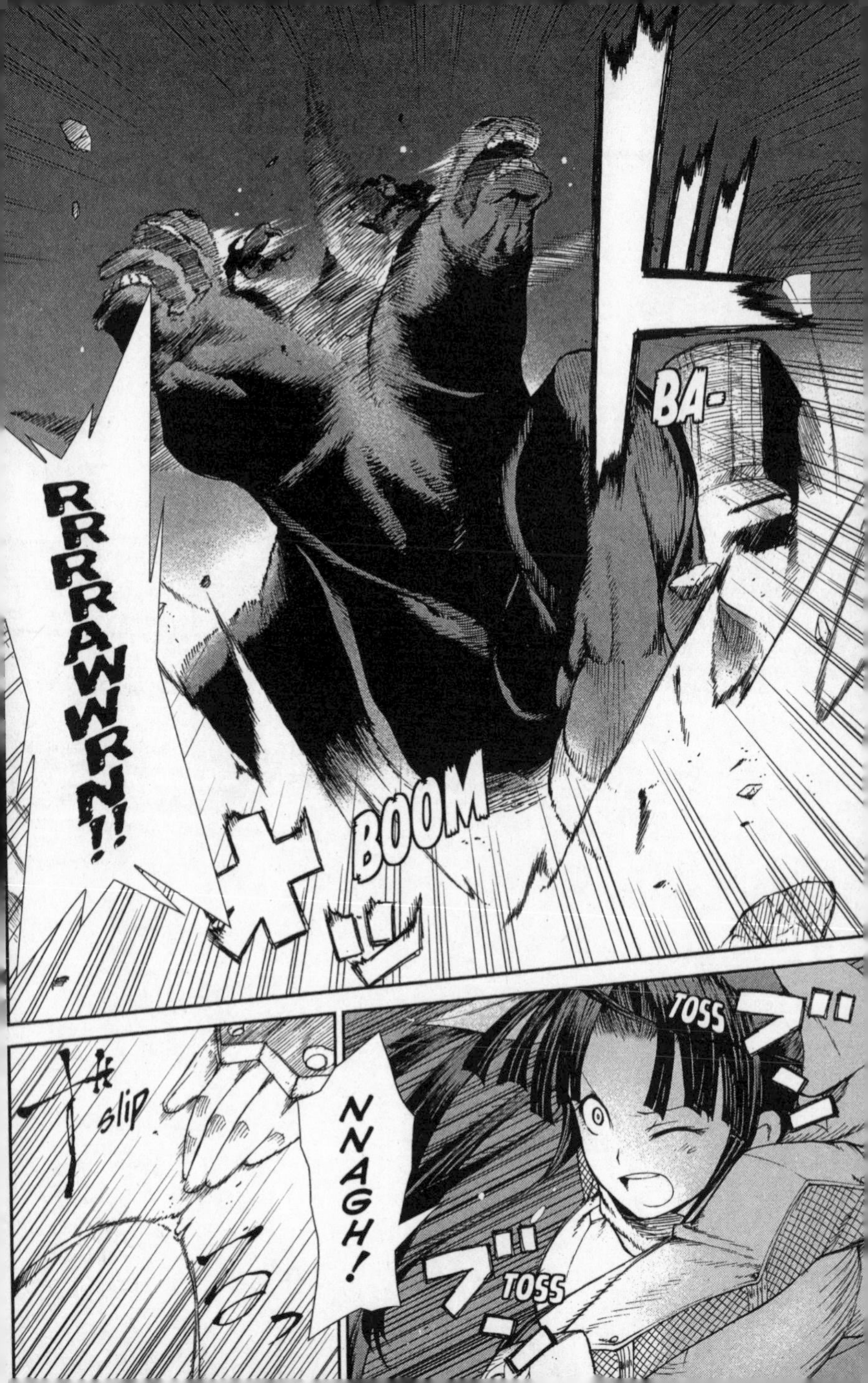
BA-
BOOM
RRRRAWWRN!!
TOSS
TOSS
NNAGH!
slip

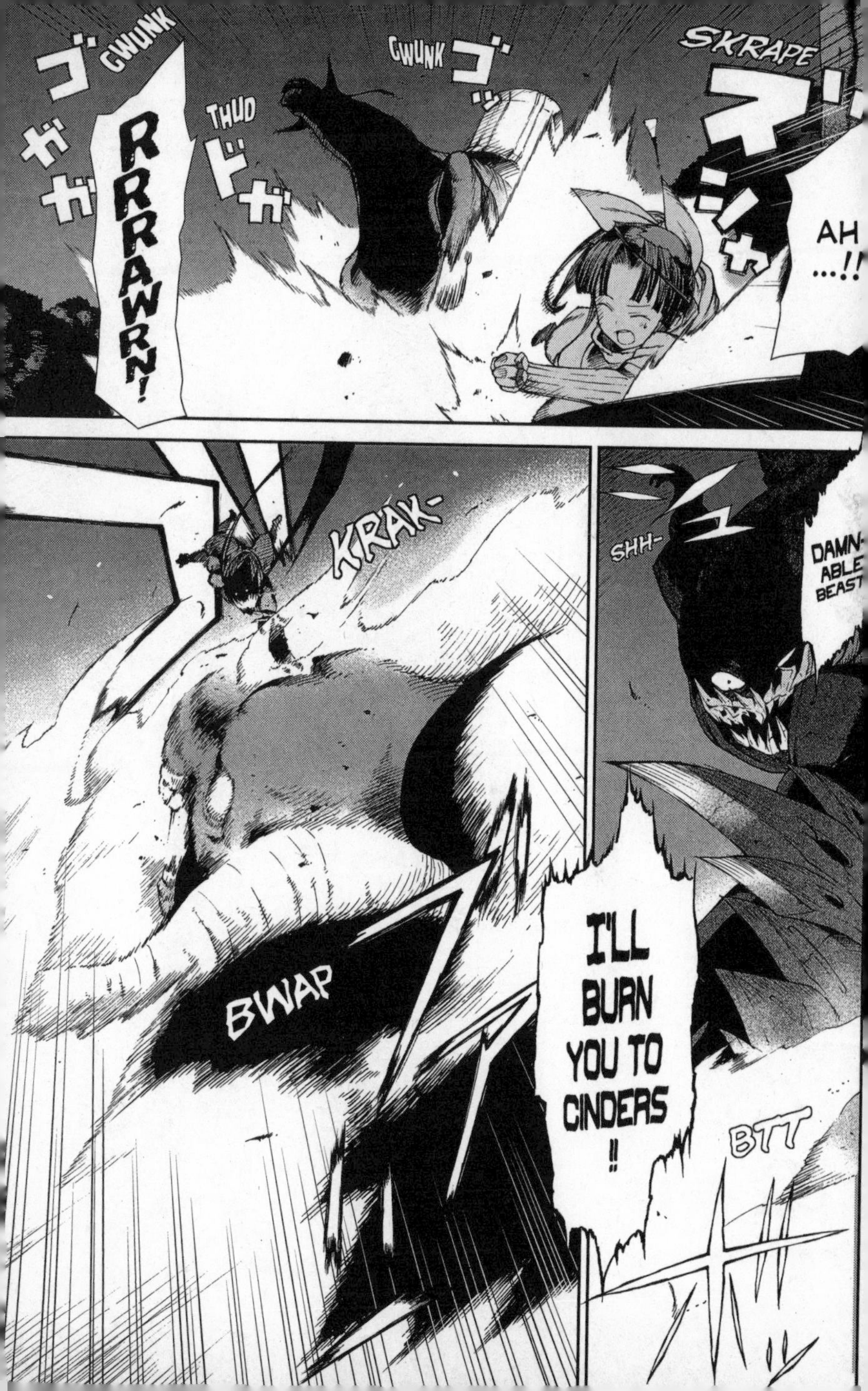
SKRAPE
AH ...!!
GWUNK
THUD
RRRAWRN!
GWUNK
SHH-
DAMN-ABLE BEAST
I'LL BURN YOU TO CINDERS !!
BTT
KRAK-
BWAP

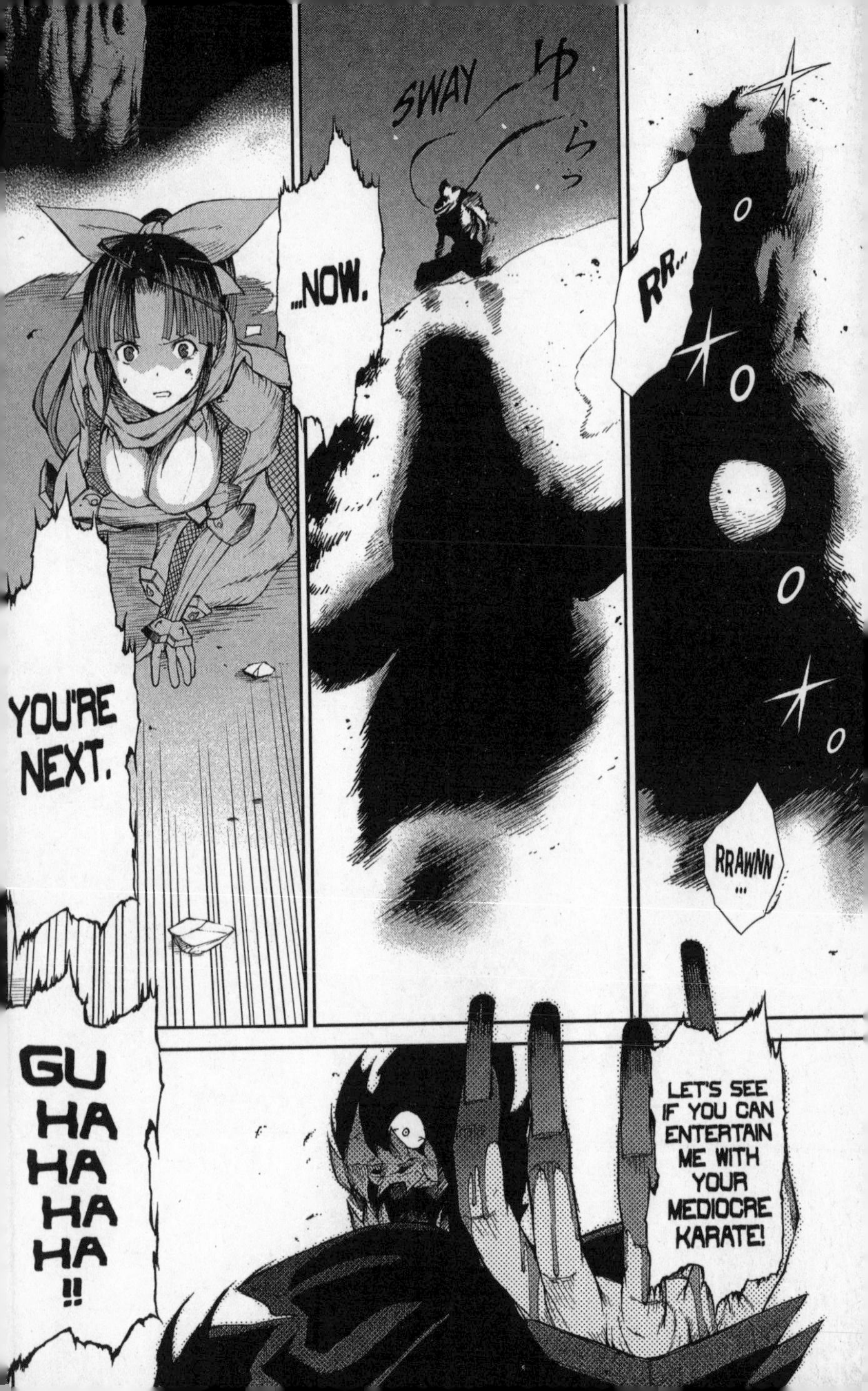
RR...
O
O
O
O
RRAWNN...
SWAY
ゆらっ
...NOW.
YOU'RE NEXT.
LET'S SEE IF YOU CAN ENTERTAIN ME WITH YOUR MEDIOCRE KARATE!
GU HA HA HA HA!!

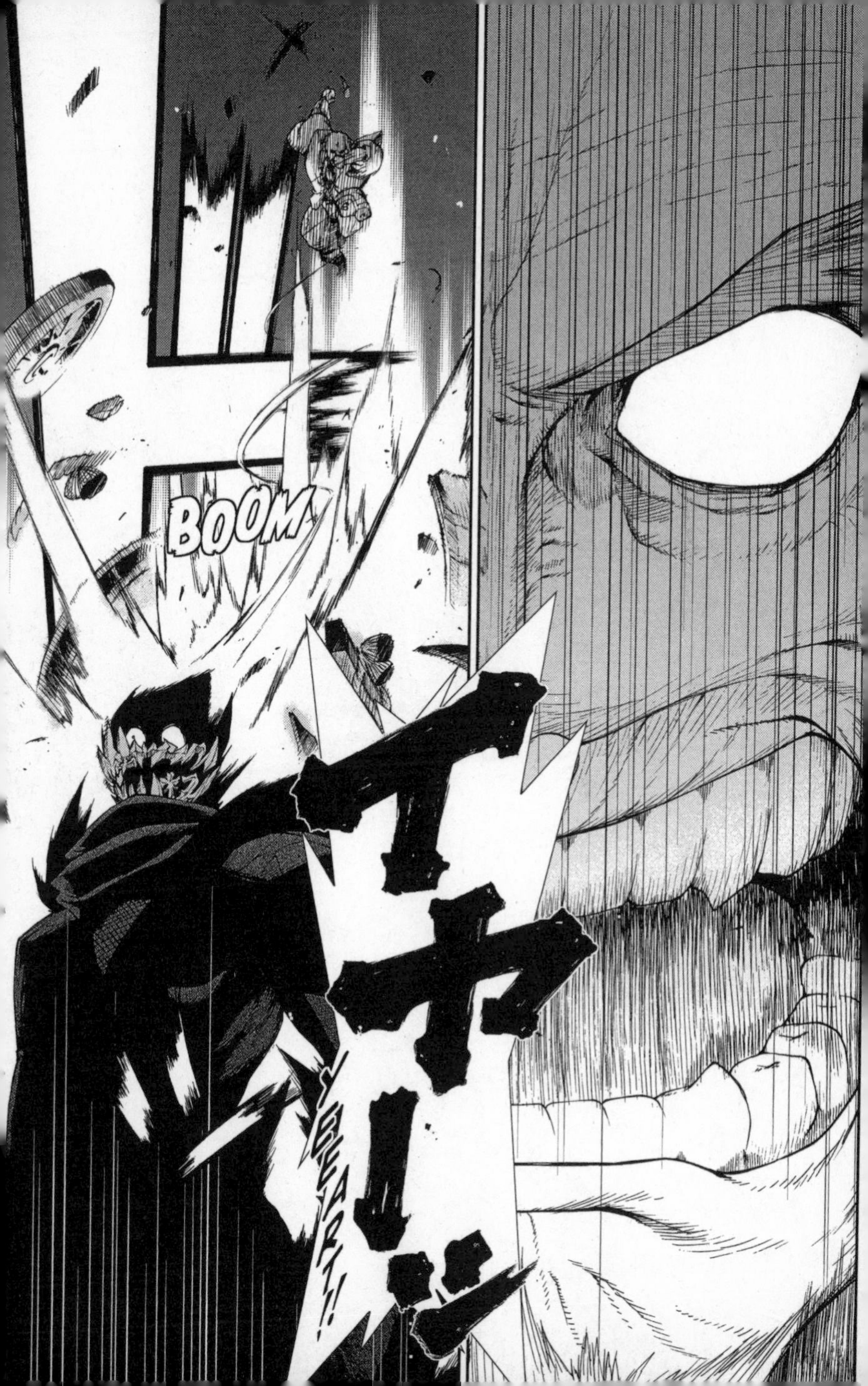
BOOM

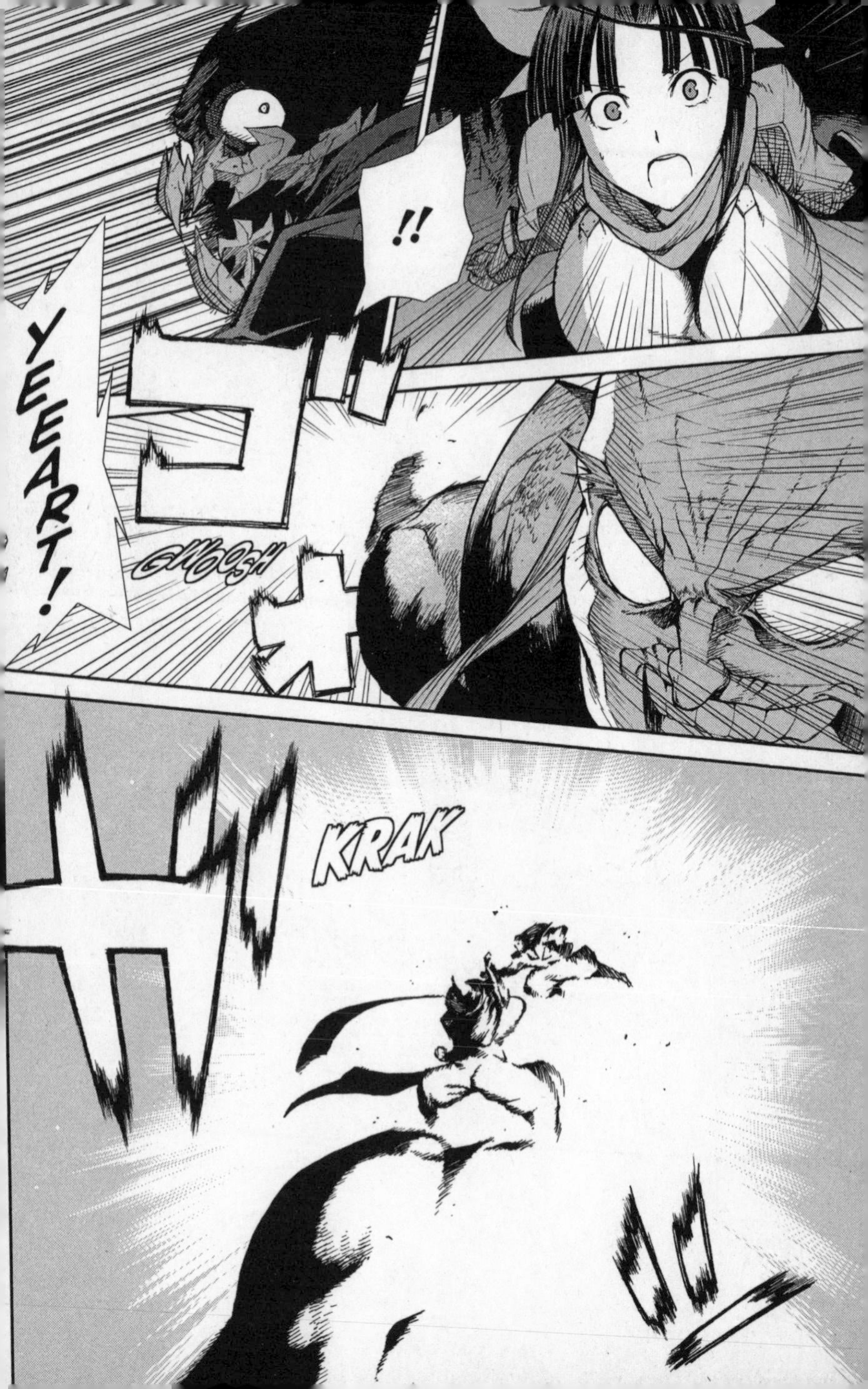
!!
YEEART!
GWOOSH
KRAK

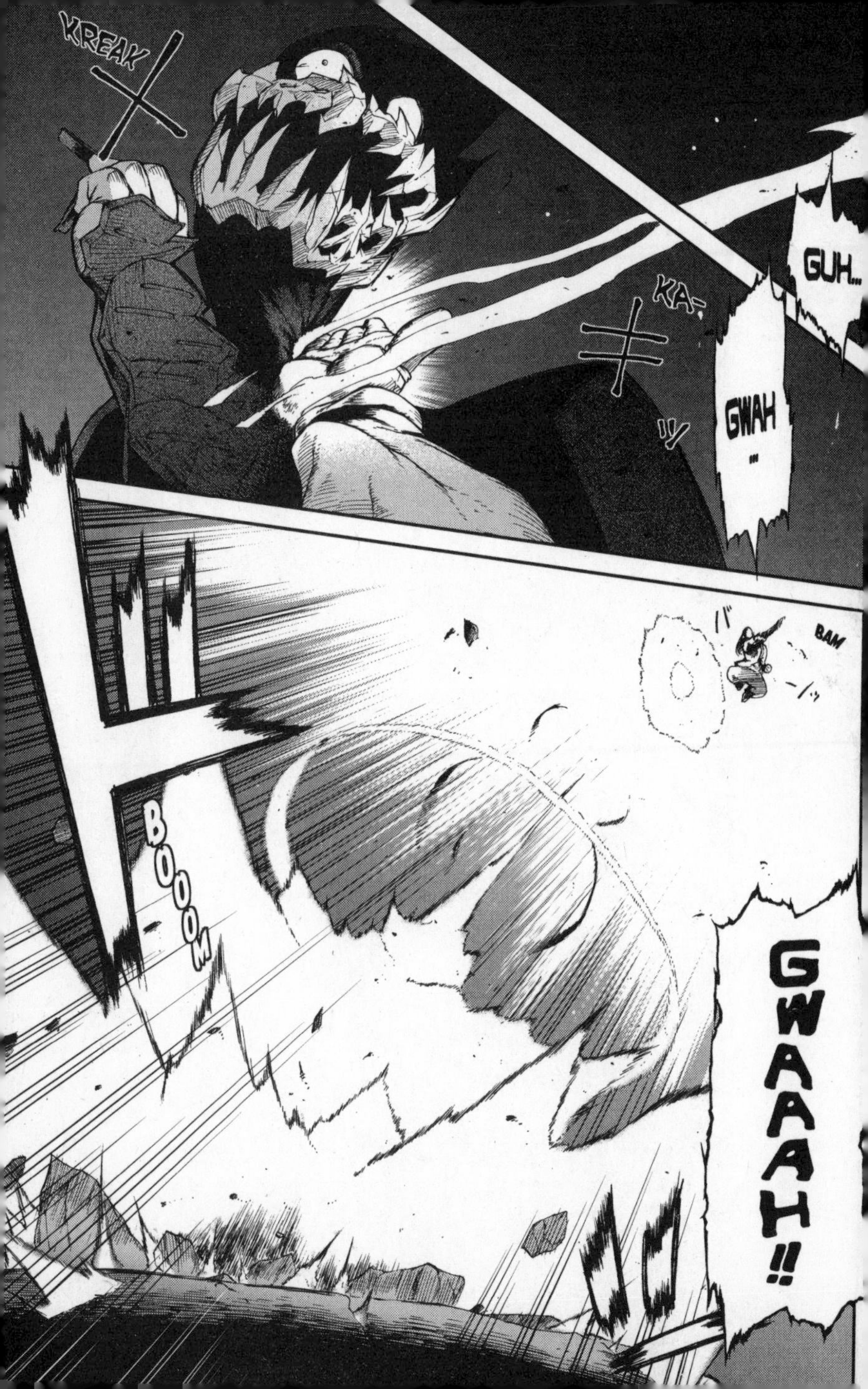
GUH...
GWAH ...
KA-
KREAK
BAM
GWAAAH!!
BOOOM

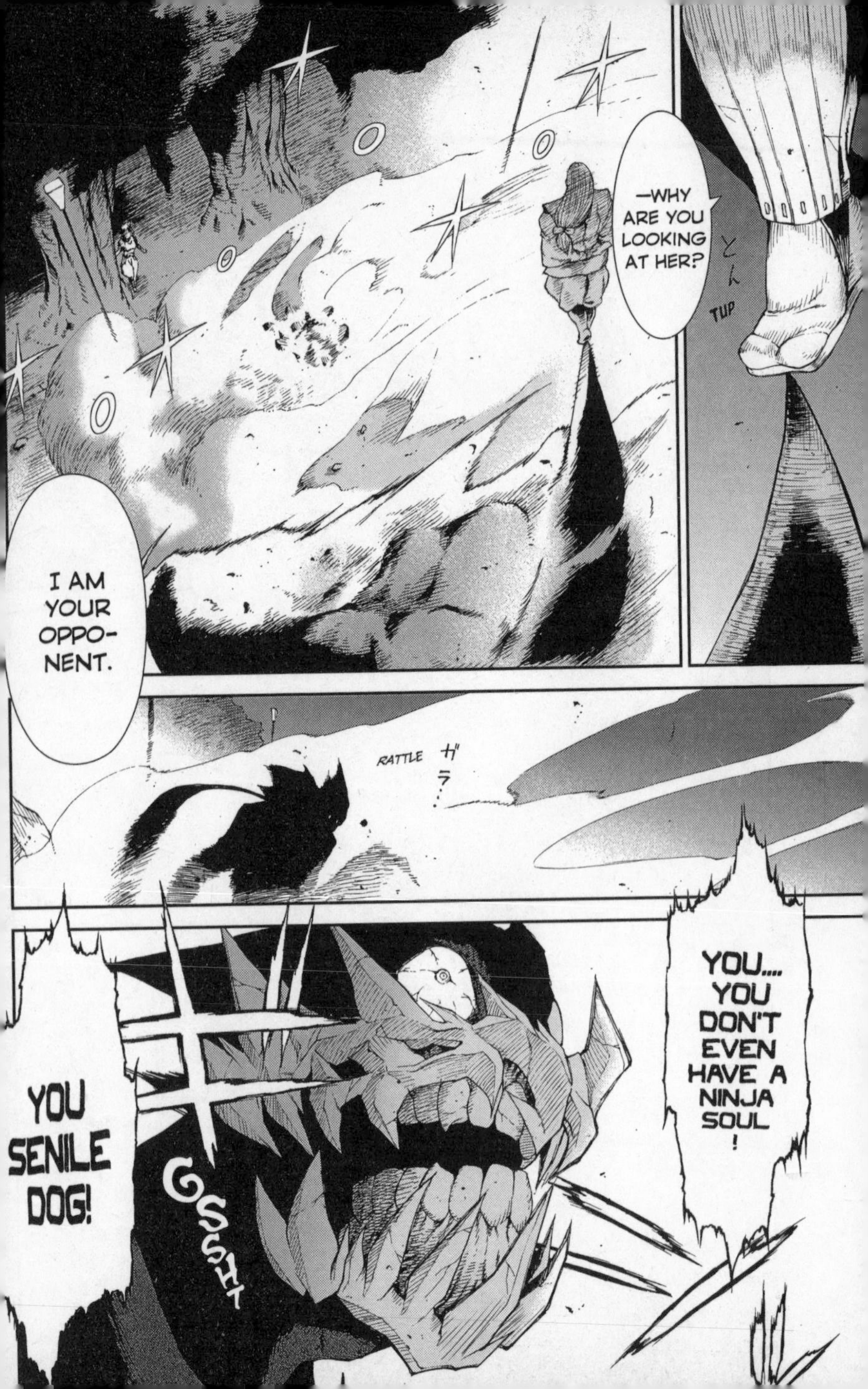
—WHY ARE YOU LOOKING AT HER?
とん
TUP
I AM YOUR OPPO- NENT.
ガラ…
RATTLE
YOU.... YOU DON'T EVEN HAVE A NINJA SOUL !
GSSHK
YOU SENILE DOG!

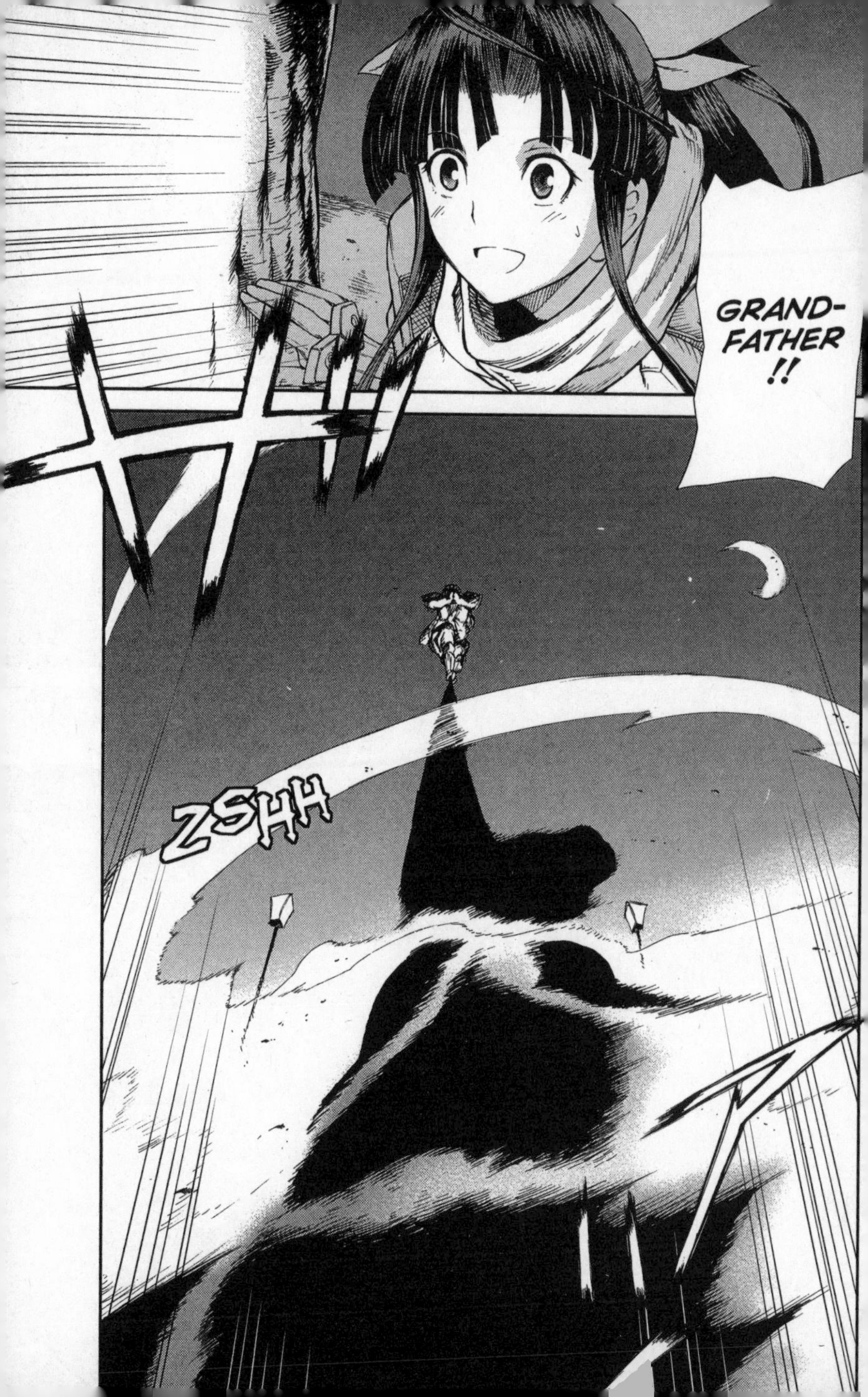
GRAND-FATHER !!
ZSHH

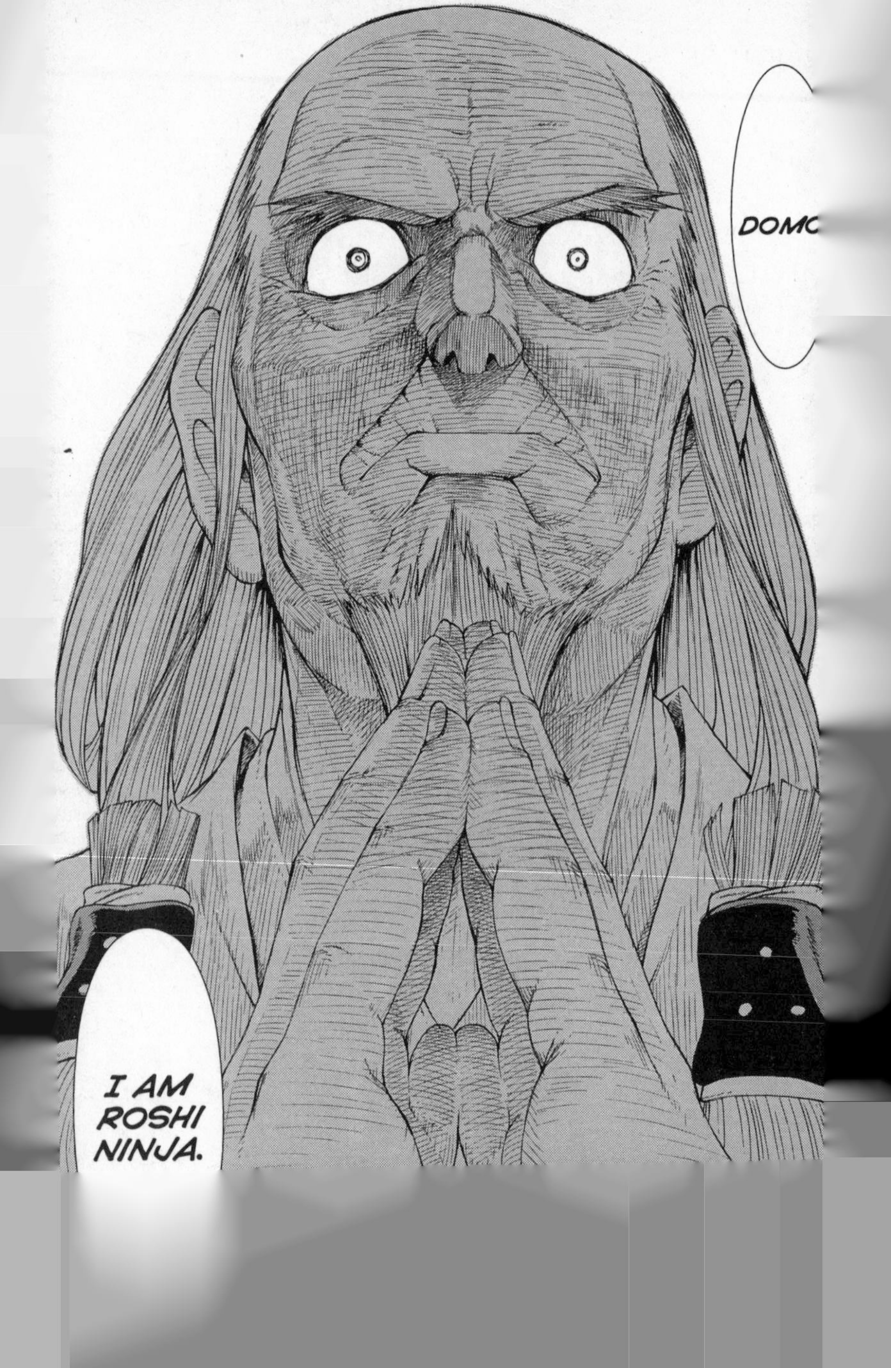
DOMO
I AM ROSHI NINJA.

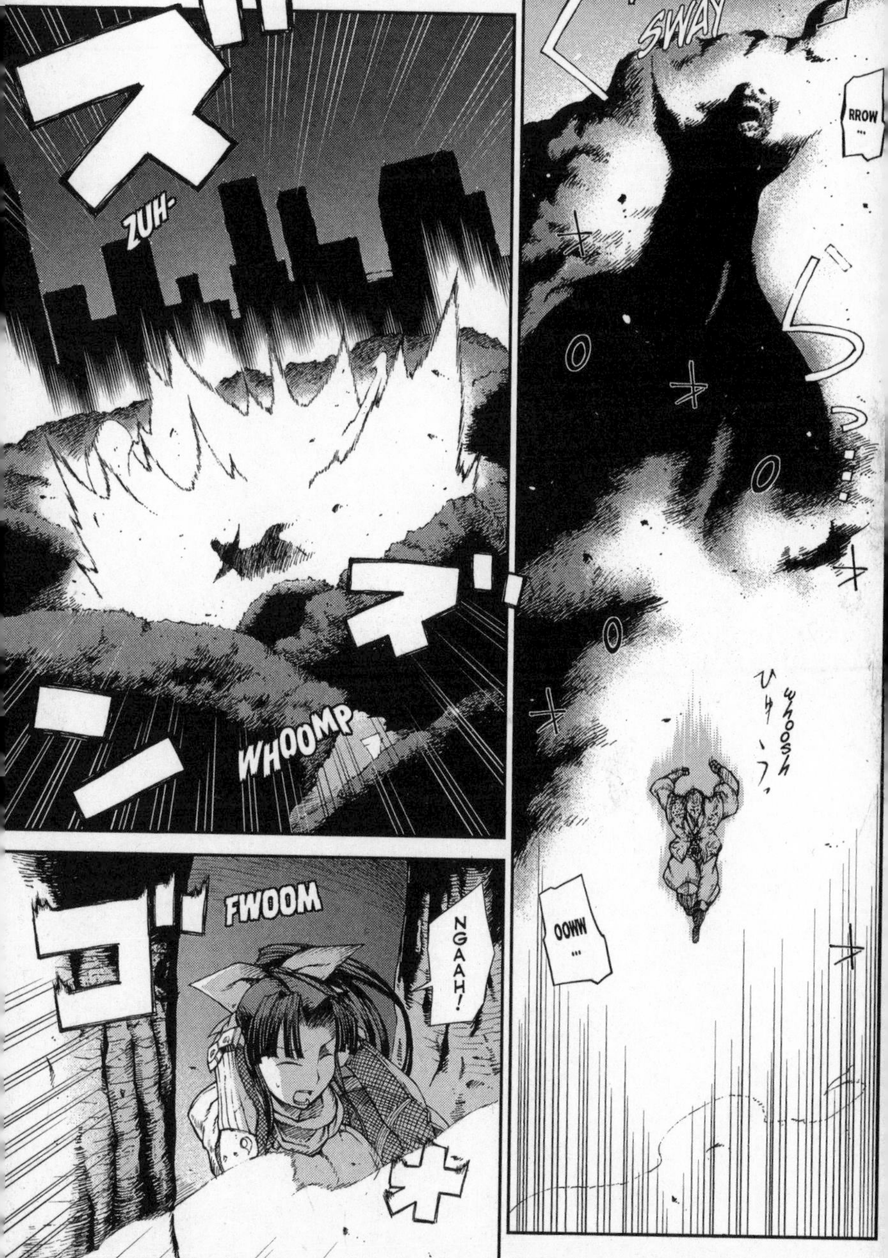
SWAY
RROW...
whoosh
OOWW...
ZUH-
WHOOMP
FWOOM
NGAAH!

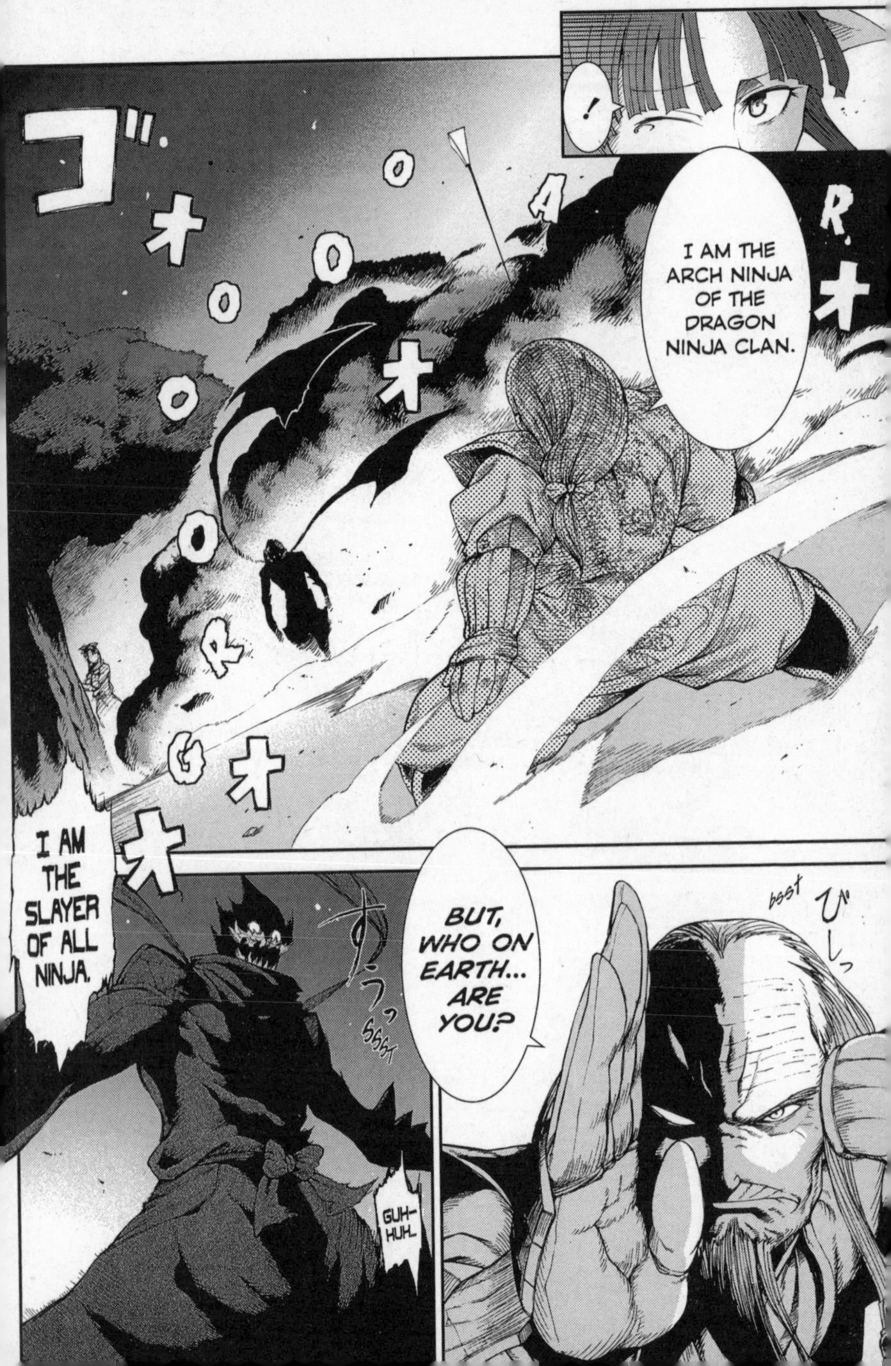

!
I AM THE ARCH NINJA OF THE DRAGON NINJA CLAN.
ゴオオオオオ
GROOOOOAR
bsst
びしっ
BUT, WHO ON EARTH... ARE YOU?
I AM THE SLAYER OF ALL NINJA.
すうっ
SSST
GUH-HUH.

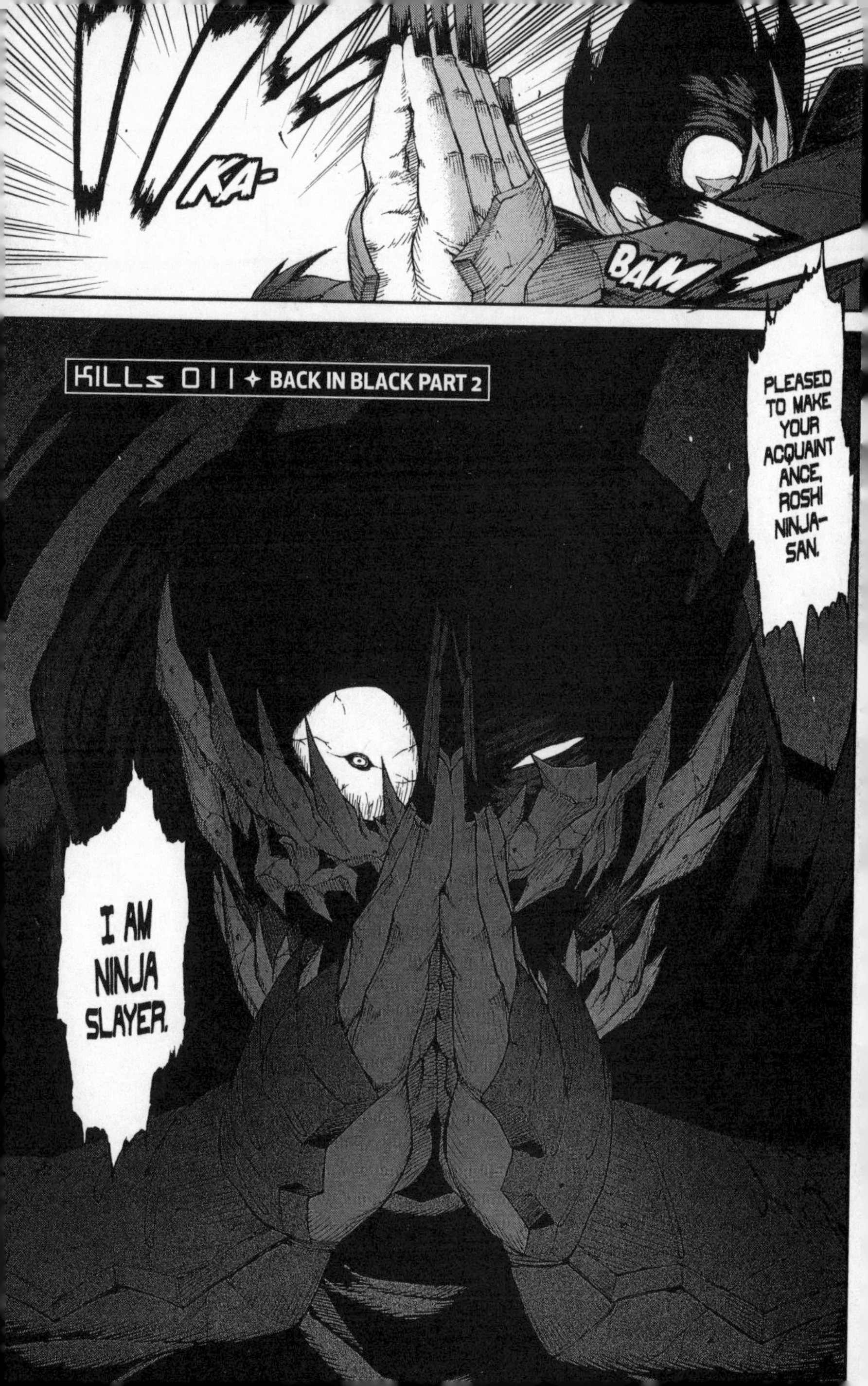
KA-
BAM
KILLs 011 ✦ BACK IN BLACK PART 2
PLEASED TO MAKE YOUR ACQUAINTANCE, ROSHI NINJA-SAN.
I AM NINJA SLAYER.

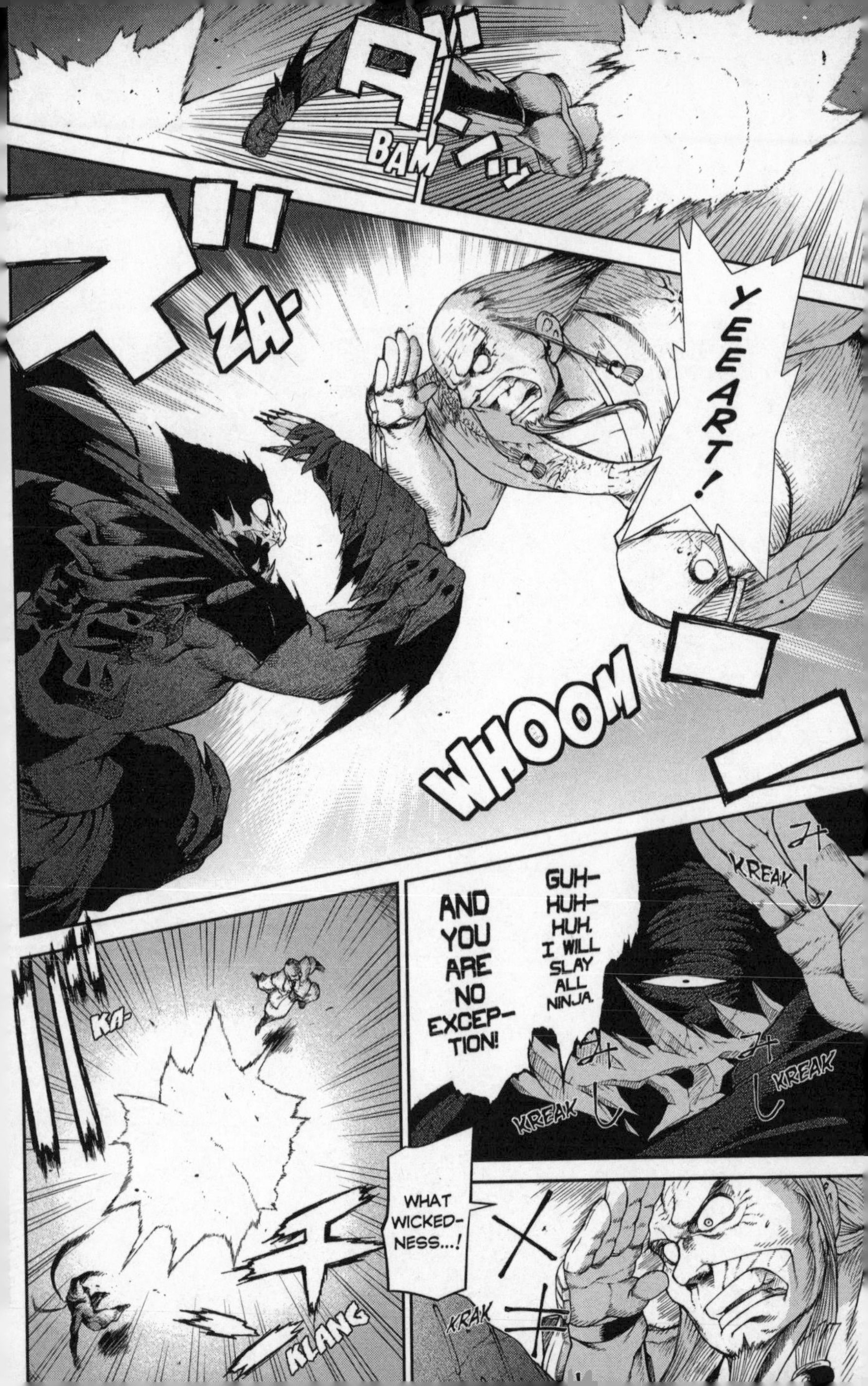
BAM
YEEART!
ZA-
WHOOM
KREAK
GUH-HUH-HUH. I WILL SLAY ALL NINJA.
AND YOU ARE NO EXCEPTION!
KREAK
KREAK
WHAT WICKEDNESS...!
KRAK
KA-
KLANG

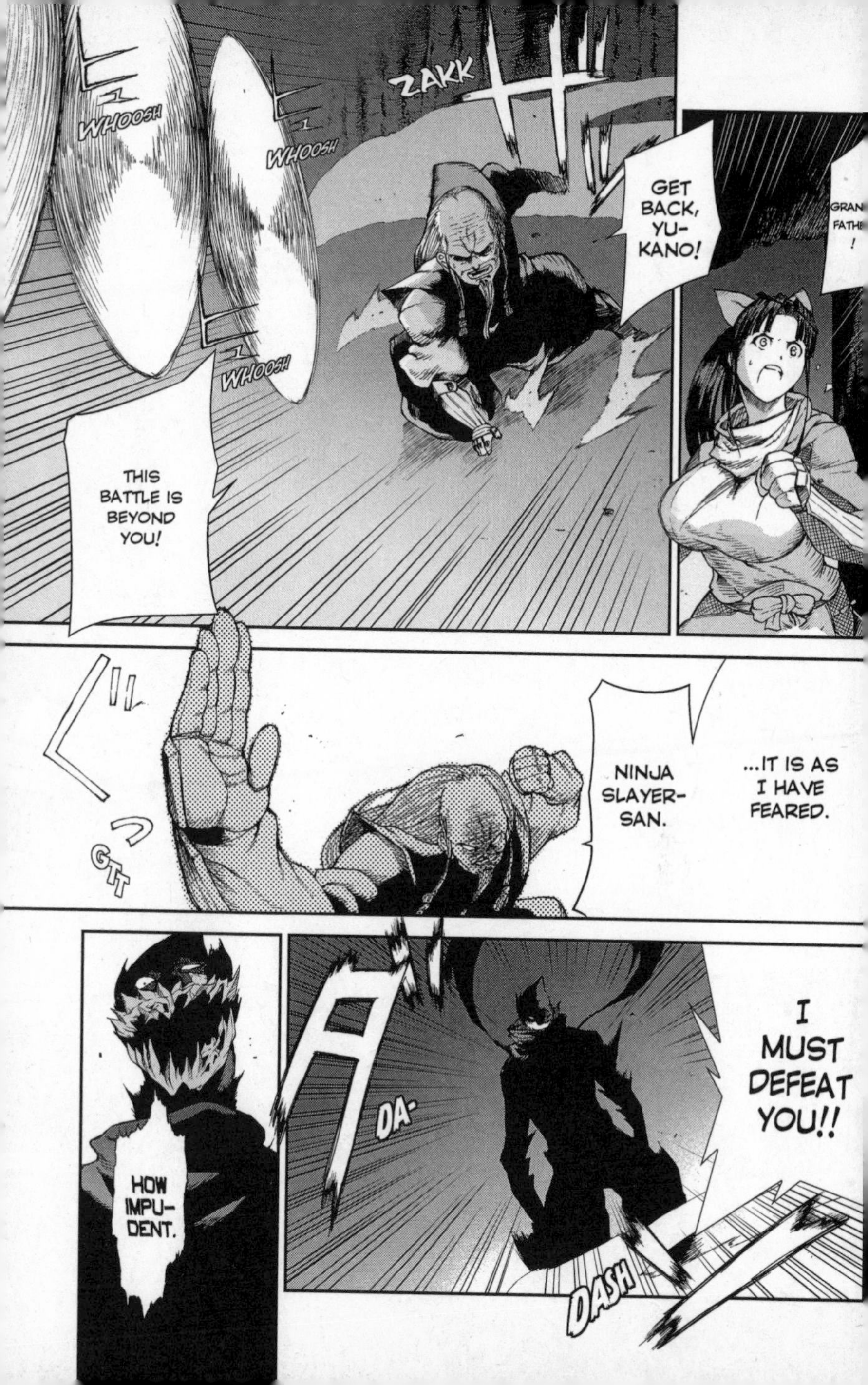
GRAN FATH !
GET BACK, YU-KANO!
ZAKK
WHOOSH
WHOOSH
WHOOSH
THIS BATTLE IS BEYOND YOU!
...IT IS AS I HAVE FEARED.
NINJA SLAYER-SAN.
GTT
I MUST DEFEAT YOU!!
DA-
DASH
HOW IMPU-DENT.

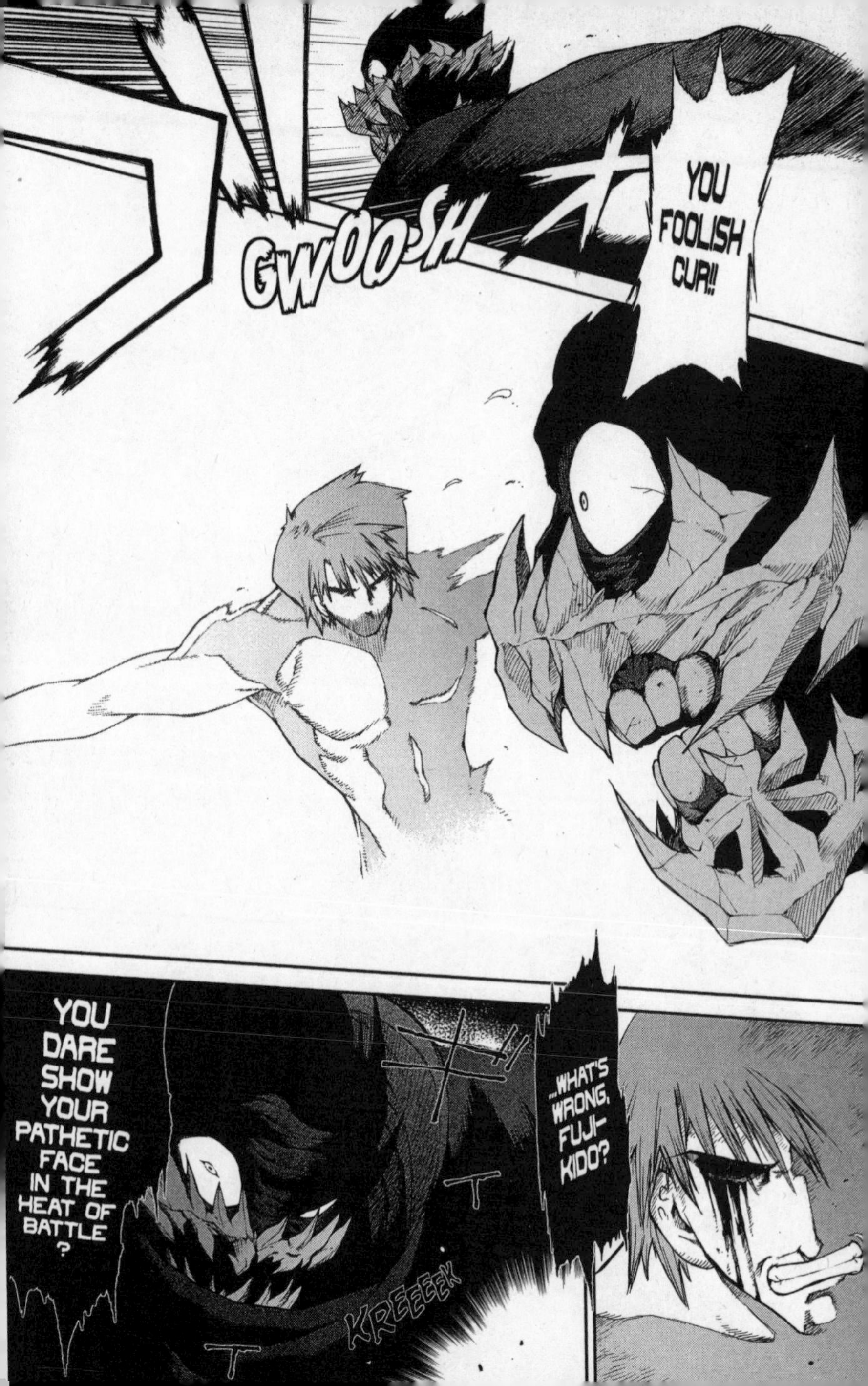
YOU FOOLISH CUR!!
GWOOSH
...WHAT'S WRONG, FUJI-KIDO?
YOU DARE SHOW YOUR PATHETIC FACE IN THE HEAT OF BATTLE?
KREEEEK

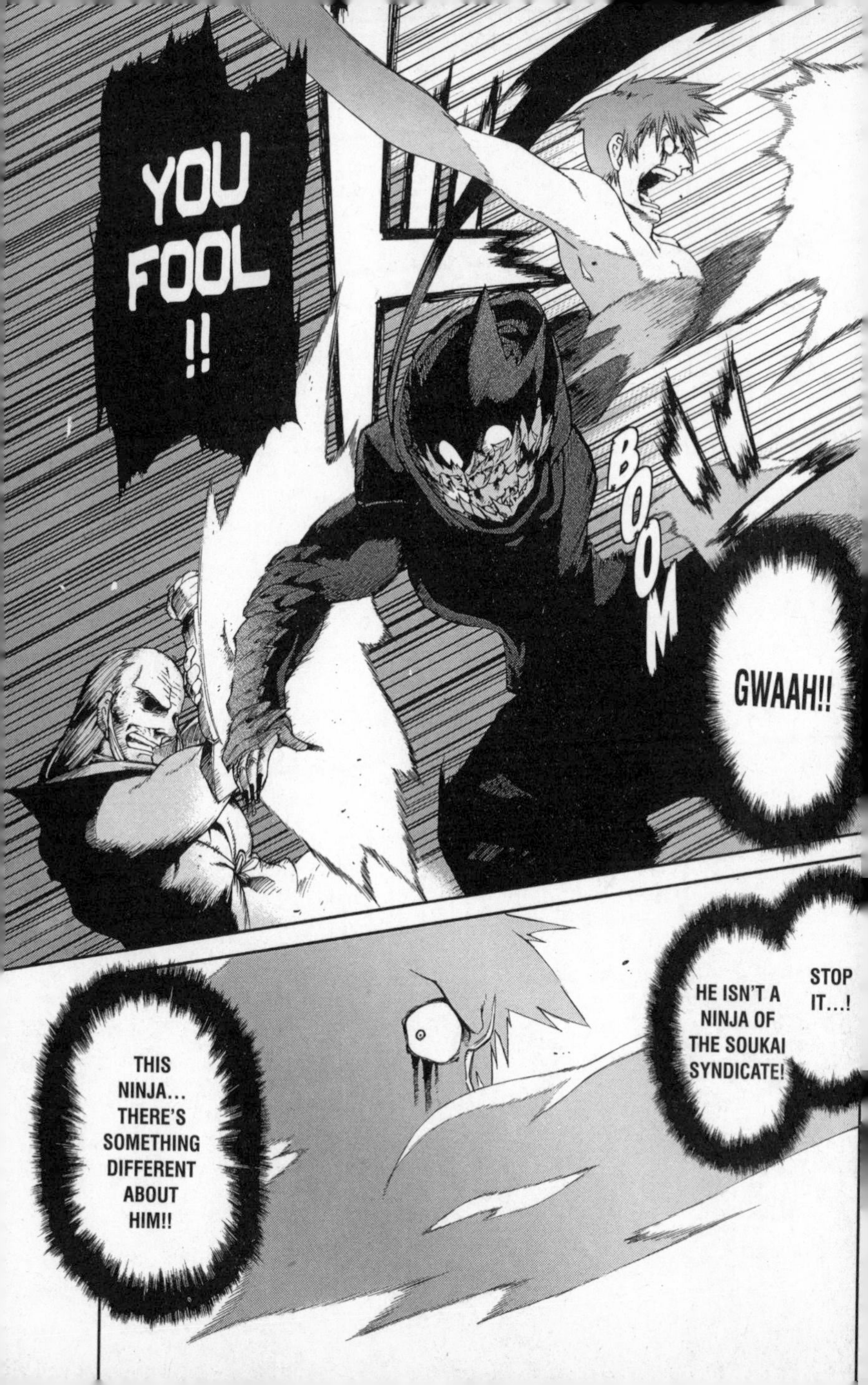
YOU FOOL!!
BOOM
GWAAH!!
STOP IT...!
HE ISN'T A NINJA OF THE SOUKAI SYNDICATE!
THIS NINJA... THERE'S SOMETHING DIFFERENT ABOUT HIM!!

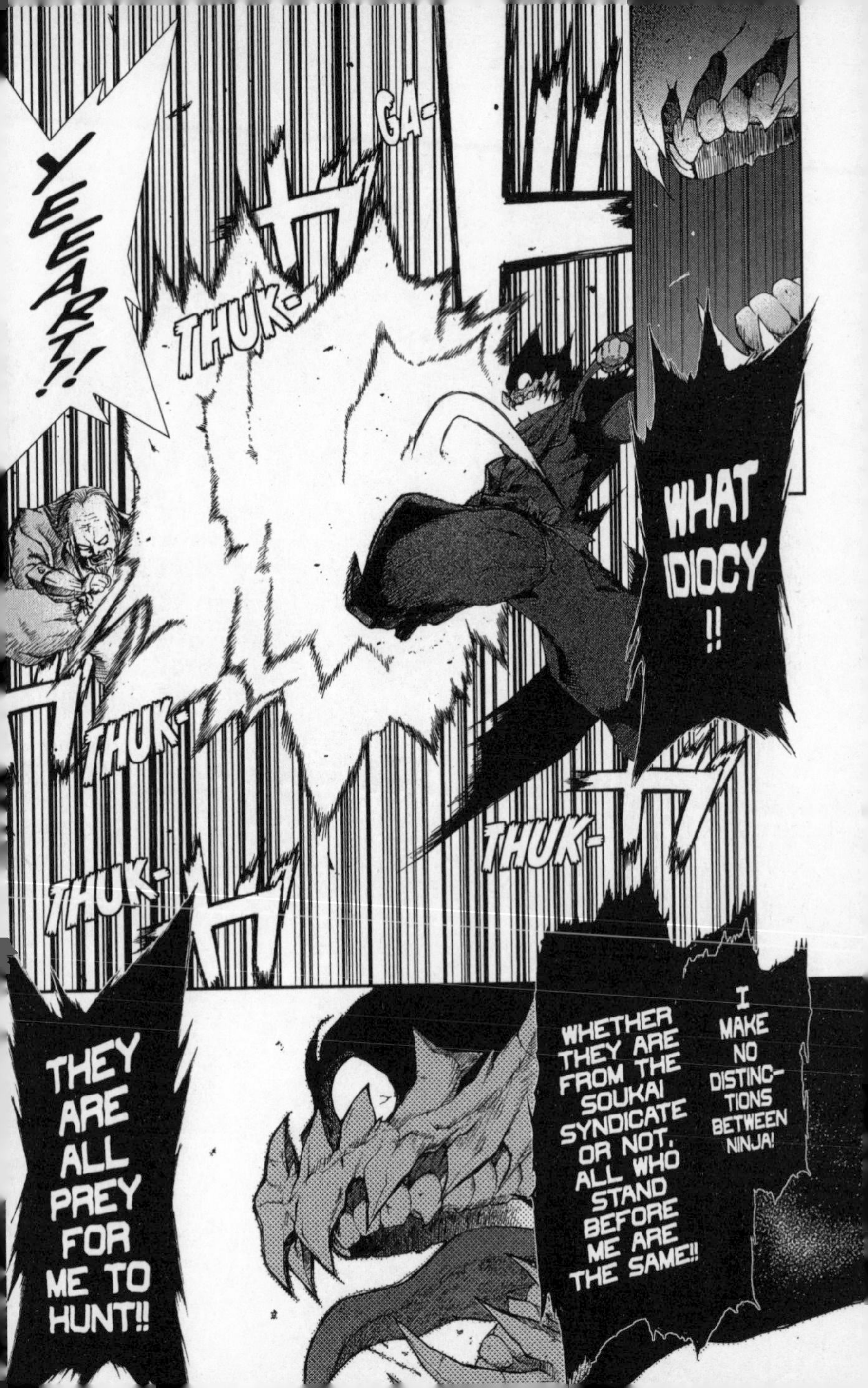
WHAT IDIOCY !!
GA-
YEEARRT!!
THUK-
THUK-
THUK-
THUK-
I MAKE NO DISTINCTIONS BETWEEN NINJA!
WHETHER THEY ARE FROM THE SOUKAI SYNDICATE OR NOT, ALL WHO STAND BEFORE ME ARE THE SAME!!
THEY ARE ALL PREY FOR ME TO HUNT!!

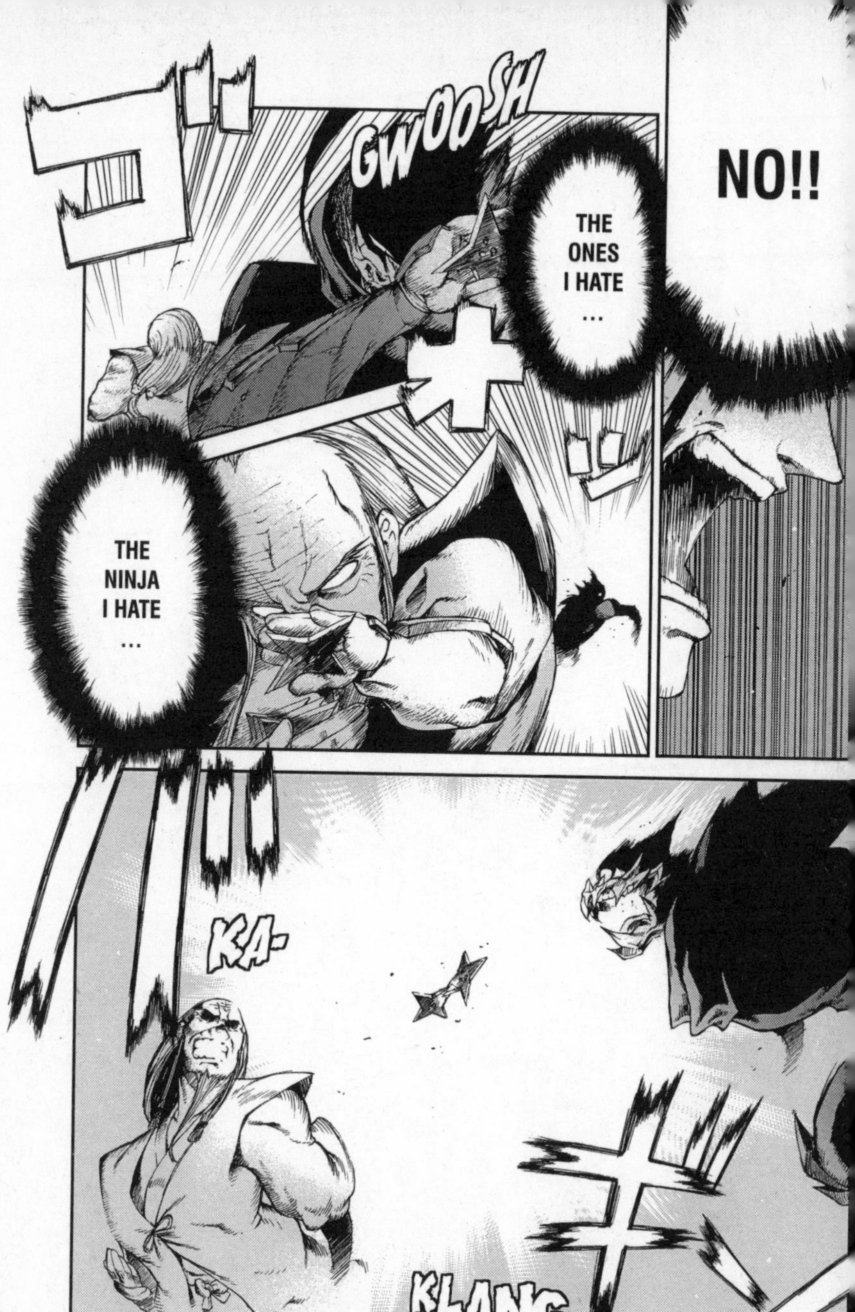
NO!!
THE ONES I HATE ...
GWOOSH
THE NINJA I HATE ...
KA-
KLANG

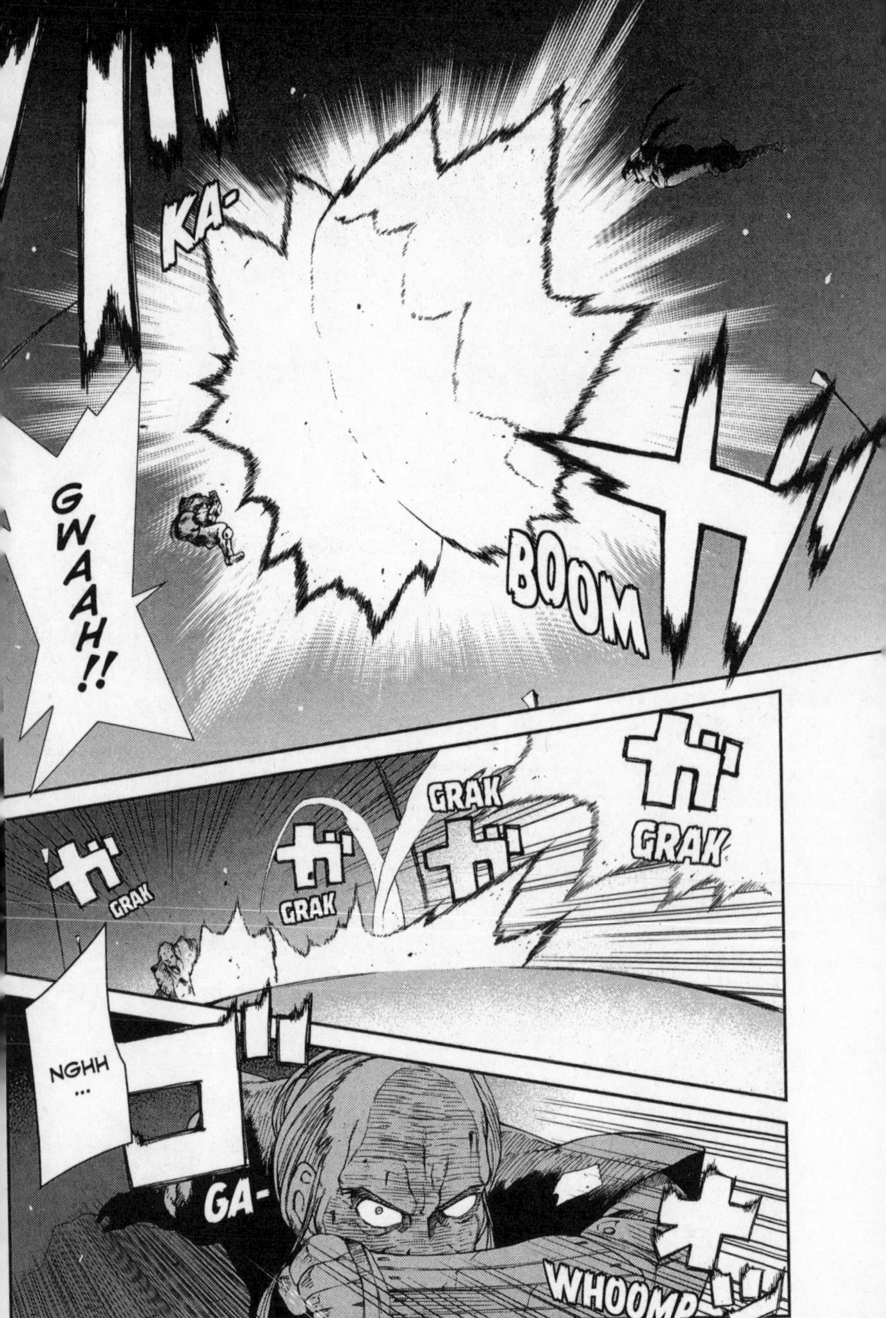
KA-
BOOM
GWAAH!!
GRAK
GRAK
GRAK
GRAK
NGHH
...
GA-
WHOOMP

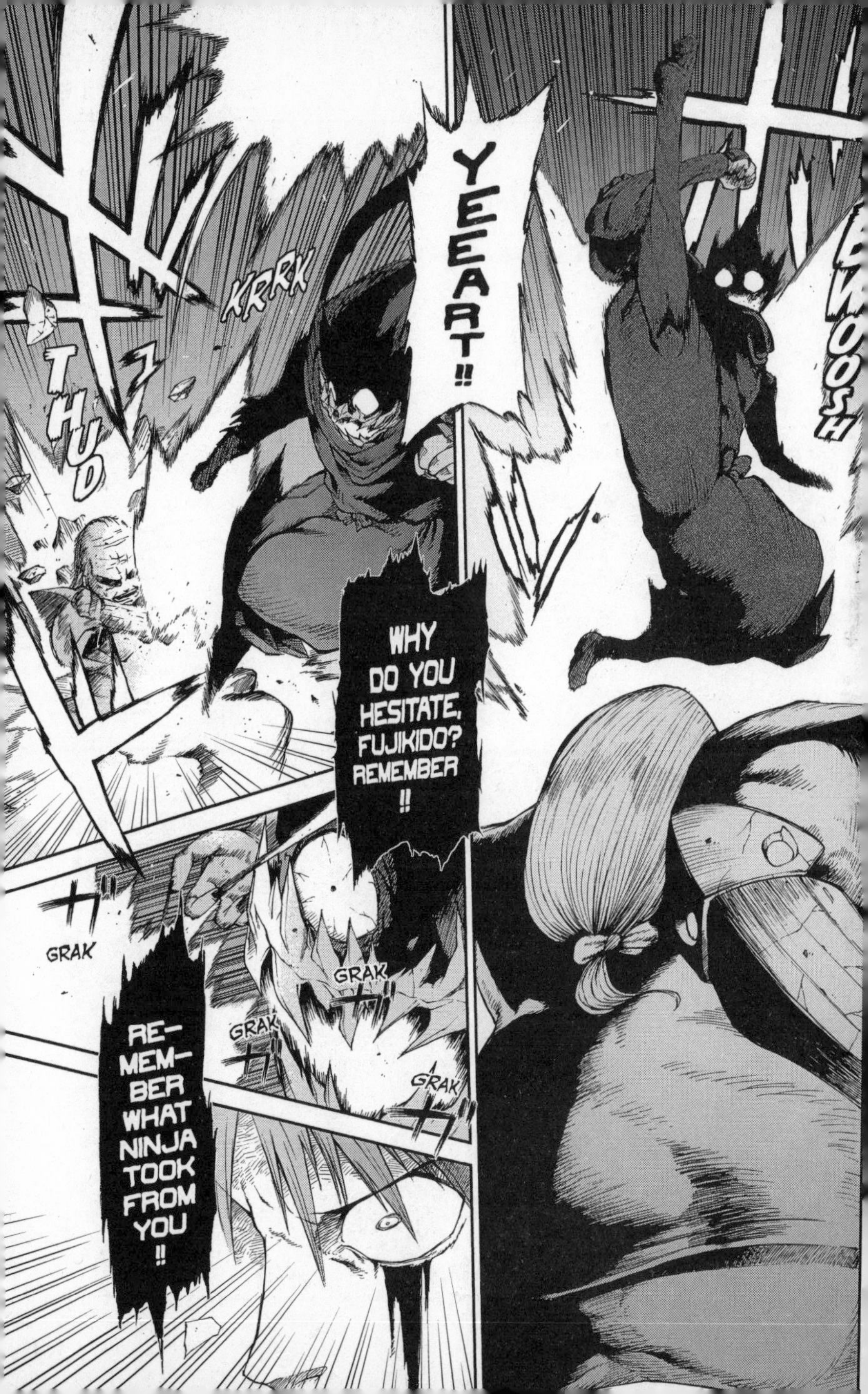
WHOOSH
YEEART!!
KRRK
THUD
WHY DO YOU HESITATE, FUJIKIDO? REMEMBER!!
GRAK
GRAK
GRAK
GRAK
RE-MEM-BER WHAT NINJA TOOK FROM YOU!!

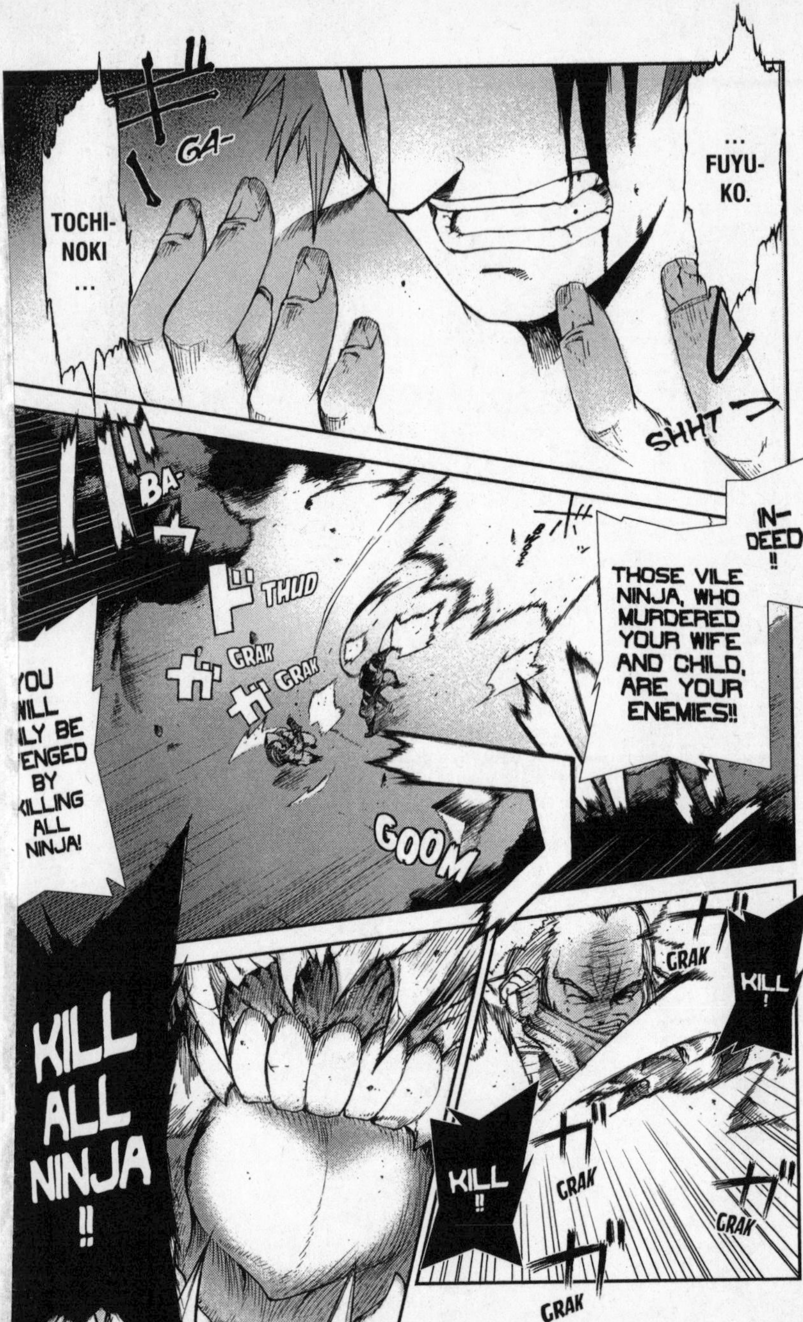
... FUYUKO.
GA-
TOCHINOKI ...
SHHT
INDEED!!
THOSE VILE NINJA, WHO MURDERED YOUR WIFE AND CHILD, ARE YOUR ENEMIES!!
BA-
THUD
GRAK
GRAK
GOOM
YOU WILL NLY BE VENGED BY KILLING ALL NINJA!
GRAK
KILL!
KILL!!
GRAK
GRAK
GRAK
KILL ALL NINJA!!

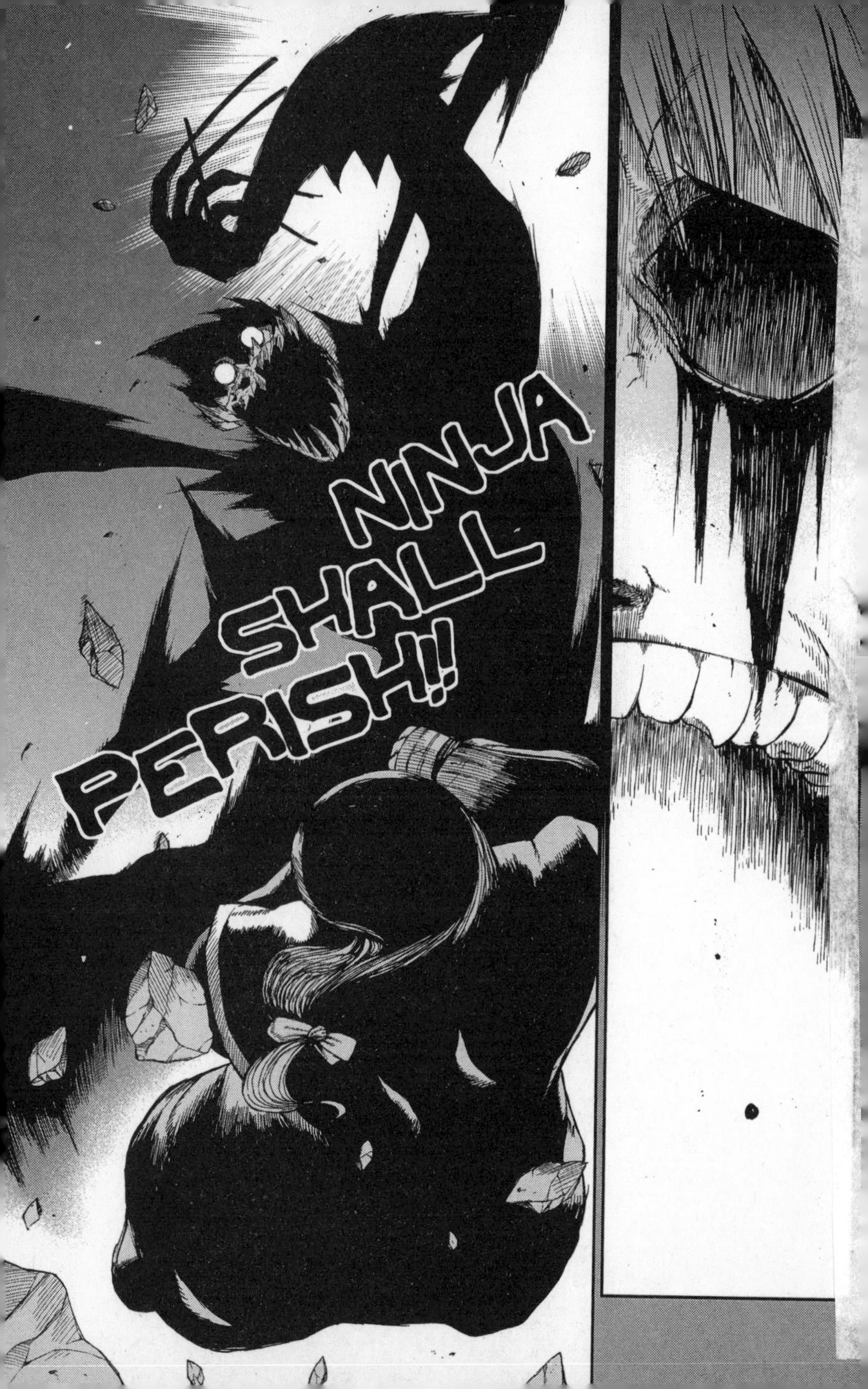
NINJA SHALL PERISH!!

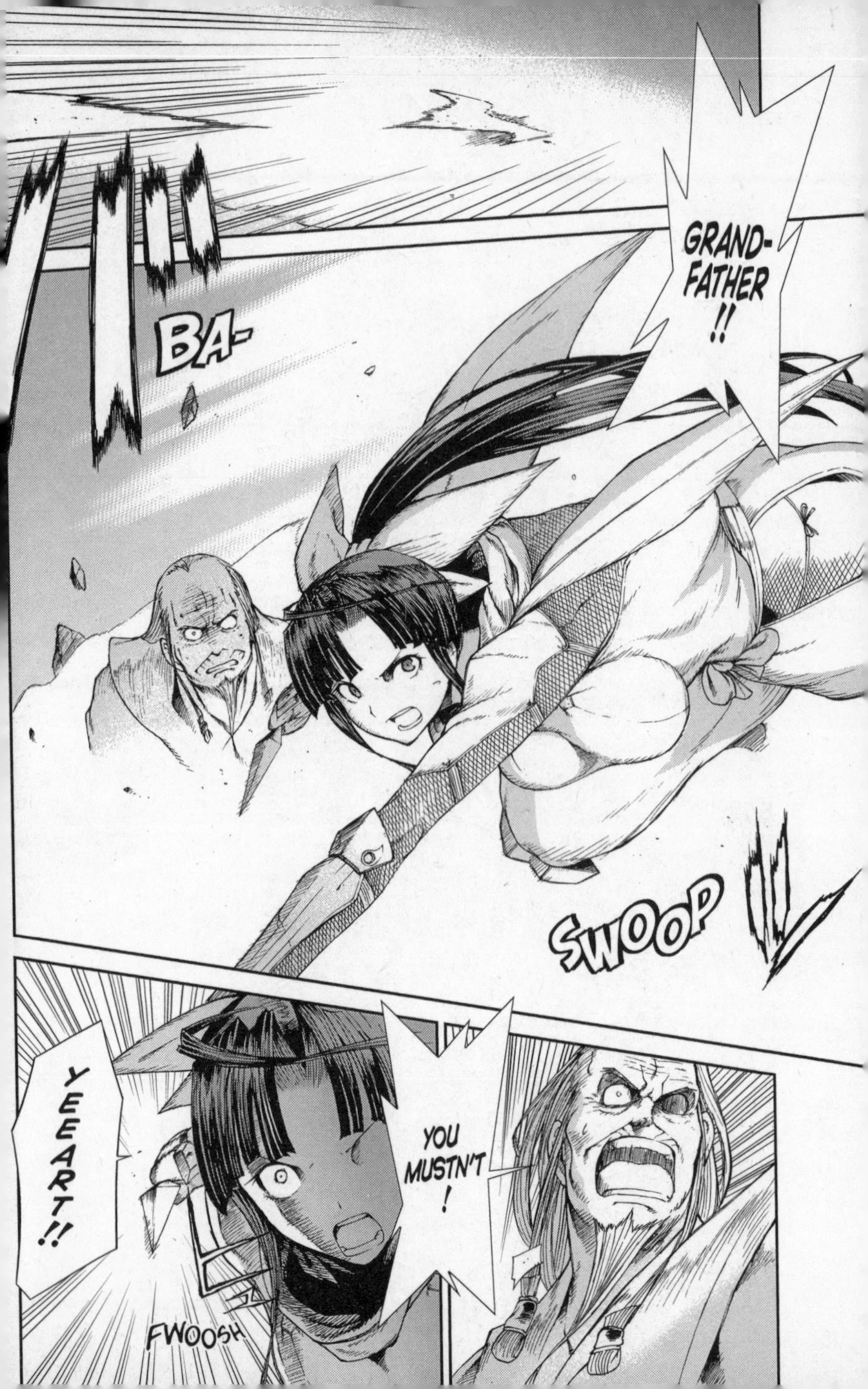
GRAND-FATHER!!
BA-
SWOOP
YOU MUSTN'T!
YEEEART!!
FWOOSH

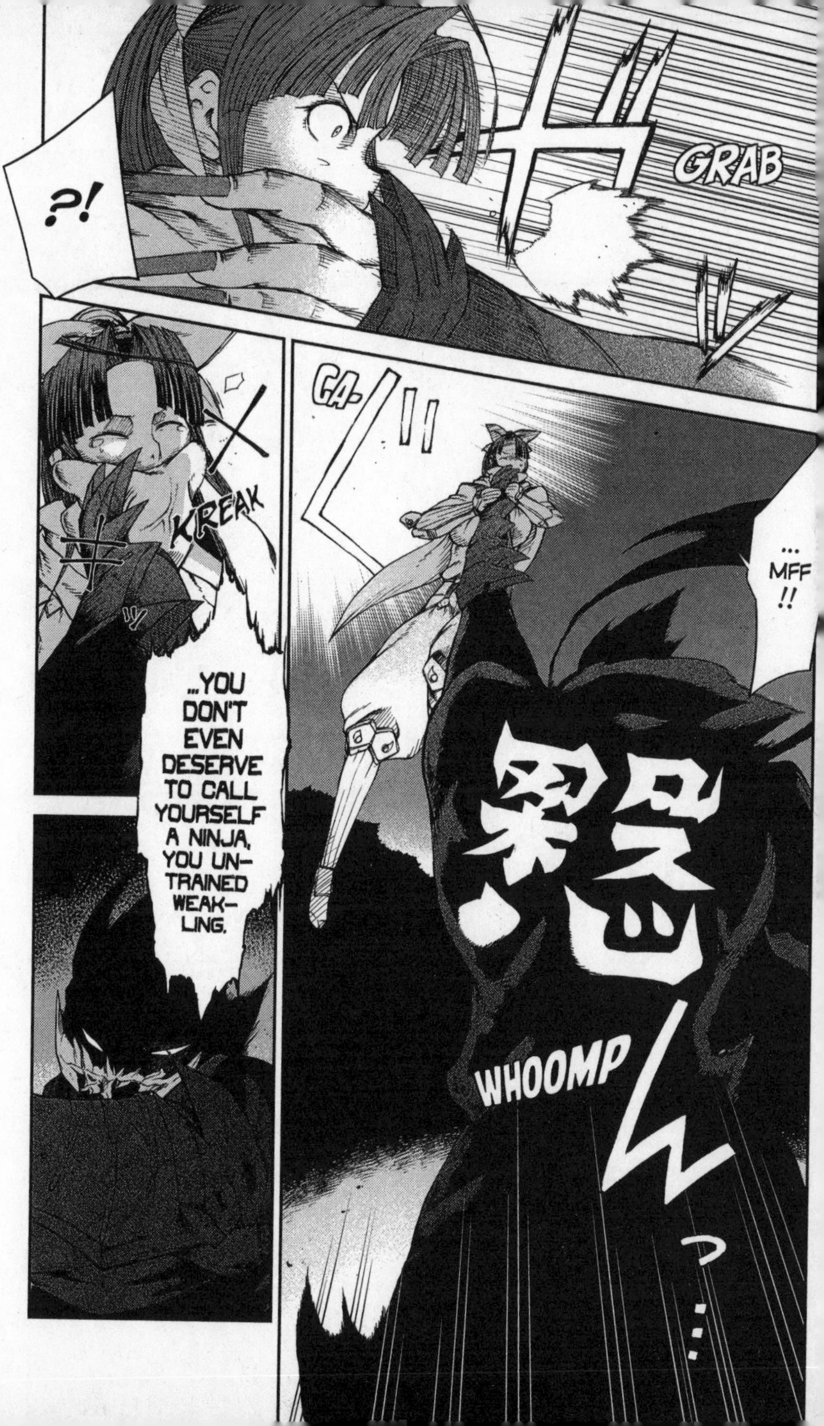
?!
GRAB
GA-
...MFF!!
WHOOMP
KREAK
...YOU DON'T EVEN DESERVE TO CALL YOURSELF A NINJA, YOU UN-TRAINED WEAK-LING.

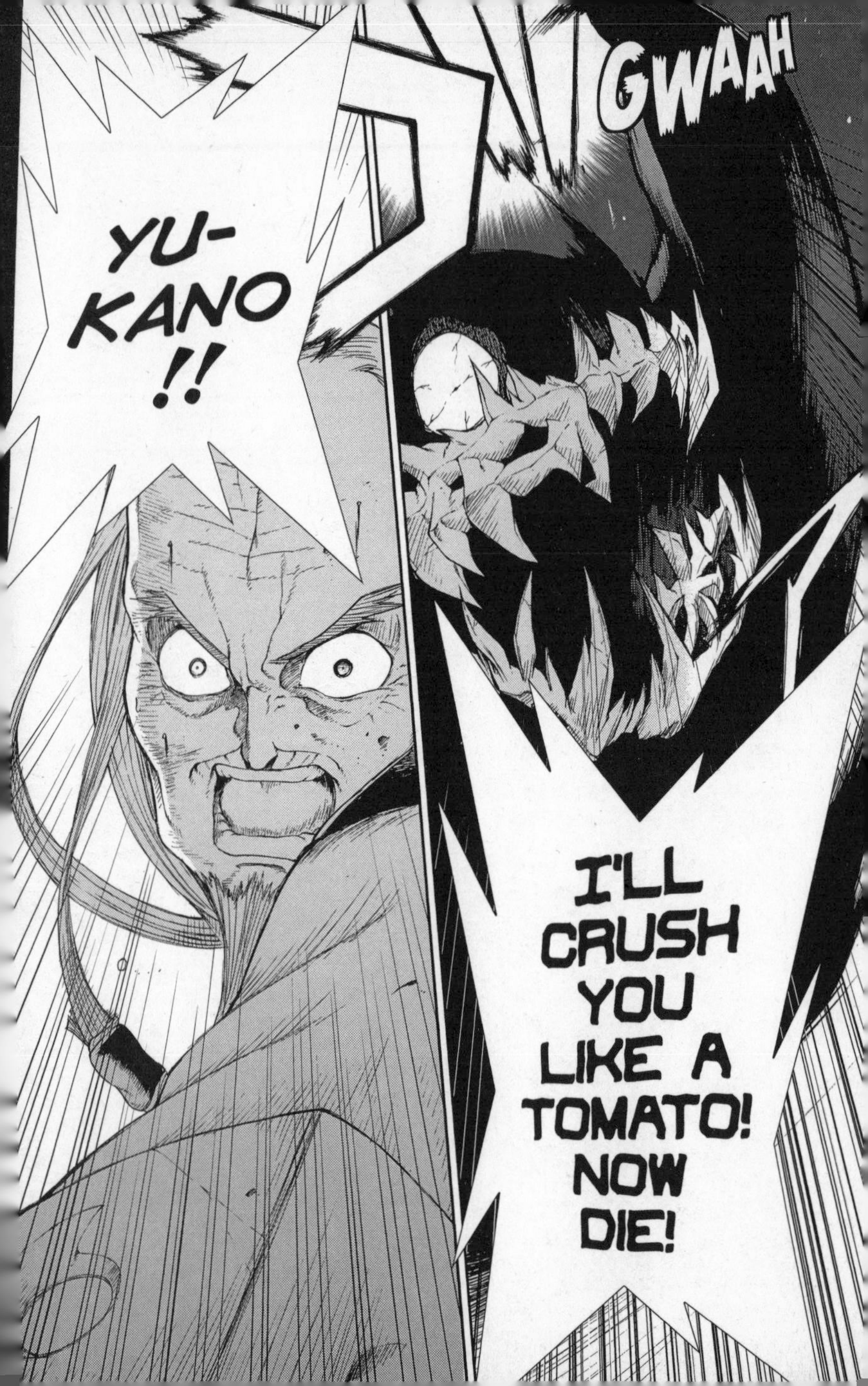
GWAAH
I'LL CRUSH YOU LIKE A TOMATO! NOW DIE!
YU-KANO!!

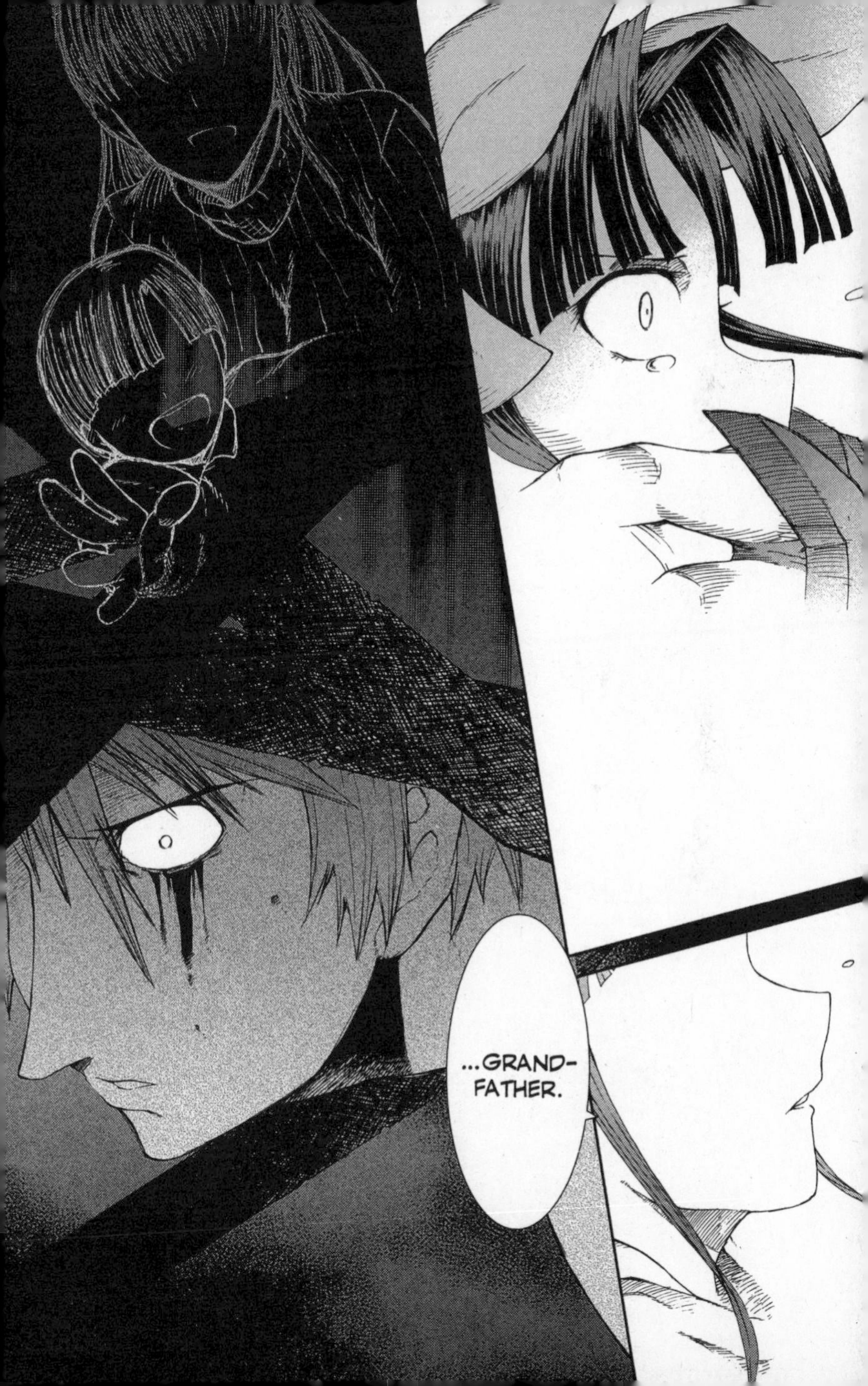
...GRAND-
FATHER.

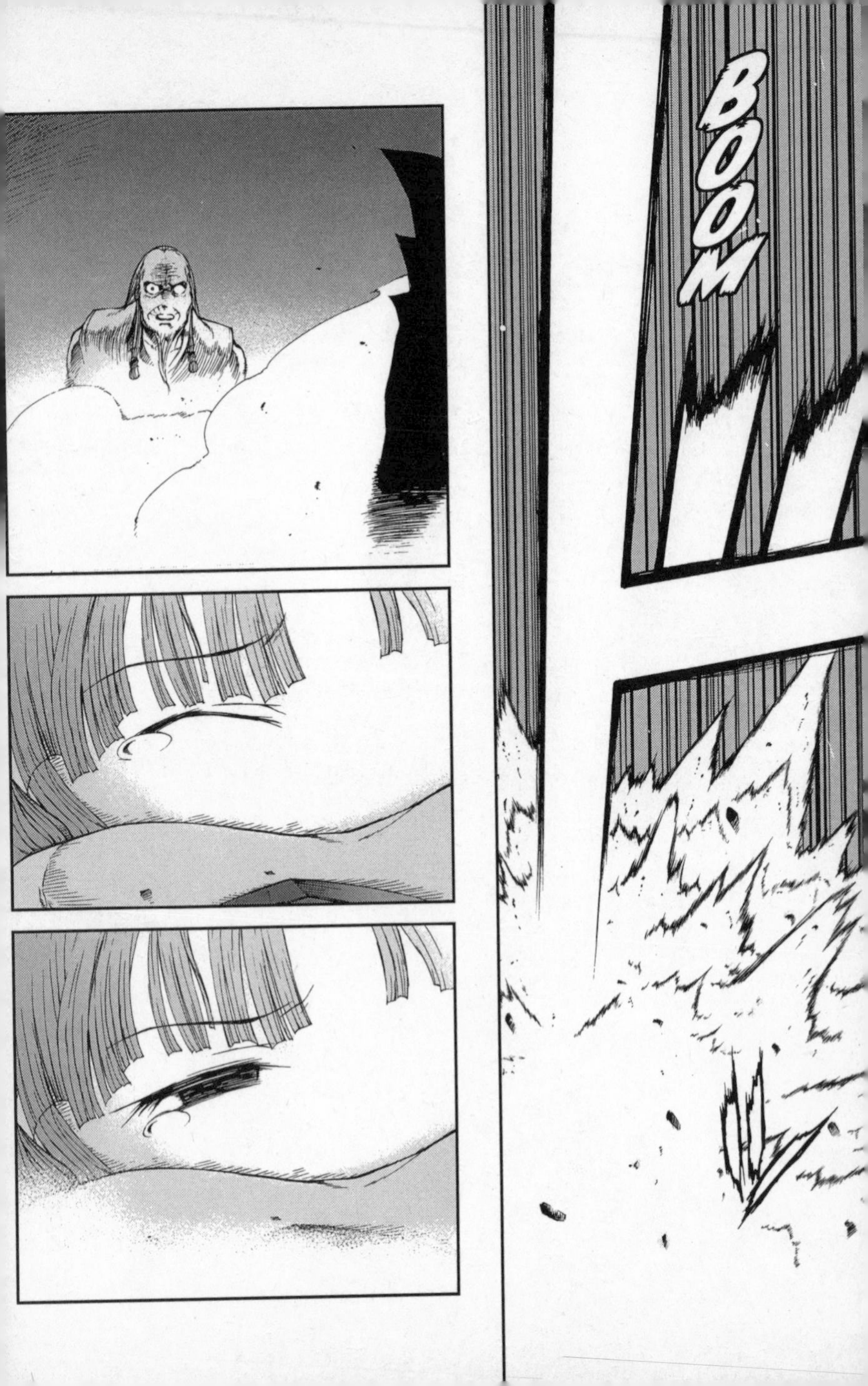
BOOM

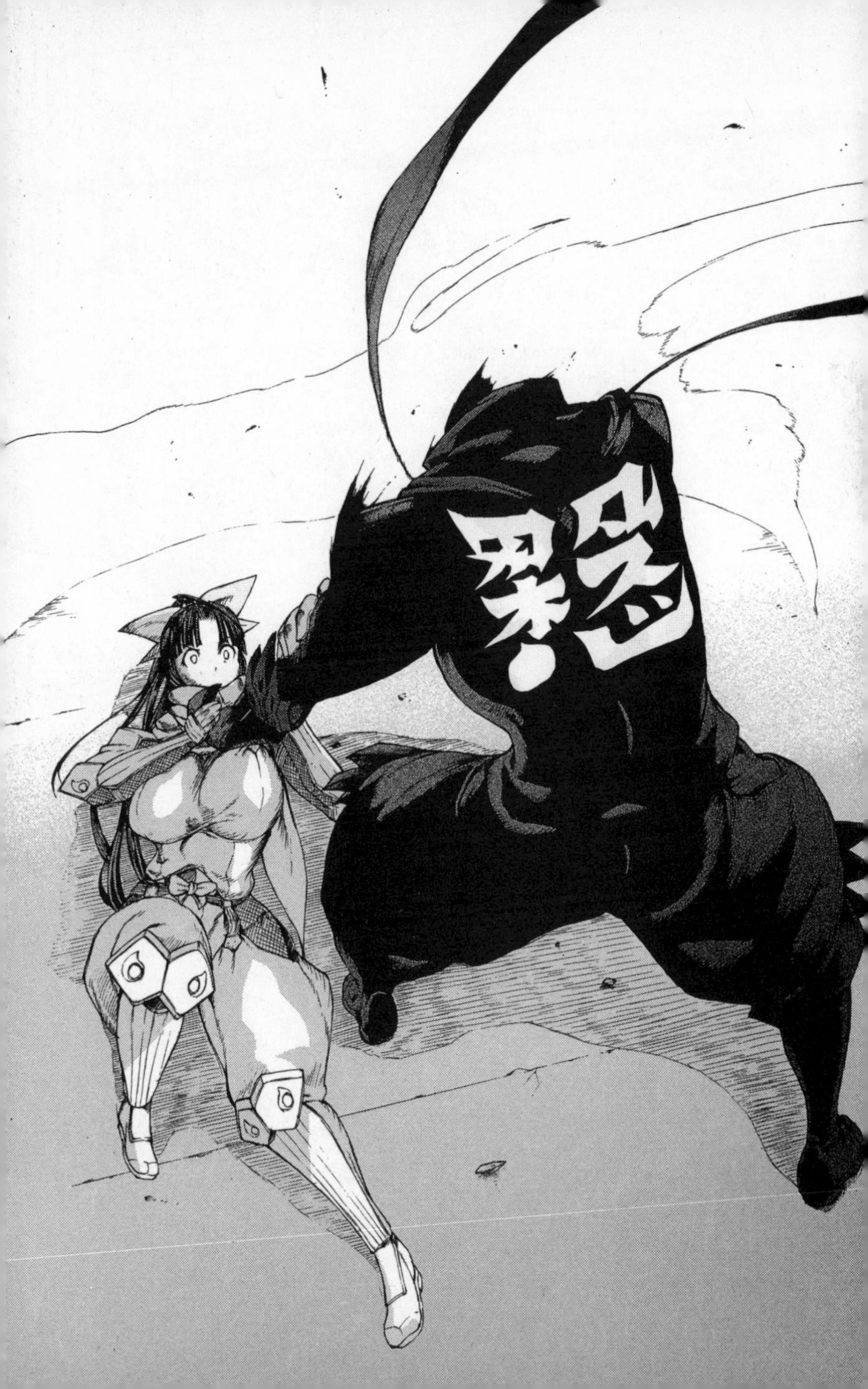

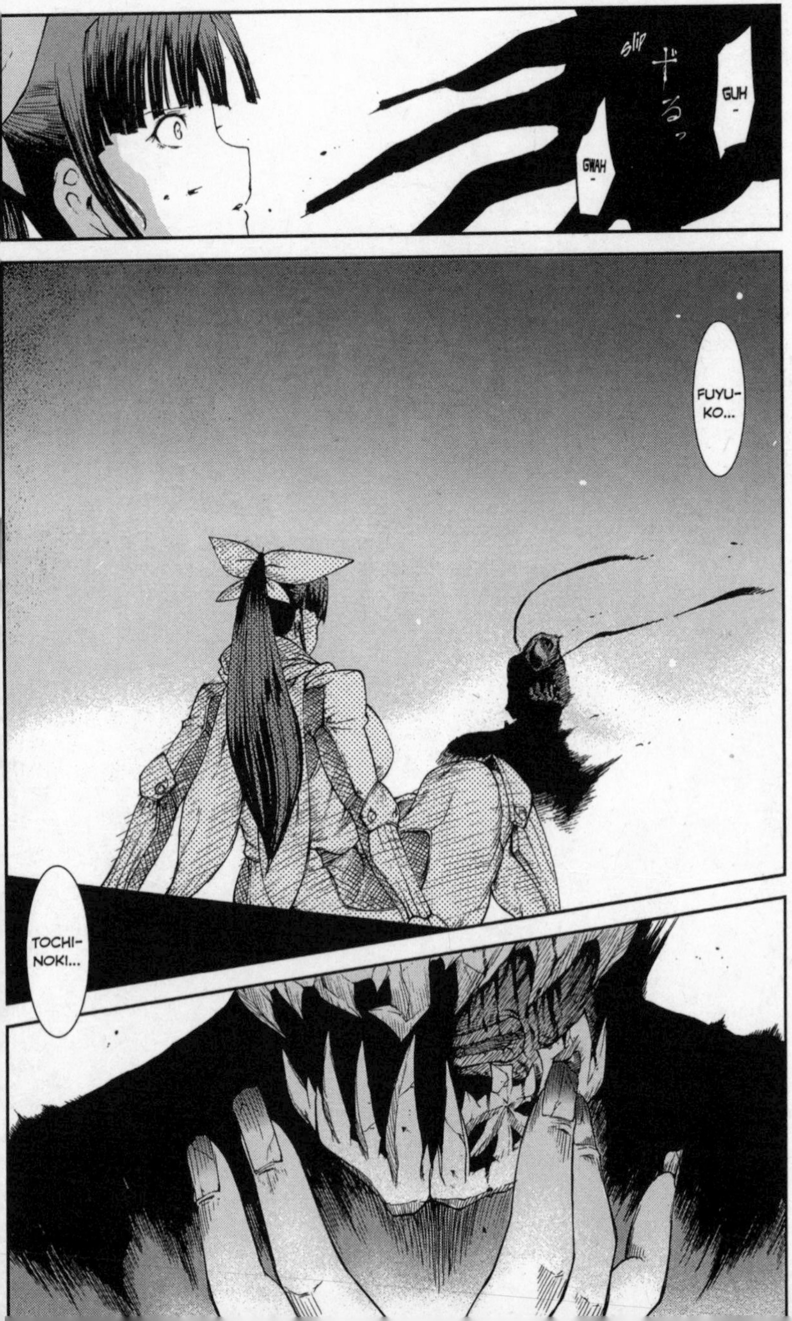
GUH-
slip
ずるっ
GWAH-
FUYU-KO...
TOCHI-NOKI...

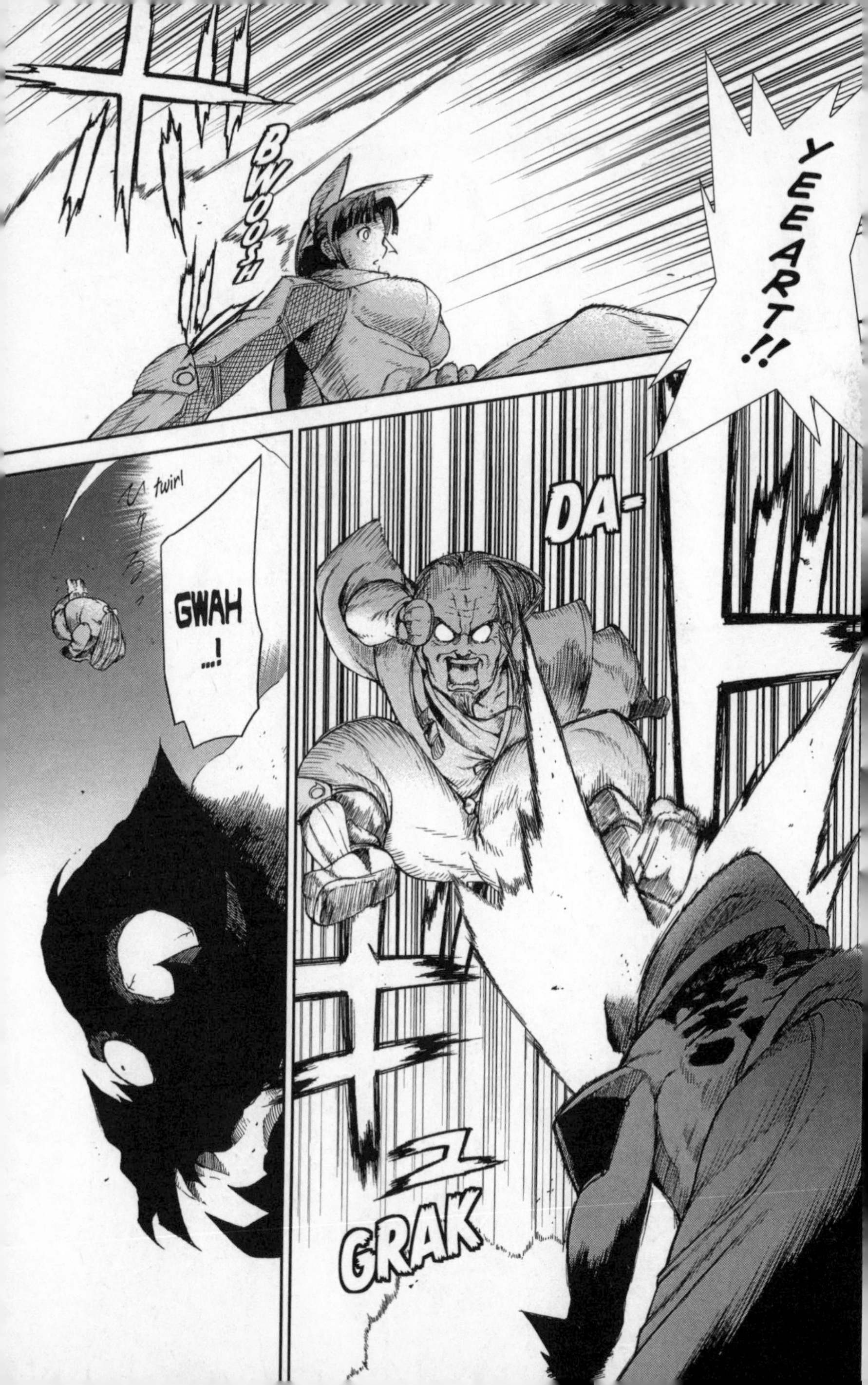
YEEART!!
BWOOSH
DA-
GRAK
twirl
GWAH ...!

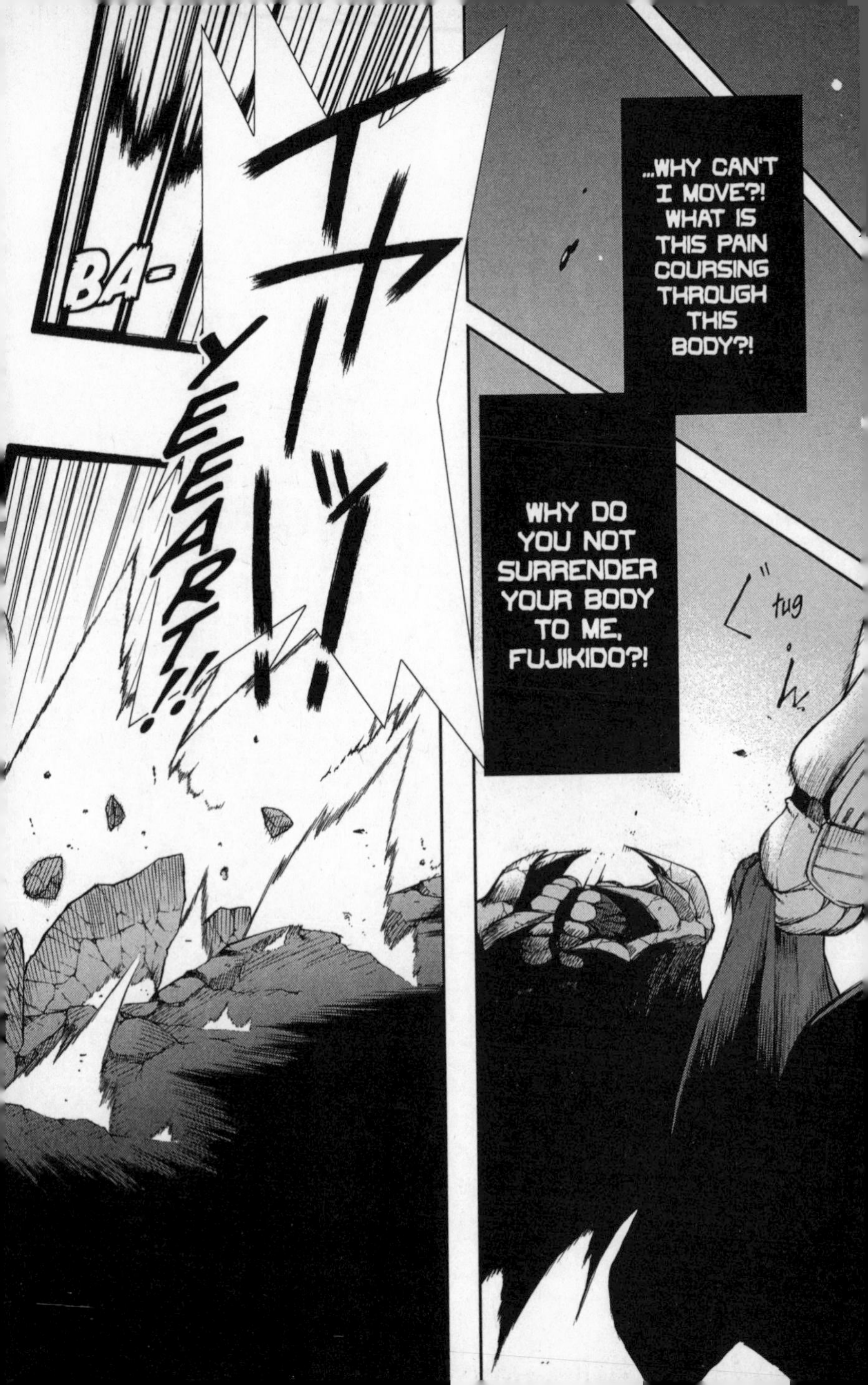
...WHY CAN'T I MOVE?! WHAT IS THIS PAIN COURSING THROUGH THIS BODY?!
WHY DO YOU NOT SURRENDER YOUR BODY TO ME, FUJIKIDO?!
ぐい
tug
BA-
イヤーッ!!
YEEAART!!

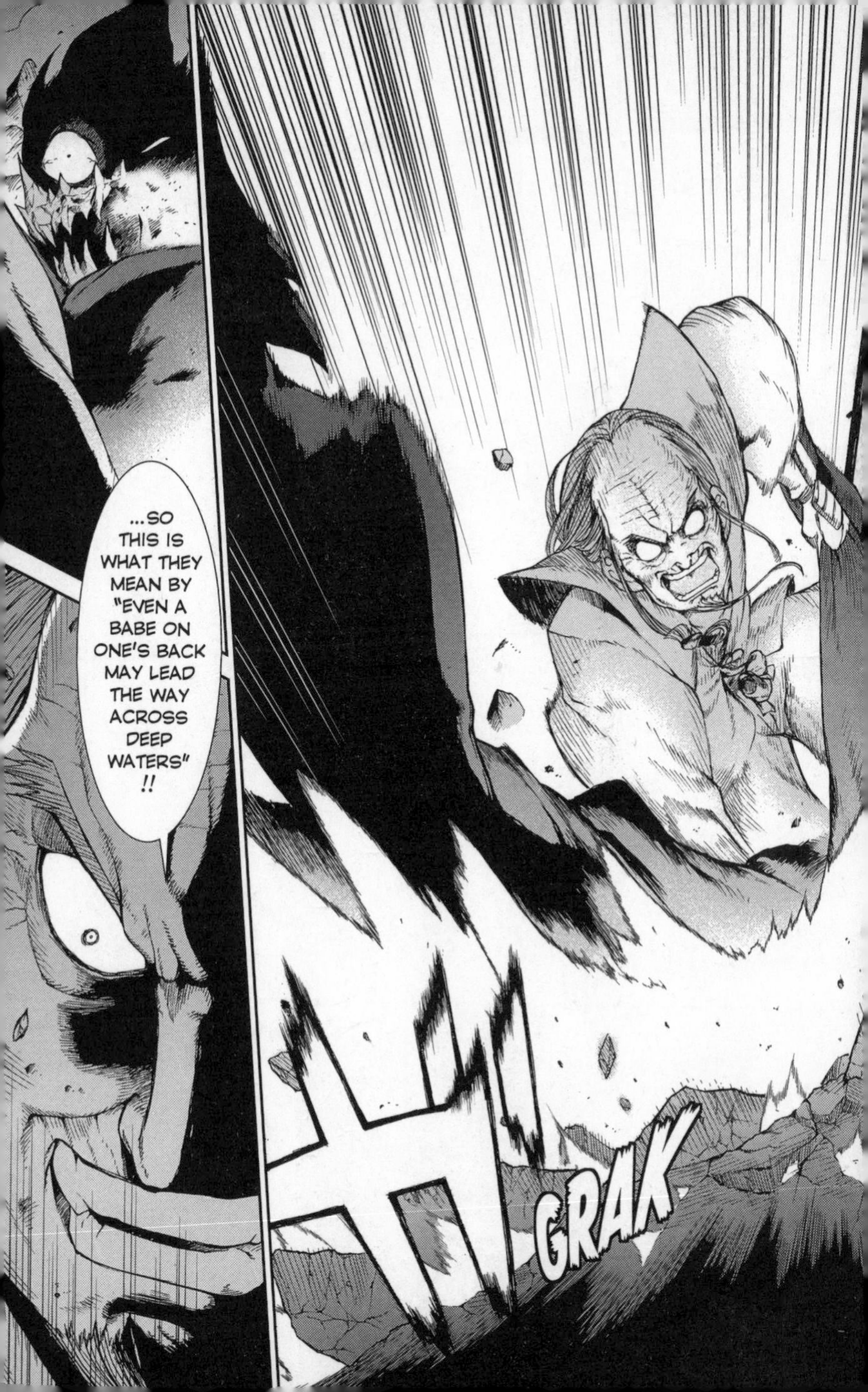
...SO THIS IS WHAT THEY MEAN BY "EVEN A BABE ON ONE'S BACK MAY LEAD THE WAY ACROSS DEEP WATERS"!!
GRAK

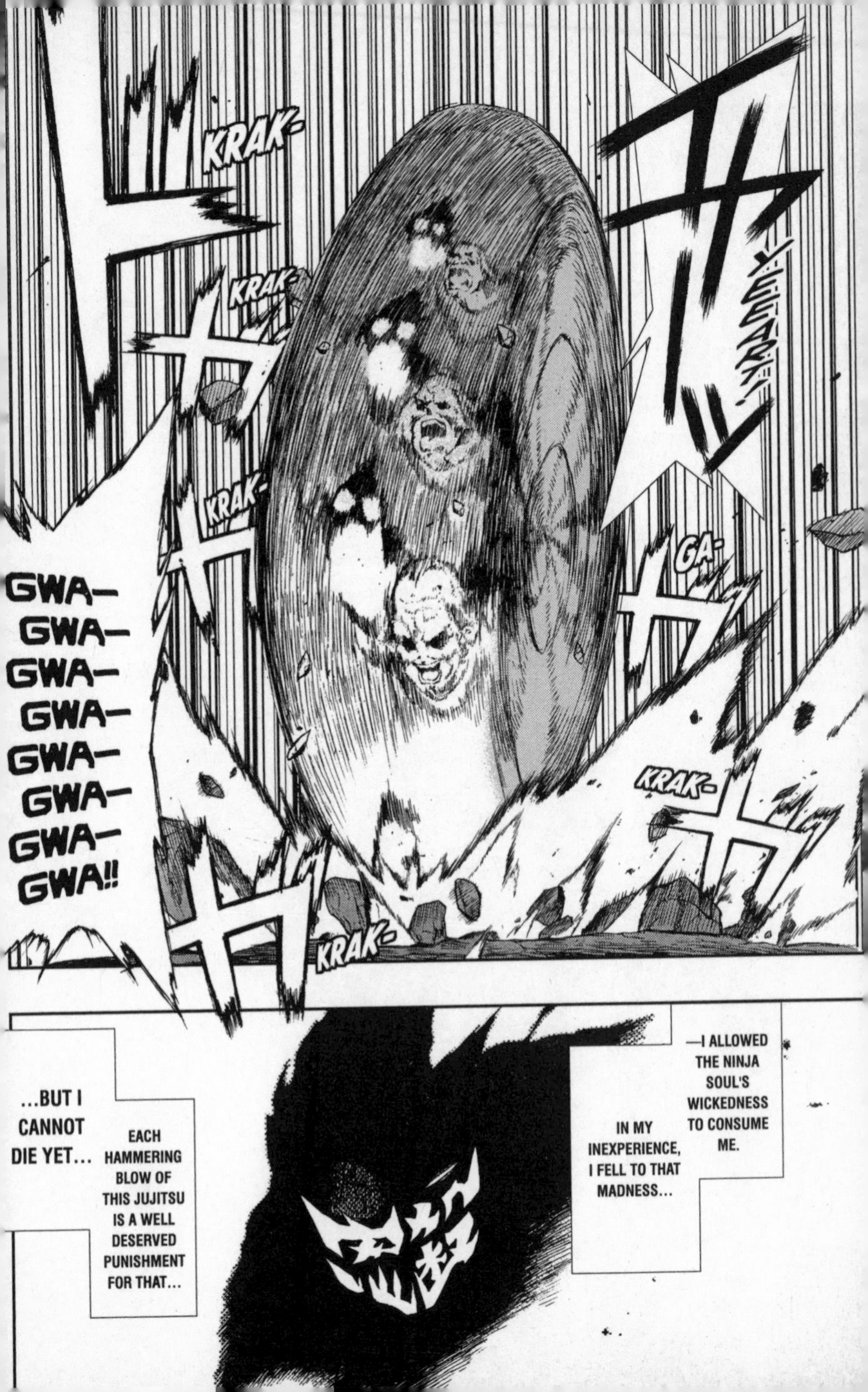
YEEARRR!!
KRAK-
KRAK-
KRAK-
GA-
KRAK-
GWA-GWA-GWA-GWA-GWA-GWA-GWA-GWA!!
KRAK-
—I ALLOWED THE NINJA SOUL'S WICKEDNESS TO CONSUME ME.
IN MY INEXPERIENCE, I FELL TO THAT MADNESS…
EACH HAMMERING BLOW OF THIS JUJITSU IS A WELL DESERVED PUNISHMENT FOR THAT…
…BUT I CANNOT DIE YET…

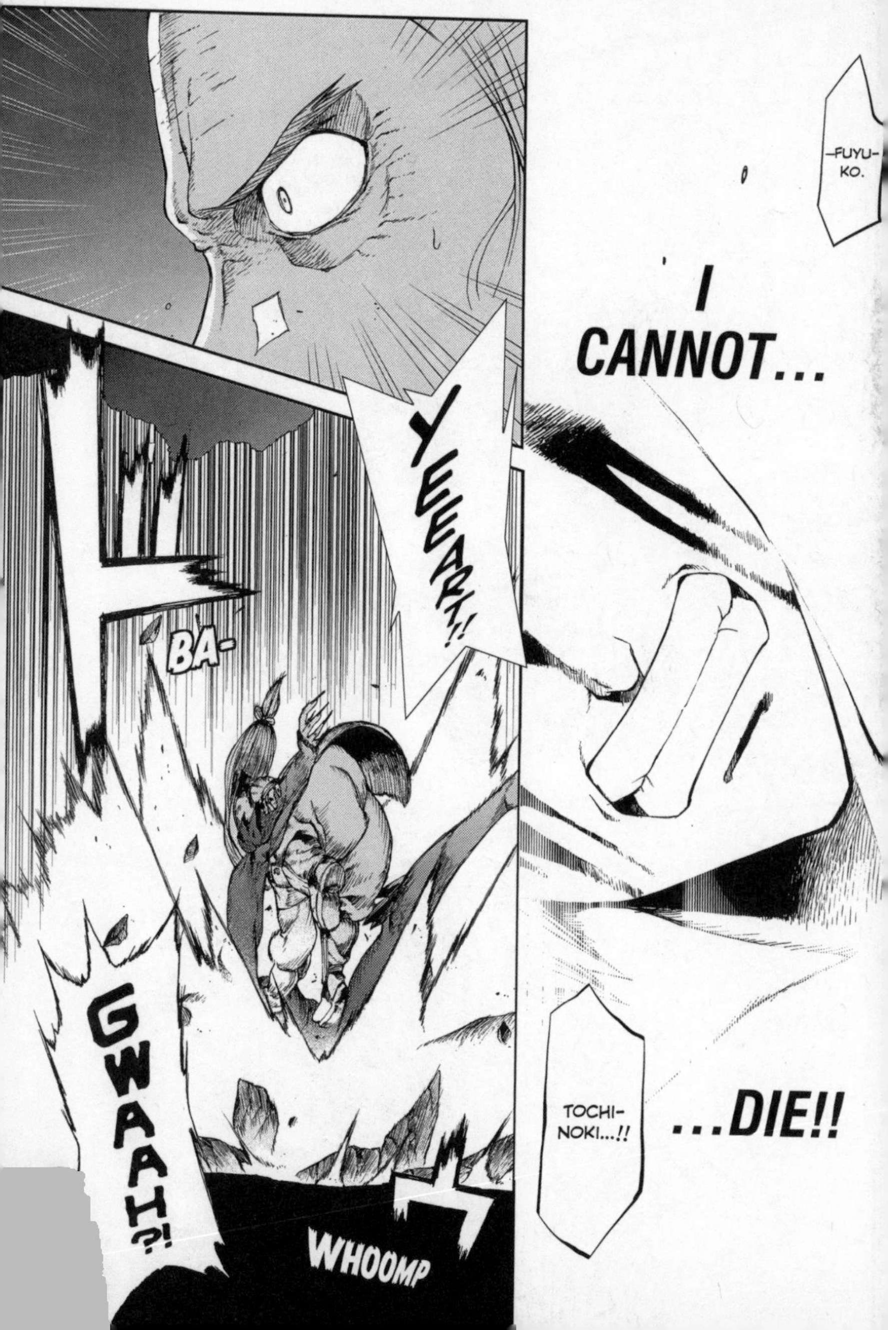
—FUYUKO.
I CANNOT...
...DIE!!
TOCHINOKI...!!
YEEARR!!
BA-
GWAAAH?!
WHOOMP

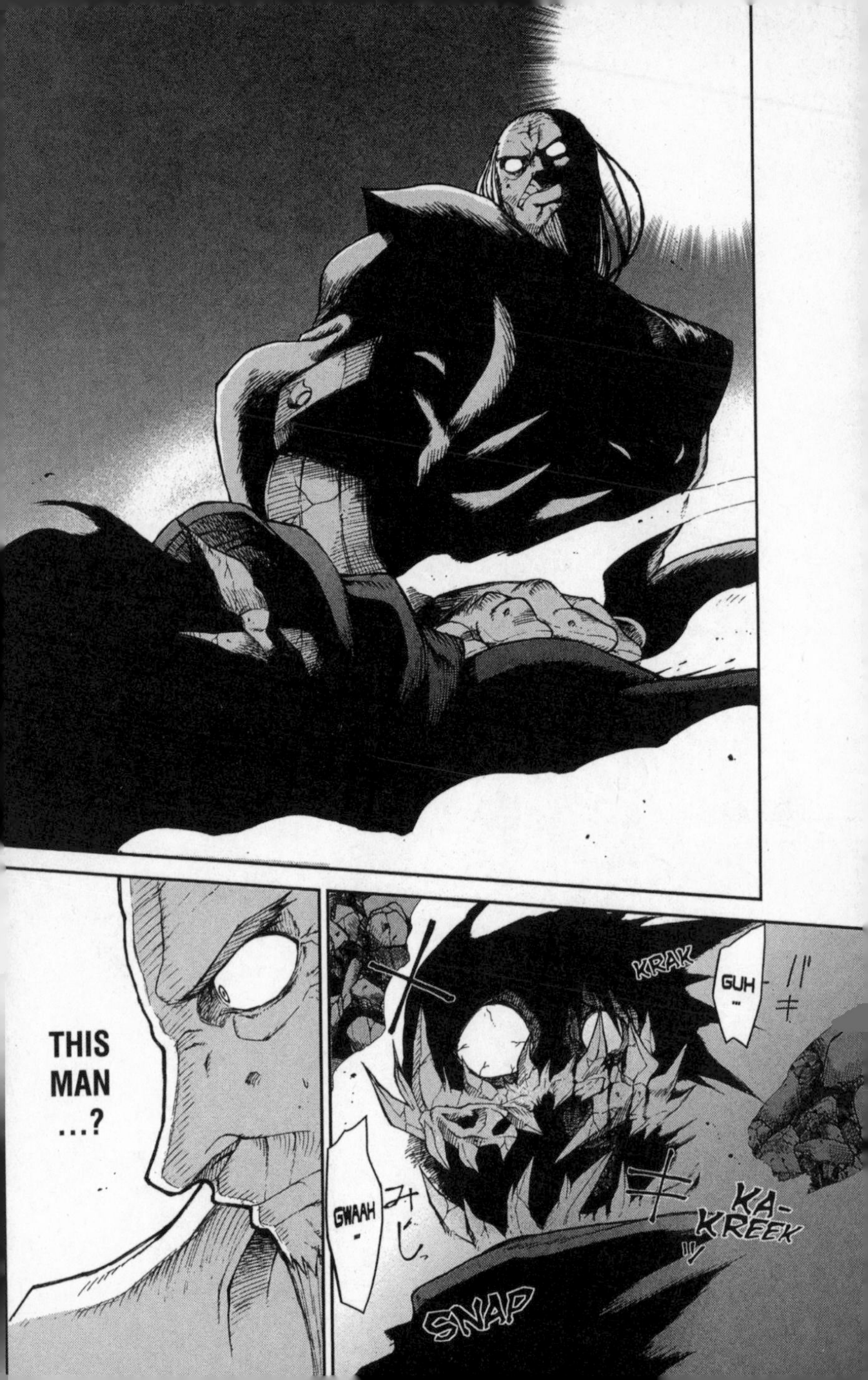
GUH...
KRAK
KA-KREEK
GWAAH...
SNAP
THIS MAN ...?

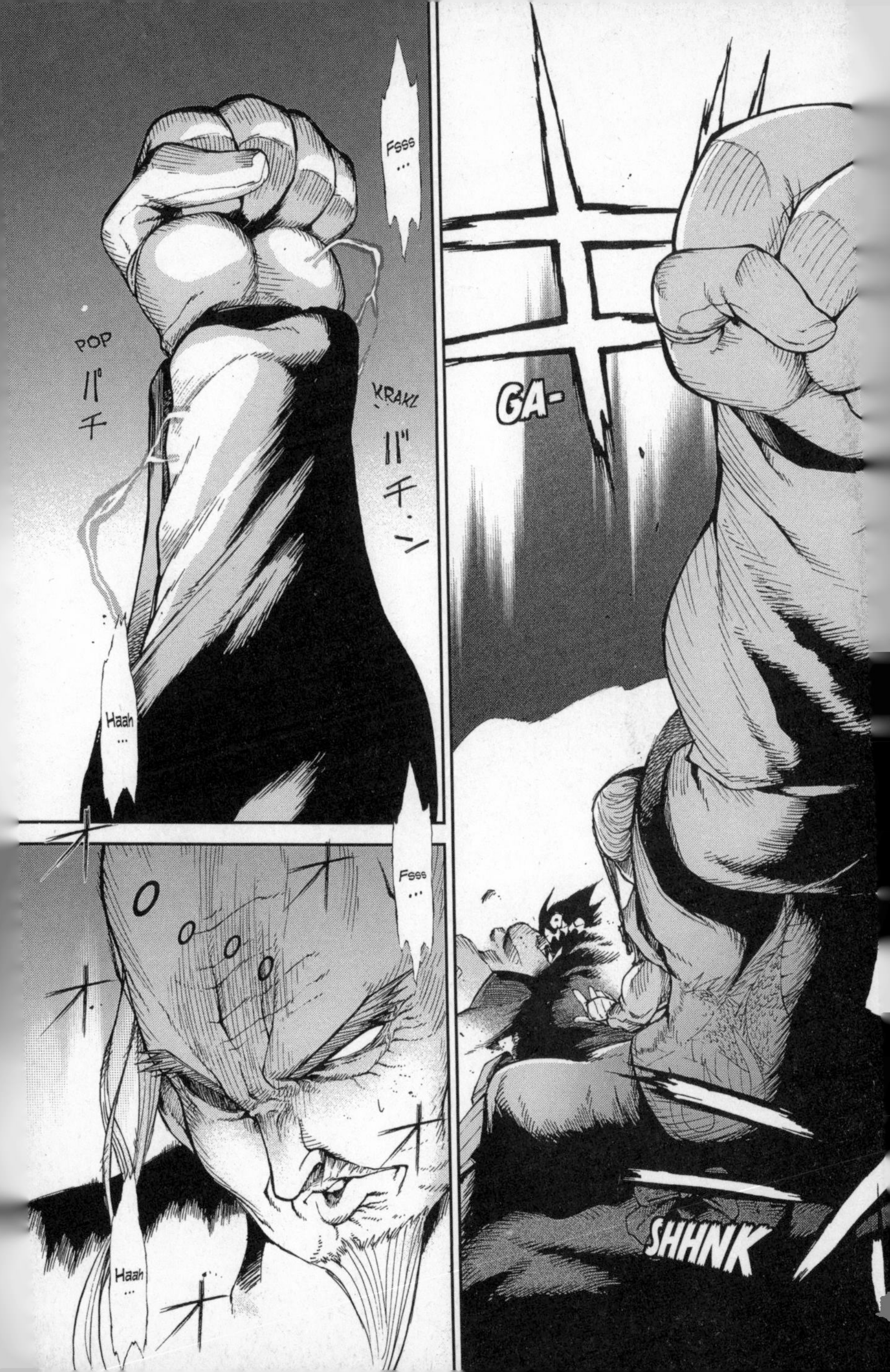
GA-
SHHNK
Fsss ...
KRAKL
バチン
POP
パチ
Haah ...
Fsss ...
オ
オ
オ
Haah ...
オ

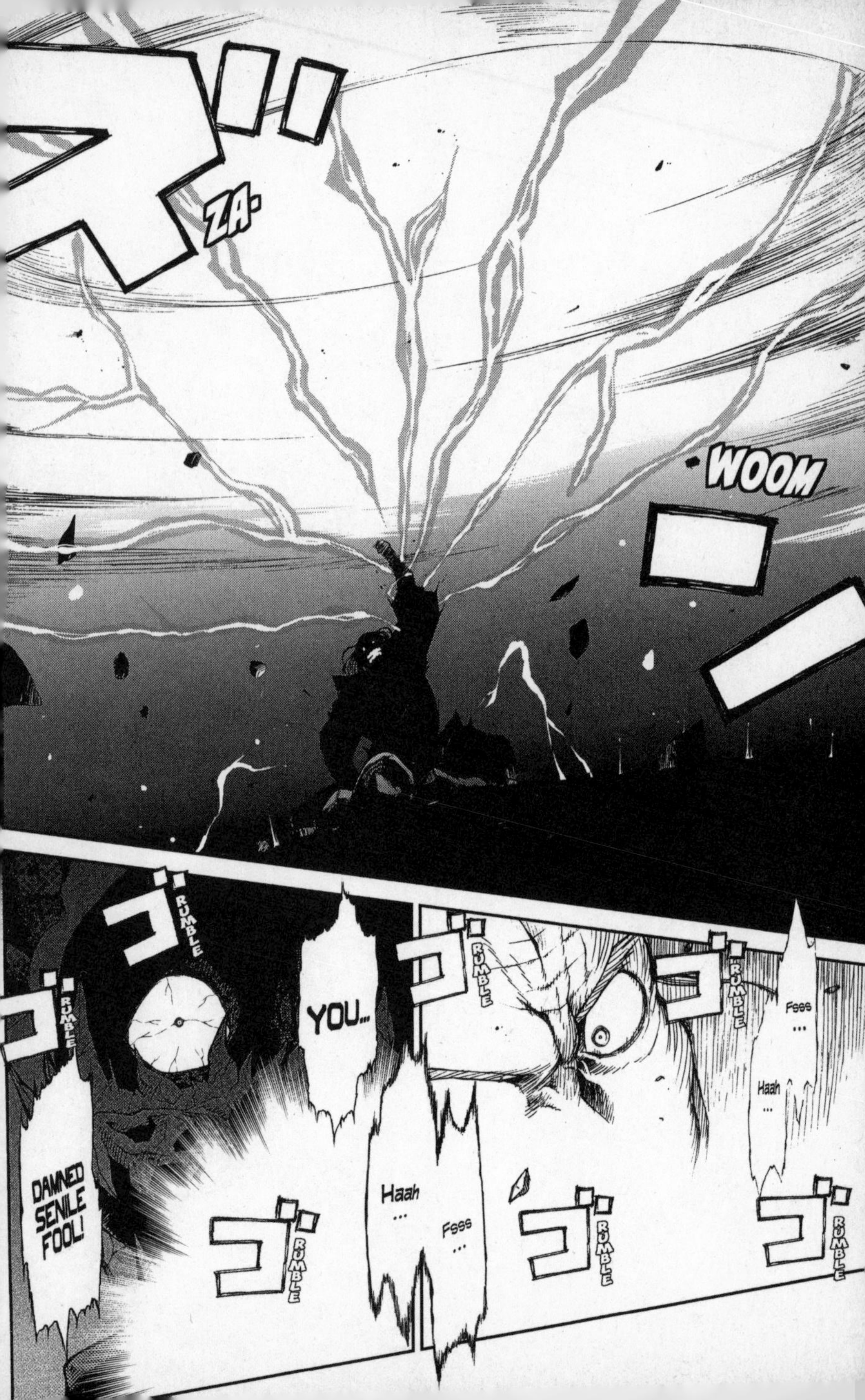
ZA-
WOOM
RUMBLE
Fsss ...
Haah ...
RUMBLE
RUMBLE
Haah ...
Fsss ...
RUMBLE
YOU...
RUMBLE
DAMNED SENILE FOOL!
RUMBLE

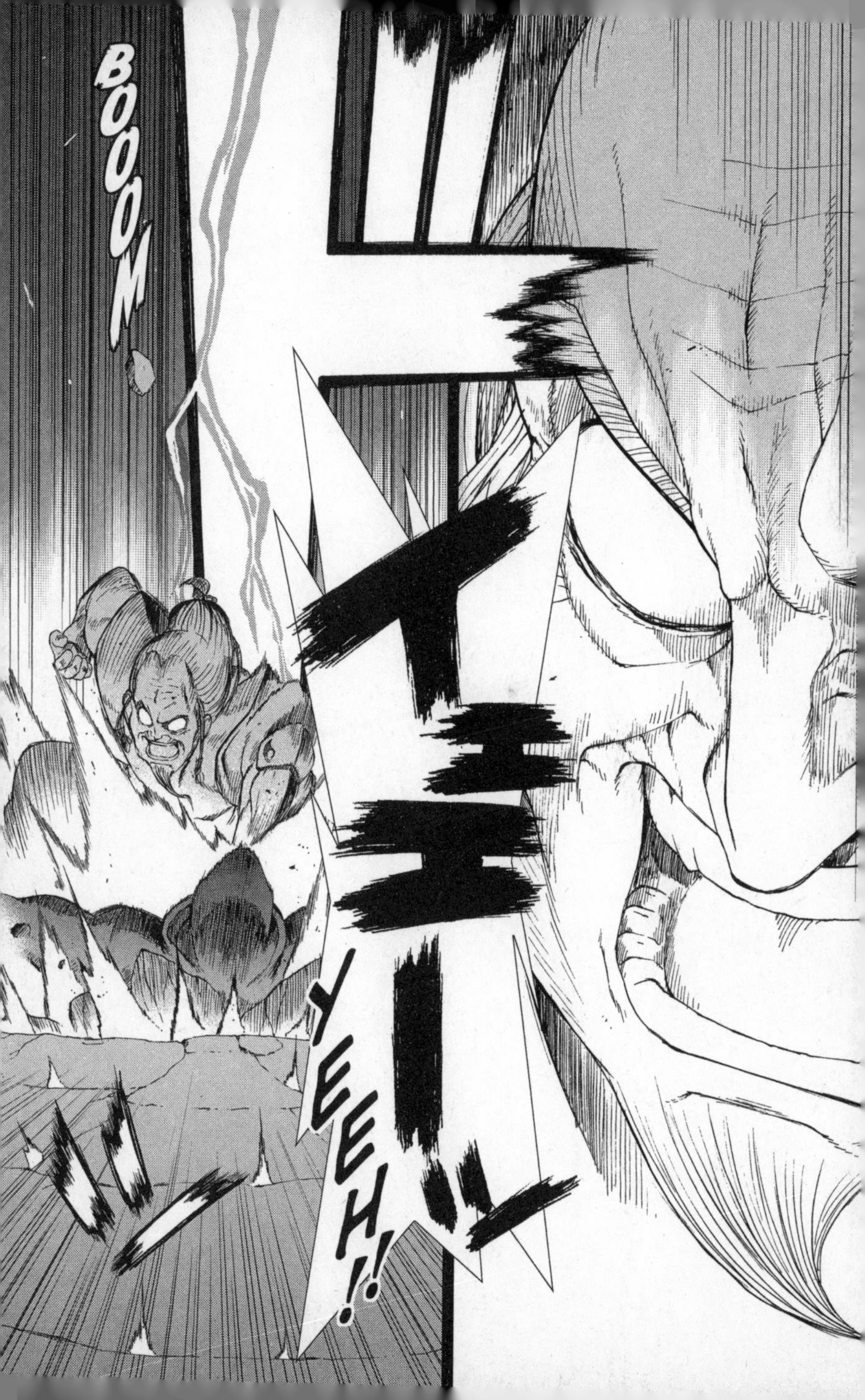
BOOOOM
YEEEH!!

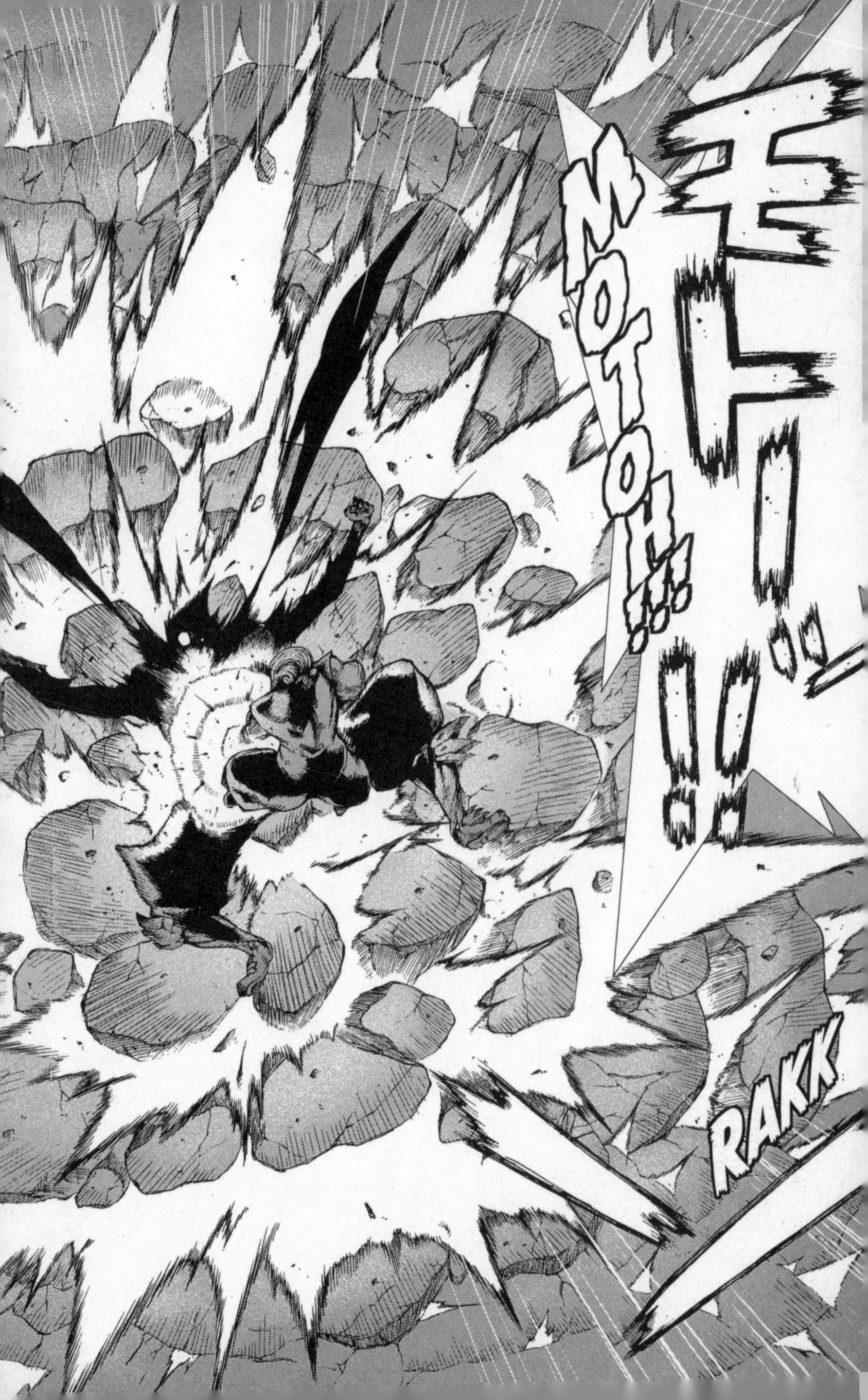

MOTOH!!!
RAKK

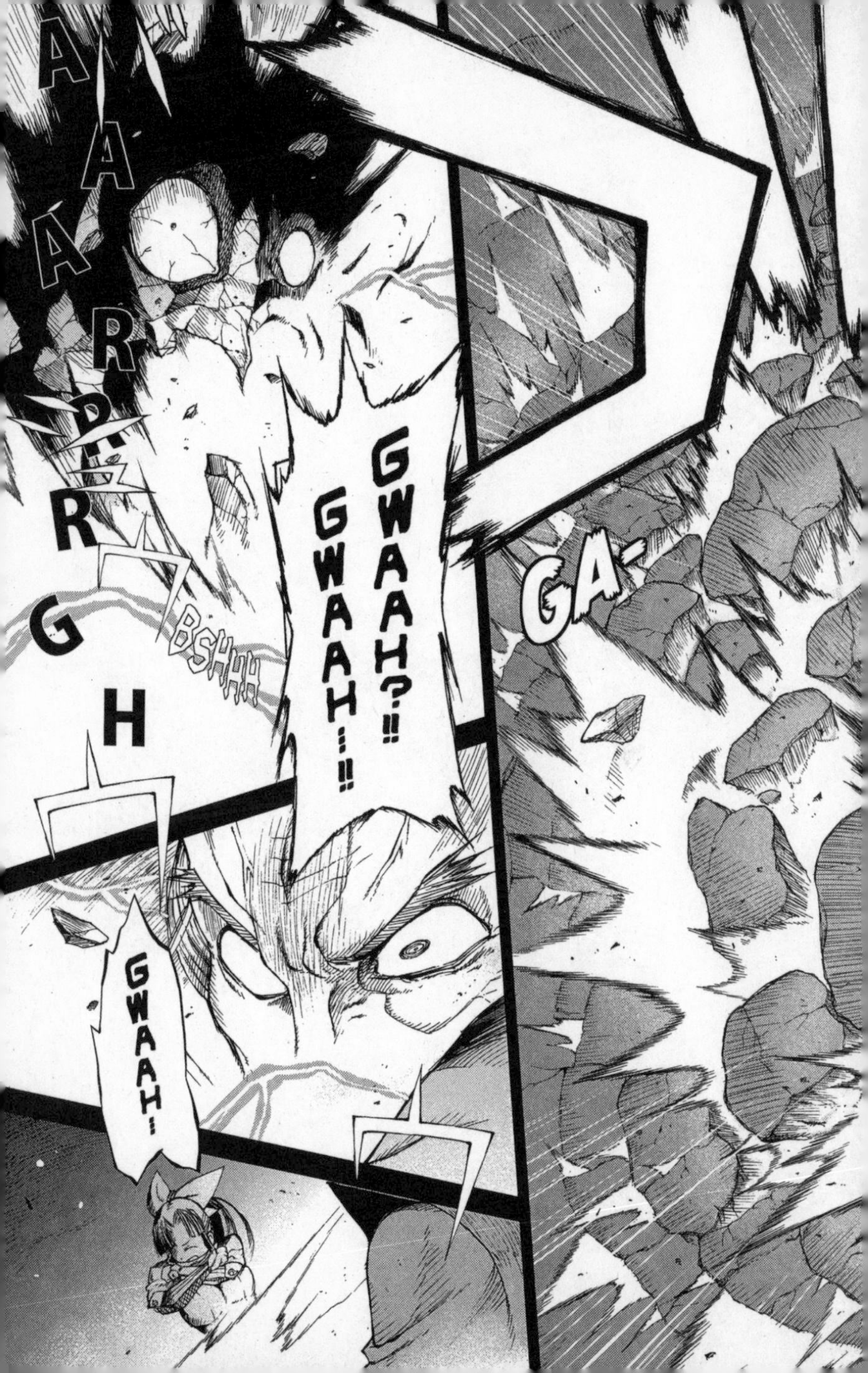
GA-
GWAAH?!!
GWAAH!!!!
AAARRRGH
BSHHH
GWAAH!!

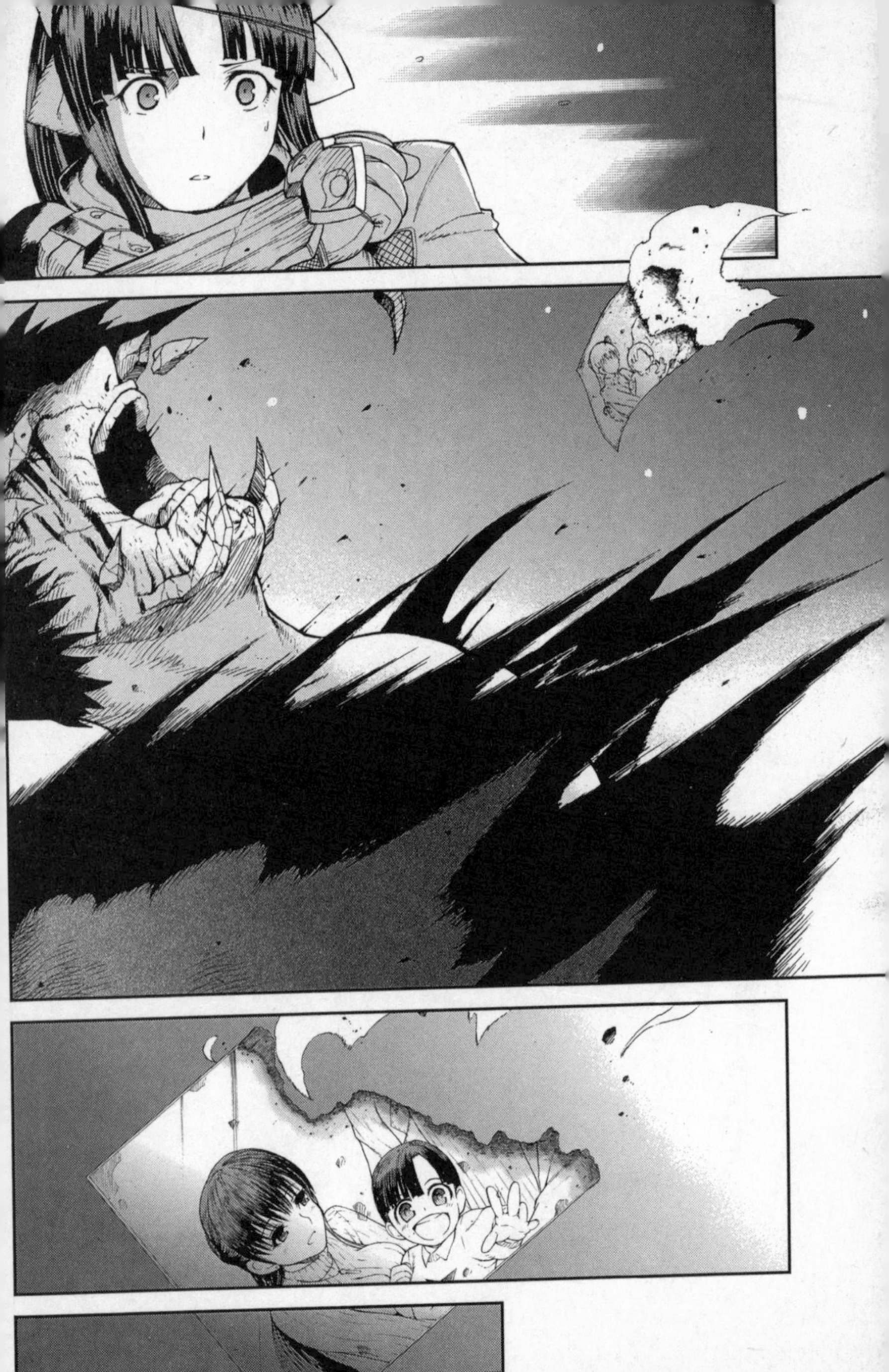

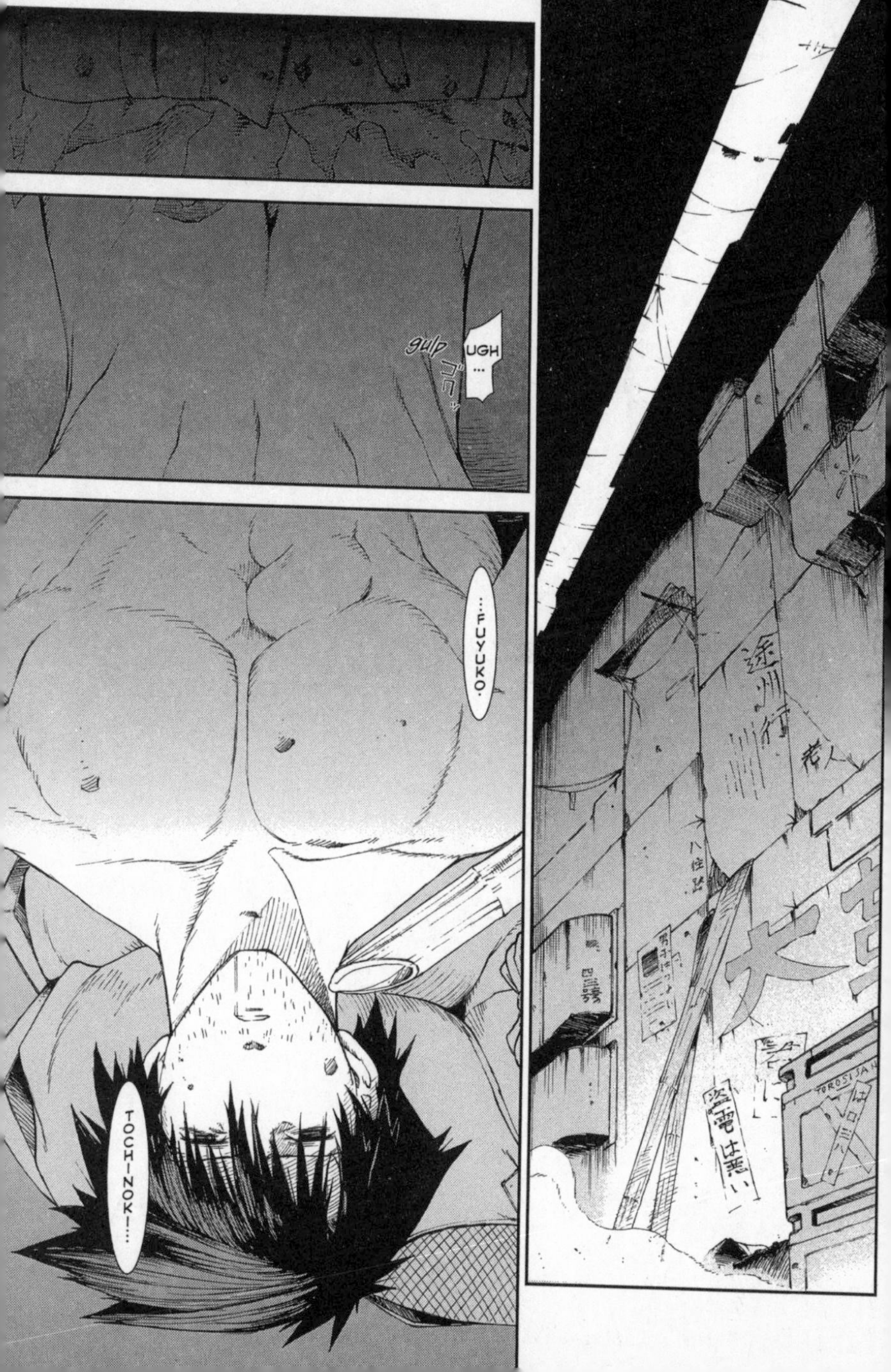
途州行
老人
盗電は悪い
TOROSIJAN
UGH ...
gulp
ゴクッ
...FUYUKO.
TOCHINOKI!...

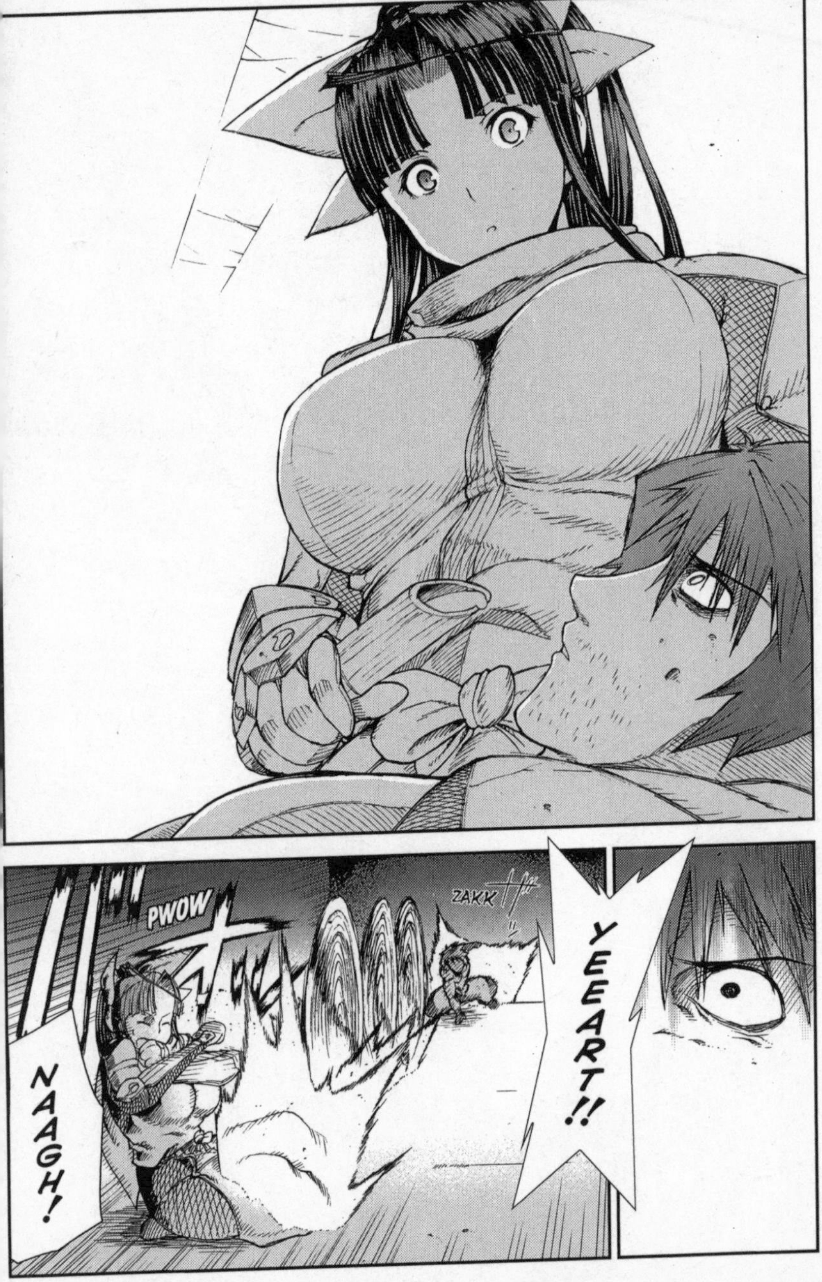
YEEART!!
ZAKK
PWOW
NAAGH!

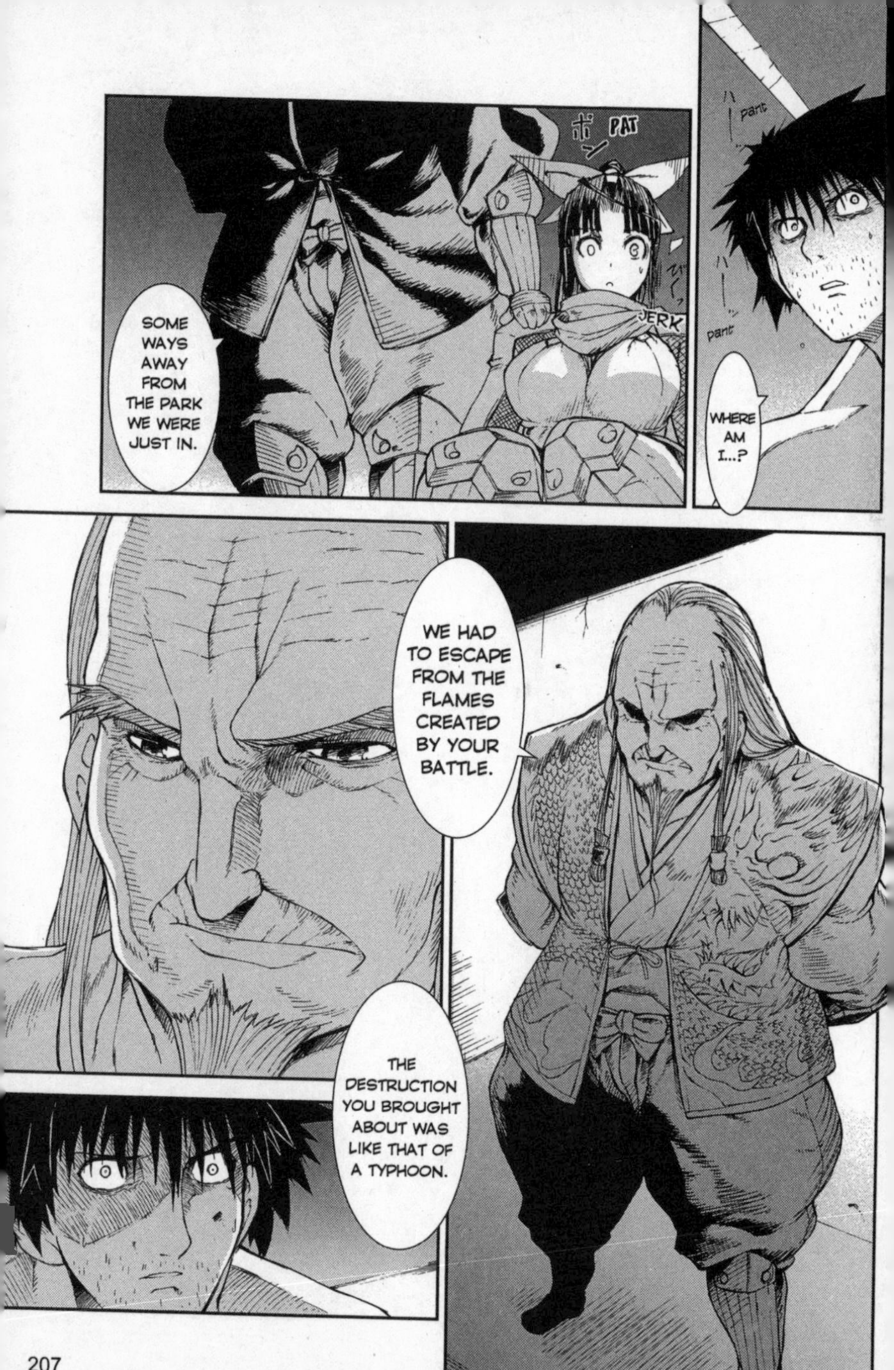
pant
pant
WHERE AM I...?
ポン PAT
JERK
SOME WAYS AWAY FROM THE PARK WE WERE JUST IN.
WE HAD TO ESCAPE FROM THE FLAMES CREATED BY YOUR BATTLE.
THE DESTRUCTION YOU BROUGHT ABOUT WAS LIKE THAT OF A TYPHOON.

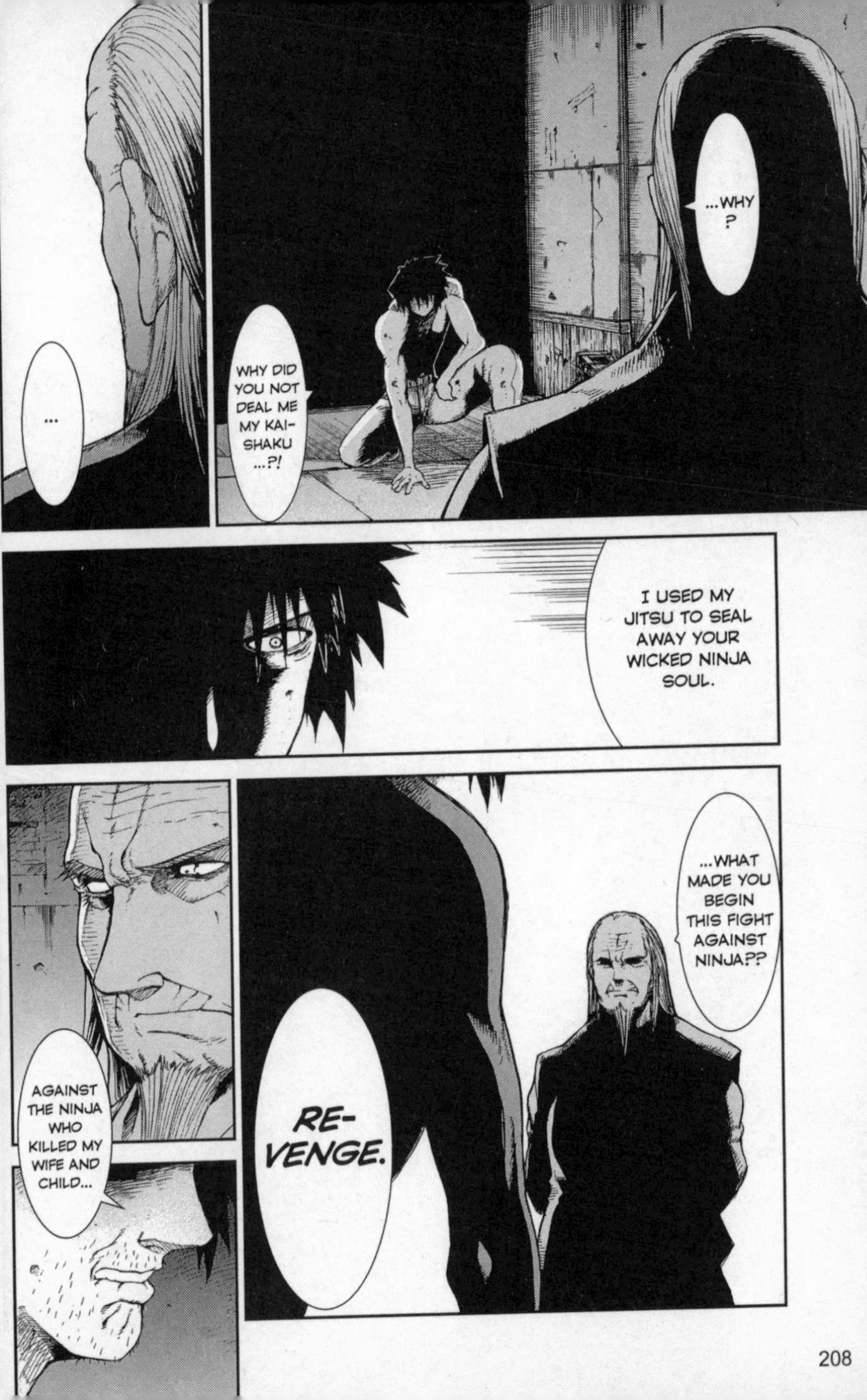
...WHY ?
WHY DID YOU NOT DEAL ME MY KAI-SHAKU ...?!
...
I USED MY JITSU TO SEAL AWAY YOUR WICKED NINJA SOUL.
...WHAT MADE YOU BEGIN THIS FIGHT AGAINST NINJA??
RE-VENGE.
AGAINST THE NINJA WHO KILLED MY WIFE AND CHILD...

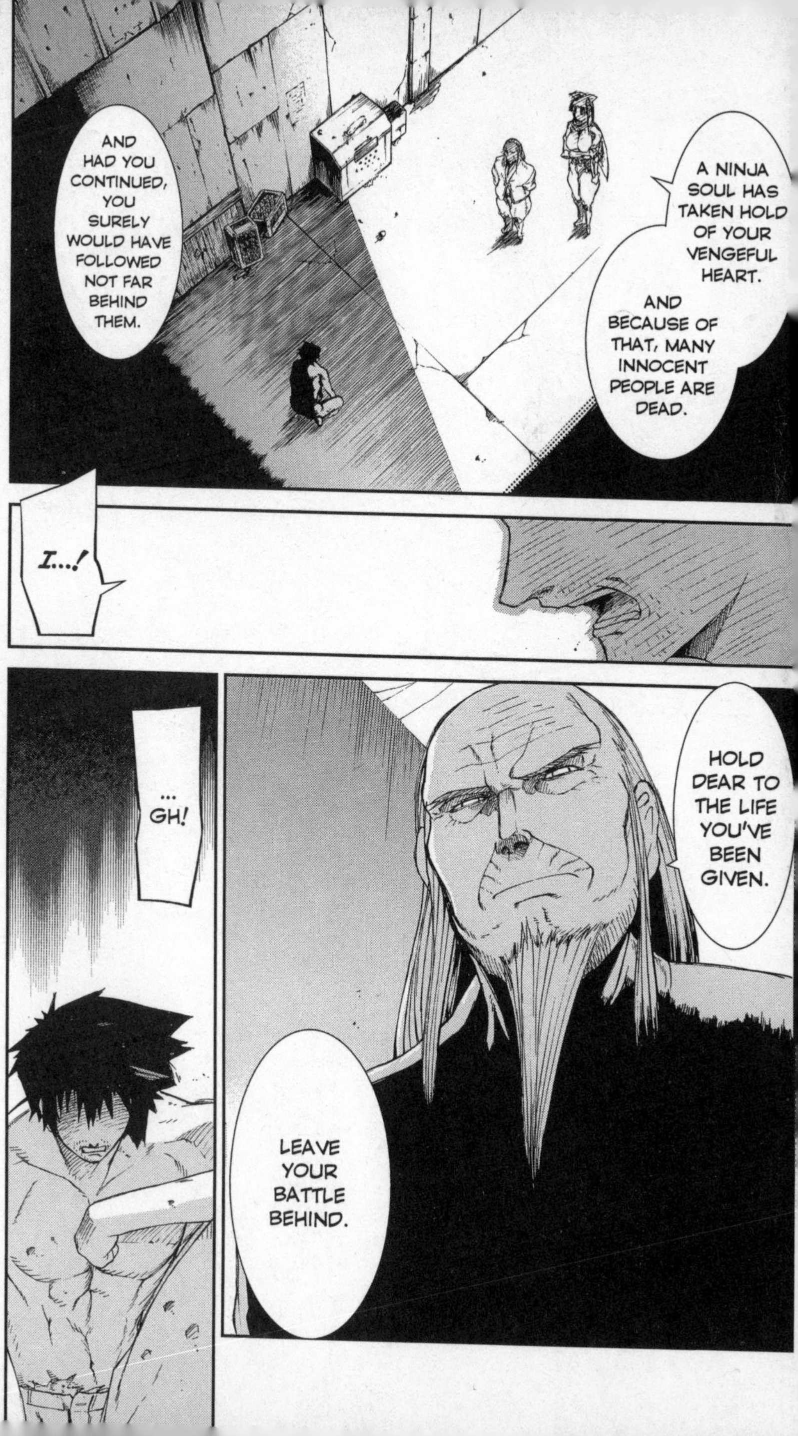
A NINJA SOUL HAS TAKEN HOLD OF YOUR VENGEFUL HEART.
AND BECAUSE OF THAT, MANY INNOCENT PEOPLE ARE DEAD.
AND HAD YOU CONTINUED, YOU SURELY WOULD HAVE FOLLOWED NOT FAR BEHIND THEM.
I...!
HOLD DEAR TO THE LIFE YOU'VE BEEN GIVEN.
LEAVE YOUR BATTLE BEHIND.
...GH!

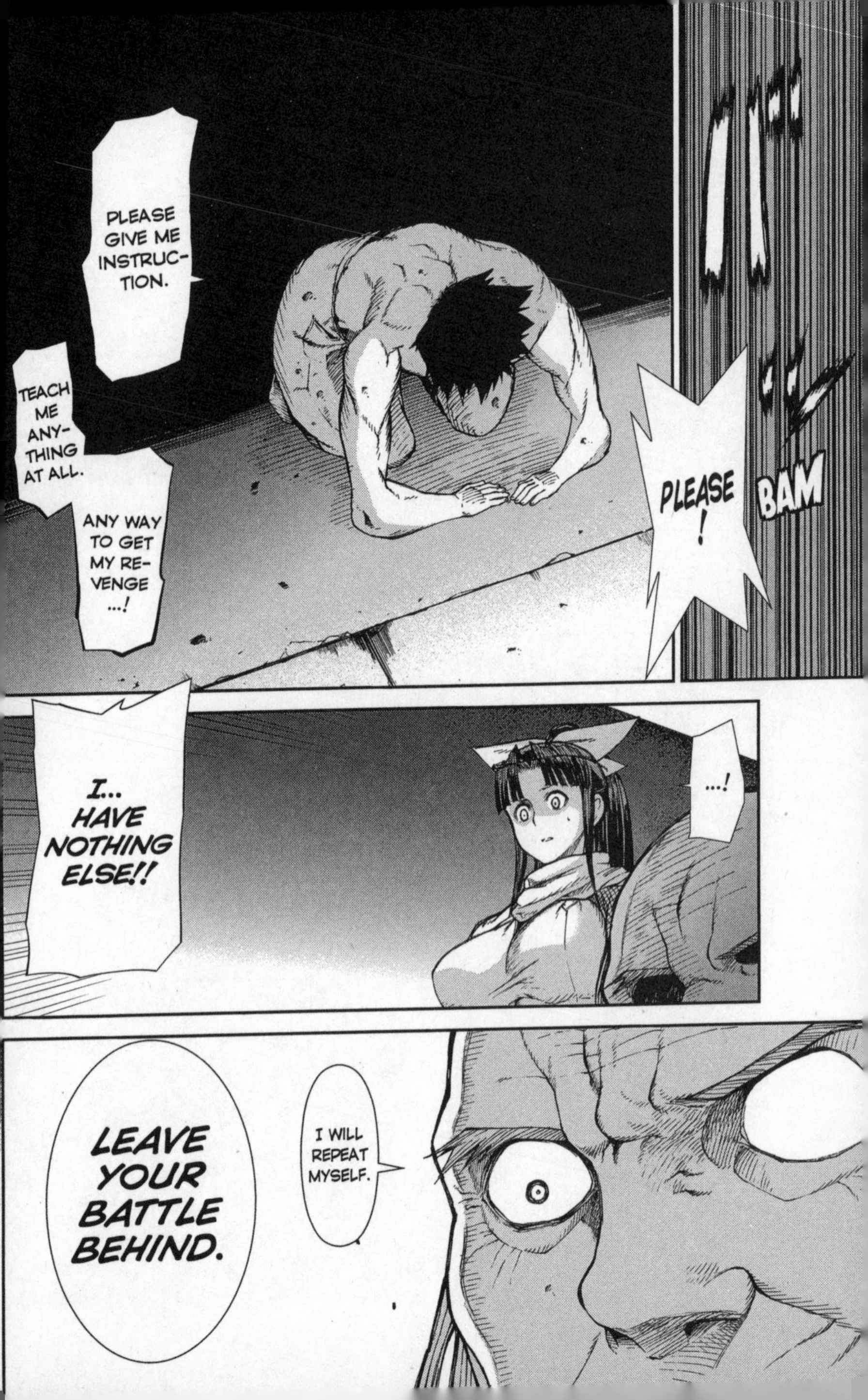
BAM
PLEASE GIVE ME INSTRUCTION.
TEACH ME ANY-THING AT ALL.
ANY WAY TO GET MY RE-VENGE ...!
PLEASE!
...!
I... HAVE NOTHING ELSE!!
I WILL REPEAT MYSELF.
LEAVE YOUR BATTLE BEHIND.

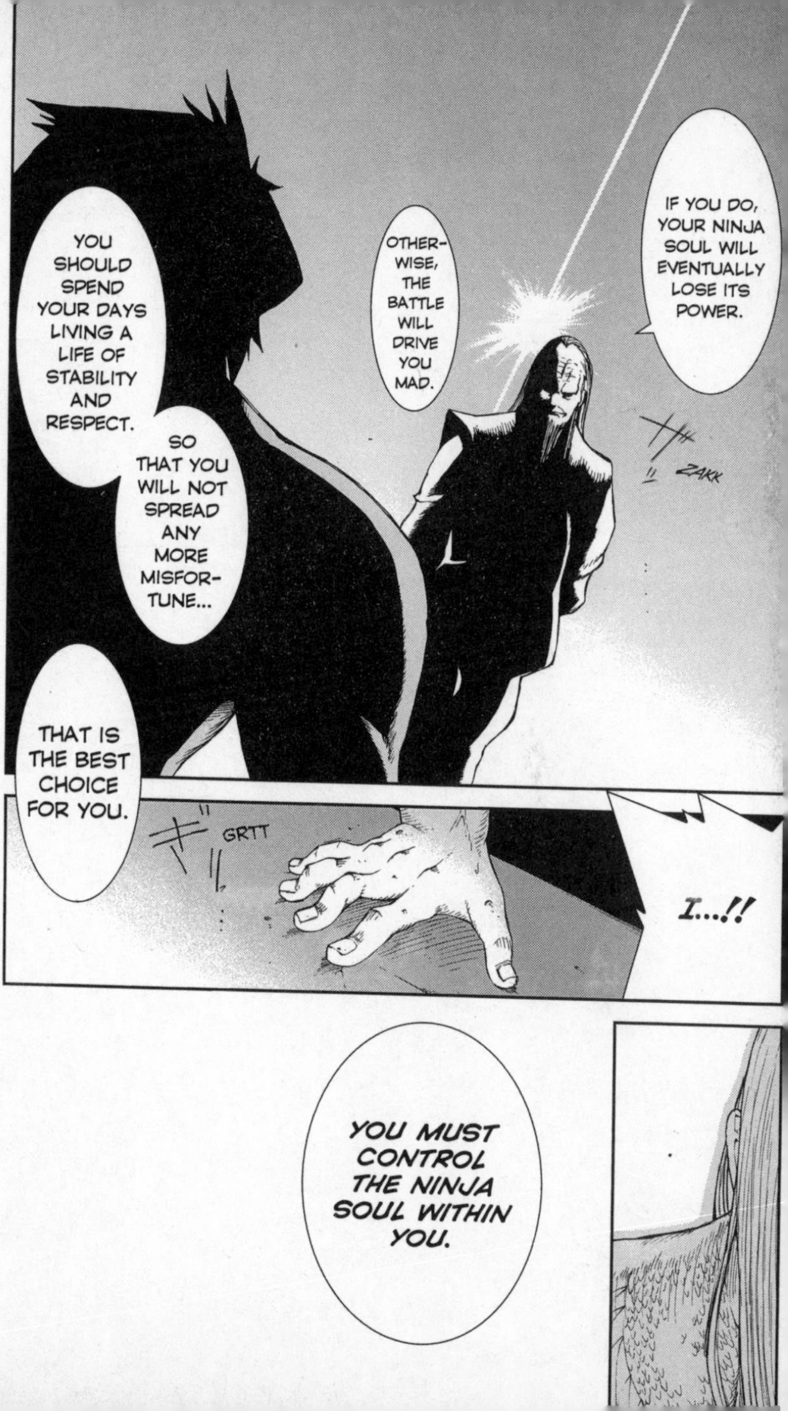
IF YOU DO, YOUR NINJA SOUL WILL EVENTUALLY LOSE ITS POWER.
OTHER-WISE, THE BATTLE WILL DRIVE YOU MAD.
ZAKK
YOU SHOULD SPEND YOUR DAYS LIVING A LIFE OF STABILITY AND RESPECT.
SO THAT YOU WILL NOT SPREAD ANY MORE MISFOR-TUNE...
THAT IS THE BEST CHOICE FOR YOU.
I...!!
GRTT
YOU MUST CONTROL THE NINJA SOUL WITHIN YOU.

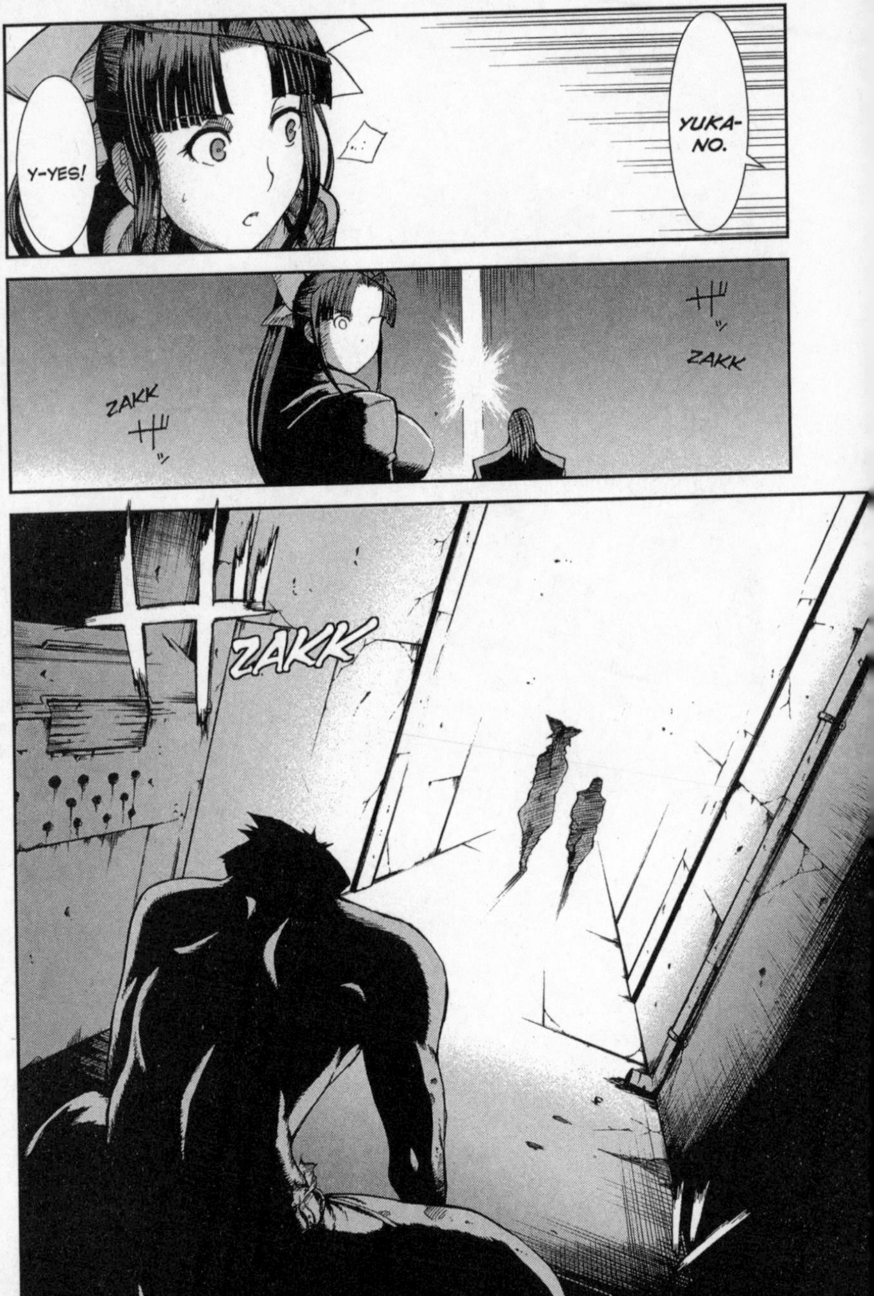
YUKA-NO.
Y-YES!
ザッ
ZAKK
ZAKK
ザッ
ザッ
ZAKK

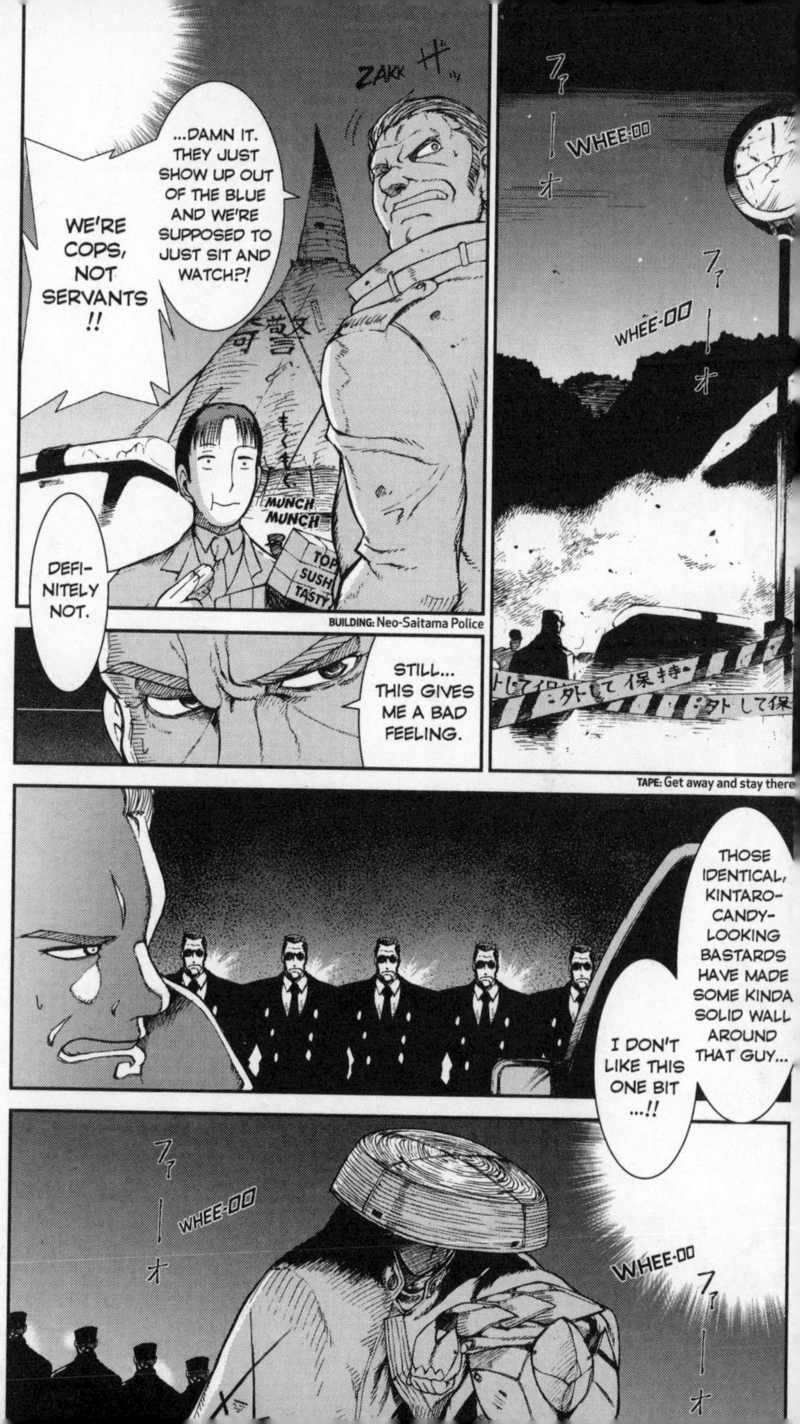
WHEE-OO
WHEE-OO
TAPE: Get away and stay there
ZAKK
...DAMN IT. THEY JUST SHOW UP OUT OF THE BLUE AND WE'RE SUPPOSED TO JUST SIT AND WATCH?!
WE'RE COPS, NOT SERVANTS!!
MUNCH MUNCH
TOP SUSHI TASTY
DEFI-NITELY NOT.
BUILDING: Neo-Saitama Police
STILL... THIS GIVES ME A BAD FEELING.
THOSE IDENTICAL, KINTARO-CANDY-LOOKING BASTARDS HAVE MADE SOME KINDA SOLID WALL AROUND THAT GUY...
I DON'T LIKE THIS ONE BIT...!!
WHEE-OO
WHEE-OO

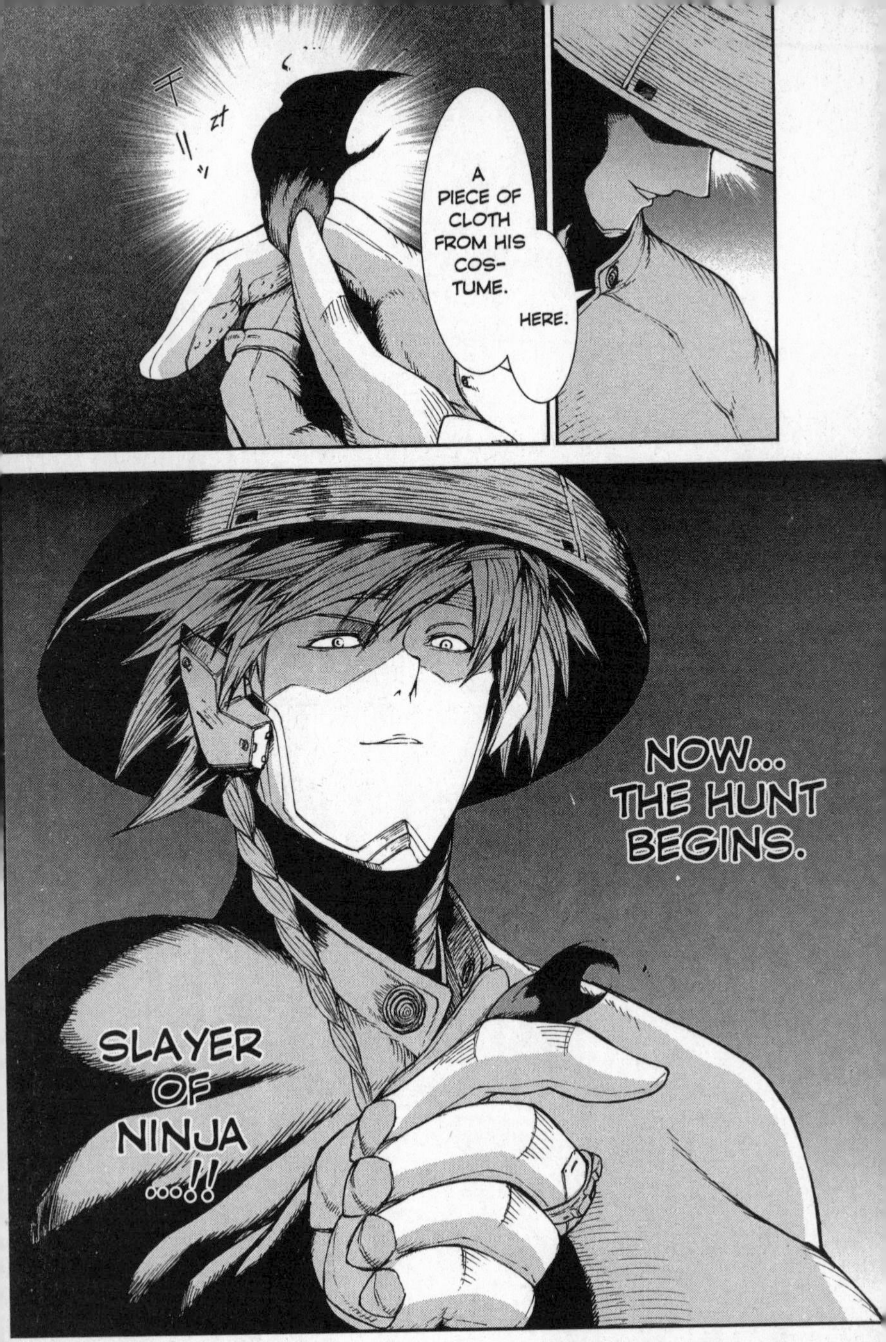
A PIECE OF CLOTH FROM HIS COS-TUME.
HERE.
NOW... THE HUNT BEGINS.
SLAYER OF NINJA ...!!

[BACK IN BLACK PART 2] • END

TO BE CONTINUED

NINJA
ニンジャスレイヤー
SLAYER
KILLS!

SETTING DESIGN COLLECTION

COMMENTARY: KOUTAROU SEKINE

NINJA SLAYER
NARAKU TRANSFORMATION

DRAGON GENDOSO

YUKANO

LAOMOTO KHAN

AGONY

CAUTIOUS

SHARPTOOTH

PAVEMENT

CLONE YAKUZA

SUBSISTENCE

PARAPONERA

HELLDEALER

WHEELDER

RUBBERDUCK

SQUASHER

TUBULAR

ROUNDERS

CYPRESS

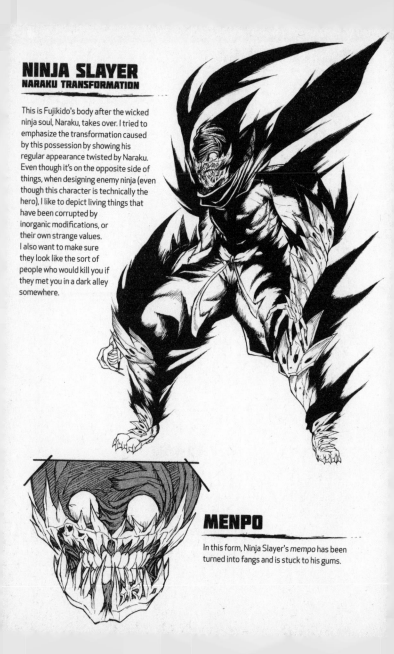

NINJA SLAYER
NARAKU TRANSFORMATION

This is Fujikido's body after the wicked ninja soul, Naraku, takes over. I tried to emphasize the transformation caused by this possession by showing his regular appearance twisted by Naraku. Even though it's on the opposite side of things, when designing enemy ninja (even though this character is technically the hero), I like to depict living things that have been corrupted by inorganic modifications, or their own strange values. I also want to make sure they look like the sort of people who would kill you if they met you in a dark alley somewhere.

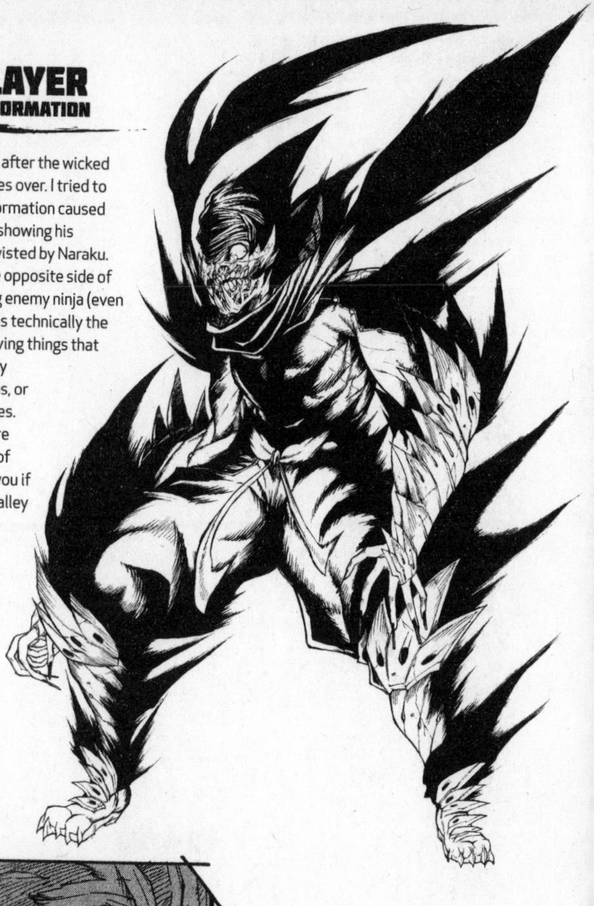

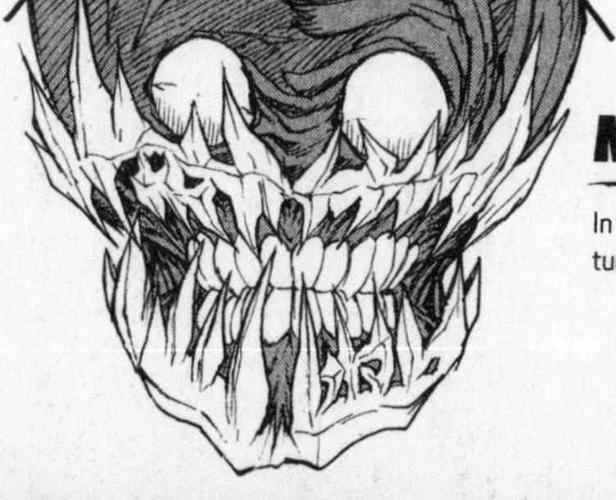

MENPO

In this form, Ninja Slayer's *mempo* has been turned into fangs and is stuck to his gums.

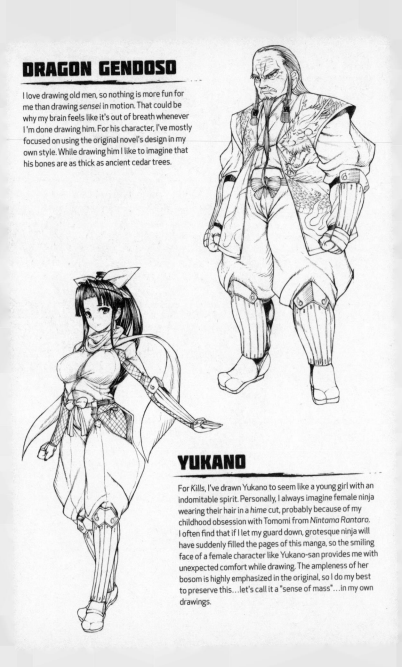

DRAGON GENDOSO

I love drawing old men, so nothing is more fun for me than drawing *sensei* in motion. That could be why my brain feels like it's out of breath whenever I'm done drawing him. For his character, I've mostly focused on using the original novel's design in my own style. While drawing him I like to imagine that his bones are as thick as ancient cedar trees.

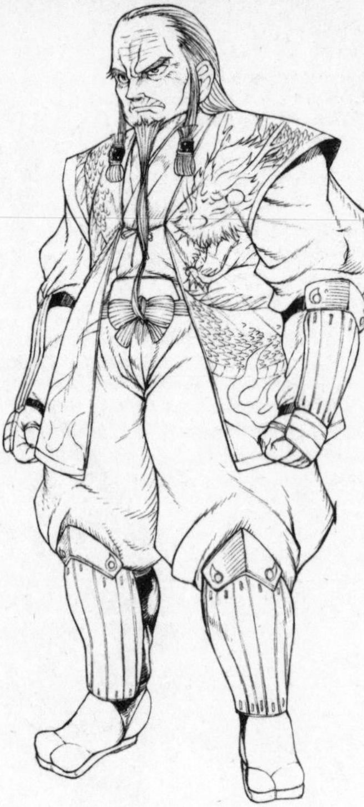

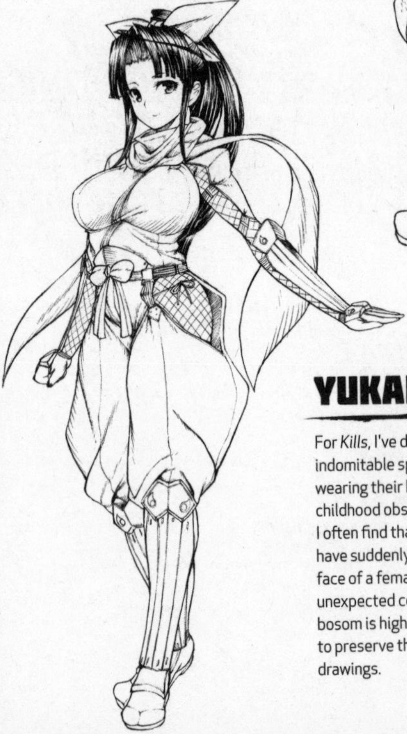

YUKANO

For *Kills*, I've drawn Yukano to seem like a young girl with an indomitable spirit. Personally, I always imagine female ninja wearing their hair in a *hime* cut, probably because of my childhood obsession with Tomomi from *Nintama Rantaro*. I often find that if I let my guard down, grotesque ninja will have suddenly filled the pages of this manga, so the smiling face of a female character like Yukano-san provides me with unexpected comfort while drawing. The ampleness of her bosom is highly emphasized in the original, so I do my best to preserve this…let's call it a "sense of mass"…in my own drawings.

AGONY

The theme here is "the walking orgasm." In my first draft, I simply took the novel's design and added that bulge between his legs, but eventually, the manga design evolved into this after I decided to play up the contrast between his groin and the rest of his body. I was afraid that I had made him too cool at first, but I was satisfied with what I saw once I started moving him around, because he was way creepier than I had imagined. The design of the bulge between his crotch is based on a pincushion used for sewing. When he runs low, supplementary *tatami* needles sprout one by one from this bulge…as if it were some perpetual motion machine…

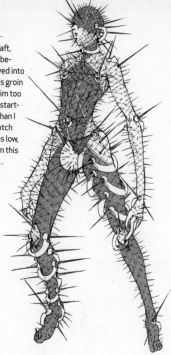

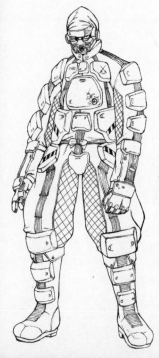

CAUTIOUS

Right around the time I started drawing him, I was also getting into flat cables. As a result, I decided to make him a kind of reconnaissance ninja with his body covered from head to toe in those cables. Come to think of it, he may be the first ninja I drew without referencing the novel at all. His entire body, from his fingertips to the cushions that line his suit, are covered in sensors. This helps him use each of his five senses to the fullest while scouting. You may wonder, then, how he ended up dying in the way he did, but… I guess all I can say is that he was blinded by his spectacular find.

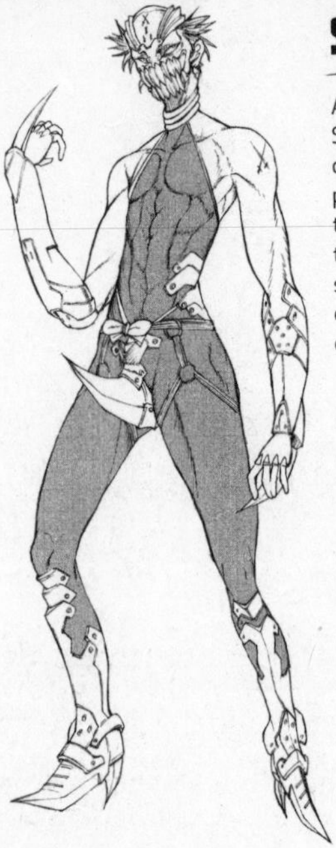

SHARPTOOTH

As this guy unleashed a *meia-lua de compasso* on Ninja Slayer, my thoughts wandered like a game of telephone from capoeira (though I realized later that I had also confused parts of Muay Thai with it) to Thailand, then to long-neck tribes plus cybernetic claws, then to some sort of general tribal feel, then to penis sacks…anyway, I drew his fight scene under the assumption that he would make use of the cybernetic claws covering his limbs with a fighting style that emphasizes high-flying, three-dimensional movement.

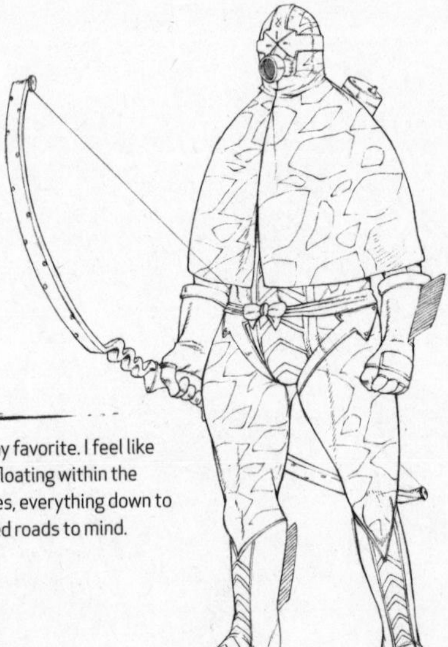

PAVEMENT

Of all the ninja I drew in this volume, this one is my favorite. I feel like I did a good job capturing his ninja ruthlessness floating within the vacuum of his stupidity. Just as his name indicates, everything down to his pavement camouflage is meant to bring paved roads to mind.

Mustard Gas Arrow Tips
Just like in the novel, the tips of his arrows explode and release mustard gas everywhere, so I designed them to look kind of like toy rockets.

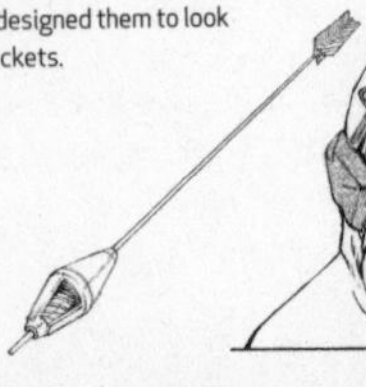

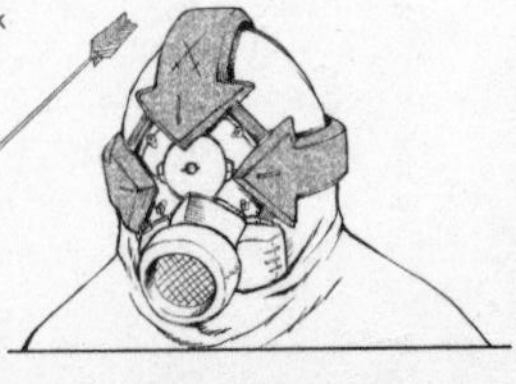

Menpo Cover Activation
His *menpo cover was designed to resemble multiple arrows coming together*, and they act as visual sensors that are able to cover all directions. When he fires arrows, this cover expands and he switches to a camera for the purpose of making highly accurate shots.

UNDERLING SOUKAI NINJA

Okay, then. The Twitter serialization of "Back in Black" features tweet after tweet of underling ninja getting blown to bits in all kinds of spectacular fashion. However, because of the structure of *Kills*, only the second half of the episode was depicted. As a result, these ninja are only shown in a scene of their memorial (?). Even so, these ninja still have both unique faces and their own *karate*, and I think it's important to remind my readers of these facts. That's why I'd like to show you what they were like when they were still alive.

SUBSISTENCE

Just a plain-looking Soukai ninja.

PARAPONERA

An impressive body, but you can probably guess how impressive his skills were.

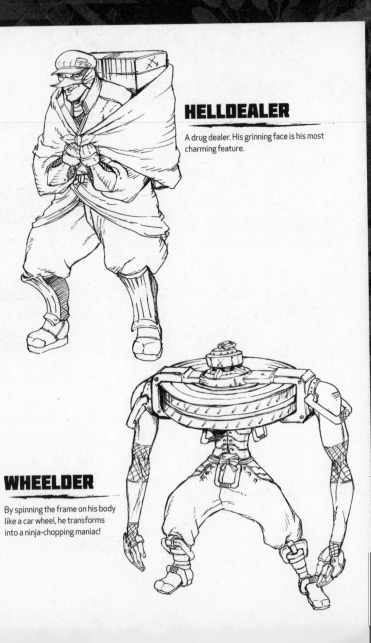

HELLDEALER

A drug dealer. His grinning face is his most charming feature.

WHEELDER

By spinning the frame on his body like a car wheel, he transforms into a ninja-chopping maniac!

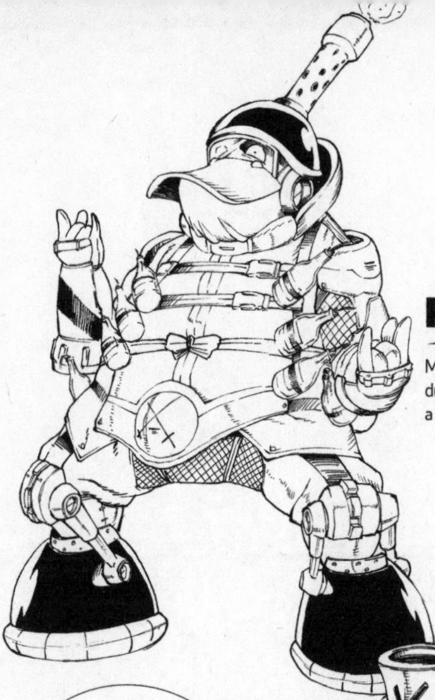

RUBBERDUCK

My thought process here went from "rubber duck" to "rubber cup" (plunger). He probably led a fun life.

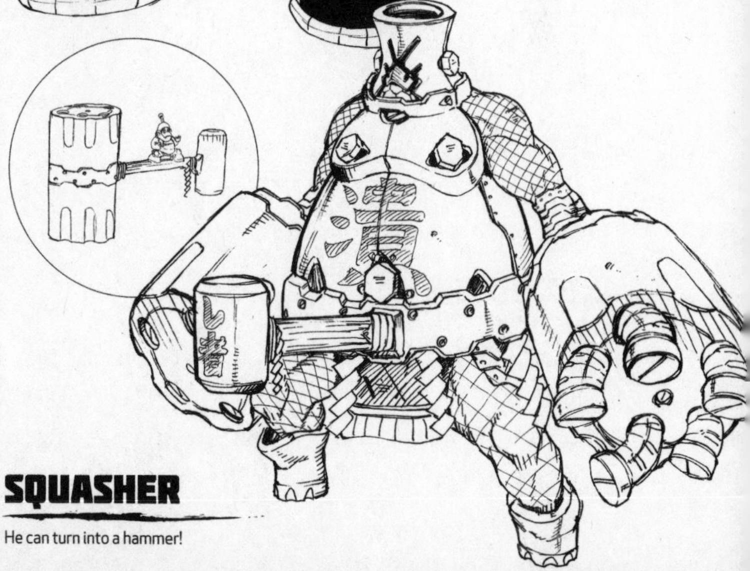

SQUASHER

He can turn into a hammer!

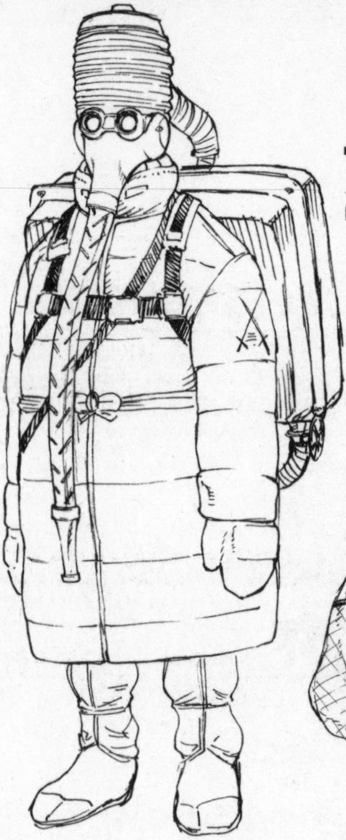

TUBULAR

I guess he's like a kerosene pump ninja?

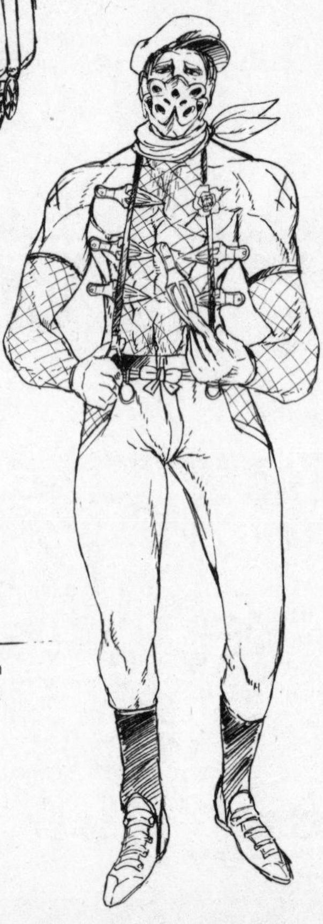

ROUNDERS

I think he's probably gay, but even I'm not sure why I think that.

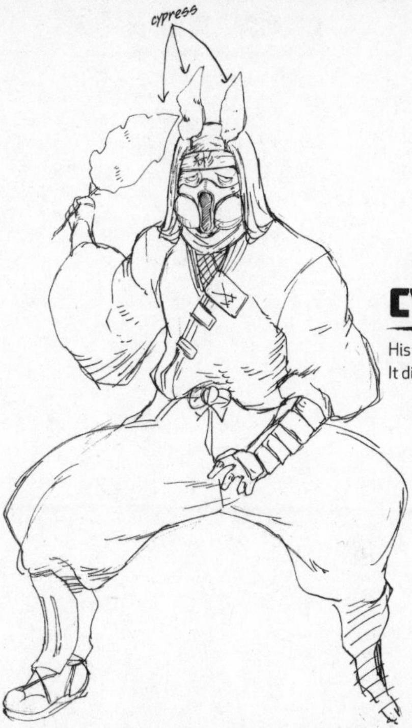
cypress

CYPRESS

His *karate* utilizes the smell of cypress. It didn't help him very much.

UNDERLING NINJA MEMORIAL PORTRAITS

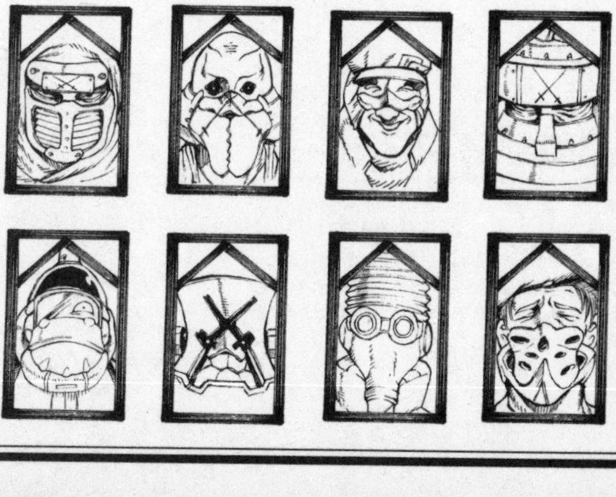

LAOMOTO KHAN

As the grand villain who stands at the apex of Neo-Saitama, I tried to depict him in a way that makes readers get a feel for his manly brawn. I had originally planned to draw him without a hood, but when I put him side-by-side with the cybernetics-heavy ninja in *Kills*, he ended up looking plainer that I had expected. Adding the hood made him feel more like the Don of an evil organization, which is why he ended up closely resembling his design in the original.

CLONE YAKUZA

These combatants are a vital part of *Ninja Slayer*. When I heard they were voiced by Tessho Genda, it only made sense to draw them like this. They have polarized tattoos of their product control tags on their left earlobes courtesy of Yoroshisan Pharmaceuticals. These tattoos can be seen by shining a special light on them.

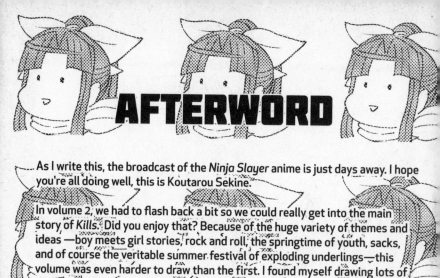

AFTERWORD

As I write this, the broadcast of the *Ninja Slayer* anime is just days away. I hope you're all doing well, this is Koutarou Sekine.

In volume 2, we had to flash back a bit so we could really get into the main story of *Kills*. Did you enjoy that? Because of the huge variety of themes and ideas —boy meets girl stories, rock and roll, the springtime of youth, sacks, and of course the veritable summer festival of exploding underlings— this volume was even harder to draw than the first. I found myself drawing lots of things for the first time, from giant oxen to rock concerts, and it seemed like every day I would say to myself, "Is this really how I should be drawing this? Yup, it's fine."

I hope that Ginichi-san is able to live his life courageously even after these experiences. He just wanted to enjoy his teenage years a little, but soon found himself caught between a ball-sack-flaunting pervert and a berserk karate monster who doesn't distinguish between friend and foe.

As for me, watching Ginichi and Ichijiku live the spring of their youth to the fullest was pretty gut-wrenching. Being reminded of my early days as a *Sister Princess-obsessed* teenager unsurfaced feelings so intense that it was like my brain and entrails were being gouged from my body. Still, I, too, hope to live my life courageously.

Okay, see you next volume! Ciao!

KOUTAROU SEKINE

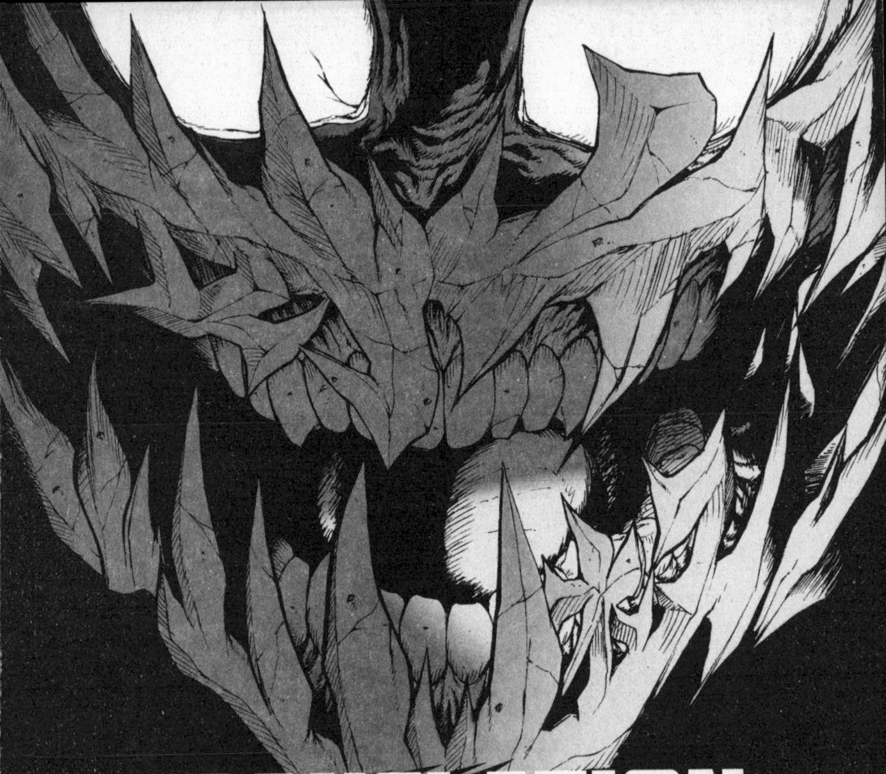

TRANSLATION NOTES

Mokugyo, page 37

A wooden gong used in Buddhist ceremonies. Directly translated, *mokugyo* means wooden fish. It is called this because it is carved to resemble two fish holding a pearl at the handle.

Itamae, page 41

A sushi chef.

Dohyo, page 45

A ring for sumo wrestling.

Kintaro Candy, page 213

Kintaro candy (Japanese: *Kintaro Ame*) is a rolled sugar candy that reveals the face of a character at its cross section when cut. For this reason, anything that looks exactly the same is said to be "like Kintaro candy."

Hime Cut/Nintama Rantaro, page 218

Nintama Rantaro is a long running anime series that has been broadcast on NHK since 1993 and has over 1,800 episodes to date. The story of the series deals with the title character Nintama Rantaro and his adventures at a school for ninja. The female character Tomomi from this series sports a *hime* cut (princess cut), which consists of long hair in the back, neck-length hair on the sides, and bangs that cover the forehead.

Meia-lua de compasso, page 220

A basic movement from capoeira that consists of an evasive, spinning kick. In Portuguese, it means "compass half-moon."

Sister Princess, page 227

A series of dating-sim games for PlayStation where the young, male protagonist can date his 12 little sisters. Most of the games have two endings; a normal ending and one where the little sister you've dated ends up not being blood-related, after which you marry her.

INUYASHIKI

A superhero like none you've ever seen, from the creator of "Gantz"!

ICHIRO INUYASHIKI IS DOWN ON HIS LUCK. HE LOOKS MUCH OLDER THAN HIS 58 YEARS, HIS CHILDREN DESPISE HIM, AND HIS WIFE THINKS HE'S A USELESS COWARD. SO WHEN HE'S DIAGNOSED WITH STOMACH CANCER AND GIVEN THREE MONTHS TO LIVE, IT SEEMS THE ONLY ONE WHO'LL MISS HIM IS HIS DOG.

THEN A BLINDING LIGHT FILLS THE SKY, AND THE OLD MAN IS KILLED... ONLY TO WAKE UP LATER IN A BODY HE ALMOST RECOGNIZES AS HIS OWN. CAN IT BE THAT ICHIRO INUYASHIKI IS NO LONGER HUMAN?

COMES IN EXTRA-LARGE EDITIONS WITH COLOR PAGES!

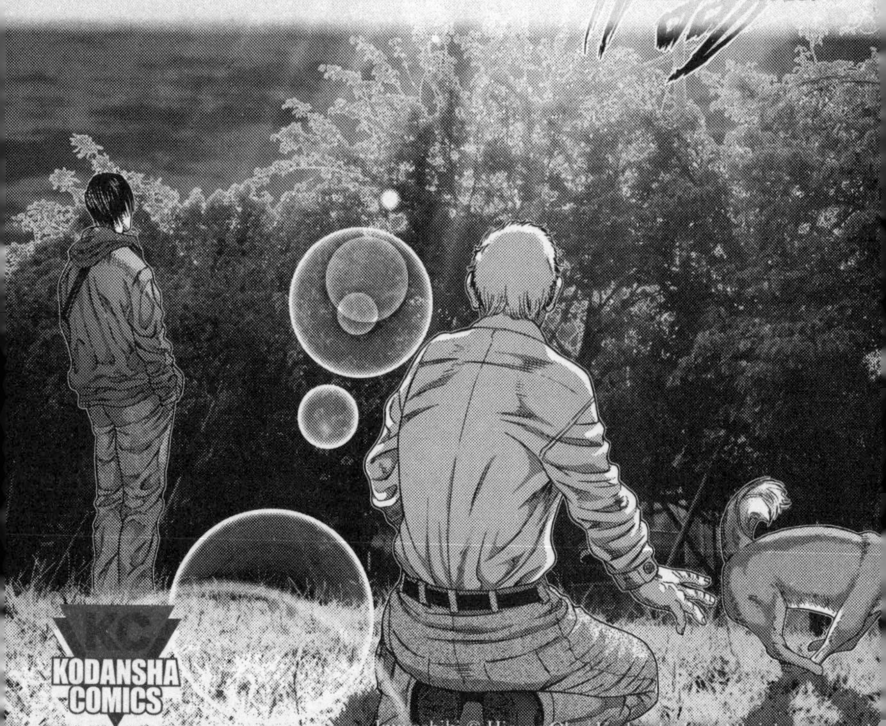

KODANSHA COMICS

Ninja Slayer Kills volume 2 is a work of fiction. Names, characters, places, and incidents are the products of the author's imagination or are used fictitiously. Any resemblance to actual events, locales, or persons, living or dead, is entirely coincidental.

A Kodansha Comics Trade Paperback Original.

Published in the United States by Kodansha Comics, an imprint of Kodansha USA Publishing, LLC, New York.

Publication rights for this English edition arranged through Kodansha Ltd., Tokyo.

First published in Japan in 2015 by Kodansha Ltd., Tokyo, as *Ninja Slayer Satsu (Kills)*, volume 2.

ISBN 978-1-63236-087-8

www.kodanshacomics.com

Localization: Ko Ransom
Lettering: Evan Hayden
Calligraphy for Kotodama: Megumi Fitzpatrick
Editing and additional material: Ajani Oloye
Kodansha Comics edition cover design: Phil Balsman